A Jewish Kapo
in Auschwitz

THE SCHUSTERMAN SERIES IN ISRAEL STUDIES

The Schusterman Series in Israel Studies publishes original scholarship of exceptional significance on the history of Zionism and the State of Israel. It draws on disciplines across the academy, from anthropology, sociology, political science, and international relations to the arts, history, and literature. It seeks to further an understanding of Israel within the context of the modern Middle East and the modern Jewish experience. There is special interest in developing publications that enrich the university curriculum and enlighten the public at large. The series is published under the auspices of the Schusterman Center for Israel Studies at Brandeis University.

For a complete list of books in this series, please see www.upne.com.

TUVIA FRILING
A Jewish Kapo in Auschwitz: History, Memory, and the Politics of Survival

MOTTI GOLANI
Palestine between Politics and Terror, 1945–1947

ILANA SZOBEL
A Poetics of Trauma: The Work of Dahlia Ravikovitch

ANITA SHAPIRA
Israel: A History

ORIT ROZIN
The Rise of the Individual in 1950s Israel: A Challenge to Collectivism

BOAZ NEUMANN
Land and Desire in Early Zionism

ANAT HELMAN
Young Tel Aviv: A Tale of Two Cities

NILI SCHARF GOLD
Yehuda Amichai: The Making of Israel's National Poet

ITAMAR RABINOVICH AND JEHUDA REINHARZ, EDITORS
Israel in the Middle East: Documents and Readings on Society, Politics, and Foreign Relations, Pre-1948 to the Present

TUVIA FRILING

A Jewish Kapo in Auschwitz

History, Memory, and the Politics of Survival

Translated by
Haim Watzman

Published with the support of the Israel Science Foundation

BRANDEIS UNIVERSITY PRESS
WALTHAM, MASSACHUSETTS

Brandeis University Press
An imprint of University Press of New England
www.upne.com

Manufactured in the United States of America
Designed by Eric M. Brooks
Typeset in Skolar by Passumpsic Publishing

University Press of New England is a member of the
Green Press Initiative. The paper used in this book meets
their minimum requirement for recycled paper.

Library of Congress Cataloging-in-Publication Data
Friling, Tuvia, author.
[Mi atah Le'on Berz'eh? English]
A Jewish kapo in Auschwitz: history, memory, and the politics of survival /
Tuvia Friling; translated by Haim Watzman.
pages cm. — (The Schusterman series in Israel studies)
Includes bibliographical references and index.
ISBN 978-1-61168-576-3 (cloth: alk. paper) —
ISBN 978-1-61168-587-9 (pbk.: alk. paper) —
ISBN 978-1-61168-577-0 (ebook)
1. Grinboim, Eli'ezer, 1908–1948. 2. Holocaust, Jewish (1939–1945) —
Poland — Biography. 3. World War, 1939–1945—Collaborationists —
Poland — Biography. 4. Auschwitz (Concentration camp). I. Title.
DS134.72.G75F7513 2014
940.53'18092 — dc23 2013049171

5 4 3 2 1

With love,
for Dina,
my wife and
companion

CONTENTS

ACKNOWLEDGMENTS

THIS BOOK BEGAN TO RUN THROUGH my mind as I was writing my previous study, *Arrows in the Dark: David Ben-Gurion, the Yishuv Leadership, and Rescue Attempts during the Holocaust*. That work offers an extensive account of the labors of the father of the subject of this book. Yitzhak Gruenbaum, a leader of the Jewish community under the British Mandate and formerly the most prominent and influential Jewish politician in Poland, was assigned major roles in the Yishuv's efforts to aid Europe's beleaguered and endangered Jews and bring as many of them as possible to Palestine. My work on that earlier history also taught me the great importance of documentation residing outside Israel, in particular that from Polish and French sources. Such evidence is critical for the re-creation, analysis, and evaluation of the convoluted story of Yitzhak's son Eliezer, the subject of the current work. This book is the story of Eliezer Gruenbaum and his time, but also a narrative of the tortuous path I and my research assistants trod to collect the necessary evidence. That search took years.

I would like to express my gratitude to the staff of the Polish Central Archives of Modern Records, and to Neli Oren, who served as my liaison to the archive. I also want to thank the staff of the archive of the Auschwitz-Birkenau National Museum, in particular the former deputy director, Teresa Swiebocka. In addition, I am grateful to those people and organizations that generously granted me access to an important French collection of documents.

Further thanks go to Henry Meyer, director of the archive at the United States Holocaust Memorial Museum, as well as to Michlean Amir and Vincent Slat of his staff, all three of whom provided me with gracious and professional assistance. Galia Glasner-Heled, Eran Turbiner, and Jeannine (Levana) Frenk, Israeli scholars who have researched and written about the Holocaust, all kindly made available to me their private collections of documents and notes that were critical in piecing together Eliezer Gruenbaum's story.

Two translators — Shmuel Katz, from the Polish, and Doron Modan, from the French — helped me delve into documents and sources in these languages. Their professionalism and patience deserve special recognition.

My colleague Shmuel Trigano of the University of Paris at Nanterre-Sorbonne, also provided me with invaluable assistance.

Special thanks go to Irena Steinfeldt, now the head of Yad Vashem's Righteous among the Nations department. She collected for me documents from different places around the world, helped translate, and offered her services as a careful reader of manuscripts. Her comments, clarifications, wide-ranging assistance, and especially her profound friendship were critical to my work.

It goes without saying that I alone am responsible for everything written in the book. But I benefited greatly from the comments and suggestions of a number of colleagues and friends who read my Hebrew manuscript. I list them in alphabetical order: Shlomo Aronson, the late Dan Bar-On, Uri Bialer, Hadas Blum, Kimmy Caplan, Galia Glasner-Heled, Daniel Gutwein, Yehoshua Porath, Smadar Rothman, Hanna Yablonka, and Lisa Yavnai.

Re'ut Ben-Horin was my associate through a large part of the research and writing of the expanded Hebrew edition. I thank her for her wonderful, dedicated, and careful work, as well as for her patience and friendship. Hadas Blum, my excellent research assistant, helped me swim through the sea of details on which the book sails, assisted in drafting the Hebrew edition, and provided essential editorial assistance for this English edition.

The book was written during my tenure as a research fellow at the Center for Advanced Holocaust Studies at the U.S. Holocaust Memorial Museum in Washington, D.C. I would like to thank Paul Shapiro, Lisa Yavnai, Rado Ioanid, and the rest of the center's staff and fellows for being gracious hosts and providing an enriching environment in which I learned a great deal.

This English version of the book is published by the Schusterman Center for Israel Studies at Brandeis University in Waltham, Massachusetts. Ilan Troen, Jehuda Reinharz, and Sylvia Fuks Fried deserve my gratitude for their confidence, assistance, and support. I am also grateful to Phyllis Deutsch, editor-in-chief of the University Press of New England, and the members of her staff for their important contribution to the process of publication. Further thanks go to Rivka Carmi, president of Ben-Gurion University of the Negev, and Avigad Vonshak, director of the Ben-Gurion Research Institute for the Study of Israel and Zionism, for their kind support. I owe special thanks to the Israel Science Foundation for its generous support for the translation of the book into English.

My sincere thanks to Avi Katzman for his important part in preparing the Hebrew manuscript for translation. I also owe a great deal to the book's

English translator, Haim Watzman, for his professionalism, fortitude, talent, and precision — all in the name of making the telling of Eliezer Gruenbaum's complex and intricate story more fluent, flowing, and clear. It would be hard to exaggerate the importance of his contribution.

My wife, Dina, accompanied me through the entire process of researching and writing this book and was a full partner in turbulent discussions and dilemmas over who, in fact, was Leon Berger. I dedicate the book to her, with all my love.

A Jewish Kapo in Auschwitz

1 Jerusalem, May 22, 1948, Morning

HAD YOU WALKED PAST THE Ta'amon Café on the corner of Hillel and King George Streets in Jerusalem on the morning of May 22, 1948, you would have spotted a gaggle of about thirty men, all in the fourth decade of their lives. Packs on their backs, they were waiting to be picked up and sent into battle. The city was under attack, with the Egyptian army advancing from the south and Jordan's Arab Legion attacking from the north and east. The soldiers had been enlisted in the city's garrison the week before and served under David Shaltiel, the controversial commander of the Jerusalem front.[1] One of them was a solidly built man who looked to be on the verge of forty. Silent and introverted, he clenched a cigarette between lips set in a bitter smile. His black beret hid a large bald spot. Few of the other men in the group were likely to have noticed the number tattooed on his forearm.[2] Those that did probably knew nothing of what the man had seen and suffered between fleeing Poland for Paris in 1931 and arriving, inadvertently, in Jerusalem in the spring of 1946. But both he and his fellow recruits knew very well that some of them would not see the end of that day and that their bodies would soon lie in the temporary military cemetery at Sheikh Bader.[3] In Jerusalem, where Jewish tradition still reigned supreme, dead men did not pass the night unburied.

Ten days previously, the men in charge of the war effort of the Yishuv had estimated the chances of a Jewish victory at 50 percent. This evaluation was given to the Yishuv's provisional government by Yisrael Galili, chief of the National Staff of the Haganah (the Jewish army that would, after independence and the incorporation of two smaller militias, become the Israel Defense Forces), and Yigal Yadin, the acting chief of staff of the Jewish forces. Golda Meyerson (later Meir) reported on the results of her frustrating meeting with King Abdullah of Jordan. He had told her that, unfortunately, he would not be able to honor the commitments he had made to her previously. Despite his promises, he declared, if war broke out, his army, the Arab Legion, would join the forces attacking the young Jewish state. In Meir's evaluation, he probably already saw himself as the king of Jerusalem. Proof of Abdullah's resolve was quick to come — in the middle of the meeting the assembled Jewish leaders received news that the four kibbutzim that made up the Etzion bloc of settlements were under attack by the Legion. The Jewish defenders were defeated two days later.[4]

The meeting, in Tel Aviv, had been called to decide whether the Yishuv should proclaim the establishment of a Jewish state. David Ben-Gurion, premier of the provisional government, was not deterred by his colleagues' pessimism. He spoke at length, explaining why the decision to declare independence had to be taken "now or never." The United States, fearing war, had proposed a trusteeship that would maintain foreign rule over Palestine. Ben-Gurion urged his colleagues to reject the American initiative. Accepting it would tie the Yishuv's hands and make its defense more difficult at a time when the inevitable war with the Arabs was already under way. An independent Jewish state should be declared, he maintained, as soon as the British left.

Word of the debate in the Yishuv leadership reached besieged Jerusalem. Even those who did not know about the plans to declare independence could hardly help being caught up in the surge of joy that overcame the Yishuv two days later. On Friday, May 14, 1948, a bit after four o'clock in the afternoon, Ben-Gurion declared, in a clear staccato voice, the establishment of the State of Israel. He and his colleagues had finished polishing the draft of the declaration only a short time before.

Ben-Gurion commenced a fresh volume of his diary when he returned from the ceremony. He opened with a somber nod to that momentous day, a single austere line that took in all the complexities he saw before him and his nation. "We declared the founding of the state. Its fate is in the hands of the military forces."[5] This may have been an expression of his inner emotions, or it may have been his version of *ab urbe condita*, written to establish a foundation myth for the State of Israel — most likely, it was a bit of each. No matter what his intentions, that story was etched in the collective memory of the Jewish state, born as it was in a storm, in blood and fire.

The soldiers waiting at the corner by the café belonged to the military forces of which Ben-Gurion had written. They did not have to stand there for long. The situation on Jerusalem's southern reaches was dire, so they, members of a regional reserve, were to be sent into battle. A truck pulled up and swallowed up the men. Menachem Richman, the commander of the fresh force, sat by the driver. The man with the number tattooed on his forearm, along with his comrades-in-arms, huddled pensively in the rear.[6]

2 Poland, Lancicia, District Prison, 1929

LANCICIA (ŁĘCZYCA IN POLISH) is a district capital in Łódź Province in central Poland, about eighty miles north of Warsaw. It lies at the crossing of two important roads, one a north-south route that runs through the Pinsk Marshes and the other an east-west route through the Bzura River valley. The prison there, formerly a Dominican monastery, is located on Pocztowej Street at the city's northwestern end, not far from a fire station and brewery and next to the King's Garden, one of the most beautiful parks in Poland. The man who would later, as a soldier in Israel's War of Independence, wait by the café to go into battle, was incarcerated in this prison in 1929. Eliezer Gruenbaum was then a member of a Communist cell in Warsaw, and, along with four comrades — Daniel Michael Warszawski, Szulim Krengel, Izrael Frydberg, and Janow Gutner, all in their mid-twenties — had been convicted of membership in the illegal Communist Youth Union. According to the indictment, their participation in an illegal gathering sponsored by the CYU in Łódź was tantamount to an intention "to carry out a crime of attacking the foundations of the Polish regime." It related that the interrogators had learned by covert means that "the Communist Central Committee in Warsaw has sent its loyalists to establish close connections with the Communists of Łódź," the first signs of a plot that had to be uprooted while still embryonic.[1] The judge sentenced the five men to four and a half years in prison. Perhaps Gruenbaum's family name and his father's position helped him. Perhaps not.

His father, Yitzhak, was a leader of Poland's Jews, the organizer and head of the Bloc of National Minorities in the Sejm, the Polish parliament. Even some of his political foes praised his courage, candor, honesty, and integrity. Others intimated that he was pedantic, tightfisted, and unable to acknowledge the limits of his power — failings that his son shared. Some suggested that, were the father prepared to rein in his criticism of the government, it might be possible to mitigate his son's sentence and that the president might view favorably a petition for a pardon. The father rejected the idea categorically. It was an attempt at political blackmail, he declared.[2]

Eliezer Gruenbaum was almost twenty-one at the time of his arrest. According to one version of the story, two uniformed policemen and two plainclothesmen forcibly entered his parents' home on Tłomackie Street in Warsaw. Yitzhak protested the violation of his privacy and of his parliamentary immunity, but to no avail. The policemen discovered a mimeograph machine and piles of placards in the son's room, proof of the young man's involvement in the outlawed Communist Party. They arrested Eliezer. According to another version, he was arrested far from home, at an illegal party meeting in Łódź.[3] The regime of Józef Piłsudski used whatever means it thought fit to fight against those it viewed as its enemies. Eliezer was interrogated, tortured, and brought to trial. The authorities were determined to prevent the Communist leadership from staging attention-grabbing demonstrations and disturbances that could produce martyrs. They had learned their lesson from the case of Naftali Botwin, a young Jewish Communist executed in 1925 for shooting a police informer. Botwin had become an icon of bravery and sacrifice, and an inspiration for other revolutionaries. Parents even named their children after him.[4]

The trials were summary. The prisoners — Gruenbaum and his four comrades were but part of a much larger group — were brought into the courtroom in groups of five to ten, or even twenty to thirty, seated on a bench, and told to give their versions of the story. Without listening to their answers, the judges convicted and sentenced them en masse, in assembly-line fashion. The trial was over even before his parents had decided which lawyer to retain. A member of the family who held a top post in the Polish Ministry of the Interior told Eliezer's parents that their son had been turned in by someone inside the party. The young Gruenbaum, who already had a reputation for bucking authority, had acquired enemies who feared his independence of thought, his critical bent, and his sharp tongue.[5]

Eliezer was born in Warsaw on November 27, 1908, a year and a half after his older brother. He attended Tarbut, a school run in the spirit of nonreligious "general" — meaning middle-class — Zionism, and, to his bourgeois parents' chagrin, he and his brother joined the socialist-Zionist HaShomer haTza'ir youth movement, which by 1930 counted eighteen thousand members in Poland.[6] Both attended the movement's "nest," as its chapter houses were called, on Rimarska Street, where they sang Hebrew songs and tried to evoke a little bit of the Land of Israel in Poland. They also held mock trials of literary characters as a means of debating issues relating to the individual's responsibility to himself and society, the Jewish question and its solution, the modern world, the Zionist pioneer movement, and democracy versus dictatorship. They discussed the role of youth in society, lifestyles, love, double standards, and collective living. From time to time they attended seminars at a training farm outside Warsaw, where they heard lectures given by the brilliant speakers who belonged to or were sympathetic toward the movement. They hiked along the banks of the Vistula and in the countryside, played pranks, and showed Polish toughs that Jewish boys weren't cowards.

The "nest" was divided into "battalions" that bore names taken from the geography of the Land of Israel, such as Tel Hai and Merhaviah. They viewed themselves as a "fighting, not a dreaming" force imbued with Zionist, socialist, and collectivist consciousness. The nest also produced many of the young people who would, just a few years hence, become leaders of the Warsaw ghetto uprising—among them Tusia Altman, Margalit Landau, Israel Gutman, and Mordechai Anielewicz.

In 1925, when he was seventeen years old, Eliezer quit HaShomer haTza'ir to join what he viewed as the "true" Left, meaning the Communist Youth Union of Warsaw.[7] His HaShomer haTza'ir friends later explained that they had opposed Gruenbaum's ecumenical efforts to bring HaShomer haTza'ir into an alliance of all left-wing and Marxist forces in Poland, one that would support the international revolutionary causes being promoted by the Comintern.[8] They demanded that he desist. It was not, they stressed, a personal matter. Other members had also been forbidden to devote their energies and talents to the world's problems. Members of HaShomer haTza'ir were expected to focus on the Jewish nation, in particular the Polish Jewish community, as a means of realizing a full, fundamental, Zionist solution to the Jewish dilemma. They were warned against "red assimilation"—that is, the loss of Jewish national identity within the socialist movement. "If we disperse along many roads, we will turn into road dust," Anielewicz cautioned. The relationships between the Jewish youth movements of the time were defined by their overwhelmingly ideological approach to all issues, both Jewish and international. No question was anything less than critical, and the fate of the world, hanging as it did in the balance, seemed to them to depend on the ideological positions they argued and carefully honed. In such an atmosphere, it was not unusual for a member to be expelled for ideological deviation. That did not happen to Eliezer, but he eventually concluded that HaShomer haTza'ir's ideology was not internationalist and revolutionary enough for his tastes.

His fervent activity in HaShomer haTza'ir and afterward in the Communist Party did not prevent Eliezer from graduating high school and matriculating as a law student. His younger brother later related that their parents viewed Eliezer as the most successful of the three sons. He was good-looking and charismatic. Girls were drawn to him, undeterred by his trademark feature, a large bald spot that developed while he was still a teenager.[9]

The older Gruenbaum had cut his political chops in Poland of the 1920s, campaigning for two goals in parallel. First, he sought full civil rights for Poland's Jews in the spirit of the Helsingsfors Program adopted by a convention of Russian Zionists in 1906, which Gruenbaum had helped draft. Second, he promoted a Zionist solution to the anomalous status of Poland's Jews — that is, the resettlement of Europe's Jews in the Land of Israel. By the time of Eliezer's arrest, Yitzhak Gruenbaum's political position had begun to erode, but many of his coreligionists still referred to him as "king of the Jews." His fiftieth birthday, in 1929, was celebrated in the community with a pomp and circumstance that even some of his disciples thought bordered on a cult of personality. In any case, both friend and foe admired his political acumen, which he exercised over a large and demographically diverse country subject to frequent political and economic reversals. No matter what the crisis, he always managed to defend the interests of his constituencies.[10]

After being partitioned between Russia, Germany, and Austria at the end of the eighteenth century, Poland did not again gain its independence until the end of World War I, when a new Polish state had been constituted on the territory of the previous Polish kingdom. But these lands were not peopled only by Poles — about 40 percent of the new country's population consisted of national minorities — Ukrainians, Germans, Belarusians, and three million Jews. The constant tensions between majority and minorities quickly undid the patchwork quilt of the Polish state. The minorities sought autonomy, while the Polish populace developed fierce animosity toward the non-Poles who threatened to unravel their new country. Antisemitic nationalist and clericalist factions that sought Polish ethnic suzerainty gained ever more support and power.

The dueling interests of so many ethnic groups paralyzed Polish politics. Governments rose and fell every few months, with a new one coming into power no fewer than fifteen times during the republic's first four years. Yitzhak Gruenbaum labored to unite minority representatives in parliament into a single political grouping that could wield serious political power, and in 1922 became the leader of the Bloc of National Minorities. A coup d'état in May 1926 made General Piłsudski, a war hero who had served as the republic's first head of state, the country's effective strongman. He dismissed the government and brutally repressed all opposition.[11]

The country's dire economic crisis make matters worse for the minorities, the Jews included. The government imposed heavy taxes, which struck the middle class in particular. On top of this, special levies were imposed on the

Jews. The worldwide depression of 1929 came to a Poland that was already in the midst of a severe economic downturn. A fifth of the working-age population was unemployed.

For Poland's Jews, the political, economic, and social catastrophe was exacerbated by official and unofficial antisemitism. While the government promised to honor the Polish Minority Treaty (the "Little Treaty of Versailles"), which guaranteed the rights of all the country's ethnic groups, the Jews included, in practice it was ignored. The state instituted a deliberate policy of discrimination that restricted the areas in which Jews and other minorities could work. Only a few government jobs were open to them. The government provided ethnic Polish businessmen with incentives and financial subsidies, such as credit guarantees, which were not available to minority groups. Since many Jews were self-employed artisans and merchants, they were thus disadvantaged against their ethnic Polish competitors. They also lost a competitive advantage when the government forbade businesses to open on Sundays and Christian holidays. The state also established monopolies in a large number of sectors, further restricting the fields in which Jews could work.[12]

The economic situation polarized the Jewish community. A small and angry wealthy minority faced off against the indigent masses who engaged in peddling and small trade. About a quarter of the population required assistance before holidays. The offices of community institutions and charities were packed with merchants and small businessmen seeking aid—people who had just recently been among the contributors to these funds. The Jews were further weakened as they split into factions that advocated different approaches to coping with the situation.

Jews from villages and towns who had lost all they had moved into the large cities, where their presence further fueled the flames of an already fiery antisemitism. Hostility toward the Jewish minority soon took on institutional form with the foundation of explicitly antisemitic political movements such as Piast and Endek, both of them Catholic and right wing. The latter attracted many members of the educated petite bourgeoisie as well as the working class. The economic and social crisis was also fertile ground for the growth of the Communist Party, which Eliezer had just joined. Yitzhak Gruenbaum, by now an experienced political warhorse, also sought to use the crisis to shore up his support, but the first signs of tragedy were already intruding into his life and that of his family.

Poland's Jews were a diverse community, culturally and politically aware and active. No fewer than forty-four different political parties competed in the Jewish community's internal elections in Warsaw in 1936.[13] The leader of such a community was hardly a small fish.

The Jews in Poland generally preferred to support a Jewish party rather than a Polish one.[14] But there were a lot of Jewish parties to choose from. Some were anti-Zionist, such as the socialist Bund and the anti-Zionist, ultrareligious Agudat Israel party. The Zionist parties were divided into four groups—left, center, right, and religious. Yitzhak Gruenbaum led the General Zionists, a liberal centrist party that represented the middle class and white-collar professionals. At the end of the 1920s this party enjoyed a large base of support. But by the time the Gruenbaums—father, mother, and all three sons—left Poland, the party had lost much of its constituency. Much of the Jewish community turned against its policies and feared that it was leading the Jews of Poland into a dead end—or so, at least, its opponents cautioned at every opportunity.[15]

The older Gruenbaum believed that the Bloc of National Minorities, with the support of some ten million Polish citizens, a third of the country's population, could impel the government to implement the minorities charter. It was essential, in his mind, that the Jews act as a unitary and stable political force in this political power game.[16] Polish Jews, he maintained, should never consent to discrimination nor accommodate themselves to "moderate" or "soft" antisemitism on the part of the state on the grounds that it was tolerable and served as a pressure valve that kept public antisemitism under control. His followers said that he tried to instill his community with a refusal to accept any kind of injustice or repression. He firmly opposed acquiescence in a withholding of some civil rights from the Jews, on the grounds that it was simply a step toward denying them all rights.

But some Jewish groups, such as Agudat Israel, viewed Yitzhak Gruenbaum as an infuriatingly blatant secularist who goaded rather than ingratiated himself with the gentile authorities. A majority of Poland's Jews were observant—in the Jewish community elections held in Warsaw in the early 1920s, religious parties had won a majority, and nationally, according to Agudat Israel's calculations, they accounted for 35–40 percent of the Jewish voting public. Yet, to the chagrin of religious political leaders, Gruenbaum was dragging the Jews, kicking and screaming, into a minorities faction at odds with the Polish government. Even worse, the bloc was led by an extremist, secularist, and militant Zionist, namely Gruenbaum himself.

Yitzhak Gruenbaum and his allies viewed their showing in the Polish parliamentary elections of 1922 as a stellar victory for their militant strategy. They held the balance of power that enabled them to ensure the election of Gabriel Narutowicz to the presidency, to the chagrin of the Right. But Agudat Israel, for its part, saw it as a Pyrrhic victory, political folly, and an unsustainable attempt to impose Jewish autonomy on the Poles in their own land. In the view of this anti-Zionist religious party, the Jewish advantage would be short-lived, and the strategy disregarded the depth of Polish antisemitism, the limits of Jewish power in the Diaspora, and the inevitable fact that any Jewish political gains would lead to a backlash that would in the end make the Jewish position all the more tenuous. As if to prove their point, President Narutowicz was assassinated soon after his election, his murderers declaring that they could not accept a president of Poland elected by foreigners, members of the country's minorities. The assassination was followed by anti-Jewish rioting and a boycott of Jewish businesses. Legislators introduced antisemitic bills, some of which were passed into law, such as a law outlawing Jewish ritual slaughter and another imposing quotas on the number of Jews in the universities. All these, the ultra-Orthodox leaders maintained, were the sad consequences of Gruenbaum's political maneuverings.[17]

Under the circumstances, it is not surprising that many of Gruenbaum's opponents were hardly sorry when Eliezer was arrested. There could be no better proof, they thought, of the fruitless nature of the elder Gruenbaum's policies, the shallowness of his view of the world, and his failure to achieve peaceful relations between the Jews and the Poles. He had even failed to ensure his family's safety and happiness.

Miriam Gruenbaum maintained contact with her jailed son, traveling to Lancicia once every two weeks. Eliezer asked her to bring him novels and books to help him learn French and Spanish. He didn't complain about prison conditions, but his pale face, his rapid loss of weight, and his bent back testified to his declining health.

Nevertheless, he helped organize activities for his fellow political prisoners, such as morning exercises and classes in the writings of Marx and Lenin. He had them read works of literature and led discussions of current events. In prison he met Communist writers who helped him broaden his acquaintance with and commitment to Communist doctrine.[18]

Miriam refused to accept her husband's advice that they all wait out the term of Eliezer's sentence. She resolved to use the family's position and connections to free her son. "We'll try to get him freed for medical reasons," she told an influential friend of the family. Bronisław W. Pieracki, the interior minister in Aleksander Prystor's new and antisemitic cabinet, was the man who could get the thing done. Politically powerful because of his long membership in Piłsudski's camp,[19] Pieracki could open many doors. Furthermore, his portfolio gave him authority over the police and the prison system. In the summer of 1931, after Eliezer had served about two and a half years of his sentence, conditions seemed right to obtain his freedom. Pieracki "acceded" to a recommendation made by the prison service's medical board that Eliezer

Gruenbaum be freed "until he is found able to continue his sentence."[20] It was clear to his parents that he had to be spirited out of Poland. He would not be capable of refraining from political activity if he stayed, and subversion would almost certainly land him in jail again.

The chosen destination was France. There was family in Paris and Grenoble, part of the Polish Jewish exodus to France. To head off the possibility that Eliezer's younger brother, Yonatan, would also run afoul of the law, the parents had already sent him to live with Yitzhak's sister in Paris.[21] Friends of the family again helped out. A passport was quickly issued in Poland, and a French visa obtained. A cover story was manufactured to explain the sudden trip. To avoid suspicion, Eliezer's stated destination was Prague; only from there would he set out for France. Members of the family traveled with him to the Czechoslovakian border—Miriam wanted to make sure that he would not run into any unexpected problems at the crossing. Furthermore, she wanted to keep an eye on her son and prevent him from taking advantage of the journey to contact friends in the underground. If he were caught in the company of other Communists, there would be no way to save him.[22] In Paris, Miriam and Yitzhak hoped, their firebrand son would lead a calm and comfortable life.

3 Paris, Fifth Arrondissement, 5 Rue Linné, 1931

Eliezer was taken in by the Polish-Jewish Communist Party cell in Paris. His comrades were members of the Polish Communist Party (Komunistyczna Partia Polski — KPP) who had fled to France either because the Polish authorities were after them or because of economic hardship — and in some cases both. As usual, he had a lover, which made his adjustment a bit easier. He also received help from members of Main d'Oeuvre Immigré, an immigrant workers' trade union controlled in practice by the French Communists. Committed to the principles of the French Revolution, *liberté, égalité, fraternité,* France opened its gates to immigrant workers and, in particular, to political exiles in need of asylum. The first wave of Eastern European Jewish immigrants, from Russia, Romania, and Galicia, had arrived there in the 1880s.

A second wave arrived in the 1920s, following the end of World War I. But this time the Jews came from a different set of countries — Poland, the Baltic states, Hungary, and Romania. A third wave flowed in during the 1930s, this time from Central Europe. When Adolf Hitler came to power, Jews fled Germany, and after the *Anschluss* many fled Austria as well. More came in the wake of *Kristallnacht*. The result was that by the end of the 1930s, France was home to about 90,000 French Jewish citizens and another 190,000 Jewish aliens. About half of this latter group arrived during this turbulent decade.[1]

The Jewish population was quite diverse, ranging from the totally assimilated who exhibited no trace of their Jewish origins to those who took fierce pride in their ethnicity. The Jewish refugees were divided by different languages and cultural practices, by their occupations, their political affiliations, and their attitudes toward their religion and its practices. Those who had been active leftists in Poland were, in Paris, taken in by the socialist-Zionist factions, the Bund, and the French Communist Party (known by its French initials, PCF). On the eve of World War II more than ninety Jewish periodicals were published in France. Of these, thirty-six were in the Yiddish language, two of which, the *Naye Prese* and the *Parizer Heint*, came out daily. Of course, some of these publications appeared for only a short time.

The PCF, founded in December 1920, attracted intellectuals, artists, and writers, but its membership and leadership were drawn predominantly from the proletariat. By 1923 the party's leadership had realized that if it wanted to absorb the Eastern European newcomers it needed a more flexible structure. To make membership easier for the refugees, it supplemented the party's central nucleus in the capital with larger circles. One was a Jewish cell that is estimated to have had two hundred to three hundred members. Beyond that, there were cells and branches located in the city's quarters, built around immigrants from different countries of origin, such as Polish and Romanian cells.

These latter cells made up the Main d'Oeuvre Immigré, the Foreign Work Force.[2] It operated among Paris's indigent workers, in the neighborhoods in which they lived, incorporating members of different occupations. Among them were leatherworkers, cobblers, tailors, clock repairmen, woodworkers, makers of cane chairs, and carpenters, as well as the headstone makers centered on the Père Lachaise cemetery. These craftsmen worked, for the most part, in tiny, bare, dark workshops in the northern, southern, and eastern quarters. The PCF was a powerful presence in these areas, creating what was called at the time Paris's "Red Belt."[3]

The complex structure of the PCF and its satellite organizations was reflected in the plethora of publications they produced. The *Naye Prese*, which commenced publication on January 1, 1934, was the most important. We do not know what newspaper Eliezer first associated himself with and when he began to write for it, but he was well aware that journalism was an important way of gaining influence in his new milieu. Two pictures emerge from what he wrote and told his family. In one version, he joined the staff of a Polish-language newspaper that, according to its editors, had a circulation of about nine thousand. This newspaper ran on a deficit, which its workers had to make up from their own pockets. Eliezer used some of the money that his mother sent him, initially from Poland and later from Palestine, for this purpose. Miriam meant him to use the money to continue his legal studies.[4] "My first series of articles," Eliezer wrote to his parents, "was on Paris's wealthy people."[5]

The other version comes from his younger brother, who wrote that Eliezer founded a new newspaper. It was targeted at the tens of thousands of Poles who had moved to Paris in the period between the two world wars to work in

France's mines and on its farms.[6] This Polish-language newspaper was written in a light and attractive style and managed to break even. Among other things, Eliezer wrote for it an anti-Nazi spy novel in installments.[7]

Eliezer met his girlfriend, Bronke Gurfinkel, at a meeting of a cell made up of Polish Jews, and a short while later they moved in with each other in an apartment they rented for sixty francs a month at the edge of the Fifth Arrondissement, across from the Jardin des Plantes and next to a small zoo filled with the noise of small children. Nearby, on rue des Arènes, was a small park containing the nearly complete remains of a Roman amphitheater, where the neighborhood's elderly residents played at *boules*. They bought the little they needed for their modest lifestyle at the local open-air market on rue Mouffetard, one of Paris's oldest, situated right next to their home. Their best friends were other young couples out to change the world and certain that communism was the way to do so — among them Yosef (Yossel) Dorembus and his wife, Paula, as well as Yankel (Jacques) Handelsman and his wife, Bella.

Eliezer managed to complete his law studies, passing his final examinations on July 31, 1935. In June and July 1936 he passed the French bar exams and received his license to practice law. Before being forced to leave France he also studied political economics, receiving a degree in this field in May 1939.[8]

His parents had reached Paris in 1932. Yitzhak Gruenbaum left Poland disappointed and frustrated.[9] All political parties feared for the present and offered, each in its own way, hopes for a brighter future. The result was a major reorganization of the political map. The Bund grew stronger. David Ben Gurion pressed his party to take over the leadership of the worldwide Zionist movement with the support of the Jewish masses in Poland. His major rival, Ze'ev Jabotinsky, who had a large following in that country, sought to do the same. Both Ben-Gurion's Mapai and Jabotinsky's Revisionists encroached on the support of the center parties that the elder Gruenbaum represented. Gruenbaum, for his part, sensed that no one was listening to him. On June 23, 1932, he rejected an invitation to attend the Polish Zionist Congress, signaling to his colleagues that this chapter in his life was over.

In Paris, Yitzhak joined his two younger sons (the eldest was living on a kibbutz in Palestine) and his sister, as well as his old friend Marc Jarblum (Yarblum) one of the founders of the socialist-Zionist Poalei Zion party in Poland. He had been in Paris since 1907. Yitzhak had been acting editor of the Polish-Yiddish-Zionist *Heint*. But throughout his years in Poland, state censorship had prevented him from publishing reports of violations of Jewish rights and of antisemitism, and protests against these.[10] In Paris, he and other writers from that newspaper founded and wrote in a new incarnation of the newspaper, the *Parizer Heint*, which became the voice of the Polish Jewish immigrants in Paris. It stood ready to serve Yitzhak as a toehold in his new city, a platform on which he could again display his polemical skills—now free of censorship. But this did not happen. A year later Yitzhak and his wife decided to go to Palestine. Their youngest son followed a short time later. But Eliezer remained in Paris along with his Communist comrades.[11]

4 Spain, March 1938–1939

ON MARCH 3, 1938, ELIEZER boarded a train at the Gare de Lyon, the huge and colorful train station on Paris's east side. His official destination was Perpignan, a city on the border with Spain,[1] but his real objective was to insinuate himself over the border and sign up for combat in the Spanish Civil War.[2] Thousands of foreign nationals — intellectuals, writers, poets, romantics, and adventurers — were volunteering to fight on the Republican side. Others arrived as journalists and observers.[3] Most of them were convinced that the war was an essential part of the rearguard battle that the forces of good in the free world were fighting against the Nazi-fascist tide.

The first battles between the opposing armies had been fought on July 17–20, 1936. The forces of the Right, supported by the church and joined by most of the army's best units, rebelled against the government. They disavowed any duty to support the official Spanish government, a center-left coalition that had taken power the previous February with a bare majority in parliament. That government, they claimed, was a sham, serving as a front for workers' militias that had organized under the sponsorship of the proletarian Left. These forces, said the Right, were destroying Spain's economic and industrial infrastructure. Anarchy and terror has spread throughout the country, the state was crumbling, and the government was but a fig leaf concealing from the English and French the unofficial dictatorship of the proletariat.[4] "Better to destroy Madrid than to leave it in the hands of the Marxists," declared General Francisco Franco, the rebels' leader. The archbishop of Salamanca, Franco's provisional capital, explained that "the Jews and the Freemasons have poisoned the national soul with absurd doctrines."[5]

Spain quickly spiraled into vicious bloodshed.[6] Many of the parties had an interest in war. For the Communists, it was a way of enhancing their influence worldwide; Moscow supported the Spanish partisans via the Comintern, enabling it to present the Spanish conflict as an international cause that would lead to the establishment of a worldwide proletarian front. For party cells in countries like Poland, where Communists were pariahs, the Spanish struggle provided inspiration and enthusiasm and helped bring in new recruits. It reinforced revolutionary consciousness, unity, and discipline. For both Moscow and other Communist parties, it provided a springboard for taking control of other left-wing factions and organizations and coloring them strongly red. The enlistment office in Paris, run by a Soviet colonel, Karol "Walter" Świerczewski, launched a process of "fusion and finishing."[7]

The Spanish conflict was also an attractive cause for the noncommunist Left, veterans of strikes, demonstrations, and "hunger marches" in many countries. They viewed the civil war in Spain as a continuation of their own campaigns against real or imagined exploiters of the working class. Romantics, who longed to do something and to change the world, found in Spain something to latch on to. As Arthur Koestler wrote, for bohemians, intellectuals, and leftists, Spain was Greenwich Village on a revolutionary junket.

For the many Jews who volunteered to fight, the Spanish Civil War was a front in the campaign against Europe's burgeoning fascism, Nazism, and antisemitism. The open support lent to Franco by Nazi Germany, fascist Italy, and Portugal under dictator António Salazar helped cloud the fact that Franco's movement did not accord with the strict definitions of fascism, Nazism, and antisemitism. But that hardly mattered if, like Eliezer Gruenbaum, you were Jewish, romantic, and a Communist as well; Spain offered all you could ask for.

For Jews of all camps, volunteering to fight in Spain was a way of shattering negative stereotypes. Conventional wisdom, among both Jews and gentiles, was that the Jew did not fight. The Jew shut himself up inside his synagogue to be martyred when the sanctuary was set afire. Furthermore, the fact that the Jews, expelled from Spain in 1492, were now returning as freedom fighters, brought color to the cheeks of the new activist Jews of the 1930s. It was a modern, secular, just, and enlightened Crusade. Few expected that the commissars and enforcers of political correctness circulating among them were in fact on the hunt for "spies" and other provocateurs for their blacklists. No one knew that some of the political supervisors could be so cruel.[8]

The idea of systematically recruiting fighters for the Republican cause was proposed by Communist leaders a short time after the conflict broke out. The Communist leadership in France and Spain were the principal advocates. Stalin gave his consent, perhaps mostly as a way of getting foreign Communists in the USSR off his back. The final obstacle was Spain's prime minister, Francisco Largo Caballero, who at the end of 1936 finally endorsed the establishment of the International Brigades.[9]

But the first volunteers were already in Spain, having arrived just a few days after fighting broke out. Several hundred non-Spanish leftists offered their help to the elected government. Some of them had been in Barcelona when hostilities broke out, where they had been participating in the alternative Olympic games that had been organized there in protest against the official games in Berlin.[10]

According to the experts, some thirty-five to forty thousand volunteers from as many as fifty-five different countries fought in the war. But volunteers came and went, and many died, so at any given moment no more than half that number were actually serving in the ranks, and many fewer toward the end of the war. Eliezer and his fellows seem to have reached Spain toward the end of the war, when there was a need for reinforcements. Over the course of the war, about seven thousand of the volunteers came from France. Another sixteen hundred came from Belgium and Holland, about five thousand from Poland, three thousand from the United States, two thousand from Britain, sixteen hundred from Yugoslavia, and five thousand from Germany and Austria. Approximately three hundred came from Palestine, mostly Jews but also Arabs and Armenians. A few came from Ethiopia, which was suffering under Italian occupation.[11] The Soviet Union tightened its hold over these forces via the senior officers it sent to France. Mothers and wives who came to search for loved ones from whom they had not heard remained and served as nurses and aides in battlefield hospitals.[12]

The war lasted thirty-two months, marked by massacres, rape, the slaughter of prisoners, and indiscriminate aerial bombings and shelling. The volunteers were badly equipped and badly commanded. Their units, at least during the first part of the war, were not proper military formations.[13] They suffered heavy losses, largely because most of the volunteers were not trained soldiers. Further casualties were caused by the weather, especially the furious heat and disruptions in the supply of water to the front line. The Republican forces, as those loyal to the government were called, lacked armored units and an air force to match Franco's. They were sent out on hopeless charges, strafed by machine guns, against well-defended enemy positions. Commanders and "military advisers" pushed for hopeless attacks, ostensibly to improve morale but actually for propaganda purposes. In retrospect, some of the volunteers reported that, in certain engagements, the Spanish forces used the volunteers as cannon fodder. Between a fifth and a quarter of the volunteers were killed; large numbers were wounded, for a total casualty rate of about 50 percent.[14] On the other side, the rebel forces included some sixty thousand African mercenaries, forty thousand of whom were Moroccans, paid for by funds given to Franco by Germany and Italy.[15] These forces made a significant contribution to the bloodbath.

By most estimates, a full fifth of the volunteers were Jewish. Jews were naturally inclined, of course, to sign up to fight against the Nazis' allies, and many were aligned with the Left. Between sixty-five hundred and eight thousand Jews volunteered to fight in Spain, among them socialists, Communists, Bundists, and Zionists. Jews also made up nearly a third of the American contingent. This disproportionate number of Jews who volunteered from all countries is remarkable by any standard.[16]

Some of them came directly from their home countries, while others were already exiles or on the run from persecution, and thus came to Spain from places of temporary refuge. Unsurprisingly, Jews made up a particularly large proportion of the volunteers' medical corps — a full 70 percent. In some of the field hospitals the working language was Yiddish.[17] The Polish Thirteenth Brigade, known as the Dombrowski Brigade, included a Jewish company named after Naftali Botwin, and it was there that Eliezer served.

Jewish volunteers also came from Palestine. But not everyone in the Yishuv was happy to see Jewish men and women setting out to fight in Spain. At the time, a huge gulf separated the Palestinian Communist movement from anything that reeked of Zionism. The Zionist parties found themselves growing ever more distant from those who were gradually coming to define themselves as non-Zionists or anti-Zionists.

Eliezer left Paris on his way to Spain at the beginning of March 1938, some two years after the war began. Why so late? Apparently he decided to volunteer in response to calls for reinforcements for the Botwin Company, which had been decimated in battles at the end of 1937 and the beginning of 1938. He may also have been motivated by the link between the Spanish conflict and the political needs of the Jewish Communists within the Parisian Jewish community.

Yonatan Gruenbaum later related that his brother left for Spain with a group of Jewish Communist volunteers led by Jacques Kaminski.[18] But in another account Eliezer left for Spain in 1936 as a war correspondent. "I watch, listen, and write," he wrote to his parents in the summer of 1938.[19] Like all the volunteers, he had to make his way over the Spanish border undetected by French and rebel guards enforcing the embargo that had been imposed on Spain and the international agreements that applied to the warring parties.[20] The volunteers were then taken to boot camp in Albecete, where they were trained in cavalry charges, artillery, and basic infantry skills. Discipline was tight. For several months, at least in the case of the first wave of volunteers, the members of the International Brigades were confined to their bases and underwent grueling training. When Eliezer and his companions arrived from France, there was no longer time for such intensive preparation, and training was reduced to a short period, perhaps of only a few days.

Whether short or long, their instruction included a brief course of ideological indoctrination that ended with a celebration and the volunteers taking an oath: "I volunteer for the International Brigades because my enemies, the fascists, are the enemies of the Spanish people, because I know that if fascism is victorious in Spain, it will come tomorrow to my country and my home. . . . I will fight to the last drop of my blood to save the freedom of Spain and the entire world."[21] After this preparation, the volunteers were dispersed to their units. Eliezer's company was, according to one source, an antitank unit.[22] When he reached his unit, the Polish Brigade was already battle-weary and very scarred. The Jews involved, both those among the fighting forces in Spain itself and those of the Jewish party cells in their home countries, had lobbied hard to be treated like other volunteer units based on national affiliation, and this had brought results. On December 12, 1937, in the city of Tardadientes on the Aragon front, the Jewish Naftali Botwin Company had been founded.[23]

As in other International Brigade units, the Jewish company had been named after a symbol of the struggle for equality and opposition to tyranny. Ludwig Renn, a German pacifist writer and deputy commander of the Thirteenth Brigade,[24] had suggested at the time that it be called the Bar Kokhba company, after the leader of the Jewish rebellion against the Romans in the second century AD, but several Communist Jews, chief among them Gershon Dua-Admani and Eugeniusz Szir, opposed this, perhaps because Bar Kokhba had already been adopted by the Zionists as a national hero. They preferred naming the unit for Botwin, who came from a new and, most importantly, different semantic and symbolic field, and they prevailed.[25] On the occasion of the founding of the Botwin Company, the commander of the Dombrowski Brigade, Janek Barvinski, and its commissar, Stach Matuszczak, issued a special order of the day:[26]

> Today . . . the Naftali Botwin Company has been added to our glorious family of fighters against fascism.
>
> Ever since we first trod on Spanish soil, we have done what all [the International Brigades] have done, first as a company, then as a battalion, and now as a brigade — Poles, Germans, Ukrainians, Belarusians, Jews, Hungarians, Spanish, and others — in brotherhood.
>
> The common struggle, the common blood that has flowed, have toughened our ranks and taught us to value and love each other. . . .
>
> Among all the volunteers, especially in the Dombrowski Brigade, the Jewish volunteers have stood out with their heroism, fighting spirit, and devotion to the struggle against fascism.
>
> At the outskirts of Madrid, at Guadalajara, at Brunete, everywhere where

> our brigade has fought . . . the Jewish volunteers have fought at the front line, serving as exemplars of heroism and anti-fascist consciousness. On the basis of our intention to underline the large number and great importance of the Jewish volunteers in the Dombrowski Brigade, and in memory of the Jewish warriors who have fallen for freedom, we have resolved that the second company of the Palafox Polish Heroes' Battalion will be, from this point forward, named after Naftali Botwin. . . .
>
> Botwin . . . gave his young life for the struggle against the forces of reaction and fascism. He fought bravely and died a hero's death . . . his name is a symbol and his life an emblem of the struggle for your freedom as Jews and our freedom as human beings. He is a symbol of international solidarity and the brotherhood of humanity.

At its largest, 150 Jews from Poland, France, Belgium, and the Yishuv served in the Botwin Company. It also included two Palestinian Arabs, one of whom spoke Yiddish. The company was put together from two sources. The first was Jews who had previously served in the Brigade's Second Battalion, named after José Rebolledo de Palafox y Melci, hero of the siege of Saragossa in the Napoleonic wars. The rest were Jews who had completed their brief training period but had not yet been assigned to a fighting force.[27] Members of the unit spoke Yiddish, Polish, Spanish, and Ladino, and like every military unit, the Botwin Company needed an insignia, flag, and anthem. They designed a flag emblazoned in large letters "The Naftali Botwin Company" and the name of their brigade, "Palafox Brigade," along with the motto "For Our Freedom and for Your Freedom" in Spanish, Polish, and Yiddish. At the center of the flag was a three-pointed star, the symbol of the International Brigades.

As one might expect in a force composed more of intellectuals than professional soldiers, the company put out a newspaper, in Yiddish. The first three issues came out under the name *Frayheyts Kemfer*, and the subsequent four under the name *Botwin*. Y. Lekhter, who had been a writer for the *Naye Prese*, served as editor. The first issue appeared on December 30, 1937, with the last of the seven issues being dated November 3, 1938. It served to reinforce morale and as a means of disseminating propaganda. At first it was handwritten and reproduced by stencil. Afterward a Hebrew typewriter was obtained from the University of Barcelona. Jewish soldiers in other battalions complained that there were not enough copies. They also wanted to read the newspaper, which they felt "should become the organ of all Jewish freedom fighters in Spain." That did not happen. Brigade commanders may have feared bolstering Jewish nationalism to a point that might exceed what was appropriate for devout Communists.[28]

Prior to the arrival of Eliezer and his companions, the Botwin Company had taken part in several bitter battles. On February 12–13, 1938, it had been nearly wiped out at the battle of Extremadura. The generous estimates are that 20 out of its 120 soldiers survived, but other accounts say only 12. In the first wave of charges, the cavalry slaughtered the volunteers. The survivors were reinforced with new volunteers, and the company went on to fight on the Aragon front, taking part in the battles of Belchite, Lesera, and Kaspe. From there the company participated in another series of battles at Lérida, on the Ebro River front, and elsewhere.[29] Some number the company's casualties throughout its existence in the thousands, attributing this to the lack of sufficient pre-combat training and faulty arms and gear. Before going into battle they were told, "The fascists have lots of arms, kill them and take their weapons." According to one source, only 10 of the company's 120 men had rifles.[30]

The company's commanders were among those killed. Company Commander Karol Gutman was killed in battle on February 13, 1938, at Extremadura. His replacement, Leon Rubinstein, was wounded at Kespe along with Moshe Misha Reger, the latter being the nom de guerre of Commissar Eugeniusz (Gershon?) Szir. Another commander was Moshe Safir, an American Jew who had originally served in the Abraham Lincoln Brigade. He was brought in to replace the wounded commanders, but was wounded himself in the battle of Lérida, afterward dying of his injuries. He was succeeded at the end of March 1938 by Emanuel Mink, at which time the company received reinforcements and returned to its original strength of 120 men. Mink went to the Botwin Company along with Eliezer. He had received the new recruits at the training base, rushed them through basic training in anticipation of coming battles, and then returned to his command of the company following Safir's death.[31]

At the end of April 1938 the Botwin Company was transferred to the Ebro River front, and at the end of May it was sent to a mustering area in the Pradel region, where it relieved another unit and prepared itself for the anticipated battle at Ebro. During this time the company invested time and effort in expanding and enriching its cultural activities. Mink was sent to an advanced course and was replaced by Moshe Halbersberg. He was killed at the battle of Ebro, and Mink was called back to resume command of the force. He managed to serve in this position for only a brief time before being wounded. Alexander Szerman replaced him.[32]

Another soldier in the company was David Szmulewski. Like Eliezer, he had been born in Poland. At the beginning of the 1930s he emigrated to Palestine, where he joined the Communist Party. Like other Palestinian Communists, he was arrested by the British and deported to Poland. When the civil war broke out, he set out for Spain and joined the volunteers. After the war he fled with his comrades to France, where he was arrested. When the Nazis conquered France he, like other Jews, Mink among them, was interred in a French concentration camp. Sometime later he was sent to Auschwitz, where he joined the Communist underground.

On September 21, 1938, Juan Negrín, who had replaced Largo Caballero as prime minister in May of the previous year, ordered the dissolution of the International Brigades and their evacuation from Spain. His hope was that the rebels would respond by sending away their Nazi German and Italian Fascist auxiliaries, enabling Spain to embark on the road to ending the war under international supervision. But the response did not come. Hundreds of thousands of soldiers, among them the members of the Botwin Company, fought on the banks of the Ebro for four months. It was the company's last battle.

Thousands of disarmed volunteers wearing red carnations marched through the streets of Barcelona for the last time on November 15, 1938. The Botwin Company, however, remained in Spain even after the announcement that the International Brigades were being disbanded, both to secure the retreat of the loyalist troops, which had decided cross the French border out of Spain, and because some of the soldiers, in particular the German and Italian Jews, had nowhere to return to.

Those that remained joined other veterans of the International Brigades and founded a new fighting force under the command of Henrik Toruńczyk.[33] This contingent guarded the Spanish civilians and remnants of the Republican army that chose to withdraw to the border town of Parafruel and from there to seek refuge in France. Some of them lived in makeshift camps on the border of France for several years. Others, those who were able to go home, did so. Still others joined up with a variety of resistance forces, disappearing in Spain, Belgium, and even Poland and the Soviet Union.[34] The British, fearing that battle-tested Marxists could be a threat to their rule, hunted down those volunteers who tried to return home to Palestine. Most were not allowed to return in the first place. These refugees from the Yishuv ended up in France, the United States, or South America. Others went to Poland and then reentered Palestine as pioneer immigrants. But they were compelled to live under assumed names and to keep their service in Spain a secret for as long as the British were in charge.[35]

Eliezer enlisted in Toruńczyk's force, remaining in Spain until the leftist factions in beleaguered and starving Madrid began to fight each other. The fascists had not succeeded in taking the capital during the war, but on March 28, 1939, it finally fell to them. Eliezer and his comrades were indignant. "If it were up to me, I would make war a required subject at school. . . . Only someone who has seen war knows how to value life," he wrote to his parents. Like many of his companions, he was disillusioned because their exertions had not roused the masses. "The bleeding hearts in Europe thought that by contributing ten francs a month they were doing their duty to us. Now they'll pay the full price — but, unfortunately, we will, too."[36]

He left Spain as an experienced but bitterly disappointed soldier, and with a nom de guerre: Leon Berger. In the lists of soldiers in the brigades he was also named Albert, Gruenbaum, and Aka, perhaps a distortion of Itche, his nickname in his family. Those sources also state that he was murdered by the fascists in the Kielce pogrom of 1946, in Poland.[37]

It is easy to understand why he changed his name. Many like him did the same, but it was not just a romantic matter — an underground organization requires false names. In his particular case, his association with his father, a famous but controversial Zionist leader, was a problem, in particular among his fellow Communists in Spain. But why did he take the name Leon Berger? Was it his choice? Or was it a name given him by his friends?

5 Saint-Cyprien, Paris, Les Tourelles, Beaune-la-Rolande, France, 1939–1942

AFTER CROSSING INTO FRANCE, Eliezer and his stateless comrades were sent to the internment camp at Saint-Cyprien, pending determination of their cases. They realized that they had left France illegally, but as far as they were concerned they had done so to fight for the forces of good. That being the case, they maintained that, now that the war in Spain was over, they deserved, despite their lack of citizenship, to be allowed to reestablish their residence in France. Wasn't it only natural for a European country with a long-standing revolutionary heritage to allow them to do so? But the French authorities and the gendarmerie thought differently.[1] The unit that had been put together from the remains of the Botwin Company and other International Brigades soldiers had secured the northern retreat of Republican forces and their supporters, serving as a rearguard for some half a million refugees who fled into France. The French authorities established several hastily built internment camps to hold these expatriates — not just at Saint-Cyprien, but also at Gurs, Argèles, and Le Vernet. The latter held those brigade fighters and Spanish refugees that the French considered the most dangerous. Some brigade soldiers were sent to a camp in southern Algeria, including all the volunteers who had come from that country. In some of the camps conditions were harsh.[2] While the camps were originally set up to take in refugees from Spain, they would, within less than a year, serve as concentration camps for the many Jews being arrested by the French.[3] The Jewish-German artist Felix Nussbaum, flushed out by the Nazis from his hiding place in Belgium, was among those sent to the camp, where he painted a series of canvases documenting life there.

Once again, Miriam Gruenbaum came to her son's rescue. This time she had to travel a much greater distance — she left Jerusalem for Paris, as her youngest son, Yonatan, said, "to free the boy," a boy who was now thirty-one. In Paris she knocked on government doors, and once again she was able to enlist the aid of influential friends and acquaintances. Marc Jarblum, the old family friend, was as always ready to help. In the end, Miriam's campaign succeeded. Eliezer was permitted to return to Paris. In March 1939, exactly a year after leaving for Spain, he returned to rue Linné to finish up his political economy degree. He received his diploma two months later.[4]

He also resumed his Communist activities, returned to his newspaper job, and reunited with Bronke. But this normal life was interrupted by war just a few months later. Hitler invaded Poland on September 1, and two days after that Britain and France declared war on Germany. For some months little happened in what was then called the Phony War, but that was just a calm before the storm of a conflict of unprecedented proportions.

But before all this happened, in August, Eliezer's father asked him about his plans and tried to persuade him to join the rest of the family in Palestine. Like other Zionist leaders, Yitzhak Gruenbaum traveled to Geneva that month to attend a packed Zionist Congress over which the threat of war hovered. During the final week, delegates received urgent cables calling on them to return home. Many left before the congress adjourned, fearing that borders would be closed. The congress's standing committee had decided a few days previously to cut the congress short by a week. But then Chaim Weizmann, president of the Zionist Organization, appeared before the standing committee on Thursday, August 24, and proposed that the congress be adjourned that very night and not the next day, and his proposal was accepted. Yitzhak, fearful and yet hopeful, had already invited his son to meet him in Geneva.[5] Eliezer again chose to stay in Europe. He consciously and freely chose "red assimilation."

When he returned to Paris, Eliezer volunteered for the French army. At this time, a Communist's enlistment in a Western army was equivalent to shattering an entire squadron of idols. The Soviet Union, his ideological motherland, had signed a treaty of nonaggression with Nazi Germany in which the two countries agreed to partition Poland once again. The Molotov-Ribbentrop Pact enabled Germany to invade Poland almost unhindered. It also forced devout Communists like Eliezer into ideological contortions that even the former Soviet people's commissar for foreign affairs, Maxim Litvinov, a Jew, had difficulty with.[6] Eliezer, who had already displayed a penchant for interpreting Communist doctrine in his own way, did not feel bound by the pact. He wanted to serve in the army of a nation preparing to fight the German-Soviet axis.[7]

But the French were willing to accept him only into the Foreign Legion. Eliezer refused, and instead enlisted, on January 20, 1940, in the Polish army organized by Władysław Sikorski, prime minister of the Paris-based Polish government-in-exile. This, too, constituted defiance of party discipline. But on June 17, France capitulated to Germany after six weeks of combat. Germany occupied northern France and set up a puppet regime, headquartered in Vichy and led by Marshal Philippe Pétain, a hero of World War I, to rule in the south. The Polish army relocated to England. Its French units were disbanded, and Eliezer was again a veteran rather than a soldier. He refused to flee France with the Polish army, preferring to resume Communist activity in Paris, this time underground. He moved to 8 rue Victor Cousin, closer to the Sorbonne and the Luxembourg Gardens, in the heart of the city's Latin Quarter.[8]

France's Jews suddenly found themselves living under a totalitarian Nazi regime. They, like France's other inhabitants, had lost all hope that Hitler could be held back. Most of the ruling elite and the public placed almost mystical faith in the fatherly figure of Pétain.

On July 11, citing a decision of the previous day, Pétain assumed legislative, judicial, and executive powers in order, he said, to reshape the character of France, "purge" it of what his supporters called the "heritage of the Enlightenment and the Revolution," the "refuse" of liberalism, socialism, democracy, and universalism. Only eighty out of the seven hundred members of the National Assembly dared vote against what they termed a putsch.[9]

The Vichy regime's supporters included traditional antisemites from the extreme Right, members of any number of conservative, Catholic, and anti-Enlightenment and antirevolutionary organizations. The regime was also supported by large parts of the bourgeois Right, who remembered with rancor the Popular Front government of 1936–1938, led by the Jewish socialist Léon Blum. They viewed the Vichy government's policies as a needed antidote to the Front's left-wing legislation.[10] Supported by this coalition of forces, in the summer of 1940 Pétain and his prime minister, Pierre Laval, pursued an antisemitic policy that quickly removed Jews from public life, culture, science, administration, and the law. Jews were required to register with the interior ministry, and their property was confiscated.[11]

But the picture grew grimmer as the differences between French sanctions and the German policy of terror and murder became evident. The German administration in the north decided, in June 1942, to require all Jews to wear yellow Stars of David. But, with the overwhelming support of the French public, the Vichy government refused to impose the same requirement in the south. When, that same spring and summer, the Germans began hunting down Jews and sending them to death camps in Poland, the French were appalled and expressed compassion and empathy for the Jews. The popularity of the Vichy regime declined. As the French grew more critical of the Germans and of the

Vichy government's collaboration with the Nazis, they displayed greater willingness to help Jews.[12]

The Germans told the Vichy regime to annul the citizenship of all French Jews so that they could be deported to death camps, but the French refused categorically. Even Laval opposed such a move, resisting pressure from both the Nazis and extreme French antisemites and collaborators.[13] In November, when Allied forces invaded North Africa, the Germans moved into previously unoccupied southern France. Yet even then the Vichy regime continued to oppose the yellow badge and, in particular, as the destination and fate of those shipped to the east came to be known, the deportation of Jewish citizens. The Germans continued to affirm that they viewed themselves as bound by the armistice agreement with France, meaning that they recognized the authority of the Vichy government and took its wishes into account. It was in the German interest not to impel the French authorities to resist the German occupation or to cause Pétain to decamp to Allied-controlled North Africa. The German occupation of France thus remained less onerous than the Nazi regime in Poland.[14] But it was only Jews who held French citizenship who benefited. The 150,000 Jews in France who were foreign nationals were prey to the Nazis' talons. The French regime arrested and interred them, and then handed them over to the Germans.

When roundups commenced in Paris, people could easily deny that Jews were being arrested simply because they were Jews. For example, British subjects, including Jews from the Yishuv, were arrested and interred in the Romainville fort just outside Paris. Several dozen Zionist activists were imprisoned at Les Tourelles. Communists were also rounded up on charges of illegal political activity. Even the detention of Jewish immigrants could be attributed to the fact that they were not French nationals. Jews who didn't trust such excuses and felt threatened moved to the city's outer suburbs. It was hard to disregard the rumors that mass arrests were around the corner.[15] But the authorities deliberately used methods that misled the Jews. In the spring of 1941 they sent out more than six thousand orders to report to clubs, sports facilities, or schools for "identity checks." In response, 3,710 Jews, mostly of Polish extraction, reported as ordered. Those who had received the order were detained, and those who had accompanied them were told to go home to bring the detainees their personal effects. The detainees were then taken by bus to the Austerlitz train station, from which they were sent by special train to camps in Pithiviers[16] and Beaune-la-Rolande, in the department of Loiret, south of Paris.[17]

Eliezer was picked up by the police on April 1, 1941. Like other Communists, he was also told that he was being arrested for his underground activity and for his participation in the Spanish Civil War.[18] In his case, the destination was Les Tourelles camp, an army base[19] located in Paris that had been converted into a concentration camp for Jews and opponents of the regime. On May 15, 1941, he was transferred, along with other Polish Jews, to Beaune-la-Rolande.[20]

Despite his prison stay in Poland and his combat experience in Spain, it was not easy to readjust to camp conditions. Behind barbed wire he registered, handed over his money and his identification papers, and made his way, along with his fellow prisoners, to the wooden barracks that were now his home. There he slept on thin straw mattresses placed on wooden bunks, with at most a single blanket. There were only the most rudimentary sanitary facilities, and a diet of 125 grams of bread and a bowl of turnip soup per day. Clothes and shoes were in short supply, especially in the winter. The camp routine consisted of morning and evening inspections separated by hours of labor. The work included chores involved with the maintenance of the camp, and infrastructure work, such as road paving, in the camp or nearby. Veterans of the French army and the fathers of large families could work on nearby farms. Some of the workers even earned a small amount of money for their labor. During Eliezer's first months at the camp prisoners were allowed to receive one letter a week, which had to be written in French so that it could be censored by the prison authorities; two packages a month, which were carefully searched; and short visits.[21]

Several friends of Eliezer's were interred with him at Beaune-la-Rolande: Ijziykléar Oléar, Martin Steg, Daniel Finkelkraut, Jacques Furmanski, and Léon (Leib) Epstein. Some of them had been members of the Polish Communist cell in Paris, others knew Eliezer from Warsaw, and still others had been comrades-in-arms in Spain. Also in the camp were German-born members of the Communist Party such as Hermann Dymanski, Walter Ballas, Max Wilner, and Walli. The group elected Eliezer chief of their prison block and later to be "camp head." He functioned as a first among equals, chairing a committee set up by the camp's Jews and serving as their delegate to the camp authorities. The committee chose an executive that included two other members in addition to Eliezer, both Parisian Communists — Sznajder, who held the title of organizational secretary of the Polish Communist cell in Paris, and another member of that cell, Wikrowiecki. The three members of the committee were party to the secret preparations for the next stage, when they learned from party headquarters in Paris that they were to be deported from France.[22]

The overt and covert political battle between the different parties to which the Jews belonged seeped into the camp life, and each faction strove to preserve its influence. Thus, having organized the prisoners and having been selected as their leadership, Eliezer and his colleagues thought it essential to present a united and determined front toward the camp administration and toward all the Jewish prisoners. The standing of the Jewish section of the French Communist Party had begun to wane years earlier, at least since the spring of 1937.[23] Now they worked to improve the daily lives of the prisoners, seeking better food, more mail privileges, and respect for Jewish religious practices for those who observed them. They also sought to support prisoners' families, which were suffering from the loss of their breadwinners. The leadership also organized wide-ranging cultural activities that included lectures on current events in French and Yiddish and classes in foreign languages, geography, and history. They also sponsored exercise groups, a choir, a drama club, a sewing workshop, and even an art exhibition. Eliezer had the benefit of his prior prison and battle experience, not to mention his natural leadership skills.

The prisoners at the camp marked French, Jewish, and Communist holidays. On July 14 they celebrated Bastille Day, on November 11 the anniversary of the Bolshevik Revolution,[24] and on May 1 International Workers Day — May Day. Eliezer and his comrades also published an underground newsletter reporting developments culled from Allied radio stations. The newsletter was carefully and confidently handwritten in fifty copies that were distributed among the barracks. They served as the basis for organized discussions of camp and larger political issues.[25]

In April 1942 Eliezer and his colleagues received new instructions from the Communist Party in Paris. They were told to organize prison breaks that would allow as many Jews as possible to flee the camp. By October, 377 prisoners had escaped Beaune-la-Rolande. The prison administration punished those who remained by taking away the few privileges they had. In May 1942 Eliezer was supposed to escape himself, but the attempt failed, and he was separated from his group, his privileges were revoked, and he was placed in harsher conditions for thirty days.[26] In fact, Eliezer disputed his party's position, which advocated escape and forbade prisoners to work on farms or do other labor that aided the Nazi cause. Eliezer reasoned that any escape plan would set the strongest prisoners free while leaving the weak behind and without leaders. Furthermore, the remaining prisoners would be subject to collective punishment. Regarding work, he understood that the French regime was short of laborers. Turning the prisoners into productive workers would reduce the risk to their lives, he argued. But he submitted on these issues to party discipline.[27]

One lecture Eliezer gave left an indelible impression on those who heard him. The subject was the political and military situation following Germany's invasion of the Soviet Union in June 1941. His audience was shocked to hear him suggest that the Communist motherland might be defeated. His fellow Communists shouted him down with cries that the USSR could never be defeated. That was an article of faith. Furthermore, they countered, even if the Red Army were to lose a battle here and there, Eliezer, as a Communist leader, must know that this should never be admitted publicly. In their prison camp, with fascists all around, every word was propaganda, and any acknowledgment of defeat could weaken the prisoners' resolve. The storm set off by the talk lasted for several days. Eliezer vainly tried to explain that "it was a legitimate lecture on war tactics . . . that it is not impossible that with the outbreak of war the Germans will achieve a few victories, but that this will certainly not determine the outcome of the war." His comrades kept attacking him until he finally gave in and declared, as the Germans were already at the approaches to Moscow, that "despite its defeats, the USSR will win the war." But his apology, verbal contortions, and revisions did not repair the damage the lecture had done to his image. His fellow Communists and his associates in the Beaune-la-Rolande camp leadership had to do everything in their power "to raise morale, because the majority understood the lecture to be defeatist."[28] Nevertheless, despite this serious deviation from the party line, he made the impression of being an effective and loyal leader. After the war, when he was in great distress, he nevertheless insisted that he had not been mistaken. "My actions at Beaune-la-Rolande should not have roused criticism. When my opinion differed from the Party position (such as when the party revoked the prohibition on escaping), I always submitted to party discipline, even though in many cases I was right."[29]

Most of the detainees in Beaune-la-Rolande were deported during the second half of June 1942. The move did not come as a surprise. Just prior to it, party representatives told the three members of the camp executive, Eliezer, Sznajder, and Wikrowiecki, how to prepare for the deportation and what to do when they reached their destination so as not to play into the hands of the Nazi-fascist war machine.[30] Eliezer was deported on June 28. In the testimony he gave after the war, he said that he and his comrades thought that they were being shipped to Germany. Only when they got off the train did they realize that they had returned to the land of their birth, Poland, and that they were in Auschwitz.[31]

6 Auschwitz, Auschwitz-Birkenau, July 1942–March/April 1944

ELIEZER GRUENBAUM — WHO WAS USING the name Leon Berger — now gained yet a new designation: *Häftling* (prisoner) 43057.[1] Unlike his previous names, this one was tattooed on his left forearm; he also wore a yellow Star of David, designating him as a Jew. There were other symbols for other categories — political prisoners received red triangles, criminals a green triangle, and homosexuals a pink one. Prostitutes and other "non-social elements" were marked with a black triangle, while clergymen and Jehovah's Witnesses with purple.[2] His number was now his primary identification. Many inmates later testified that the humiliation of being reduced to a number was worse than the physical pain the tattoo caused. It indicated that all those who entered should abandon hope, "the brand burned on slaves and cattle for slaughter, thus you have become."[3]

Like others sent to the death camps, Eliezer and the rest of the Jews in shipment 5 were packed into cargo and cattle railcars.[4] The degree of packing depended on the origin of the shipment — if it came from an "inferior" country, 150 were pushed into each car. Prisoners sent from places like Italy and France, however, were granted better conditions, traveling only sixty to seventy per railcar. Women, men, children, old men and women, pregnant women, the handicapped, entire families were loaded on together, and the car bolted shut, without food, water, any place to sit, without any sanitary facilities, for a trip that could take several days.[5]

While the Nazis kept their victims in the dark about the nature of the trip, they did give the deportees one piece of advice: deportees should bring good-quality winter coats, with fur linings if possible, as well as silver and gold, diamonds and jewelry, anything easy to carry that could be used in time of need. When the Jews arrived at the camps, the money and valuables were confiscated, sorted, and sent to a storehouse. The prisoners sarcastically referred to the storehouse that held the plunder stolen from prisoners as "Canada" — that is, a land of wealth and plenty.[6]

Auschwitz was a huge complex of exploitation, arbitrariness, humiliation, and murder. The Nazis did all they could to cover their tracks, burning most of their documents when they evacuated the camp. Konzentrationslager Auschwitz, as it was officially known, was named for Oświęcim, which would otherwise have remained anonymous and unknown. The town lies beside the Soła River in Polish Silesia. The camp was built less than a mile and a half from the town, using as its nucleus sixteen one-story structures that had served as a military camp for the Austro-Hungarian army. It was no coincidence that it became the most important of the more than one thousand concentration camps constructed by the Nazis in the lands they occupied in Europe. Its physical and geographic characteristics made it a good choice. It lay in swampland, so the terrain was hard to navigate except on paved roads. The wetlands harbored typhus, malaria, and rheumatic fever. The climate was harsh and extreme; the available drinking water was turbid. Taken together, they made it a perfect location for a Nazi death works. Nearly 180 miles from Warsaw, it was sufficiently out of the way to stay hidden from the rest of the world. Yet it lay at a crossroads and was served by a train line, and was close enough to the Austrian, Czech, and Hungarian borders to make shipping people there convenient.[7]

Auschwitz opened in May 1940, about nine months following the Wehrmacht's blitzkrieg in Poland. Rudolf Höss was appointed its commander. By this time the SS had gained experience in running concentration camps. The first, Dachau, had been set up in March 1933, and its commander, Theodor Eicke, devised the operational model that was copied by all the rest. The central element was a hierarchy of prisoners, which was called "prisoner administration." When Auschwitz was founded, a vanguard of thirty veteran prisoners was brought in from the Sachsenhausen camp. Criminal prisoners who had previous training and experience in the way Nazi concentration camps were run, they served as its first *kapos* — prisoners who supervised other prisoners — and in other administrative roles. They were responsible for controlling the masses of prisoners and took part in fashioning the perverse rules according to which the camp operated. The role of the kapo, according to SS commandant Heinrich Himmler, was

> to see to it that the work gets done . . . to do so he must pressure his people. The minute we are no longer satisfied with him, he will cease to be a kapo and will return to the rest of the prisoners. He knows that when he returns they will beat him to death on the very first night. . . . Since we don't have enough Germans

> here, we use others — of course a French kapo for the Poles, a Polish kapo for the Russians; we pit one nation against another.[8]

At first, Auschwitz was meant mostly for Poles. The first Jews sent there were leaders of the Bund from Łódź and Jews from Warsaw suspected of involvement in the Polish resistance. But, within a year, they were followed by hundreds of thousands of Jews, who were slaughtered there with terrifying efficiency.[9] The original camp was referred to as Auschwitz I, or the main camp (*Stammlager*). By 1941 it had been built up to house eighteen thousand prisoners. At the end of 1941 the Nazis rapidly built, on the Raisko marshes, near the village of Brzezinka, some two miles away from the main location, another camp — Birkenau, or Auschwitz II.

Birkenau was huge — it could hold more than one hundred thousand prisoners. Beyond these two main camps, the complex included another forty-five extensions, the most distant of them being located in the Sudetenland, some 210 miles away.[10] The Auschwitz complex of camps operated until January 22, 1945. By the time of its liberation five days later by the Red Army, 1.3 million people had passed through it. Prior to the German evacuation of the camp there were sixty-four thousand inmates. A few were sent to Germany before the camp was abandoned, and only a small number of these survived. The rest were murdered or died of hunger, exposure, and illness. And these were the "lucky" ones who had not been exterminated immediately on arrival. Eliezer Gruenbaum was one of the few survivors.[11]

Auschwitz I also served as part of a deception. Its administration took care that, externally, it could be presented as a model camp. The prison blocks were two-story, redbrick structures, and its inner roads were stone-paved; it was kept spotlessly clean, and trees and flowerbeds were planted near the blocks. It looked entirely innocent. A foreign visitor would not grasp the horror of what actually took place there. The orchestras that played at the main camp, Birkenau, and in the sub-camps, which included famous musicians, were the ultimate absurdity.[12]

Auschwitz II, Birkenau, was surrounded by wetlands. Its access road led to the Red Gate, a broad structure in a long building with a tower at its center. The building housed the camp administration; the prisoners passed through the gate on the way to their deaths. Those selected to remain alive were housed in windowless rectangular wooden, or sometimes brick, barracks (in the women's camp there were also brick structures). The only light came in from narrow slits in the roof, much like in stables. The roofs were covered with a thin layer of tar paper. The floors in most of the buildings were earthen, so when the rain came in through the roof it formed puddles on the water-soaked ground. In the summer the barracks were unbearably hot and filled with clouds of dust. The inside walls were lined with sleeping platforms three high, with the boards of the lowest bunks lying directly on the ground. Six to ten prisoners slept on each shelf, sharing two mattresses stuffed with a bit of straw. Drinking water was always in short supply, and thirst tortured the prisoners even more than hunger. In the entire women's camp there were only two faucets. With nothing else to drink, inmates were reduced to drinking swamp water.[13]

Mass extermination began on July 28, 1941, when SS personnel used carbon monoxide to suffocate a group of non-Jewish psychotics. On September 3 a trial run was made using Zyklon B gas. It was even more successful than expected.[14] The four crematoria at Birkenau began operating in the summer of 1943, ending the practice of burning the bodies in nearby fields. But this practice was resumed in the summer of 1944, when the annihilation of Hungarian Jewry commenced — the crematoria could not keep up with the output of the adjacent gas chambers. By this time, the number of *Sonderkommandos* — prisoners who were forced to remove the bodies from the gas chambers and burn them in the crematoria — reached more than one thousand.[15] Scholars estimate that a total of 1.1 million human beings were murdered in the Auschwitz complex — mostly Jews, but also Roma, Soviet prisoners of war, and French, Polish, and other foreign nationals.[16]

Eliezer spent two years and nearly seven months in four of the Auschwitz camps. Upon arrival he was in Auschwitz I for three days. At the beginning of July 1942 he was sent to Birkenau and stayed there until March or April 1944, when he was transferred to the industrial Buna-Monowitz sub-camp (also called Auschwitz III). Afterward he spent time at the Jawischowitz coal mine, until January 1945, when he was sent to Buchenwald.

According to later testimonies from his comrades, his fellow inmates from Beaune-la-Rolande asked that he serve as their interpreter and representative before their keepers, all of whom were German criminal inmates. During his three days in Auschwitz I he was beaten twice by these superiors. His attempts to defend his comrades and his manner of speaking to the keepers were not acceptable at the camp.[17]

After the confiscation of all their belongings, Eliezer and several of his fellow prisoners were sent to Birkenau, which was called "Paradise" in the camp argot.[18] There they were crammed, along with fifteen hundred others, according to one witness, into a closed prison block. The heat and hunger were unbearable. The SS officer responsible for their transport told them: "Damn Jews, you haven't come to Auschwitz to live. Not one of you will get out of the camp."[19] The "welcome" to Birkenau generally also included a first encounter with the prison block's Jewish kapo, who would tell them: You are in the Birkenau death camp. Here you will work hard and receive little food. If you behave well, you will last for three or four months, and if not, you'll die within a few days.[20]

They were then given their camp uniform—shirt, pants, overcoat, and wooden clogs. They were marched to the block where their numbers were tattooed on their arms, and then to the one that served as their living quarters. Eliezer was assigned to Block 9, the chief (*Blockältester*) of which was Ludwik (Ludwig) Konczal, a Polish thug who had gained a name for himself as a murderer of Soviet prisoners who had been sent to Auschwitz to labor on the construction of Birkenau.[21]

Konczal asked for a representative of the newcomers to join the block officers, in keeping with the camp's "self-government" policy.[22] In their few days at Auschwitz, Eliezer and his fellows had learned that this needed to be someone they knew, whom they could trust, who was resilient enough to resist the pressures that would be placed on him. They chose Eliezer. They may have hoped, as they did when they chose him as their representative at Beaune-la-Rolande, that the fact that he was the son of one of the leaders of Polish Jewry would given him added standing at the camp.

Daniel Finkelkraut and Herman Freilich recommended Eliezer to Konczal —Eliezer was sleeping at the time. Konczal agreed and ordered that Eliezer be brought to him. His friends woke him, notified him that he had been chosen, and asked him to accept the post. The beatings he had taken at Auschwitz I made him realize that the job would be a dangerous one. He thus did not volunteer for the post of kapo or push to get it—his friends decided for him.[23] This was testified to by those who would become his accusers in the postwar investigations of his actions.[24] But, at the time, he was their natural leader, and he spoke both Polish and German. They believed he could serve as a buffer between Konczal and the prisoners and save them from the Pole's arbitrary violence. They already knew that block chiefs routinely murdered prisoners.[25]

Eliezer's leadership was put to an immediate test, and as far as his comrades were concerned he passed it. He managed to serve as a buffer between them and Konczal. But three weeks later many of them were moved to Block 8, to be replaced in Block 9 by a new influx of inmates. The picture changed. Eliezer now found it harder to do his job, so he took an opportunity to move to Block 4. A Polish friend helped him get appointed to an office job that enabled him to sink into anonymity.[26]

But he did not remain in that position for long. His remaining friends in Block 9 wanted him back. From the time Eliezer left, they told him, Konczal had turned even more ferocious, killing several prisoners each day. If

Eliezer returned, they believed, he could reduce the deadly tension between the *Blockältester* and the prisoners. Eliezer had his doubts, but he returned to Block 9, only to come down with typhus. The disease, which was rampant because of the camp's unsanitary conditions, killed many of the inmates. For two weeks he was on the brink of death. He later wrote in a moment of despair that he wished the disease had taken him then. At the end of October 1942, after he recovered, he returned to his post in Block 9, serving for another four months.[27]

During this time he was beaten several times by Konczal and SS men, partly because of their whims and partly because of his insistence on exempting himself and the members of his group from some of the most arduous disciplinary actions and labors. This favoritism gained him enemies among the prisoners as well, and some of those who felt that he treated them inequitably would later, after the war, number among his accusers. Then, in January 1943, he was moved to Block 39. He later claimed that he had not wanted to move. He understood that there he would have no choice but to act in concert with the SS guards. He refused, but only for a short time, and in 1943 was appointed chief of the isolation block, Block 20. Why did he win this "promotion"? Was he once again voted into it by his friends, or by the leaders of the camp underground, as part of their efforts to gain better conditions for the prisoners? Or was he moved up because his SS superiors were impressed with him and thought he was the best candidate to enforce the camp rules? Gruenbaum claimed that he was asked to take the post by Hermann Dymanski, a veteran of the International Brigades and a former inmate at Beaune-la-Rolande who was then Block 9 chief and later camp elder. The underground's leadership believed that "our comrades should not turn down positions of responsibility."[28]

Block 20, the isolation compound, held people — in somewhat better conditions — that the SS had an interest in keeping alive and in relatively good condition. The inmates there were neither sent to the gas chambers nor used as slave labor. It was thus considered a lucky assignment. Upon arrival, the existing testimonies say, Eliezer succeeded in replacing the criminals who served as block officials with political prisoners.[29] These latter men formed a network that, over time, established links between resistance figures from different national groups and political movements. According to some later testimonies, Block 20 served as a meeting place for the leaders of the underground. This may indicate that these men felt they could trust the people running the block. A while later Eliezer was sent to be chief of Block 30, a position he held until January 1944. At that time, with the SS increasingly fearful that Jews in positions of power could lead an uprising, all the Jewish block chiefs were replaced with non-Jews.

On January 20, 1944, he was assigned to a *Kommando*, a work detail designated for a project to divert the flow of the Vistula River and to broaden and deepen its channel. A few weeks later, in March or April 1944, he was sent to sub-camps where the Nazis exploited the slave labor of Auschwitz prisoners — first to Buna-Monowitz, and then, a few days later, to the coal mines at Jawischowitz, near the city of Brzeszcze.[30]

He first worked as a digger, but was then transferred to a desk job. He managed to hold on to that for a few months, but then lost the relatively easy assignment and was sent as punishment to a labor detail for two months, after which he was returned to digging. He remained at Jawischowitz until the end of January 1945, when the camp was evacuated in the face of the advancing Red Army. His next stop was Buchenwald, where he first faced semiformal accusations relating to his conduct at Auschwitz.[31]

||| EVALUATION OF ELIEZER'S VERSION of events, and comparison of his with other accounts, can only be accomplished on the basis of an acquaintance with the human and political geography of Auschwitz — the composition of the prisoner population and, in particular, a map of the different rebel groups that operated in the different parts of the camp. The Polish-Jewish Communists from Paris, among whom Eliezer numbered, were central actors in the underground. Eliezer's accusers would later claim that he had been excised from the underground and its activities, while Eliezer would insist that he had played an important role. His contribution had, he argued, been obscured, and some of the credit due to him had been appropriated by his former comrades.

Conditions in the camp, and the fact that different groups of prisoners were isolated from one another, meant that underground movements developed independently in different locations in the camp and among different national groups. Later, these groups managed to establish a unified international command, establishing the Kampfgruppe Auschwitz — the Auschwitz Resistance Group.

The first people to be sent to Auschwitz at its founding in 1940 were, for the most part, Polish political prisoners, some of whom were Jewish. Some were leftists, members of the antifascist front that had been active in that country prior to the war. Others of these prisoners were members of the Polish elite, among them senior officers from the Polish army, allied with the country's right-wing parties. The prisoners were thus divided among the entire range of Polish political factions, from the Communists and the Polish Socialist Party (PPS) on the left to the right-wing National Democrats (known as the Endeks).[32] There were also priests and officers allied with the Union for

Armed Combat (zwz).[33] Right and Left vied with each other in the camp, and the different factions on each side of the political map were also at odds. The Nazis exploited these ideological differences and the mutual distrust between the members of the different parties to divide the prisoners. It was only in the spring of 1943 that the warring factions began to evince a willingness to talk and cooperate with each other. But this cooperation remained a surface phenomenon, with hostility still running deep and strong beneath. The Poles at Auschwitz were thus divided into two or three antagonistic groups.[34]

The Czechs formed another distinct group. The first Czechs arrived at the camp on January 21, 1943. Later, when their underground activity began to take shape, their group consisted of 735 men and 411 women. Unlike the Poles, they were united, establishing a common front that included members of Edvard Beneš's National Social Party along with Social Democrats and Communists. Many survivors of the camp expressed their admiration for the profound solidarity displayed by the Czechs and, to a large extent, by the Slovaks as well.[35]

The Germans were diverse. They received somewhat better treatment than the foreign prisoners and thus enjoyed a higher survival rate. As such, they served as an island of continuity throughout the camp's existence. Some were well-known anti-Nazi political prisoners respected by their colleagues of all persuasions. But there were also common offenders, some of them violent criminals, who had been brought in to fill camp positions in the "self-governing" system that the Germans established. As Eliezer would later relate, the leaders of the other groups had to fight long and hard to remove the criminal elements from positions of authority. Eliezer's appointment to the positions he held, at least at first, and the contact with him initiated by Hermann Dymanski, leader of the German group, were part of this process.

The Yugoslavian and Soviet inmates, unlike the others, were prisoners of war. Most of the Yugoslavians came from the partisan force commanded by Josip Broz Tito. These women and men displayed notable fortitude, courage, and solidarity with their comrades. The women, for example, refused to shed their military uniforms and wear camp garb, and continued to do so even when some women were executed for this infraction. While most of the Yugoslavians were quickly exterminated, some of the women played a role in the united underground and served as members of the international committee in the women's camp.[36]

The Soviet prisoners of war numbered 450 when the underground began forming. These were all that remained from the twelve thousand Soviet captives who arrived in two transports, in October or December 1941. All were Red Army soldiers, among them officers of various ranks, including one general. Some of them established ties with the unified underground, but others displayed a great amount of wariness toward prisoners of other nationalities, even the Communists among them. Some were Jews who managed to conceal their origin. These prisoners displayed great heroism and played an important role in the underground.[37] Karol Suttor (Sudor), one of Eliezer's contacts among the Russians, seems to have been one of them.

Most of the French prisoners were Communists, but there were also representatives of other parties. Some were natives of France, while others were immigrants who had lived there for a decade or two prior to the war. Many had known one another before the war, serving as party activists together and as comrades in the International Brigades in Spain.

The rapid turnover of the Jewish population made it difficult for them to maintain a resistance movement. Continuity was provided largely by those Jews who accepted positions of authority. Many of these came from among the Jewish-French Communist group to which Eliezer belonged. That group's decision to disobey the orders they had received from their party's Paris headquarters, and to take on positions of authority on the grounds that by doing so they could help their party comrades and other prisoners survive, turned them into a linchpin of the united camp resistance.

All prisoners, even the most courageous, lived in constant fear of death and betrayal. Understandably, they tended to trust only those closest to them, and their first priority was to help members of their own small cluster of associates. This was all the more true of the French-Jewish-Polish Communist group to which Eliezer belonged, where personal loyalties were reinforced by a tradition of party discipline. The members of this group first looked out for each other, then for other Communists from other groups. Such assistance inevitably came at the expense of others, but the Communists justified this by arguing that, as the vanguard of the resistance, they needed to keep their men and women alive and in leadership roles, for the benefit of all prisoners and of the antifascist struggle. Many of the accusations made against Eliezer were precisely of this kind — that he had sacrificed other prisoners in order to keep himself and his close associates alive and in power.

The resistance group most important to Eliezer's story — and one of the most active and broad-based ones at Auschwitz-Birkenau, was the Jewish antifascist underground led by David Szmulewski and Emanuel Mink, his former commander in Spain. Most of its members were seasoned political fighters, veterans of covert and open Communist or leftist activity in Poland or, after emigration, in Paris's Red Belt. Some had fought on the Republican side in Spain and in the French resistance under Nazi occupation. A handful came from places other than Poland, and the group also included Jews without party affiliations, independent antifascists with activist spirits and characters that enabled them to take action at times of crisis.[38]

The composition of this group and the range of its actions provide an outline of the united resistance movement and its great weight in its central leadership. Like the Polish and German groups, it had a certain influence over the camp management, as it was able to place its members in a number of administrative positions, especially those of block clerk and kapo. They accepted these positions despite the prior instructions the prisoner leadership at Beaune-la-Rolande — Eliezer, Sznajder, and Wikrowiecki — had received, forbidding them to accept any official roles and not to integrate themselves into camp life. Eliezer was quick to disregard this rule as soon as he understood that it was not appropriate to the situation they found themselves in. This transgression, like his pessimistic speech at the French camp, would be held against him and listed among the true and imaginary charges he faced.

Not long after Eliezer reached this conclusion, his associates also came to understand the twisted nature of Auschwitz and realized that the party's orders needed to be set aside and that they had no choice but to accept camp positions. If you had a profession that the camp administration needed, it was best to say so even if, serving in such a position, you would be helping manage the murder machine. It would increase your chances of survival and perhaps also give you an opportunity to help others.[39] Eliezer was a member of the central group, and his appointment was part of its new policy.

The group did much in 1943–1944. It pursued self-help and rescue operations, in cooperation with other national groups, among them Soviet and leftist Polish prisoners. It extended essential help to the Soviet resistance group at Birkenau, led by Stepan Tiszczenko from Leningrad. The Jews supplied the Soviets with food, clothing, and other vital goods, as well as with reports of developments at the front. They also tried to inform the world that Jews were being exterminated in gas chambers in Auschwitz I. In addition, they supplied money and valuables to the resistance movement as a whole, and in particular to the Polish movement. Beyond that, they helped prisoners escape and maintained ties with the Sonderkommandos and took part in their uprising, persuading the crematoria workers to put off their rebellion when the leadership felt the time was not right. In the latter half of 1944 some of its members planned a rebellion as part of a general uprising in the entire camp. Mink played a central role in this.[40]

But the ranks of the resistance were decimated as time went by. Many of its members died of hunger, typhus, other diseases, and abuse. Eliezer later claimed that he played a central role in the group and that this was kept from the public after the war because of the efforts of his former associates and current antagonists. They, he charged, had become disillusioned with him because of the way he had done the jobs assigned to him.

The Mink-Szmulewski group maintained ties with the rebels in the Warsaw ghetto. Toward the end of the spring of 1943 it made connections with Jews who had been deported to Auschwitz from the razed ghetto, among them leaders of the rebellion. News of the rebellion also reached the Jewish leadership at the camp through Polish prisoners and was disseminated there by Polish leftists. The idea was to establish another resistance group made up of Jews from the ghetto, who had become symbols of courage, self-sacrifice, and heroism. Yisrael Peled ("Robert"), who had been born in Rymanów and had later moved to Belgium, and the Polish Communist Jozef Szpilski, who was from Warsaw, were appointed as liaisons and organizers. Szpilski would later defend Eliezer, testifying that he had served in a pivotal position, connecting the group with the Polish underground outside the camp. Little information about the Warsaw Jewish group is available, and we may assume that it was quickly wiped out.[41] When Israel Gutman, one of the Warsaw ghetto fighters, arrived at Auschwitz from Majdanek shattered and wounded, he was carefully looked after by the camp underground thanks to the aura of heroism that surrounded him. It may have been the secret of his survival.[42] The Mink-Szmulewski group established contact with Jews, mostly from Plonsk, in Block 9, with their main goal being to combat the corrupt kapos and the rest of the sadistic officials in the blocks and the camp. The group of Jews from Plonsk in Block 9 also declared open war against Eliezer. But the group also had other goals, such as saving its own members, and to achieve them it established contact with a group of Jewish women from Belgium. Most of these had arrived in Auschwitz on February 11, 1943, from the Drancy transit camp in France. They knew each other from their underground activity in France and Belgium. Some of them worked in "Canada," the warehouse of valuables taken from prisoners, and at great risk smuggled considerable amounts of money, gold, and diamonds, as well as other valuables, medicine, and food, to the underground and others in need. The underground tried to use its influence in the camp to place some of its members in relatively easy jobs, such as working in this facility. Sometimes it failed. It was unable to rescue women who were sent to work under especially harsh conditions in work details outside the camps, and many died.[43] Some of the women served as messengers and couriers, conveying orders and information from one side to another, as well as valuables, food, and whatever else could be smuggled out of "Canada" to be delivered to those designated by the leadership. The women also maintained contact with the general organization and the men's camp via members of the underground who gained entry to the women's camp as skilled workers and experts. Szmulewski, who worked on the *Dachdecker* (roofing) detail, was one. Sometimes Mink also gained entry as part of the carpentry detail, as did Karol Suttor, a member of the group and a kapo. The roofers managed to smuggle out a camera hidden under the false bottom of a teapot and used it to photograph the burning of bodies in the crematoria. The film was then smuggled out of the camp.[44]

During the second half of 1944 instructions arrived from the leadership of the general resistance organization to make preparations for an armed struggle. Prisoners prepared bottles filled with gasoline, cuttings of barbed wire, and other weapons. Masha Ravin-Speter, a member of the Paris group and of the underground in the women's camp, conveyed to Mink a diagram of Birkenau prepared by Vera Foltynov, a Czech-Jewish architect who worked in the camp's building administration.[45]

Jewish women who served as physicians and nurses also played an important role and were instrumental in saving many lives. At least some of these bold women, those who came from Paris, knew Eliezer and Bronke, his lover, from the city's Communist cells.

As Soviet forces approached, some members of the group began to feel, if not regret, at least a certain amount of doubt. Was it worth taking risks when the Soviet liberators would soon arrive? But rumors also spread that the Nazis planned to kill all the prisoners and burn the camp to the ground. Some of the prisoners favored taking up arms, trying to put the camp to the torch, and fleeing. They were led by a German Jew, Leon Weiner, a foreman; a Polish Jew named Yos (or Yosek), a deputy kapo; and an Austrian Jewish doctor who was called Nalkan. The group collected a large sum of money and gold, with which it tried to buy weapons. The leading figures among the prisoners supported this plan when their hopes were up, but when the hopes for a rapid liberation receded and the prisoners' spirits sank, the leaders lost their taste for a fight.[46] Eliezer was well aware of what the group was doing, and may well have been part of it.[47] Another group, centered in Block 8, with a membership made up mostly of Polish Jews who had been deported from France, called itself "Solidarity." It was headed by Haim Idel Goldstein, a left-wing activist, and Nachman Feinstein (Wilner). It organized self-help and rescue activities, considered the possibility of active resistance, and began to purchase arms. Both Goldstein and Feinstein knew Eliezer well, and both took part in the proceedings against him, with the former speaking in Eliezer's defense.[48] There was also an international group in Buna-Monowitz. It included Polish and German Jews, and non-Jewish Poles and Germans, many with considerable seniority in the camp, and concealed itself well.

The resistance and aid activities carried out by the Auschwitz underground were sometimes interlinked. One example is an operation involving the Sonderkommandos carried out by the French-Polish group led by Szmulewski and Mink, in which Eliezer was also involved. These prisoners were responsible for the practical operation of the gas chambers, the evacuation of the bodies, the pulling of gold teeth and removal of rings, earrings, and other effects from the bodies.

The Nazis realized that they were forcing the Sonderkommandos to do unthinkable work. To make sure it was done properly and that the items being harvested from the bodies did not get pocketed by those disposing of the bodies, the SS imposed three safeguards. First, as with every other task assigned to prisoners, the Nazis enforced fear and terror, making it clear that any Sonderkommando caught pocketing valuables would be killed immediately. Primo Levi told the story of four hundred Jews from Corfu who were assigned to the gas chamber detail in 1944. They unanimously refused to do the work and were immediately gassed. According to Levi, several other individuals also refused, and each died a horrible death. Filip Müller, one of the few Sonderkommando survivors, related the story of a friend whom the SS pushed into the ovens alive. There were also people who committed suicide when they were given the assignment, or a short time after beginning the work. On his scale of hatreds, Primo Levi categorized this as "directed hatred." It did not stand on its own but was aimed at a "practical goal."

The second measure was high turnover. Anyone who could not take the emotional stress was sent straight to the gas chamber, and another prisoner was brought in to replace him. Every few months the entire Sonderkommando was gassed, with the SS using a different trick each time to prevent resistance. Twelve contingents served at Auschwitz in succession. The first job assigned to the new prisoners in the detail was burning the bodies of their predecessors. This changing of shifts achieved another goal as well — getting rid of any witnesses to the enormity of the systematic Nazi death machine.

The third measure was a carrot rather than a stick. The Sonderkommados were promised improved work conditions. They received decent rations and, especially, an unlimited supply of liquor. This dulled their senses, detached them from their surroundings, and made them unfeeling, unthinking, and brutish, as their job required.[49]

The first two Sonderkommando details of 1942 were composed of Jews from Slovakia and France. At the end of the autumn of 1942 these were replaced by Jews from Ciechanów and Małków, two towns near Białystok, from the Grodno ghetto, Łomża, Zambrów, Ostrołęka, Racyonez, and elsewhere. As the pace of the killings accelerated, the units were increased from two hundred to eight hundred men and included Jews from Slovakia, Greece, Hungary, and

Holland. In mid-1943 the Jews from France, in particular ones of Polish origin, were assigned to the job, and these included members of the antifascist camp and veterans of the Spanish Civil War.

The nature of the job and the behavior of those who did it made its members the targets of anger and accusations by prisoners and survivors. But survivors also acknowledged that the details included some extremely brave individuals who played a role in providing aid to prisoners, and passed on information about the nature of the camp to the free world. The Sonderkommando even led one of the most important uprisings at Auschwitz.[50]

Even though the composition of the Sonderkommando changed frequently, and despite the constant fear felt by members of the underground that the ranks of the Sonderkommando included traitors who would turn them and their plans over to the SS, it was the members of these death details who first advocated rebellion.[51]

The first members of the Sonderkommado to propose the idea to the resistance movement were Lemberger, a man called Hetzkel (his last name is unknown), and Goz. All three were Polish Jews who had emigrated to France and belonged to the left-wing camp. In other words, they came from the same organizational, geographical, and ideological environment that Eliezer did. They founded the first resistance cell in the detail. In their wake, beginning in late 1943, four others came to promote the idea, in close coordination with the resistance movement at Birkenau. The first of these was Daniel Ostbaum, a tailor who had fought in Spain. The second was called Dziobaty — which means "pockmarked" in Polish; his real name is unknown. The third was Alter Fajnzylber, a veteran of Spain and a Polish-Jewish émigré to France. The fourth was Jozef Warszawski. In Eliezer's version of the story, Fajnzylber, whom he knew from Spain, was the link between him and Warszawski, a central figure in the attempted uprising.[52]

Fajnzylber served as liaison between the Sonderkommando and the resistance movement in Birkenau. With the help of prisoners whose jobs brought them to different camps and Polish civilians who worked in the camp, he conveyed a large part of the money and jewelry that he and his fellows removed from the bodies to the general and Polish resistance, as well as to the Polish Workers Party, the PPR — Poland's Communist movement — outside the camp. Szmulewski wrote in his memoirs and in interviews that he had done this. Eliezer offered a different account. While fighting to defend his good name, he related that he had been assigned to be liaison and that he had been deprived the credit he deserved.[53] At one point the resistance tried to arrange Fajnzylber's escape so that he could tell the world the truth about the gas chambers and crematoria. The plan failed. A kapo turned him in, and Fajnzylber was given a thousand lashes, but miraculously survived.[54] Eliezer told of other escape plans, including two cases in which he was designated to flee.

The Sonderkommando's central location in the heart of the death industry of the "secret Reich," the gas chambers and crematoria, gave its members special importance in the attempts to alert the free world about the Nazis' annihilation of the Jews. The idea was to photograph the killing process and to smuggle the photographs out of the camp. Mink, a member of the carpentry detail, was a central figure in this effort. The resistance movement assigned members of the underground who worked in "Canada" to find a camera among the personal property stolen from the victims. The plan was to get the camera to a member of the Sonderkommando, who would take the necessary pictures. A camera was found and smuggled to a member of the detail, and two photographs were taken, one of a group of naked women being chased into the gas chambers, and the second of bodies about to be shoved into the fire. Szmulewski managed to get the film and deliver it to Józef Cyrankiewicz, one of the leaders of the resistance movement at Auschwitz. He passed the testimony on to a courier, Teresa Lasocka, code-named "Tal." Eleizer would later claim, over and over, that he had been involved.

These operations, and the principal attempt at rebellion, were carried out when Jozef Warszawski and Jankiel (Yankel) Handelsman were members of the Sonderkommando. Warszawski was the code name of Yosef Dorembus, born in 1905 to a poor family in Żyrardów. He was a cobbler who had been active in the underground leatherworkers' trade union in Poland. Like many of his colleagues in that organization, he had been hounded by the authorities and was compelled to flee. When he arrived in Paris he continued his left-wing labor activity, joined the Communist Party, and rose to the leadership of a Yiddish-speaking cell. He was also a member of the Central Committee of the CGT, France's left-wing labor federation, and a notable figure in Jewish immigrant labor circles. His wife, Paula (born Paula Pilreis), was a teacher, Communist, and an activist among Jewish immigrant women. When the war broke out Warszawski enlisted in the French army and was sent, unlike Eliezer, to the front. In June 1940 he was taken prisoner by the Germans, but was released. Upon returning to occupied Paris he joined the resistance. In February 1943 he and Paula, also active in the underground, were arrested and sent to Auschwitz. They were unable to save Paula from being included in a selection; he was sent to Birkenau, where, in the summer of 1943, he was assigned to the Sonderkommando.[55]

Yankel Handelsman was born in Radom, Poland, and emigrated to France in 1931. By profession he was a presser of women's garments, a trade he followed in Paris as well. He did not belong to the Communist Party, but was an active left-wing sympathizer and in 1936 joined the secretariat of the association of Friends of the *Neue Presse*, a left-wing Jewish group organized around the Communist Party's Yiddish-language newspaper. During the occupation he joined the resistance and took part in sabotage operations and in organizing a strike of the glove-making industry. The strike disrupted production of gloves that the Wehrmacht needed during the invasion of the Soviet Union. His wife, Bella, also took part in resistance activities, including distribution of the newspaper. They were both apprehended on February 12, 1943, and, after interrogation, were sent to Drancy and from there to Auschwitz. Bella was murdered there. He was assigned to the Sonderkommando, where he linked up with Warszawski.[56]

When these two men arrived at the furnaces, they found resistance cells already organized within the Sonderkommando. The members were Communists and nonmembers of the party, religious and secular Jews, from different countries of origin. The initial contribution of the two newcomers was to mold these cells into an underground organization capable of coordinating its actions and uniting around a single plan of action. They also reinforced ties between the Sonderkommando resistance and the leadership of the general resistance in the camp, as well as with other Polish Jewish activists from France. This latter group included Haim Idel Goldstein and Nachman Feinstein, leaders of the resistance in Block 8, and David Szmulewski and Emanuel Mink, who headed a group of their own. Eliezer later claimed, repeatedly and insistently, that he had been in constant contact with them. He contended that he had connected them with the Russian and Polish undergrounds in the camp.[57] The two men also established contact with the French Jewish women's underground.[58]

The situation on the front in mid-1944 raised the hopes of Auschwitz's inmates. Even those who had been devoted collaborators with the SS began to think about the need to prepare for liberation. The members of the underground sought an opportunity to stage a successful uprising. The Soviet forces were steadily approaching from the east. Lublin, 175 miles from Auschwitz, was liberated. The Polish uprising in Warsaw broke out on August 1. The AK, the right-wing Polish resistance organization outside the camp, had a year earlier shelved plans for an attack on the camp to release its prisoners. Now these were dusted off and put back in active mode by the AK and the local Peasant Brigades. The operation was given the name *Burza*, meaning "Tempest." The hope was that the attack would set off uprisings throughout Poland, including in Auschwitz.

Instructions were sent to the undergrounds throughout the Auschwitz complex of camps. Two principal forces commenced preparations — the united military organization of the camp resistance, which comprised all the national antifascist groups, including the Jewish underground; and the AK's branch in Silesia, along with local members of the Peasant Brigades and others. According to the plan, the Sonderkommando was to play a primary role — setting fire to or blowing up the gas chambers and furnaces. The explosions would be the sign for the uprising to begin.[59] They were to obtain explosives and get them smuggled into the gas chamber and furnace compound. Clearly, they needed the cooperation of people they could trust. Eliezer would later make this argument against his accusers: If everything you charge me with is true, how is it that you knowingly worked with me on all this?

By August 1944 the preparations were in their advanced stages. The uprising in Warsaw was seen as a good sign, and the prisoners at Auschwitz eagerly anticipated Operation Tempest. One Sunday — the day the SS left the camp to enjoy their day off — the resistance leadership at Birkenau met. The participants included Zygmunt Balitzki, a prisoner who belong to the PPR; Valentin Pilatov, a Soviet prisoner; Mink, representing the German underground; and a representative of the Jewish-French group. They resolved that Balitzki, who worked, along with other engineer-prisoners, in the construction administration detail, would obtain further blueprints of the camp and that Pilatov and the Soviet major Antitipov would prepare the military aspects. Everyone was to do his best to further the efforts to obtain explosives and arms. The plans were conveyed to the Sonderkommando underground, as well as to the underground in the women's camp led by Tzipora Shapira (Gutnik), Masha Ravin Spcter, and a Yugoslavian partisan. It was planned that when the uprising broke out, during the initial chaos, the women were to cut through the barbed-wire fences and flee in every direction. The camp leadership contacted the AK outside the camp and asked to be supplied with the necessary explosives.[60]

But the optimism was short-lived. By the beginning of September the Warsaw rebellion was fading. The AK leadership in Silesia began to waver, and then pulled out of the plan. On September 29 the Germans apprehended Stefan Jasienski (his nom de guerre was Urban), who served as the liaison between the Silesian AK and the Auschwitz underground. He was viciously tortured. While he apparently revealed nothing before he died, his arrest was a cause for concern and impelled the AK to defer the plan. After the defeat of the rebels in Warsaw, the Silesian group no longer wanted to launch a new local uprising that would, it believed, have no hope of success.[61]

In the meantime, the Auschwitz SS command got wind that something was being plotted in the camp. They did not know any details but took preventative measures. They began evacuating most of the men in the camp to Germany

—the Poles in particular, but Jews as well—on the assumption that they could serve as the nucleus of an uprising.[62] These developments, coming from the outside, split the underground between those who advocated putting off the uprising and those who maintained that the plan should go forward no matter what.

The dividing line ran more or less between the members of the general resistance leadership at Auschwitz I and the rebel groups at Birkenau. The most outspoken in their demands to stick with the plan for an uprising were the men of the Sonderkommando. The opponents demanded restraint and warned that an uprising under the prevailing conditions would induce the Germans to liquidate immediately all the prisoners in both parts of Auschwitz. Bruno Baum succinctly summed up the difference between the two factions: "We could not take part [in an immediate uprising] because what was for them the only hope of being saved was liable to be for the others an act of suicide." A member of the international underground leadership, the Austrian Ernst Burger (or possibly Hermann Langbein) was sent to speak to the Sonderkommando to appease them. The previous roles were reversed. Warszawski, Handelsman, and Fajnzylber, the Sonderkommando leadership, demanded action, while the general resistance leadership demanded restraint and patience.[63]

Realizing that there was no chance of a general uprising, the Sonderkommando decided to go it alone. They would take the SS guards by surprise when their shifts changed, grab their guns, kill as many as they could, set fire to the crematoria, cut through as much of the camp's fence as they could. As many of them as could manage it would flee: Zalman Gradowski, Alosh Malinska, Fajnzylber, and Warszawski would lead the uprising.

The reason the Sonderkommandos were so anxious to take action was their knowledge that time was against them. As the Soviet forces continued their advance, the chances increased that the Nazis would decide to wipe out all the principal witnesses to the murder machine. This fear intensified in the autumn of 1944, when the number of transports to the camp diminished. The men in the death details suspected that they would become redundant, too risky to keep alive. They feared that they were no longer an essential part of the annihilation operation.

The Jewish resistance leaders in Birkenau realized that they could not bridge the gap between the opposing views. They resolved not to prevent the Sonderkommando from carrying out its plan, turning a blind eye to events as they unfolded.[64]

The uprising broke out on October 7, 1944. The diary of one of the rebels, Zalman Lewenthal (Leventhal), and other sources indicate that, after realizing they were on their own, the Sonderkommando rebels redoubled their efforts to obtain arms, explosives, and everything else they needed. A religious Jewish member of the detail, about forty years old — the witnesses referred to him as "the Judge" but did not know his real name — offered to blow himself up alone inside one of the crematoria. That, he said, would set off an uprising throughout the camp. The rebels managed to obtain a few pistols and to manufacture some hand grenades that Jewish women working in the camp's Union munitions factory had fashioned out of pieces of barbed wire, gunpowder, and explosives.[65] But disputes that arose within the Sonderkommando itself made execution more difficult.[66]

On the designated day, October 7, and at zero hour, 4 p.m., 120 relatively fit Sonderkommandos were assigned, in groups of five, to overcome the SS sentries at the changing of their guard. After taking their arms, the Jews would put the crematoria to the torch. "*Hurrah*!" was chosen as the code word that would start the operation. But something — it is not clear what — went wrong. The Germans got suspicious and started arresting members of the detail. The rebels were cast into confusion. Only three men — Handelsman, "the Judge," and one other — remained in one of the crematoria (Leventhal does not say which one) that was slated to play a central role in the action.[67]

The preemptive arrests, the difficulties in coordinating the various parts of the plan properly, and the problem of adjusting the plan to the changing situation enabled the SS to isolate some of the rebels and to snuff the uprising out easily. The Sonderkommandos in Crematorium 3 were surrounded and neutralized for all intents and purposes at the very beginning of the uprising. But the men in Crematoria 2 and 4 managed to set Crematorium 4 and the gas chambers on fire, throw grenades, and to fire bullets, creating the sense of a rebellion and terrifying the SS guards. The ideas that the underground had been tossing around for more than a year became a reality. But the uprising did not live up to the hopes of its organizers.

The panic lasted for only a few minutes. The guards fled, some of them running for the places where they had secreted gold and valuables they had stolen. But the Nazis quickly recovered. Some three thousand well-armed soldiers surrounded the crematoria compound and opened heavy fire on the grove of trees behind Crematorium 4, where most of the Sonderkommandos had gathered. One group of rebels managed to break through the siege, heading toward the Vistula and reaching Rajsko, about five miles from Birkenau. There they were surrounded. The rebels fortified themselves in one of the shacks there and returned fire. The SS set fire to the shack with flamethrowers.[68]

The outcome was no surprise. About two hundred Jews fell in the uprising. The rest of the Sonderkommandos who were captured were forced to lie down and were shot dead. A few of the rebels managed to hide out within Birkenau itself, in "Canada," among other places. Of the 663 men who had been in the Sonderkommando at the time, 212 remained alive. Three SS men were killed in the battle, and three more wounded.[69] But some rebels were not killed. Handelsman was captured alive, but was shot after interrogation. Fajnzylber and Erlich of the small Parisian group survived, as did the Judge and Alush Malinka. At a ceremony at which five SS men received the Iron Cross for their heroic suppression of the rebellion, the camp's commander, Richard Baer, declared that this was the first occasion on which *Reichsführer* Himmler had awarded such high honors to low-ranking soldiers.

Despite its failure, the rebellion made a huge impression on the camp's prisoners. Otto Kraus and Erich Kulka, two survivors who later wrote about the Holocaust, wrote that two hundred Jews from the Sonderkommando fell fighting for human freedom; but Tadeusz Hołuj, a prisoner who later wrote of his experiences, emphasized that, when the uprising began, none of the other prisoners came to their aid. Cyrankiewicz and the leaders of the Polish underground in Auschwitz I immediately conveyed a brief appeal to the forces outside the camp, calling on them to come to the aid of the Jewish prisoners who had managed to break out of the camp. Assistance should also be granted to those who did not know Polish, they said. But they did no more.[70]

By the time the uprising began, Eliezer was no longer at Birkenau. The previous spring he had been transferred to Jawischowitz. If he knew of the uprising at Birkenau, it was only from afar.

7 Jawischowitz, March 1944–January 1945

IN MARCH 1942 HERMANN GÖRING Industries (Reichswerke AG für Bergund Huttenbetriebe, known as the "Hermann Göring Werke," or HGW) signed a contract with Wirtschafts Verwaltungshauptamt, the economic-administrative arm of the SS, according to which Auschwitz would send six thousand prisoners to labor in the Brzeszcze-Jawischowitz coal mines, about five miles from Auschwitz.[1] HGW and the camp management together built barracks to house the prisoners and the SS personnel who guarded them, creating the Jawischowitz sub-camp.[2] A first shipment of 150 Jews was sent there on August 15, 1942. The population grew steadily, and by mid-1944, when Eliezer arrived, twenty-five hundred slave laborers were at work, most of them Jews from Poland or Western Europe, as well as Poles, Russians, and Germans.[3]

Jawischowitz's first commander was SS-Unterscharführer Wilhelm Kowol. Kowol liked to get drunk in his office and then go out to shoot indiscriminately. He took part in the selections that singled out those who had grown too weak to work. These filled the sub-camp's monthly quota for the gas chambers and furnaces at nearby Birkenau.[4] He was removed from his post because of complaints about his behavior — his drinking, his fraternization with women, his connections with prisoners, along with negligence and contemptuousness of his responsibilities. Kowol was replaced by SS-Hauptscharführer Josef Remmele, who took over the job in July 1944 and held it until the evacuation. He had previously served at Dachau, Auschwitz, and Auschwitz's Eintrachthütte sub-camp. Remmele was later brought to trial in an Allied court in West Germany and was convicted and executed. Kowol's fate is unknown.[5]

Eighty percent of the camp population worked in the mines, most of them in tunnels deep underground. They extracted the coal, loaded coal and coal dust on carts, pushed them up out of the shafts, and took the empty or gear-loaded carts back down. The prisoners spent nearly all their shifts wielding picks while lying on their bellies in narrow tunnels just thirty to fifty inches high, or on their knees, with a miner's lantern clenched between their teeth. Yitzhak Liber, who worked there, later said it was called "walking into the wall" in camp parlance.[6] The rest worked at various maintenance and support roles above, in what was called "the yard." They unloaded boards used as supports in the tunnels, rails and ties for the carts, and other operating equipment. The prisoners were also responsible for keeping the site clean and orderly — a Nazi obsession — and some were used as construction laborers at the camp or at nearby sites such as the Andrez power station in Brzeszcze. In nearly all work details a few dozen laborers were expected to achieve production quotas that normally required hundreds of workers. HGW offered construction services to other companies in the area, most of which were part of the mining and steel concern Deutsche Bergwerks- und Hüttenbau Gmbh.[7] Another seventy to eighty prisoners — especially children and teenagers between the ages of thirteen and seventeen — stood on either side of a conveyor belt to sort the coal. They had to pick out the shale from the coal and coal dust. Any of them who could not keep up with the belt's pace was beaten. Like the adults, they worked in two twelve-hour shifts.[8]

Professional Polish miners and prisoner foremen, mostly Germans, oversaw the work. Outside the tunnels, the prisoners were guarded by seventy soldiers from the SS, Wehrmacht, camp guards (*Werkschutz*), and auxiliaries (*Hilfswachmannschaft*).

The prisoners working underground were at least, most of the time, out of sight of the SS and their fellow soldiers, who descended into the tunnels only for spot checks to ensure that the prisoners were working according to the rules and meeting the quotas set by the mine's professionals. With rare exceptions, the German overseers treated the Jews badly, sometimes thrashing them for no reason.

As the end of the war approached, members of the prisoner underground tried to indicate to those who beat, humiliated, and mistreated them that they should give some thought to the accusations they would face after liberation. The professional administrator of the mine and its support services was a German named Otto Heine.[9] Several witnesses later testified that at times, in particular in the facility's early days, Heine was more reasonable than the SS men. Prisoners were able to submit grievances, and in some cases he dealt with the issues to their satisfaction.[10]

Unlike the German overseers and managers, nearly all the foremen and the Polish civilian miners did their best to ease the prisoners' workload, despite the risk to themselves. Each Polish worker had a Jewish prisoner who served as his assistant. Some Jews later related that the Poles regularly brought sandwiches and other food that they ate together.[11] But when the Nazis were not satisfied with the coal production, they put pressure on the Polish miners, and this worsened relations between the latter and the prisoners.[12]

Injuries and death were routine. Overseers also murdered prisoners at random on a daily basis. Some prisoners took their own lives, throwing themselves under the wheels of the railcars inside the tunnels. Prisoners often emerged from the mine at the end of their shifts bearing the bodies of their dead fellows on their shoulders. A kapo named Biele (apparently the notorious Block 2 chief, Hans Biele or Biell) did his best to make his work group the champion in this regard.[13]

The camp's food supply was grossly disproportionate to the number of prisoners. Provisions were not augmented when more prisoners were brought in, and their rations grew steadily smaller. What food was available was short on calories, meaning that Jawischowitz was no different from other concentration camps. But its isolated location and the relatively long distance between it and its mother camp meant that there was little way of topping up the rations covertly, as was done at the larger sites. Famished prisoners picked through garbage at the camp or on the roads, searching for anything edible. They ate local plants—chicory, chamomile, whatever could be chewed—while they prepared to return from the mine to the camp. The SS beat anyone caught doing this.[14] The camp infirmary, which the prisoners called the "Ka-Be" (short for *Krankenbau*), mostly held prisoners who had been injured at work and those who suffered from influenza, typhus, ulcers, and acute diarrhea brought on by malnourishment.

Every four weeks the SS doctors would conduct a selection in the infirmary. Patients found unfit for work—often more than a hundred at a time—were sent to Auschwitz-Birkenau to be gassed, or killed with an injection of phenol in the heart. Dr. Horst Fischer generally ran the selection, joined by Kowol. Heine took part in at least one. From the end of October 1942 through December 1944, at least eighteen hundred prisoners were sent from Jawischowitz back to the main camps.[15] New arrivals topped up the population as needed. The bodies of those murdered at the camp or who died in work accidents, of hunger, or of disease were sent to the crematoria.[16]

Jawischowitz became notorious among the prisoners at Auschwitz. The conditions there were especially horrible, and the mortality high. Anyone who lacked connections enabling him to gain easier conditions turned within months to a *Muselmann*—a prisoner who had been defeated by starvation and exhaustion and was simply waiting to be selected for transport to the gas chambers.[17] The word among the prisoners at the main camps was that Jawischowitz was the destination for anyone who had lost the favor of the

Auschwitz administration. The power station at Brzeszcze was also known as a brutal place, and the prisoners referred to it as "the death trap." Germany's severe labor shortage made the skilled workers at Buna-Monowitz more valuable, so they enjoyed relatively better conditions. But this did not apply to Jawischowitz, where most of the prisoners were unskilled and thus of little value to the Nazi regime. A short time after the camp was built, the number of prisoners grew and the barracks became severely overcrowded. Some prisoners "went for the barbed wire," meaning that they cast themselves deliberately on the electrified fence that surrounded the camp.[18]

Underground cells operated at Jawischowitz in 1943–1944, led by several dozen prisoners of Austrian, German, French, Polish, and Russian origin. Some of them were Jews. A larger circle of about 150 prisoners cooperated with this leadership. The rest withdrew and focused on their daily battle for survival. In conjunction with the international underground at Auschwitz and with the members of the Polish Socialist Party underground at the camp and elsewhere, they made contact with the resistance units fighting in the surrounding countryside. With this help they sabotaged the mines, helped ill prisoners, protected the younger prisoners, and planned escapes. Some prisoners gained their freedom thanks to this help.[19] The Polish Socialist Party (PPS), as well as members of the AK, the Communist PPR, the Peasant Brigades, and unaffiliated Polish patriots, cooperated with the Jawischowitz underground despite the danger.[20] When escape attempts failed, both the prisoners involved and those who helped them were killed. Eliezer later tried to prove that he took part in this activity during his time at Jawischowitz and that he was one of the architects of the communications lines with resistance cells outside the area. He claimed that at Jawischowitz, as at Birkenau, he had pushed for the underground to organize escape operations.

Eliezer arrived in Jawischowitz in March or April 1944.[21] Before he left Birkenau for Buna-Monowitz, his initial destination, his associates Warszawski and Szmulewski briefed him on the underground activists in the latter camp. He was to establish contact with the resistance at his new camp, tighten the contact between the two camps, and examine areas in which the undergrounds at both camps could cooperate and reinforce each other.[22] But in the end Eliezer spent only a few days in Buna-Monowitz before being sent on to Jawischowitz.

Upon his arrival at the mining camp he was first assigned to the earthwork detail. It is not clear whether he worked inside or outside the mine. After a while he was transferred to a desk job. Apparently this was, once again, thanks to his connections. While we do not have any direct evidence of what block Eliezer was assigned to, he had a previous acquaintance with one of the block chiefs, Ijziykléar Oléar, and presumably it was Oléar who took him in and helped him get this position.[23]

As a clerk his life was easier. He performed a job that was vital to the camp bureaucracy and one that put him in an influential position. By adjusting a detail on the list of candidates for the gas chambers — revising a prisoner's age downward or replacing it with another name — he could save a man's life. He was in a position to get wind of the camp management's intentions and plans and thus enable the underground to make preparations to save prisoners. Of course, the capacity of the underground to do so was severely limited, but they were able in some cases to protect those close to them, those with connections, those who were considered "important." These actions raise difficult moral issues that deserve serious discussion, but they are not our concern here.

Eliezer managed to hold on to this job for several months before being sent once more to a penal detail. The administration either found out that he was engaging in subversion, or perhaps he was caught falsifying records. But it could simply have been a chance whim of his superiors. Those close to him testified that his infraction was helping to smuggle letters from Polish prisoners out of the camp. After about two months of this punishment, he was sent back to the excavation *Kommando*, where he remained until the camp was evacuated and its prisoners sent on their final death march.[24]

He was critical of his activity in Jawischowitz. He had hoped to achieve better results and that ties between the underground activists at the camp would produce results more quickly.[25] He also wanted to take the same central role in the Jawischowitz underground as he had, at least in his own eyes, played at Birkenau. But this did not happen. The process of transport to the new camp disrupted the communications networks used by the underground, and when he arrived, Eliezer did not know which members of the resistance were in the new camp, where they were located, and how to establish contact. It took time to find them and reestablish ties with them. The task was made all the more difficult because, beset by fear and terror and bereft of the support networks they had benefited from in Birkenau, these people tried their best to remain inconspicuous. Even when a member was, with great effort, located, it took time to confirm his identity. Great precautions had to be taken to ensure that Gestapo agents and informers were not taken into the underground ranks.

||| BUT RUMORS HAD FOLLOWED Eliezer to the camp. It was said that his actions had been questionable and that he had established overly close relations with Nazis and other doubtful characters. On top of this, the underground groups that had already organized at Jawischowitz were closely knit

and had no urgent need for immediate reinforcement. They saw no reason to take a chance on placing themselves at the disposal of such a controversial figure. Before being sent away from Birkenau, Eliezer had been involved in attempts to establish a common leadership for Polish, Jewish, Russian, and other prisoners. These were in part motivated, in his case, by a desire to repair the bad impression made by his opposition to just such an effort during his early weeks in Birkenau. But the project remained uncompleted when he was transferred, and news of it did not reach Jawischowitz.

In any case, by the time Eliezer arrived at Jawischowitz, the underground there was already active. It contained many experienced resistance activists, some of whom had been among the camp's original 150 prisoners and others of whom had arrived later. The underground's leadership and members numbered between 50 and 100 men, while another 150–180 knew of the underground and were prepared to take part in its activity. The founders were mostly Germans and Austrians who had been augmented later by Poles, then by Yugoslavians, Russians, French, Czechs, and Hungarians, as members of each of those national groups arrived at the camp in succession. The underground was divided into national cells that were governed by an international command that set its goals and initiated its actions. The innermost nucleus was made up of Communists, but anyone who was willing to join the antifascist struggle was welcomed, without regard to nationality or ideology.[26]

To maintain secrecy and prevent the organization's collapse in the case of a mishap, the underground's nucleus was structured hierarchically out of teams of three members, one of whom was designated as team leader. Each of these leaders belonged to a further triad on the next level up, which had its own leader, and so up to the top of the pyramid. The top level, the international committee, was composed at the end of 1944 of representatives of all the above-mentioned national groups.[27] The organization, like its parallels in the main camps, set itself several goals: to sabotage Nazi plans and interests; to reduce coal production to every extent possible; to integrate members of the underground into essential management positions in the camp; to foster solidarity and support Communist Party members and other anti-Nazi activists; to fight against the inhuman conditions and brutal treatment of prisoners at the camp, in the mines, and aboveground; to fight those who consciously or unconsciously collaborated with the SS, including criminal detainees, kapos and others in positions of authority, factory managers who employed slave labor, and others; to establish and maintain contact with Polish partisan forces outside the camps and all other resistance forces; and to prepare escape plans for all the anti-Nazi forces in the camps and their attachment to the partisan ranks.[28]

The goals were adjusted in accordance with the developing situation in the camp, in the mines, at the building sites, and the international situation. Links were maintained with other camps and with Auschwitz itself, mostly through Herbert Kreutzman, the administrator of the infirmary, whose work took him from one camp to the other. Contacts with the Polish underground were maintained through the Polish miners who worked there, as well as through a *Kommando* of Polish prisoners who were sent to the dairy and bakery at a nearby village to bring provisions for the SS. They would covertly meet Polish resistance fighters and sympathizers who gave them medicine, food, and information.[29]

The underground scored an impressive success in its effort to remove collaborators from positions of power and replace them with members of the underground. It used a number of means to persuade the SS to make such appointments. One was bribery; another was convincing those who understood that they were involved in actions for which they could be punished after the war to help the underground as a sort of "insurance policy." It was a gradual process, but by the end of 1944 the resistance had insinuated its personnel into a number of key positions. For example, four out of the ten workers in the kitchen, including the kapo, were from the resistance. This enabled the underground to obtain food and distribute it to those who needed it, especially the weak. The organization also had a great deal of influence over Baldus, the SS kitchen captain. He allowed members of the underground to listen to Allied broadcasts on his radio. The underground conducted its meetings in the showers. The person responsible for this facility was their associate Hans Patocki, a German prisoner.[30]

The underground also held sway over most of the camp's fourteen kapos. Three of them were members, and five were under its sway. The kapos led the prisoners to their work sites and supervised them there. Their role was critical — on these trips and at the work sites the prisoners were under the thumb of the SS guards, and the prisoners were thus at high risk. Two of the twelve block chiefs were from the resistance, while another four were under its influence. Nearly all the deputy block chiefs were under its influence or actual members. The blocks were divided into rooms, with each room under the authority of a room warden (*Stubendienst*). Four out of twelve of these were members of the underground, and six under its influence.

The infirmary was a vital location. The camp was a breeding ground for routine seasonal illnesses, as well as more serious diseases like typhus, dysentery, diphtheria, scarlet fever, tuberculosis, and skin rashes of all kinds that plagued the hungry and weak prisoners. Such prisoners were prime candidates for selection for the gas chambers. The underground had two people there — Kreutzman and one other. All the prisoner-doctors were under the influence of the underground and took action to save prisoners. When the underground learned what criteria the SS doctors had set for the coming selection, it made sure to keep sick prisoners from going to the infirmary. When a selection approached, the doctors released all patients who were capable of working, even if only for a few days. Once the danger passed these prisoners were hospitalized again. When word came that a large selection was on the way, one that could not be avoided, *Muselmänner* were sent to the infirmary, while others were kept out in an attempt to save them. Sometimes the underground was able to save a prisoner from the gas chambers by getting him classified as a skilled worker or a diligent and vital one.[31]

The camp's barber, electrician, gardener, and tailor were also under the underground's influence or sympathetic to its goals. Some of the German and Austrian prisoners who served as typists and administrative workers were under the underground's influence or at least aware of its demands and willing to help so long as it did not involve any great personal risk.

The situation of the prisoners at Jawischowitz was dire. How much worse might it have been without the underground's activity?[32] Certainly in the absence of the resistance the prisoners would have been much less well informed and more subject to the deliberate campaign of disinformation pursued by the SS, and unmitigated terror and hopelessness would have reigned. Members of the underground collected information and disseminated what they could confirm. They had several sources of intelligence — the Polish miners; the Nazi newspapers in which the miners wrapped the sandwiches they brought from home; newspapers they found in the camp office's trash; visits by prisoner officers whose jobs enabled them to enter in the village of Jawischowitz and other villages in the area; and Allied radio broadcasts they heard clandestinely on a radio constructed by the camp's prisoner-electricians, on private radios that SS men gave to the electricians for repair, and on Baldus's kitchen radio. Another source was the prisoners who continued to arrive in the camp in the unceasing shipments.[33]

The underground did its best to convince the Polish laborers that they and the prisoners were allies. It took a long time to do so, but the longer the two groups rubbed shoulders, and the more they came to understand that the war was going against the Third Reich, it began to succeed. However, the underground had only limited success in its efforts to use threats of retribution after the war and other means to gain influence over SS personnel. It was very difficult to get through to those who had been enlisted from among the German minorities in Romania, Hungary, and Yugoslavia. Some of them had been forced into service, and their families were being held hostage to ensure their good behavior and efficiency.[34]

In Jawischowitz, as in Birkenau, escape operations were considered a prime objective. In both locations the underground sought to get out prisoners who would be able to establish contact with the resistance outside, to carry out important information, and help prepare the escape of others. This was the reason Eliezer had been included in two of the breakout operations from Birkenau. At least three of those attempts succeeded in enabling a few prisoners to flee.[35]

There were also larger escape plans. The first idea was to spark a general rebellion in coordination with armed partisans outside the camp. The latter would help get prisoners out of the camp, escort those prisoners who were able to escape, and to conceal them until they could organize themselves as a fighting unit. But the plot was never carried out. It was difficult to obtain agreement across the board from all the underground groups; there were fears and clashing interests; and the good news they heard from the front affected different people in different ways — it energized those who supported an uprising but redoubled the apprehensions of those who felt that they had something to lose.[36]

A second escape plan involved digging a tunnel from Block 7, Oléar's block, to outside the camp. Its location near the fence made it a good place to begin a tunnel under the fence. According to the plan, a large group of prisoners would crawl through and be met on the other side by armed partisans who would, again, conceal them until the prisoners could form an armed resistance unit of their own. The conspirators succeeded in completing the tunnel, and a date for the escape was set. As luck would have it, however, a group of German prisoners from another block began to dig their own tunnel without any coordination with the Jews. One of the Germans informed on his fellows to the SS, setting a snowball rolling that led in the end to the arrest of Karl Grummer, the camp secretary, and then of Oléar and one of his room wardens, Eliewitch. The latter was one of the senior members of the underground, a veteran of the Spanish Civil War and member of the group that was involved in the conspiracy. They were interrogated and beaten ruthlessly but, despite their knowledge of and involvement in the plan, did not incriminate their comrades. In the end they were transferred to Monowitz and punished, but survived. The punitive action taken by the SS — increased surveillance, the dispersal of prisoners to other blocks, and later the dispatch of others to other camps, along with the Gestapo's efforts to uncover the underground network, led the resistance to abandon the plan and cover its tracks. Meetings between different cells were abandoned, and even more-stringent precautions were taken not to allow unknown people to gain any knowledge of the underground's work.[37]

In a third operation, Polish partisans were to attack the convoys from the camp to the work sites. The armed militias would kill the guards and enable the members of the underground — and any other prisoners who wanted to join them — to flee in all directions. The partisans would then hide the escapees, as in the other plans. But this never came to fruition.[38]

The French-Jewish section of the French cell, led by Henri Krasucki, was also involved — a Communist cell of Polish-born French prisoners who had been arrested after the Nazi occupation of France and sent to Beaune-la-Rolande, Drancy, and other detention camps, and in the end reached Auschwitz. It was in this framework that the Polish Jews from Paris operated. In the spring of 1944 they still trusted Eliezer.[39]

They were the first prisoners from France to join the resistance in the camp, and they filled the French slot on the international committee. Later they were joined by other Frenchmen; at its height the group had about thirty members. Krasucki, an impressive young man of eighteen or nineteen, was the group's leader and its representative in the underground leadership. Spending his nights in the mine, he engaged in underground activity during the day. He established contact with the Polish miners and participated in sabotage operations in the mine, despite the fact that these led to the imposition of sanctions on the prisoners and civilian miners, who were unable to fill their quotas. Along with other members of the cell, he worked to keep the prisoners' spirits up, to show them how they could, despite everything, and especially their hunger, "behave properly and maintain moral values . . . to keep in mind the goal of fighting the Germans." He also worked to curb the brutality of the kapos and other officials, and to set an example of good and humane behavior that could inspire others. Along with allies in other underground groups, Krasucki sought ways to help their fellow prisoners, but in particular other members of the Communist Party or those close to them. They sought to supplement the prisoners' rations, to get them easier work assignments, to give them enough rest, and to defend everyone they could against the kapos and others — always within the unwritten law of the camp, in which aid was extended first and foremost to the members of one's own group.[40]

This group was Eliezer's natural environment, and he enjoyed the imprimatur of the revered Handelsman.[41] When he arrived he tried to establish contact with the activists at the camp, but several members of the leadership gave him a cold shoulder. He attributed this to the rumors of the inquiry that had been conducted about his actions — rumors he had heard about while still in Birkenau from his friend Majcher Langman. Eliezer had transferred Langman to Block 20 after being appointed its head and had named him room warden. Langman had told him about the in absentia inquiry about his actions as a block leader in Birkenau. The inquiry took up his relations with the Nazis and violent camp officials. It also examined allegations of violent behavior by Eliezer himself and considered whether all these actions had indeed been unavoidable, in the best judgment of the underground, in the framework of the missions it had assigned Eliezer or ones he had initiated with its approval.

Eliezer did not take the treatment he received at Jawischowitz sitting down. He turned to Herman Achsen, a Communist and Spanish Civil War veteran, and other senior figures in the underground in an effort to find out what was being kept from him — in other words, what had been the outcome of the inquiry and what it meant for his future. He received an ambiguous response. Josef Regliszyn and Achsen told him that the charges against him had been found to be baseless. But others, Victor Majzlik among them, intimated or told him explicitly that the party had issued a ban against him for "killing, tormenting, and beating his defenseless comrades at Birkenau."[42] Both versions of the collected recollections of the members of the French group at Jawischowitz mention Eliezer only in passing, in a footnote, and in a negative light. His absence from their accounts is telling and certainly not coincidental.

Oddly, Jawischowitz was, for his family, a ray of light for a while. Like many others, Eliezer had disappeared in the rush of events, and after he was sent to Auschwitz, his family had no idea where he was or what had happened to him. His father, by then a central figure in Yishuv politics, was the permanent vice chairman of the Jewish Agency Executive, a member of the Polish-Jewish community's "Committee of Four," and, from the end of 1942, also chairman of the Jewish Agency's Rescue Committee.[43] He did all he could to find out what had happened to his son. He had at his disposal means to do so that ordinary people did not, and he had no hesitations about taking advantage of his position.

The family began looking for him in the summer of 1942, when they learned that he had been deported from France. In the spring of 1944, his father's efforts to obtain information brought in a surprising piece of news. He had spoken to Gerhart Riegner, secretary of the World Jewish Congress in Geneva, who decided — despite his hunch that it would be useless — to send ten packages addressed to Eliezer Gruenbaum to the ten concentration camps he knew of. On May 1, 1944, he received a postcard from Eliezer, which had been sent from Jawischowitz on April 29, saying that he had received "three food packages" from "Relico," the World Jewish Congress's welfare arm. Despite the war, it took only three days for the postcard to get from Jawischowitz in Upper Silesia to Riegner's desk. Richard Lichtheim, who worked with Riegner in Geneva, immediately sent a cable to Jerusalem, telling the family that Eliezer was alive and in Jawischowitz. "For all intents and purposes it is Birkenau," he added. The elder Gruenbaum and his colleagues in the Yishuv leadership in Jerusalem knew the location of Auschwitz-Birkenau, but they would learn the nature of the place only two or three months hence.[44]

Who else in the camp knew that Eliezer had received the packages? The fact could not easily have been concealed, given the crowded conditions and the hunger that prevailed there. If it was known, it could have had two opposing results. Some may have been angry at and jealous of this "prince," son of a famous Polish Jewish leader, who was once again getting preferential treatment. The fact that a small number of other Jews received packages as well would not have mollified these critics. On the other hand, the packages could have reinforced the belief that Eliezer had special status and connections in the camp, which could be an asset to his fellows. Some other prisoners later testified that this was the reason they chose him for leadership positions.[45]

The information on what kind of camp Auschwitz indeed was was not long in coming. It came from Rudolf Vrba and Alfred Wetzler, two men who had fled the camp.[46] This information did not cause Yitzhak Gruenbaum to ease up on his insistence that the Jewish Agency Executive demand that the Allies bomb the death camps and the roads leading to them. Up to that point he had been unable to gain the support of a majority of his colleagues in the Executive. Two months would pass, until the end of June and beginning of July 1944, before the Jewish Agency in Jerusalem and London would make his position its official one. Now that Gruenbaum had solid information that his son was located in the network of camps that he was demanding be bombed, the situation became even more convoluted and dramatic.[47]

Even though Eliezer was acquainted with leaders of the underground cells, was in contact with them, and was in the know about some of their activities, he was at most a supporting actor. Perhaps this was because he had been rejected and ostracized by the group. Or it might have been that he realized that, given the rumors flying about regarding his past actions, he needed to keep a low profile, focus on his daily struggle for survival, and wait for the furor to pass.[48]

During the last third of January 1945 a flurry of activity, restlessness, and tension was evident at both Buna-Monowitz and Jawischowitz. Even those Nazis who succeeded in shutting out the thunder of the Soviet artillery that had already deployed in nearby Kraków and the reports on the radio and in the newspapers about the advance of the forces of the Soviet general Ivan

Stepanovich Konev along the Vistula could hardly ignore the thunder of the bombs that U.S. aircraft were dropping on the camp's factories and in the area, or the air raid sirens that went off whenever masses of combat squadrons screeched over the camps on their way to bomb strategic targets. The Western powers had told the members of the Jewish Agency Executive, Yitzhak Gruenbaum among them, that the Allied command could not afford to allot planes to bomb the camp because this would divert them from vital targets. Furthermore, the Executive was told, bombs on the camps were liable to kill Jews.[49] On January 17–19 the Jawischowitz camp prepared for evacuation.[50]

The last prisoners to descend into the Jawischowitz mines were the contingents that began their shift on the night of January 17. The next morning the SS and camp administration began burning all the documents and archives in the camp offices. At about 3 p.m. all the prisoners were ordered to assemble outside. In an atmosphere of total and uncharacteristic disarray the guards doled out bread, margarine, and sausages. Some of the ravenous prisoners managed to grab a double portion. Others did not get a full ration. The guards ordered each prisoner to take a blanket — the prisoners estimated the temperature at between plus five and minus twenty-two degrees Fahrenheit. Again, some seized several, but in the end the blankets turned out to be more of a burden than a benefit. As snow fell, the blankets absorbed moisture and became so heavy that the prisoners cast them off during the march.[51] On the morning of January 19 the Jawischowitz prisoners joined the tail end of the Auschwitz-Birkenau death march. About a hundred prisoners, the ill and others who could not walk, were left behind at the camp. Two doctors remained with them, but bereft of medicine, food, or coal for heating. Only a handful of these were alive by the time the Soviets liberated the camp on January 25.[52]

By one account 1,948 prisoners set out on the death march; another source puts the number at 1,998. They were divided into groups that took different routes, passing close by Polish villages and towns. Some of the prisoners were forced to pull and push sleds loaded with gear and spoils that the SS men had taken with them. On the evening of January 19, the groups converged on the towns of Poremba and Brzeszcze. In the latter, the prisoners slept outside, with only a few finding shelter under the roofs of unfinished houses. Most of the prisoners, especially the weaker ones who were not able to push themselves into such relatively protected spots, had no choice but to lie down in the snow. Many of them died of exposure during the night.[53] The following morning, when the prisoners were ordered to continue the march, the SS gathered together all the weak and dying and sprayed them with machine gun fire.

Concentration camp prisoners, group by group, continued to walk the frozen and muddy roads of Eastern Europe throughout the month of January.

Exhausted, they froze at night and starved by day. Their icy feet swelled and were covered with blisters from their wooden clogs. Anyone who could not keep up was killed—in individual cases by a shot to the back of the head, in groups by automatic fire. Thousands of bodies were left in piles along the roads. The prisoners trudged between the rows of snow-laden trees that lined the roads, interspersed by hedgerows of bodies frozen solid like sculptures, displaying the final spasms of death.

The prisoners from Jawischowitz who survived these horrors were eventually led to train stations. After a long wait, they were told to board a set of open coal cars, full of snow that melted when it made contact with the prisoners' bodies, soaking them in the freezing weather. When the train set off, the wind froze the wet rags the prisoners were wearing, killing many.

One group, which was taken to the Wodzisław station, was herded into the railway engine depot, where the prisoners waited for a train to arrive. They, too, were packed into coal cars so tightly that they could neither sit nor lie down. There they waited in the cars, until the train started to move on January 22 or 23. The train trip lasted several days and nights, depending on the route. The trains had to stop at busy road crossings, and were further delayed by mechanical problems, more urgent trains, and the general confusion and disorder that typified the final stages of the collapse of Nazi military and logistical systems. The cold remained unbearable, and no one thought to provide the prisoners with food or drink. In many cases, the meager provisions they were given when they left Jawischowitz were the only food they ate during the entire ordeal. In some places compassionate civilians tossed loaves of bread at the convoy. A prisoner who caught one would share it out with those around him—if he did not, those around him would grab it out of his hands. In some cases, the SS men who put them on the coal cars threw some bread in as well, but in the resulting chaos some prisoners were unable to lay hands on even a small piece.

The trains took the prisoners to Mauthausen or Buchenwald and their satellite camps.[54] Eliezer was in one of the groups sent, on foot and by coal car, to Buchenwald. Later, fighting for his good name, he would testify, as would others, that during the death march he bore on his back an exhausted Communist comrade, caring for him the entire way. Without his help, he and his supporters said, this man would never have survived the march.[55]

In June 1944 there had been about three thousand prisoners at Jawischowitz. At the time of evacuation there were, as noted above, slightly fewer than two thousand. In other words, during the camp's final six months, a third of the prisoners disappeared. They either died of exposure, hunger, disease, and exhaustion, or were beaten and murdered by the Nazis and their collaborators. According to the best scholarly estimates, only about five hundred survived the death march that set out from Jawischowitz. Those who arrived at the Mauthausen and Buchenwald camps lived to endure another terrible stage in their suffering.[56]

Eliezer reached Buchenwald toward the end of January 1945. As he had at Auschwitz, Birkenau, and Jawischowitz, he sought out acquaintances from the underground cells. In his new location, he had to do this in the midst of utter chaos, to find them among the tens of thousands of long-standing prisoners there and tens of thousands more who had arrived from other camps. Yet, by push and shove, he managed, within just a few days, to locate the underground's leaders, and they managed to find him. That did not mean that the rumors that had plagued him in Jawischowitz did not make it to Buchenwald — they did, but were not as much of an obstacle. He again busied himself with the overt aid and covert underground activities, usually with the knowledge and agreement of the leadership. Yet, as he acclimatized to the new camp he became more and more aware that the accusations that had pursued him had not disappeared or been dismissed. On the contrary, they gained force and weight, and, he realized, they could overwhelm him.

8 Buchenwald, January–June 1945

BUCHENWALD'S ORIGINAL NAME had been the Ettersberg Concentration Camp, after the nearby mountain of that name, located about five miles north of Weimar in Thüringen, in east-central Germany. A group of 149 men, most of them convicted criminals but some of them political prisoners, had arrived there on July 16, 1937, to lay the foundations for what would eventually become one of the largest concentration camps on German soil. At its height, Buchenwald was the center of a network that included 130 sub-camps and external units. A total of 238,980 prisoners from thirty countries passed through it during its period of operation, and 43,045 of them, including Soviet POWs, were murdered there or died of other causes.[1]

The camp had three branches. The so-called Large Camp held long-serving prisoners; the Small Camp was a detention center where prisoners were held until their fate was decided; while the Tent Camp was designated for Polish prisoners incarcerated there after the German invasion of their country. These three branches were supplemented by administrative buildings, an SS barracks, and factories built on site. During its final period, a special block was built to hold child prisoners. Hermann Pister served as the camp's commander from 1942 through its liberation in April 1945.[2] Since 1942, tens of thousands of slave laborers from the camp had been employed in an arms factory located next to the camp. But hardly any of them were Jews — on October 17, 1942, an order mandated the transfer of all Jewish prisoners from concentration camps located in Germany to Auschwitz. Only 204 Jews, who had skills vital to the camp's operation, remained. This changed only in 1944, when Buchenwald began to receive shipments of Hungarian Jews from Auschwitz. After a brief stay in the main camp, most of these were sent on to the sub-camps to be used for arms production.[3] Thousands of more Jews, including children and teenagers, began to arrive on January 18, 1945, after Auschwitz and other camps in the east were evacuated. A special block was built in the Tent Camp to hold them — Block 8, which held more than six hundred prisoners. Most of them survived.[4]

Some of Eliezer's former associates from the other Auschwitz camps also survived their death marches and made it to Buchenwald. They found an already operating prisoner underground there, one that had been formed in the camp's early years. The group's original goal had been to plant members in central positions of influence, provide mutual support, and to remove the camp's criminal elements from positions of power.

Some of the criminal prisoners enjoyed the backing of the SS and some figures in the camp administration. Nevertheless, the underground was gradually able to insinuate its own members into positions of influence, even if their standing was always tenuous. After the war broke out the Germans arrested masses of political prisoners in the countries it occupied and sent them to Buchenwald. As a result new underground groups formed by prisoners of different national groups sprang up. In 1943 the different groups united under an International Underground Committee. As in Auschwitz, Jews were members.[5]

In addition to saving the lives of prisoners and, in a modest way, improving conditions, the Buchenwald resistance scored some impressive successes of other kinds, in particular by carrying out sabotage operations in the arms factories. These were pursued in nearly all the factories in which prisoners were employed. The underground was also able to disrupt the evacuation of the Jewish prisoners during the camp's final days. The SS sought to remove the Jews from areas that were in danger of being taken over by the invading forces so that the annihilation of these prisoners could continue at a time and under conditions amenable to the Nazis. Furthermore, the SS wanted to do away with all witnesses to the atrocities its forces had committed. The Nazis also believed that they might be able to use the Jews as bargaining chips.

The evacuation of Buchenwald began on April 6, 1945, and reached its climax the next day, when tens of thousands of prisoners were removed from the main camp and sub-camps. The underground did its best to disrupt the process by scrambling SS orders and creating bureaucratic, logistical, and other tie-ups. It also used the arms and ammunition that members had managed to smuggle into the camp. Taking advantage of the demoralized state of the Nazis and the fact that most of the SS personnel were already gone, the underground was able to take control and capture the SS soldiers who had been left behind and block the roads out, all this before the arrival of the U.S. forces that liberated the camp on April 11. The Americans freed about twenty-one thousand prisoners who remained there, among them some four thousand Jews — about one thousand of whom were children and teenagers.

The Nazis had nevertheless managed to remove 28,250 prisoners from the camp. About seven thousand to eight thousand of these were murdered or died of other causes during the evacuation. Another seventeen to eighteen thousand were murdered or died in the sub-camps. The underground's disruption of the evacuation process saved many lives.[6]

Eliezer and other prisoners later testified that during his few months in Buchenwald he became involved in the underground and took part in its operations in the period before the liberation.[7] He had reached Buchenwald at the end of January.[8] Throughout the death march he had cared for and carried his friend Shimon (Szymon) Rutkowski, a leader of the Polish Communist cell at Birkenau and later a leader of the party in postwar Poland.[9] When Eliezer arrived at Buchenwald he had sought out his underground associates from Birkenau, as well as those from Jawischowitz who had not rejected him. These may have included Jozef Szpilski, Suttor, Achsen, Dymenski, and Blass. He may also have contacted Henri Krasucki and Roger Trugnan of the French cell.[10] Szpilski had been a leader of the Polish Socialists at Birkenau; Dymenski had served as chief of Block 9, and when Eliezer was transferred out of Block 9, Dymenski pressed him to reassume command of the block. Eliezer had met Blass, a German Jew, when Dymenski brought him to Block 9, and Blass later became block chief himself. Suttor had been an underground activist in Birkenau. Achsen was a German Communist, a leader of the nucleus of the underground at Jawischowitz, and had been involved in the inquiry into Eliezer's actions.

Eliezer's efforts to connect up with them aroused mixed feelings. Some wanted him involved and cleared the way for him; others continued to have reservations. Eliezer asked Blass, whose courage and integrity he trusted, whether he had gone over the line and done things that should not be done. On the whole, it seemed as if the pall hanging over his head had just grown darker.

Eliezer chose not to look the other way. Maybe he thought that he had nothing to lose, or perhaps he presumed that if the accusations against him had any foundation, it would be better to have it dealt with in the framework of the underground's institutions and procedures before any particular individual with an ax to grind took advantage of the chaos of the Nazi collapse to close real or imagined accounts with him.[11] He may well also have thought that it would be better to have the matter out with other scarred survivors of the inferno rather than to be judged after the war by people who did not understand the rules by which the concentration camp world operated. Whatever the case, he asked the leaders of the camp's Polish Communist cell to conduct an official, open, and thorough inquiry. He asked to be informed of the specific charges against him, to be informed who was testifying against him, to examine the evidence, and if necessary to contend face to face with his comrades from the underground, who had also taken on posts in the camps. If there were skeletons in his closet, he maintained, they should be aired out, along with everyone else's skeletons as well.

As the inquiry got under way, Eliezer recalled that when he arrived at Auschwitz his comrades from the leadership at Beaune-la-Rolande had intimated to him that he should be wary of prisoners whose underhanded dealings — for example, the theft and sale of food rations on the camp's black market — had suffered from the efforts of Eliezer and other members of the leadership to stop them. The leadership had done so because these activities had put all the members of the underground at risk and had encroached on the few rights that they had.[12]

This second inquiry was as transparent as it could be, given that it was conducted while the prisoners were still under the thumb of the Nazis. Prisoners in many camps conducted their own improvised inquiries and trials during the final period before liberation, and afterward. Sometimes punishments were meted out before an inquiry was completed. Prisoners took revenge on fellow prisoners who had mistreated them, sometimes lynching them at the first opportunity. Natan Orbach, who encountered Eliezer at Buchenwald, was a witness to such an incident involving Eliezer. "Two *shkotzim*[13] began to beat Gruenbaum fiercely," he related. "I heard him shout 'Save me! They're killing me!'"

This attack was part of a campaign that prisoners carried out to pay back kapos and other prisoner functionaries. Orbach ran to a block, 23 or 24, where French prisoners lived, some of whom were, like Eliezer, veterans of the Spanish Civil War. Orbach alerted them to what was going on. Eliezer's friends intervened, and the attackers let him go. Orbach testified that Eliezer was a rank-and-file prisoner at Buchenwald who worked in sanitation. He also related that both he and Eliezer had received packages and that they shared the food they contained with their fellow prisoners. Orbach had not been at Birkenau and did not know how Eliezer had acted there. But when he asked other prisoners about that, he was told "Don't ask unnecessary questions."[14] Did Eliezer become a target of such attacks simply because it was known that he had been a block chief, and vengeful prisoners went after anyone who had been involved with the Nazis? And if they believed him guilty, why did the members of the French group save him rather than taking advantage of this convenient opportunity to be rid of him?

Two inquiries into Eliezer's actions took place in Buchenwald. The first was conducted by Stanislave Kisiel, Stefaniak from Zagłębie, and Baruch

Goldberg, all three of them members of the camp's Communist underground. Kisiel was assigned to seek out Eliezer's accusers and to collect their concrete accusations. The major accusers were the surviving Czech prisoners, principal among them a barber named Karol. This group made four accusations against Eliezer — that he had acted roughly and had beaten prisoners without cause; that he had given preference to Poles and had mistreated Czechs; that he had stolen food rations from their rightful owners; and that he had taken part in pressuring the Czechs to hand over money and valuables.

Eliezer denied most of the charges, but admitted that a few of the counts were correct. He had indeed beaten a Dr. Niedzwiedz, one of the Czech group's leaders, he said, but had done so "without being acquainted with him or knowing who he was." The victim was actually a prominent figure among the Czechs, Dr. Miloš Nedvěd, born on September 21, 1908, in Prague and killed on March 23, 1943, at Auschwitz; Nedvěd was a physician and researcher, an underground activist, and a son of a senator in the Czech parliament. As a member of the Czech underground he had secretly provided medical care, money, and other things to the resistance against the Nazi occupation. Underground groups, the Communists in particular, met in his clinic and laboratories. In March 1942 he was turned in to the Nazis by a physician colleague who informed on his resistance activity and his connections in the underground to his father-in-law, Professor Nejedlý, a leading Communist and anti-Nazi propagandist in Moscow. This relationship had granted the doctor further cachet among the members of the party in Czechoslovakia and in Auschwitz-Birkenau. He was interrogated and cruelly tortured by the Nazis in the hope that he would turn in his colleagues and lay out his connections with the Communist cells active in the Czech provinces. Apparently he did not break. In fact, during his imprisonment, Dr. Nedvěd seems to have managed to convey to the underground information that came his way in prison. On December 15, 1942, he was deported with his wife to Theresienstadt, and in January 1943 he was sent to Auschwitz, where he died two months later of typhus.[15] Eliezer confirmed that the doctor had been in his block at Auschwitz, and that he had beaten him, but without knowing who he was. He admitted striking others without cause, but denied stealing food from other prisoners or extracting money from Czechs. He also said he had never insulted prisoners because of their national origin, although he did use the Czech epithet *pepiki*, a diminutive used to refer to Czechs that the members of that nation find offensive. But, he maintained, he quickly changed his attitude — in January 1943, when all the Jews were removed from Block 9 and replaced by Poles, Eliezer, then Konczal's deputy, sent the Poles out to do hard labor and kept the Czechs in the block. When Konczal, the block chief, found out about this, he beat Eliezer.

Karol, his chief accuser, had been present during this incident, he claimed. All this happened when there were about one thousand prisoners living in the barracks, during a very difficult and tense period at the camp.

Things changed afterward. The brutal Konczal had been transferred to another barracks, to be replaced by Dymenski, a good friend to members of the underground. The change in the block command and the replacement of several other block officers brought about a change in the atmosphere. Dymenski, Eliezer said, had confirmed at the time that no complaints had been lodged against him by the Czechs who had been in the block then or thereafter. "I also want to mention," he told his interrogators, "that a few Czechs who have made accusations against me have confirmed that in the spring of 1943 I was a block chief at the camp and that my behavior was unexceptional." One of the Czechs told him then that this period, when Eliezer had taken out his anger and frustration on that group, had been three black weeks in his life.[16] The judges noted his confession about beating prisoners and acquitted him on the charges of theft and taking money from prisoners. While we know the results of this proceeding only from sources close to Eliezer, they seem to be reliable in reporting that the judges in this proceeding found that, in the large picture, Eliezer had done nothing exceptional in pursuing his responsibilities at that time. This is reinforced by the fact that he continued to serve as a block officer under Dymenski, at the latter's request, and with the support of his party comrades.

Yonatan Gruenbaum concisely referred to this stage in Eliezer's tribulations as a relief. His brother, he wrote, had been accused of beating some of his block mates, but that was the end of it. Eliezer's counsel in a later proceeding, André Ballot, offered more details: "The commission of inquiry was set up by a covert underground organization. After collecting about a dozen depositions, it ruled in Gruenbaum's favor, pointing out the great work he had done at Birkenau." Furthermore, the lawyer said, after the commission found that his actions as block chief had not gone beyond what was reasonable in those circumstances, he was permitted to once more join his friends in the energetic resistance activity that was then being pursued at Buchenwald. He was party to the plans for an armed takeover of the camp, using ammunition and arms that members of the underground had stolen from the Gustloff-Werke factory.[17]

As the German army collapsed, the lawyer went on, Eliezer took part in planning the uprising and "was even among its leaders." On April 11, 1945, he took part in cutting through the barbed-wire fence when the camp was liberated. That same day, he was placed at the head of a Polish unit that was assigned to scour the camp to catch fleeing SS personnel. This uprising saved the lives of thirty thousand prisoners, the lawyer claimed (in fact, twenty-one thousand were saved).[18] Following the liberation of the camp, Eliezer was elected a member of the committee that represented the camp's Polish residents. This was one further piece of evidence that Eliezer and those who defended him had been successful in persuading the members of the commission of inquiry of Eliezer's innocence, and that the problems had been resolved at least for a time. Otherwise he would not possibly have been named a member of the Polish cell and one of its representatives on Buchenwald's International Underground Committee.

Another fact supports the claim that, at least at that stage, the underground accepted Eliezer's word that he had carried out all these actions in the liberated camp at the behest of the Communist-dominated Polish government-in-exile that had taken control of Poland with Soviet support. He had been tasked with persuading former prisoners who were Polish exiles to return to their homeland and to participate in the construction of a new Poland. To carry out this assignment he was sent to Paris to speak to his friends there.[19]

In addition to this inquiry by the Communist activists at Buchenwald, and apparently slightly in advance of it, a group of "reactionary" Poles, as Eliezer and his associates called them (meaning Polish nationalists of the AK and other right-wing groups), conducted its own investigation at the camp. In the background to this move were the ideological and tactical differences among the Polish former prisoners. Those from the center and right claimed that their leftist compatriots had been involved in killing prisoners by injections of poison and other means, charges that grew out of the fact that the left-wing group gave priority to helping its members and those close to it. When they had to top up a quota for the gas chambers or assign prisoners to an especially arduous work detail, the right-wingers charged, the leftists did all they could to save their own people. That meant replacing them with political opponents. But this inquiry also ended up not convicting Eliezer of any crime.[20]

After Buchenwald's liberation, Eliezer's family and friends received word that he was safe and, all things considered, healthy.[21] The news had come from Isaac (Ignacy) Schwarzbart, a Polish-Jewish leader and a former member of the Sjem, and his wife, who had immediately sent the family their best wishes from London. Schwarzbart said he had found out that Eliezer was alive when he read a report filed by Florian Sokolov, military correspondent for a Polish daily newspaper, *Deziennik Polski*, on April 25, 1945, saying that Eliezer had been found among the inmates at Buchenwald. Schwarzbart passed the information on to Palcor, the Jewish Agency's news service, and to the local correspondent for the London *Morning Journal*. He requested that another Polish Jewish leader, Anshel Reiss, a member of Mapai who was preparing to travel from England to France, ask Marc Jarblum to look after Eliezer. He also asked another acquaintance, a Polish government official in London, to see after him. Schwarzbart also applied to the Polish Red Cross. He reported all these efforts to Yitzhak Gruenbaum. He also said that he had notified Ben-Gurion, who had been overjoyed. "The most important thing," Schwarzbart wrote, "is that your son is alive. I am so happy that in the midst of all these catastrophes and pain you have been given some happiness."[22]

On June 2, 1945, Schwarzbart updated the worried father about his son. He said that he had met with Sokolov and "interrogated" him about Eliezer's condition. Sokolov "spoke to him [Eliezer] for a fair amount of time," Schwarzbart reported. Sokolov's impression was that "Eliezer looks well." He was wearing civilian clothes that fit him, seemed to be in full possession of himself and acted coolly, keeping his "old demeanor." Schwarzbart seems to have wanted to signal to Yitzhak that he should get used to the fact that his son remained a staunch Communist. Eliezer was already in contact with his associates in Paris, planning out his future, but apparently had no intention of joining his family in Palestine. Schwarzbart did not know if Eliezer was still in Buchenwald, where Sokolov had apparently seen him, but promised that when he himself got to Paris he would check out Eliezer's status and plans. Eliezer had given Sokolov a letter for his father, which was already in the mail. "The most important thing," Schwarzbart reassured Yitzhak, "is that after such horrifying events he is still alive, healthy, and ready to get back into action."[23]

Eliezer was eager to resume his party activities and enthusiastic about carrying out faithfully and successfully the mission to Paris that had been assigned to him. But the next round in his campaign to stay alive and protect his good name was gathering steam. This time the arenas would be Communist Party headquarters in Warsaw and the Polish party's branch in Paris.

9 Warsaw–Paris, Paris–Warsaw, June–September 1945

A NEW INQUIRY INTO ELIEZER'S conduct in the camps got under way on May 25, 1945. Once again it was a panel sponsored by the Polish Communist Party. Its members included two men named Kowalski and Eisner.[1] The inquiry was conducted in Warsaw, Buchenwald, and Paris, and was divided into three principal parts that were carried out in parallel in these different locations: the presentation of the accusations, the collection of evidence, and the examination of witnesses. This first part was concluded on September 7, by which time Eliezer was already preoccupied with the subsequent French investigation. The second part began the following June 3, with Eliezer's opening statement and questions put to him in person and in correspondence, and lasted until August 22. The third part, which took place on August 13, consisted of a rigorous inquisitorial cross-examination. The verdict was written in September 1945. Each point in the verdict included a one- or two-line summary of the evidence that the judges considered critical. The verdict itself was concise, just a line and a half long, and it sealed Eliezer's fate.[2]

This time the charges were much more detailed, there were many more witnesses, and the proceedings were much longer. Eliezer's responses to the commission were also more detailed, and a reader cannot help but be impressed both by the extent of his knowledge about underground activity in Auschwitz and the centrality of his involvement, to the extent that a prisoner at Birkenau could play a major role in such a terrifying and compartmentalized environment.

The evidence presented to him outlined an "indictment" centered on his transgressions against Communist Party ideology and policy; verbal violence and viciousness; withholding assistance from members of party cells; commerce in food stolen from prisoners; preventing those under his sway from receiving medical care; abuse of prisoners in his block via his helpers; direct abuse of prisoners; beating prisoners and causing permanent injury; dispatch of prisoners to the gas chambers; abetting manslaughter and murder; and manslaughter and murder.

He responded to these charges in writing and orally, at length and in detail, in his opening statement, under cross-examination, and in his summing-up. He questioned witnesses and wrote personal letters to the coordinators of the inquiry, urging them to bring it to a conclusion. All this was carefully documented in party documents that eventually made their way into the Polish national archives, where I hunted them down. The files contain dozens of pages in Polish, most of them typed on manual typewriters, with the addition of handwritten proofreading marks and notes. The file also includes documents relating to the trial conducted against Eliezer and his Communist cell comrades in Łódź in 1929—during the postwar proceeding, some witnesses referred obliquely to his youthful transgressions against the party.[3]

In his lengthy opening statement, Eliezer surveyed his actions from the time he and the other members of his group were taken from Beaune-la-Rolande, through his time in Auschwitz, Birkenau, Buna-Monowitz, Jawischowitz, and Buchenwald. Here and there he referred to his time in Spain, Paris, and Poland. His aim was to place his endeavors in the context and inform his judges of the background to his deeds. He clearly understood that not only his place in his Communist cell and his right to remain part of it were at stake, but his life as well. He did everything in his power to respond to the entire range of accusations that had been leveled at him, both minor and major. To every extent possible, he sought to make distinctions between different kinds of offenses, from the seemingly mild to the more serious. In doing so, he sought to place his actions in perspective and proportion. It was an environment where denying a prisoner shoes, a slice of bread, or a shirt, or assigning him to a hard-labor detail, might have been the equivalent of sentencing him to death.

Here and there the proceeding extracted very personal emotional reactions to the inexorable way in which the prisoners in the camps regressed into a herd mentality and into their basest animal instincts. He also spoke of his personal sense of betrayal, his frustration at what he saw as a lack of appreciation for his efforts. Implicitly but also explicitly, he accused his comrades of hypocrisy. He talked about what leadership, devotion, self-sacrifice, and courage meant in a place like the camps, where being a leader meant becoming part of the Nazi hierarchy.

He acknowledged the facts of some of the charges against him, in most cases seeking to explain why he had been unable to act in any other way. His opponents would later maintain that criminals generally deny the accusations against them. Eliezer intimated that some of his accusers, ones who had also served in problematic positions in the camps, had joined the campaign against him out of fear that the skeletons in their own closets would be taken out and inspected. He posited a conspiracy — he had been abandoned, sacrificed, made into a scapegoat. A reader of his opening statement can easily dismiss all this self-justification — after all, most criminals insist that their hands are clean.

But it clearly shows that he was well-informed about what was going on in the camps. He knew the underground in great detail — the names of its major players, activities, what had been achieved, and what had failed. He maintained assiduously that he had played a central role in all this. At some points in the statement he accused his comrades of seeking to take credit due to him. For the most part, he spoke fluently and cogently, presenting a chronological account of events. At certain places, however, an association led him off on a tangent. In some places he made claims that he later contradicted. In some passages the reader gets the impression that rather than describe what actually happened, Eliezer constructed an account of events that put him at the center and in the best possible light. In some places his self-possession cracked.[4]

Sznajder and Wikrowiecki, his partners on the underground executive, had been sent with him on the transport from Beaune-la-Rolande to Auschwitz. Before their departure, the party organization in Paris had conveyed to them specific instructions about what they were to do when they reached Germany. Both the prisoners and the party leadership assumed that Germany, not Poland, was the destination. The instructions, which had been smuggled into the camp in France, stated that all activists who accepted the party's authority were to act in accordance with four principles, all based on a common logic. They were to take every measure, actively or passively, that could undermine Nazi policy — sabotage, the refusal to accept any assignment, to pretend to be ill at every opportunity, and refusal to provide any information at all about one's profession, especially regarding any profession that could be of use to the Nazis or which they could exploit for their war aims. And, in fact, Eliezer and his colleagues initially acted in accordance with these instructions when they reached Auschwitz. When they were asked about their professions, all of them refused to respond. About 250 prisoners remained in Auschwitz I, most of them people who had nevertheless provided information about their skills. The rest were sent to Birkenau. The conditions in Auschwitz, Eliezer reminded his examiners, were better than those they found at Birkenau.

Since many of those who had been on the transport knew Eliezer and his capabilities, they asked him to serve as "mediator and interpreter" of the camp kapo who had received them. Immediately upon his arrival he was beaten, Eliezer related. The reason was that he had instructed his men to sit when the kapo had ordered them to stand as a punishment.[5]

They spent three days at Auschwitz, Eliezer recounted. Despite the fact that they were kept in isolation and despite the prohibition against making contact with other prisoners in the camp, Eliezer said that he was able during this time to converse with veteran prisoners. He learned from them the extent to which the instructions he had received from Communist Party headquarters in Paris had been based on ignorance of the conditions prevailing at the camp and the rules of the game there. They had, it transpired, been sent to an annihilation camp, not a labor camp as they had presumed. The upshot was that to evade work by pleading a lack of expertise or illness was to be sent to the gas chambers. The only way to survive the initial selection was to exploit connections with prisoners in positions of authority who could arrange for a relatively easy job or ensure that the newcomer be placed in a relatively tolerable environment such as a workshop. Furthermore, in Auschwitz the conditions, and thus the chances of survival, were better.

He told the judges what he had heard among his comrades, that they also understood that following the instructions they had received in Paris would put the group in mortal danger. Anyone who concealed his profession would face certain death, whereas anyone who had a needed skill had good chances of survival. Following instructions would mean dooming themselves and their fellow Communists to certain death. Despite all this, they did not agree on the need to set aside the instructions. It took Eliezer several days to persuade his comrades to take a different approach. This was not the only time, he implied, that his colleagues had carried out the party's instructions to the letter, no matter what the facts of the situation were — at least until the real world whacked them in the face.

They were shipped to Birkenau on July 2, 1942.[6] Upon arrival, during the long wait imposed on them as part of the different stages of the camp's intake process — registration, having their number tattooed on their forearms and sewed on their clothes, and so on — they collected information on the place and its rules. The more they learned about what awaited them, the clearer it became that what they had heard about Birkenau in Auschwitz had been "much too rosy" and that "the instructions [from Paris] had been written on the assumption that we were going to perform civilian labor, in which case the orders would have been meaningful." They were simply not "practical in a concentration camp." These were, Eliezer said, "the first crises with the instructions from Paris," which brought him by that time — with his comrades falling in line with him gradually — to the decision to set aside his orders.

To save themselves and to be in a position to save others, they resolved to do everything possible to obtain service positions at the camp, if at all possible in the blocks where they were to be housed.[7]

Eliezer related that at Birkenau they found people they knew from their former lives in Paris, people who were willing to help. One of these was Herman Freilich, who helped install Eliezer in his post in the first block he was assigned to. Other witnesses corroborated this. On the same principle, Eliezer claimed, he and Freilich also tried to find a position for Ijziykléar Oléar — a member of the group from Beaune-la-Rolande whom Eliezer had known in Warsaw — but without success. Nevertheless, as his position grew stronger, he and his associates — Eliezer did not say who — were better placed to place people close to them in vital positions. They were able to assign doctors from their group to the infirmary, at the same time that physicians who had arrived a few days earlier in a different group were unable to get placed in the infirmary and were sent to perform hard manual labor. The assigned doctors, Eliezer told his interrogators, included Dr. Fajgenbaum, a party member, in whose favor Eliezer personally intervened. Before long, Eliezer was able to get Freilich an even better job as overseer of the prisoners who prepared and distributed food. This enabled Eliezer and his associates to secretly divert food to those they believed deserved help. Similarly, they were able to place members of the Beaune-la-Rolande group in office jobs, which gave them further influence over the placement of prisoners. He did not explain how he managed to achieve such power in just a few days — in fact, he may have jumped ahead of himself, referring to his position at a later date.[8]

According to Eliezer, such initiatives of his, or ones he was involved in, produced a situation in which he and his associates were able to ensure that his group, made up of Polish Jews who had emigrated to France — along with being veterans of the Spanish Civil War and active Communists — were given preference over prisoners who arrived on other transports. "I wish to note that this cannot be seen as special achievement that our transport was given preference over others, and obviously I feel bad about them [the people in the other transports], but it produced for us several points of support in the concentration camp that enabled us in a later period to save an entire group of our comrades." He did not try to adorn the facts. He understood very well, as did the judges, that the preference given to Eliezer's group and their placement in better positions meant that others who did not belong to or were not close to the group received worse assignments. Under the conditions prevailing in the camp, such preference could mean living days, weeks, or months longer, or even surviving until liberation.[9]

He offered an account of his placement in Block 9, and how he fashioned his relations with Konczal. He was able to get on the block chief's good side by taking advantage of Konczal's vocal objections to the overall set of Nazi policies. This enabled Eliezer to play on the Pole's patriotism and even, Eliezer said, his "human feelings." If you knew, he said, "how to play his game, you could get some things done." His brother Yonatan would later add that Eliezer had also been able to get on Konczal's good side by telling him pornographic and other spicy stories about life in Paris — Eliezer knew such stories well and was even better at telling them. This enabled him to get Konczal's consent to placing other men from his transport as block officers. But he was unable to keep the block chief from beating whomever he wanted to whenever he saw fit.[10]

He was able to use the position he gained to help his friends, he said. He could sneak a few extra slices of bread and other food to Sznajder and Wikrowiecki, as well as to Langman and Oléar and others. He obtained shoes for some. Had he been caught, his life would have been at risk. As soon as he heard that a new detail was being put together to perform jobs at the camp — easier and safer work that did not involve the long exhausting daily march to a work site and back — and that the commander of the detail would be their block commander, he was able to assign Oléar, and with the latter's help also the three other previously named men and one other.

Oléar was later chosen for a new job — filling mattresses with straw. "This made it possible for him to offer friends preferential work conditions and helped them with food as well," Eliezer related. Oléar, he made a point of mentioning, would also become a controversial figure when he was promoted to block chief — a brutal one, even if at a certain point he changed his ways. Eliezer said that his own main job was to seek out possibilities for cooperation with the Poles and Russians interred at the camp, as well as with German political prisoners. It was, he stressed, difficult, complex, and dangerous work. "One careless word and they would have turned us over to the SS, who would have shot or murdered us."[11]

He realized that by accepting a position like the ones he held in the blocks and camps made him "part of the SS system of persecution. But we took that into account from the start of our time in Birkenau" as part of the conscious decision "to insert [our] people into those positions." To the same extent it was clear to him that to justify his involvement in the SS structure he had to undermine that system everywhere he could. He also had to work to make conditions easier for the prisoners and "to do everything possible to save" prisoners, but first and foremost members of his group.

"I tried to do my jobs," he declared. To succeed as a mediator between the Germans and the prisoners, he explained, he had to consent to enforce clear rules of conduct in the block and to do everything to inculcate these rules in the members of his group. They would be better off if they understood that it was in their best interest to follow his instructions, which were aimed at enforcing good behavior in the block. Obedience would avoid giving the block chief an excuse to beat them, and his beatings could have dire consequences. It was necessary to make the members of the group realize that if they wanted to preserve some sort of autonomy in the block they had to keep the camp rules. Nor could they circumvent his authority by applying directly to the block chief. Doing so not only undermined Eliezer's position, but infringed on the group's self-government by making Konczal less willing to permit them to manage their own affairs. What was done to those who were not willing to keep the rules, Eliezer asked, and answered his own question bluntly: "I considered the matter and reached the conclusion that it was best to punch some people in the face or cane them in order to keep things quiet."

Breaking the rules was liable to have serious consequences. Konczal or a delegate of his might take matters in hand, and Konczal's punishments were always worse than anything Eliezer imposed, up to and including the death of the prisoner in question. But there was also another consequence, perhaps a worse one — collective punishment, a method "very popular in the camp." In other blocks, the prisoners were allowed into the barracks only after the lights-off bell rang, but were then woken up and sent outside for hours, sometimes until the wake-up call. Many survivors have provided accounts of such endless inspections, during which they were forced to stand in the cold, wind, rain, and snow. The practice, Eliezer explained, was a simple punitive measure used to enforce order and hygiene. But he did not use it himself and sometimes even managed to dissuade the block chief from doing so. In his block, unlike others, prisoners were allowed to stay inside when they returned from work, and after they were counted they were also allowed to eat there and were not forced to do so outside, as in other blocks. He himself, Eliezer said at the conclusion of this part of his statement, had been beaten "several times by the block chief for not using force to enforce silence in the block."[12] This was not an answer to the question that had been posed during the Buchenwald inquiry — whether there had been cases in which he had beaten prisoners without reason. Neither was it the response he had offered then, when he admitted that there had indeed been such cases.

Speaking to the issue of sick prisoners, he responded both directly and indirectly to one of the most serious charges that had been leveled against him — that he had mistreated and withheld medical care from sick inmates of the blocks in which he had held positions of authority. "Going to the doctor," he explained to the panel of inquiry, "was for all practical purposes a death sentence." But not all prisoners knew this and would go "to the doctor for all sorts of stupid things (flu, scrapes on the legs and so on)." Such ailments were liable to get them categorized as lacking in "economic value" and thus as prisoners that were not worth keeping alive — which meant getting sent straight to the gas chamber. It was thus imperative, Eliezer maintained, to prevent prisoners whose medical condition did not warrant hospitalization from seeing a doctor, despite the suffering this caused. Better for them to try to get over their illnesses in the block, to hope that they would pass, rather than take the risk of going to the infirmary, from which they might not return. The old-timers at the camp were well aware of this, but the new ones were not. "I tried, within the range of possibilities available to me, to have only hopeless cases sent to the infirmary." Such prisoners, he said, had nothing to lose. But block officials could not share this information because doing so could lead to charges from their superiors that they were trying to disrupt camp procedures and rules. He nevertheless did inform the members of his group about this, and "our comrades had instructions not to go to the infirmary even though some of them came down with serious diseases." When it came to the rest of the prisoners, Eliezer said, he would "send them off to work despite their objections. Sometimes I was able to leave them in the barracks, without permission [from the block chief]." But this itself was risky.[13] At the end of 1942, the camp instituted a new procedure regarding sick prisoners. Prisoners could submit forms (*Blockschonung*) that were forwarded to the doctors. A doctor's signature could authorize a prisoner to remain in the block for several days to rest, instead of reporting for work. But when the trucks showed up to take the periodic shipment to the gas chambers, they had a quota of unfit prisoners that they were supposed to collect. The number was determined by the camp staff on the basis of the certifications of illness that the prisoners received. So the gas chamber crew would go through the blocks and take any prisoners who had not gone out to work. Sometimes the block chiefs loyal to the underground were able to obtain inside information secretly from their comrades working in the camp offices about when the trucks would be arriving. They would then compel sick prisoners to go out for work despite the authorization they had received. At times, Eliezer declared, "I had no choice but to banish them [from the block and send them] to work by force, and sometimes by beating them. . . . When we returned from work the sick prisoners whom I forced out to work saw what had happened and most of them came to thank me."

But at other times the SS raids on the blocks were canceled because the quota had been filled, and the prisoners who had been sent to work despite their illnesses came back from a day of forced labor to find that there had been a false alarm. In such instances they were furious at having been denied a day of rest. They blamed Eliezer and attributed it to his habit of senselessly mistreating and brutalizing prisoners.

They did not know and could not understand that, by forcing them out to work, he may well have saved them from being sent to the gas chambers, and that in doing so he had incurred no little personal risk. Eliezer testified that he had, in fact, been beaten badly by the block chief for "playing games with the sick."

Eliezer took the same approach in explaining his treatment of prisoners when an SS soldier arrived in the block to prepare a list of candidates for the next shipment to the gas chamber. He asked the prisoners, ostensibly innocently, who was ill, and suggested that anyone who thought he was could sign up for sick call. The prisoners did not know that in adding their name to the list they were signing their own death warrant. "I'd kick them or scream that they were faking" and eject them from the line — thus saving their lives, he told the judges.

The block sometimes held a thousand or more prisoners. In these overcrowded conditions prisoners began coming down with typhus and dysentery. There were many prisoners who would not listen to his explanations about hygiene, people who were apathetic about their condition, people who lost their wits, people who simply lay and stared into space in pain and anguish, people who lay in their own excrement. Only fear of the rod could force a man sick with dysentery who was so weak that he could barely stand to climb down from his ledge at night rather than make use of one of the bowls that everyone else would have to eat from the next day. Other prisoners took the clothing from the bodies of their fellows who had died of infectious diseases just so that they would have another shirt and pair of pants. This was tantamount to suicide and murder of the prisoners who shared their sleeping ledge. The contaminated articles had to be taken from them by force, and they had to be punished publicly, in front of all the prisoners in the block, in order to deter others from doing the same.[14]

The soiled clothing had to be disposed of and clean clothing obtained. Eliezer told the judges that he took advantage of his acquaintance with a group of Russians who worked in the camp laundry where the uniforms and clothing of the soldiers and SS men were washed. He obtained several hundred extra prison uniforms from them, which he distributed to the men in his block. The Russians also undertook to launder these extra garments secretly. The result was that, in Eliezer's block, prisoners had a spare set of clothing and that they could send soiled clothing to the laundry without remaining unclothed. "This was how, at my initiative, I was able to send in people's laundry twice," Eliezer explained. "Many didn't agree to hand over their dirty, lousy clothing, and we had to use force against them. They wanted to keep both suits with them because of the cold." It was the only Jewish block that operated in this way, he said, and the only block that received extra blankets. "But I [kept] watch over them as if they were my own eyes and punish[ed] those who ripped up blankets to make scarves and such," he related. "Blankets were always in short supply and difficult to obtain."[15]

During his time as Konczal's deputy in Block 9 (July–August 1942 and from the end of September 1942 until February 1943), he said, he managed to help other members of the Polish-French group and a number of Russian prisoners. But his efforts were not always successful, he confessed — when the block chief got wind of what he was doing, he beat Eliezer badly.

One of the camp commanders, named *Hauptscharführer* Moll, set off a bloodbath on Christmas Day 1942. After Moll charged both Jews and non-Jewish prisoners with "dumping sand on the camp roads," non-Jewish prisoners rioted, attacking Jews. Eliezer testified that he hid several dozen prisoners in his block to save them from Moll's wrath. Since there were also other prisoners hiding out in the block for other reasons, Eliezer had to stand at the door and keep out others who sought refuge. Had he let them in, the SS would have realized where they had disappeared to and would have broken into the block and killed everyone. Here Eliezer again sought to bolster his claim that he had saved prisoners and explain the extenuating circumstances that forced him to deny help to others.[16]

Eliezer told the panel that he faced a similar dilemma when the block chiefs were ordered by the SS to submit lists of prisoners for the gas chambers and to include all Jews over the age of fifty. Eliezer claimed that he had put his life on the line to save his associates and the other prisoners in his block. On various pretexts he managed to remove his people from the list of those slated for death. But the quota had then to be topped off with unsuspecting Poles. A short time later the camp commandant told the block chiefs that they had to leave the Jews and Aryans unfit for work in the block when everyone else went out for work. "We knew that that meant certain death for the Jews," Eliezer related. "They weren't taking Aryans to the gas chambers by then, even those who couldn't work. The commandant also announced that if he saw a single *Muselmann* among the details exiting the gate that morning, the commander of that block would go to the gas chamber himself. He said that he and the other kapos decided that only non-Jews would be left behind in the block. On the fateful day, Eliezer said, he was among those who hid the weak Jews among the members of a *Kommando* that was assigned to work in the camp, thus evading being caught at the gate. They saw to it that weak non-Jews were washed, shaven, dressed in clean clothes and shunted, during inspection and the march to work, into the inside ranks. He passed on instructions to the rest of the chiefs of the Jewish blocks, most of whom were Poles and a few of whom were Germans — to do the same. The only block chiefs who carried out the commandant's orders to the letter were ones who were German criminals. "According to the statistics of the block clerk," Eliezer summed up the matter, "only small numbers were selected from my block, which held more than three hundred Jews. It was a dubious success because the quota was filled with others." He did not tell the committee of inquiry, and its members did not ask, how the Poles reacted to his replacement of his people with theirs. Whatever the case, from the autumn of 1943 onward, block officers no longer took part in the selections.

Eliezer said that he began checking out the possibility of escape during this period. Toward the end of 1942, he learned from Russian prisoners of war that they wanted to plan a breakout. They thought that, for operational purposes, it would be a good idea to have members of the Sonderkommando involved, and Eliezer put them in touch with one of his acquaintances from Beaune-la-Rolande who belonged to the crematorium detail. The plan was to carry out the escape during a night shift. But it failed when a member of the Sonderkommando informed on the plotters. The conspirators from that detail were executed, and, Eliezer told his interrogators, he then waited for the next opportunity. Presumably he wished to prove that he had been involved in covert activity and had been linked to the camp underground.

He also enumerated the price he sometimes paid. The block chief beat him when, during a treatment for lice, Eliezer exempted two sick prisoners from having to take a cold shower. He was beaten on a winter day when, against regulations, he conducted an inspection inside the block rather than outside. The camp kapo clubbed him on the head until he was senseless because he had turned a blind eye when certain prisoners evaded the morning inspection and the march out to work.

The end of 1942 and the beginning of 1943 was, he told the judges, "personally, a very difficult time." This was the difficult period that had already come up during the inquiry held after the war at Buchenwald, where it was found that he had indeed behaved brutally toward prisoners at that time, especially the Czechs. The group he had come to Auschwitz with had dispersed, and his activity was restricted to contacts with just a few of its members. A number of rescue attempts had failed, he had heavy responsibilities on his shoulders, and did not always have anyone to consult with. An attempt to organize an escape also failed. His job in the block caused him "revulsion." It was a hopeless time, he said: "My goal was to wait for an opportunity to die with honor."[17]

Nevertheless, Block 9, he claimed, was considered the best Jewish block in the camp, with only half the mortality rate of the others. If the accusations against him were true, he asked, how could that have been the case?

He told the panel how difficult it had been to have the job of linking up the different underground cells in greater Auschwitz, both because of the constant fear of betrayal and informers and because some of the people he was able, after great labor, to establish contact with were then sent to the gas chambers or died from disease or other causes. There were also those who became introverted and stopped responding. In one case, Eliezer said, he established a connection with a Pole named Marian, from the Lublin region. But then Marian escaped from the camp with four Russian prisoners. There were also efforts to make contact with German political prisoners, including some who knew him from France. Some of these men were in very serious condition, broken both mentally and physically, and at least at that time evinced no desire to fight. "The best of them isolated themselves from us, did not want to hear about friendship with Jews," and did not want to be involved in mutual aid and resistance efforts. Others degenerated into being "everyday criminals or murderers."

The situation in the camp was horrible, he recalled. Dozens of prisoners were murdered while participating in work details. Hundreds died of dysentery, typhus, hunger, exhaustion, and infected sores on their feet, some of them caused by their wooden clogs.[18] Many of the members of his group from Beaune-la-Rolande died just a few weeks or months after arriving at Auschwitz. His two fellow leaders from Beaune-la-Rolande, Sznajder and Wikrowiecki, fell ill and died. During the latter's illness, Eliezer hid him in the block for two days, in violation of the rules, but to no effect. Despite all his efforts to save people, "first of all our comrades," as he did not cease to stress, the most he was able to do was to extend their lives by a few weeks or months. He and his associates wondered whether it would not be better "to murder [sick prisoners from their group] humanely (with injections)." Perhaps "that would have been a good deed for the victims, to shorten their suffering." Those who remained alive were dispersed. Some were assigned to the Sonderkommando, and were thus isolated from the rest of the camp; many of these did not last for long and died. Others were transferred to the infamous Block 8, and it was difficult to maintain contact with them.[19]

He claimed that he also tried to help people from outside his close circle. One such case was when a transport of fourteen hundred Parisians arrived. "While they were treated better than the Jews," Eliezer said, "they were in horrible condition and dying like flies." He did his best to intercede on their behalf with the Polish foremen he knew, who agreed to enlarge the list of French prisoners who were assigned to work details at Auschwitz. But of the six hundred sent, ninety were still alive when he left Auschwitz in 1944, he said. Of those who remained in Birkenau, who were sent a few months later to Auschwitz, only thirty survived, he pointed out. He managed to persuade Albert Hammerle, the well-known German criminal and murderer who was chief of Block 5, to accept as his deputy responsible for the French group a baker that Eliezer had known at Beaune-la-Rolande. But he was unable to persuade Hammerle to appoint other members of the group to positions in his block.[20]

Two uprisings were attempted in 1942, Eliezer reported. The first broke out in the block that held Jews from Slovakia. It produced nothing but general carnage. The second started during work hours among Lublin Jews who had been put in a punitive *Kommando*. But the SS and camp guards quickly suppressed it, and some one hundred prisoners were exterminated. Yet, Eliezer said, twenty-six prisoners managed to flee, and even though some of them were later captured, the proportion "between the escapees and the dead seemed reasonable to us," which, he said, "opened up a different point of view for us." They began to think of rebellion and mass flight. It was decided at that point to "bring together resolute comrades, supporters, and people" to form a nucleus for such an action. The first idea was to have a group that would, at an auspicious time, assault SS guards, steal their weapons, and flee.[21] Eliezer testified that his partners in this operation were his friend Majtek Michrowski, whom he had had previously transferred to his block and appointed to a position of authority, and Mirecki. These two men began seeking out appropriate candidates for the attack team. But the plan was short-lived because Michrowski died soon thereafter and because "'good' news began spreading through the camp that the war was coming to an end, that the Jews would be ransomed and sent to Palestine, that there was an order from up high prohibiting the further use of gas to kill [prisoners] and so on." It later transpired that the rumors were spread by the SS and informers in order to suppress the winds of rebellion among the prisoners. The Nazis presumed, correctly, that "a wave of reports that liberation was approaching" would lead to the postponement of any planned uprising. "In those circumstances our attempt shattered. The group [*Kommando*] fell apart and we had difficulty putting together another one," he said. The planned Sonderkommando rebellion of spring-summer-fall 1944 also dissolved as the anticipation of liberation mushroomed, leading more and more prisoners to reason that there was no point taking a risk when they had so much to lose.[22]

Keep in mind, Eliezer stressed, that at the end of 1942 they had not been "in a situation in which we could have taken over the camp." Many blocks were out of bounds to prisoners belonging to other blocks, and prisoners in other blocks were forbidden to leave their own compound. The regular influx of transports, from which prisoners were taken to the gas chambers and sent on to sub-camps, along with frequent changes in the composition of work details, "led to people not knowing where they would be or sleep the next day. . . . We lost comrades without knowing where they had disappeared to, whether they had been taken in a transport, put to death, or had fallen ill." He did not add a detail that needs to be taken into account — most of the prisoners assigned to work details set out early in the morning and returned, exhausted, in the late evening, after which they had to endure inspections, punishments, and other tribulations. Simply getting people together to talk and plan was often impossible. The camp's reign of terror made it difficult to maintain contact between members of Eliezer's group dispersed among the tens of thousands of prisoners in different blocks, and those who had been assigned to the Sonderkommando were isolated and inaccessible.[23]

In the summer and autumn of 1942 and the early winter of 1943, Eliezer began to understand that "Canada" could be a critical resource for the underground. When Meir Kalinski, one of the Paris Communists, arrived at the camp, Eliezer assigned him to a detail that received the transports. Kalinski provided Eliezer with further information about "Canada," where the valuables that were confiscated from the prisoners arriving on the transports were stored. New arrivals were relieved of their gold, silver, jewelry, and other items of value as soon as they descended from the trains to the platforms where they were sorted, and anything remaining — including gold teeth — was taken off their bodies after they were killed. Kalinski also witnessed the trading and dealing that some of the members of the "Canada" *Kommando* conducted with the money and valuables they stole from the Nazi thieves, taking items that had been classified as property of the Reich or appropriated by senior figures in the camp. Kalinski and others sought to put an end to such pilfering for personal gain and to replace it with an organized system in which items were taken to support activities that benefited all prisoners — the purchase of food, medicine, and, later, weapons for defense and rebellion. While they soon realized that they could not thwart individual theft, the underground cells were indeed able to use some of the stolen money to fund assistance and subversion.[24]

At the end of August and the beginning of September 1942, Eliezer began to weary of his post in Block 9. "The work brought negligible results in the context of saving people, made me nauseated, and I found it difficult to maintain humane standards and so on," he told the panel. An opportunity for a change presented itself when the camp administration announced that it was opening a training school for block chiefs. Eliezer asked to enroll.

For reasons he did not spell out, the program was shut down a short time later, and the trainees dispersed. Eliezer managed to arrange to stay in Block 4, where the course had been conducted, and obtain the post of block clerk, settling back into routine.[25]

In September 1942, a short time after arriving in Block 4, he learned of a transport that had arrived in Birkenau from Auschwitz. It contained about a thousand prisoners who had been classified as unfit for work. In other words, they were destined for extermination, but instead of being sent immediately to their deaths they were confined in a waiting area. Later that day SS soldiers arrived with trucks and demanded to take 150 of the new arrivals to the gas chambers. Eliezer testified that he managed to warn the group of the danger and to advise them to run for it and to try to lose themselves among the prisoners in the camp. Some of the people "still had the strength and energy to try to flee," he reported. Eliezer said that he was caught and beaten by an SS soldier. Luckily for him, however, his assailant let him go and joined those who were looking for the prisoners who had fled. But, again, "in enabling them to flee I didn't help save a single person, because in place of each one who fled they immediately took another one to top up the quota."[26]

Knowing that work meant life, he tried to manufacture jobs. He proposed to the camp kapo, Anton, a German criminal and murderer, the establishment of a *Kommando* to pave more roads and walkways in the camp. Anton agreed, and a group of two hundred prisoners was assigned to this relatively easy labor for two weeks. This also made them eligible for a food supplement that was given only to workers. While the *Kommando* was disbanded after a short time, its members were transferred to other work details and were thus able to remain alive, at least for a time. At about that time, in cooperation with his acquaintance from Paris, Jacques Furmanski, who had been made a foreman, Eliezer managed to transfer Communist comrades to workshops at Auschwitz, where they were employed as tailors and shoemakers.[27]

But Eliezer did not manage to remain in his block clerk job for long. Michrowski, representing the members of the Paris group, asked him to return to Block 9 "and not hide out in the clerks' room. I thought to myself that it was my job to return to the block, even though it was better for me in Block 4 and the office where I worked was quiet, clean, and without confrontations with the SS. Also, I wasn't responsible for other people." Since his departure from Block 9, Eliezer learned from friends who had remained in that block, Konczal had gotten more violent. The prisoners preferred Eliezer, with his outbursts, to Konczal and his accessories. He agreed, and his return to Block 9 was approved by Konczal and his superiors. But a short time after his return he came down with a severe case of typhus. His friends, in particular Langman, who had managed to bring him back from Block 8 when he was transferred there soon after their arrival at Birkenau, took care of him. They designated him as night guard in order to relieve him of the need to go out to work; and to ensure that his illness was not discovered, twice a day, morning and evening, they dragged Eliezer, exhausted and barely conscious, out for inspection. Everyone knew that if his illness became known and if he did not report for inspection, he would be sent to another part of the camp and from there to the gas chambers. It took two months for him to recover, and he was able to resume his duties only at the end of November 1942—but then Michrowski came down with the same disease and was transferred to Block 7, known as the Death Block. But there, under the care of David Szmulewski, Eliezer's comrade-in-arms in Spain, Michrowski beat back the disease — only to be felled by a complication from dysentery. Typhus killed Kalinski. Sawek Kirszenbaum, for whom, Eliezer claimed, he had arranged work in a tolerable detail, also came down with typhus. He too was cared for by Szmulewski, but died of the disease.[28]

At the end of January more changes came to Block 9. Most of the Jews were moved out, to be replaced by Poles. A few days later a transport of Czechs arrived, and they were housed in the block as well. Konczal was transferred elsewhere, and was replaced by Dymanski, a German who had close relations with the Paris Jewish Communists. Blass and Wilner arrived with him. The changes in the leadership and the prisoner population led Eliezer to conclude that he should ask to be relieved of his position.

He was appointed head of Block 25 (or, according to another account, Block 39), which was empty at the time and had to be prepared to take in prisoners. But he did not remain there long. Just a few days later he was returned to Block 9, where he served under Dymanski until February 1943. At the end of February, he left Block 9 again, after spending, intermittently, a total of some four months there. Once again, he saw the move as an opportunity to divest himself of the complications brought on by responsibility, and perhaps to take a distance from the reputation he had developed.

But he was no more able to influence events in Auschwitz than any other prisoner. In mid-1943, SS-Rapportführer Ludwig Plagge, an official who oversaw a number of block chiefs, reassigned Eliezer to be commander of a new block that had been placed in isolation. He found "horrible conditions" there. It was in this block that the *Lagerälteste* (a prisoner appointed by the Nazis as the senior "trustee" of a camp), SS-Rapportführer Plagge, and other German block chiefs, all of them criminals, got together to get drunk and kill. Eliezer tried, he told the panel, to oppose them, but they took him out one night and beat him, and then did the same the next day. The Germans planned to do away with him, but before they could he was transferred again, this time to the main camp. Eliezer told his interrogators that Comrade Bobryk, who had been in the block with him and whom he later ran into at Buchenwald, could confirm this.

The inquiry, of course, could not help taking an interest in how it was that Eliezer was able to switch from posting to posting so rapidly over such a short span of time. He confronted these questions.

In March 1943 he was given a new position, chief of Block 20, the quarantine block. Once again, he claimed, he had not wanted the position, but Dymanski and others had impressed on him that he would be able to increase the likelihood that prisoners in the block could survive.[29] Presumably, Dymanski and his associates would not have asked Eliezer to once again assume a position of responsibility had they considered him disreputable.

Block 20 was known as the Block of Murders. Its previous chief, Leon Stakhoviak from Posen, and the room wardens that worked with him were all murderers. Eliezer tried to replace the latter with his own men. But any such change required the consent of the camp elder. The camp elder proposed new men for the job, but they were no more than "new criminals," Eliezer said. He did manage to get rid of a room warden named Mazgay, who stole from prisoners, and Frank (Frantisek) Krasiewicz, the block clerk, a loyalist of both Stakhoviak and the camp elder. Gradually he was able to insert his own men into important positions. One of them was Avraham Berneman, a member of Eliezer's group. Eliezer told the panel that the staff changes took place over several weeks.

His next project was to change the block's routine. "I permitted people to go inside the block and lie on their platforms immediately after inspection," he said. His predecessor, like other camp officials, had kept prisoners standing at inspection for hours on end.[30]

When he arrived in the block, it contained Jewish prisoners from the latest transport, which had come from the Polish town of Radomsko, the seat of a well-known Hasidic dynasty. The most serious accusations against Eliezer involved his treatment of religious Jews such as these Hasidim. A transport of Czechoslovakian Jews arrived at the same time, soon to be followed by one from Łódź and another from Greece. In the summer of 1943 a transport arrived from Radom,[31] a city in central Poland, as well as one of a shipment of Dutch and French Jews. Eliezer appointed officials from these groups as well, mostly to the post of room warden. He chose the son of a Jewish activist from Salonika from the Greek transport. From a Polish transport he chose a dentist named Edek from Bicêtre. He also managed to find easy assignments for a veteran of the Spanish Civil War, a comrade from Greece, and also for a group of Polish political prisoners who arrived at the end of the spring in 1943 and were placed in Block 26. He made Jan Kędzierski, a member of the Workers' Cultural Organization (TUR), a room warden.[32]

It was at this time that Eliezer managed to establish a network of connections with new arrivals at the camp, and through them with other people and the organizations they were associated with. He got to know Franz Kejman from Vienna, a member of the KZM (Kirche zum Mitreden, a Christian organization that rescued Jews), as well as Konstantin (Kostek) Jagelo, who was moved into Block 20 in May 1943. He asked Kejman to make contact with forces outside the camp, via both local civilians with whom the prisoners had contact in the course of their labors and SS men with whom Kejman conducted black-market dealings within the camp. Jagelo updated him about the state of the Polish Communist Party, the changes it had undergone with the establishment of the PPR (Communist Party) in 1942, its delegation in London, and other matters. Another person Eliezer was talking to at the time, by his account, was a Polish officer, Korwin Piotrowski, in connection with his role in the underground force the Union of Armed Combat (Związek Walki Zbrojnej—ZWZ), which placed itself under the authority of the Polish government-in-exile. Piotrowski had been in contact with the ZWZ in Radom. In addition, he established a good relationship with Jozef Szpilski of the Polish Socialist Party, who spent five weeks in Eliezer's block. He also told the panel about his contacts with Szmulewski, who was responsible for the Auschwitz underground's communications with the women's camp. Karol Suttor, who was also a kapo in Birkenau, helped him maintain contact with Polish and other forces outside the camp.[33]

The new arrivals from Radom were infested with typhus and lice, which Eliezer and his team managed to eradicate. He also took in another transport, this one from the Majdanek concentration camp, and a transport from Greece. He begged his interrogators to call in witnesses from these groups to testify about his treatment of them. He referred specifically to a doctor from Block 65 who had been present when Eliezer testified at Buchenwald. Eliezer told the panel that in the spring of 1943 he had a severe altercation with Perschl, a block chief who demanded that Eliezer provide him with food. After being turned down by Eliezer several times, Perschl initiated an inquiry, which discovered wire cutters in Eliezer's possession. Luckily, he got off with a relatively minor sentence, being sent "for only ten nights in solitary."[34] In telling all this, Eliezer tried to show that after "a few black weeks" he changed his ways and worked, as block chief, to do all he could for the prisoners in his charge.

In July 1943 the entire men's camp at Birkenau was relocated into a new camp. Eliezer was made chief of Block 30, and brought his close associates into that block as well. Among these were Zygmunt Swierdłowaki from Austrowitz, a member of the KPP. In the autumn of 1943 he was also able to bring in Langman, who had cared for him so devotedly during his illness.[35] After the war, Langman was apprehensive about providing his version of the story, and there were those people who reinforced his apprehension.

Eliezer managed to keep looking out for his friends and comrades in his new position. He made Balevski, a Polish friend from the Radom region, a night guard in Block 28. As block clerk he appointed Aaron, a Romanian Communist who had arrived in the block with Eliezer's group from Paris, and for others from the same transport he arranged positions in his block, in other nearby and good blocks, and on relatively easy work details. Eliezer had first turned Aaron away when he presented himself as a party member, suspecting that he was an SS agent planted in the group. He asked Szmulewski to make inquiries, and when it turned out that Aaron was telling the truth, Eliezer took him on. Wilner, whom he had known in Block 9 and who had since become clerk of Block 5, helped with the placements.[36]

Eliezer also recounted his efforts to purchase weapons for camp officeholders, by which he apparently meant a group of leading prisoners that included Leon Weiner, a Jewish-German foreman; Yos (or Josek or Yosef), a Polish-Jewish deputy kapo in the clothing depot; and Nelkan, a Jewish doctor from Austria who worked as a cook in the kitchen. They approached him at the end of 1943, offering money and gold in exchange for weapons for "organizing an uprising and setting fire to all the blocks at night." Eliezer passed on their request to other underground activists. Eliezer added that the money came via Berneman, who had replaced Meir Kalinski, a member of the covert operation in "Canada," who had died of dysentery.[37] Eliezer was not able to obtain any weapons for the group, but the attempt strengthened his ties with Suttor and other Russian and German underground activists, and through them with members of the SS, who became his collaborators in planning an escape operation. With their assistance, he sought to make it possible for the escapees to vanish as quickly as possible.

Other members of the group were Petia, who worked in the camp laundry; Dima, a former naval officer who worked on the burial detail, and Nikolaj Iwanow, a Belarusian Communist who worked in the food depot, all members of a group of Soviet prisoners with whom he had connected in the fall of 1943. With and through them he sought to obtain arms, establish contacts with the partisan forces outside, and organize an escape.[38] It was through this group that he learned, at the beginning of 1944, about a plan to attack the guard post at the camp's entrance gate. A German Jew who cleaned the post provided details about the structure and the weapon cache there. Eliezer told his questioners that he had opposed the plan, which he defined as "unrealistic . . . suicide." One of the Russians Eliezer was in contact with informed the SS, and Iwanow and a Soviet colonel who was part of the conspiracy were arrested, held in solitary confinement for a period, and then sent to Flossenbürg, a concentration camp on the Czech-German border. Eliezer's ties with Suttor were so close that both of them, along with Aaron, considered heading a new leadership for the underground, but the plans were abandoned both because Aaron came down with typhus and because Eliezer was transferred out of Birkenau.[39]

In the autumn and winter of 1943 another underground activist arrived — Gustaw Miciol (or Micol), commander of the Gwardia Ludowa, a Polish Communist resistance organization, in the Kraków area. He had also served as an officer in Spain. Another arrival was Roman Sliwa. Szmulewski sent them to Eliezer, who arranged for them to work in Suttor's group. Eliezer said that he also arranged an easy assignment for another, unnamed member of the underground, in the carpentry detail where Mink was a central figure. Eliezer, Mink, and Szmulewski notified Blass, a block chief, that this man was one of theirs.[40] Eliezer testified that they also decided to bring Miciol into the escape plan — his status and his connections outside the camp would be key to ensuring that the escapees were taken in securely by the partisan forces or others who could protect them. Szmulewski supplied the necessary gear — a watch, compass, and money, while Eliezer connected him with Dima and his partners. Three men took part in the escape attempt. They were able to get out of the camp, but after making their way for nearly twenty miles they ran into a search party and were shot dead. Members of the Communist underground received the three bodies at the crematorium. It was a heavy blow not just because the escape attempt failed, but also because it had raised such high hopes. Just before the plan went into action, Miciol had received precise instructions about locations at which he could join up with the partisans. Everyone had been sure that the attempt would succeed and that it in its wake "we too could make contact with freedom." Eliezer would later insist that his involvement in taking Miciol in and in helping prepare the escape operation were further examples that disproved the claims that the underground leadership had considered him unreliable and had kept him out of the loop. Another man involved in a breakout attempt was Franz Kejman, from his block. Kejman, Eliezer said, had been forced to serve as the block chief's sex slave, a position Eliezer was able to extricate him from. Through Kejman, Eliezer claimed, contacts were also established with a Croatian member of the SS who wanted to defect to the partisans. He also told the panel about another escape operation he had been involved in, which involved digging a bunker to hide out in. The bunker was prepared, and all that was left was to set a date for the escape. He added no further details.[41]

Letters were sent to underground and partisan groups in an attempt to obtain information and develop connections that could serve in later operations. Sliwa, Suttor, and civilian workers who were willing to serve as paid couriers were involved. Payment was made in watches and other valuables that Szmulewski passed on after receiving them from his associates in the Sonderkommando.[42] When questioned by his interrogators, Eliezer always made a point of saying that he involved members of the underground leadership, and Szmulewski in particular, in all his activities and special contacts.

He also told of a move to bring together forces in the Sonderkommando and elsewhere for joint action. According to the plan, one force would charge at SS personnel when the guard shift changed at one of the crematoria. This force would take possession of the guards' weapons and then attack the guards in the guard towers and at the guard posts by the main gate. In parallel, the barracks would be set aflame, and prisoners would rush the fences. The contact people in the Sonderkommando were Fajnzylber, whom Eliezer had first met in Spain, and Warszawski (later known as Dorembus), a member of his circle in Paris. According to Eliezer, these two men plotted the uprising with others in the Sonderkommando and outside it. The underground leadership discussed the plan and decided that it was a good one, "but it was clear to me that the plan could go into action only when the front got closer, or when the situation in the camp was desperate not only for the Jewish prisoners," Eliezer related.

He was not wrong in his estimation that the differences between the disparate underground groups could unravel the consensus that the plan was logical and well-timed. Zero hour was the changing of the guard at the beginning of the night shift. The day chosen had to be an auspicious one, when most of the prisoners were desperate enough to take such a huge risk. The choice of day became the subject of major disagreement. Neither was it easy to put together a "decisive" group, as Eliezer termed it, in the Sonderkommando. The active nucleus there, he said, did not manage to put together a group that could meet the uprising's needs and expectations.[43]

Eliezer's opening statement concluded with an account of the end of his time in Birkenau, his transfer to Buna-Monowitz, and then to Jawischowitz. He explained that he was not writing about his period there, which lasted until the end of January 1945, "because as far as I know no accusations have been made against me regarding that period." He described the rumors regarding the in absentia proceeding against him and its findings, of which he learned from Herman Achsen. He also spoke of the Buchenwald inquiry into the complaint lodged by the Czech group. "The commission, to the best of my knowledge," he wrote, "heard several dozen Polish, German, Russian, Czech, and Jewish witnesses. The decision was, more or less: we recognize the fact that, in the difficult conditions in Birkenau, you did positive work, but while you were doing that work, in exceptional cases, you made mistakes." Wanting to know more, he explained, he had asked them to be "more specific." There are two kinds of mistakes, he said — those done inadvertently while carrying out one's duties, and those that are done maliciously and which involve turpitude. "I was told that the second type was not under consideration and that it was clear that they continued to consider me a comrade."[44]

Before concluding his testimony with a list of substantive and character witnesses, he said that he wanted to cast light on an issue that applied to everyone who had filled a position in the camps. "Was it permissible," he asked, "for comrades in the camps to accept the post of block chief, kapo, and foreman and to place themselves in a position in which we would be part of the SS machinery of persecution?" Everyone, he said, knew the answer: "Communists, as well antifascists of all nations, adopted this tactic, without exception, in all the concentration camps." What consideration guided all these people to take on such assignments even though they understood that they were, in doing so, becoming part of the terror apparatus? "This tactic made it possible to do much good," he asserted, "and first of all to save the team." Furthermore, in choosing this course of action, these people had to make it look as if they were "carrying out the SS's orders." This was the policy they pursued during the deportation from Buchenwald. After the SS crushed the initial resistance, the camp administration, made up of prisoners, resolved to manage the transports itself so as to sabotage them and thus gain time and to keep in the camp, for the moment of truth, the pillars of the antifascist resistance. The result, Eliezer said, was the emergence of a group of overseers composed mostly of party members from all the national groups. The strategy made it possible to save the lives of thousands of antifascists from many countries, but it could not have been pursued without blows and kicks and their consequences.[45]

Had they not used force, he argued, the Nazis would, from the start, not have allowed these officials to become part of the system. Had they not been willing to use such measures they could not have broken through the Nazi cordon and acquired authority. Notably, however, he did not address the corollary issue of where lay the dividing line between cooperation and collaboration, between integration into the system in order to assist and aid other prisoners and assimilation into that system and addiction to the power it provided.[46]

Another such issue was that the prisoner officials had no power to set and shape the rules of the game, which were entirely dictated by the Nazis. Saving one prisoner thus inevitably meant sending another one to his death. There was no way not to fill the quotas for the gas chamber and no way to give everyone an easy work assignment. It was not possible to share out to everyone the extra rations that officials were able to obtain. One cannot help but recall Primo Levi's agonizing over which of his two friends to share drops of water from a leaking faucet with.[47] The question, then, was — and this was not always at the discretion of the block chiefs — whom to use to fill the quotas, before whom to slam doors, and who was to be left to his fate.

Eliezer did not wait for his questioners or attackers to put all these issues on the table. He raised them himself and tried to give answers, some of which were difficult to digest, answers that stabbed deep into living flesh.

Who was on the list of witnesses he gave to the investigatory commission? They were people who had been with him and who should know very well what he had done and not done, or so he thought. He wrote down David Shmuelevich, meaning Szmulewski; Aaron the Romanian Communist; Jacques Furmanski, one of the Paris Polish-Jewish Communists; Leon Shechter, who spent a few months during 1942 in Block 9 and had testified before the committee convened at Buchenwald; and Lazare Etlinger, who had been a room warden in Blocks 20 and 30 under Eliezer's direction at the end of 1943. He also included Martin Steg, an acquaintance who had been a friend of the Block 9 clerk, David Pastela. This latter was a Polish-born French Jew who had been a leader of the covert group active in an isolated camp in the Auschwitz complex and had acted, along with others, to promote the idea of an uprising. We may assume that he did not mention Pastela, who had been killed on the death march, for nothing. It was an attempt to link himself to a highly regarded figure. He also included the controversial Ijziykléar Oléar. Eliezer stressed that he did not know "what the opinions of these people are of me at this point in time and I do not know whether some of them are not among my accusers. In any case, they can confirm a range of facts that I have cited." If necessary, he said, there were others from Buchenwald, party members and nonmembers, who had known him in Auschwitz and Birkenau.[48]

The collection of testimonies and hearing of witnesses, along with the questioning of Eliezer and witnesses and confrontation between the two lasted for several months. This comprehensive documentation covers tens of pages. The questions were tough, and many of them uncomfortable ones for Eliezer. Both the facts that the two sides could agree on and the interpretation of those facts offered by the witnesses were often quite different from those presented by Eliezer in his opening statement and at other stages in the proceeding. Nevertheless, some witnesses openly stood by him.

Kowalski and Eisner also headed the next stage of the inquiry, serving as both judges and interrogators. They questioned him about his early days in the party, asking whether his membership had been continuous, what positions he had held at its behest before the war, how he had acted in the party's name at Beaune-la-Rolande, and the nature of the previous Buchenwald proceeding. As the proceeding went on, they focused on the specific accusations made against him — beating, abuse, theft of and commerce in food, the use of antisemitic language, dispatching prisoners to the gas chambers, and the murder of prisoners. The judges pressed him more and more intensely on a number of questions. To the best of his knowledge, had there been others who served as kapos but had not been accused of the offenses he had been charged with? Did all the complaints come from resentful and injured people, or were some of them objective? And how did he explain the fact that some of the accusations had been made by senior members of the party cell at Birkenau, in most cases by people who had been with him over an extended period?

In some instances he was able to deflect the accusations easily. In others the questions hit him square in the face, and had we film footage of the hearings we almost certainly would have been able to make out beads of sweat on his bald spot. The questions were open ones, but others were leading questions that presumed the truth of the charges against him.[49]

In their first question, the judges sought to get Eliezer to position himself among his comrades, and it threw Eliezer completely off balance. What, he was asked, did he think his fellow Communists at the camps had thought of him then, how did he think their opinions of him had changed over time, and what had he learned only later about his standing among them? His answer was confused and contradictory. He had been a member of the leadership and had seen that leadership dissolve during the initial period at Auschwitz-Birkenau, he acknowledged. But he also confessed that the party organization continued to operate thereafter, at least partially — and that he had been excluded from it. During the entire period at Beaune-la-Rolande, he said, he had been a member of the party's troika of leaders there. He had continued in that leadership capacity during the first six weeks at Birkenau. But the party leadership had then fallen apart, and for the four remaining months of 1942 there had been, to the best of his knowledge at the time, no party organization in the camp. He had tried, with the help of several comrades, to reconstitute it, but without success. He maintained contact with "certain people" from the party during 1943, he claimed, but only toward the end of that year, he said, "did we begin to form a party organization, and I was largely in contact with Polish and Russian members." He later learned, he related, "that during the above-mentioned period the organization had [in fact] been in existence," but "apparently because of lack of confidence, the comrades thought it best not to bring me in. Whatever the case, during this entire period I was in close contact with our people — Poles, Russians, Jews, and Germans." He had first heard of the charges being leveled at him in 1944, at Jawischowitz, "ostensibly about 'inhumane treatment,'" and was told that a committee had been set up, without his knowledge, to look into the accusations that were the reason he had not been included in the new leadership. The committee, he said, did not find anything against him, and when it was over, Achsen had explained to him that "we did not take you for the job because of the accusations against you. I think they aren't true and now you can cooperate with us." Eliezer said they assigned him "to a special task with the Poles."

From the beginning of the judges' interrogation he was thus compelled to admit that his standing in the group had been shaky, that his associates lacked confidence in him, and that he had not been aware of this at the time. At the beginning of their term in Birkenau, something in their relationship with him had broken, something deep enough to bring them to exclude him. He had only learned after the fact, and by chance, that they had sought to dissociate themselves from him and that they had established a committee to look into his actions. At the end of his first response he stressed that, for this reason, he should be allowed to name further witnesses — Blass, Langman, a man named Alexander, Epstein, Szpilski, and Stepan Tiszczenko, a Russian military engineer who had fled Birkenau and been captured in Poland. The judges should also remember what had been said by Szmulewski, who was a central member of the group, "that even though I wasn't in the party, I provided it with very significant services." They could also ask "Oléar, against whom, as I know, there are also accusations," and who had sought out every knoll or hill or shadow of a hill to hide behind.[50]

This answer made it clear that, at a very early stage, for better or for worse, Eliezer had functioned as a one-man cell of his own, as a contractor or "freelancer." He had worked independently because he wanted to take part in initiatives others had begun, or projects he thought up himself, in actions he took part in with members of his own group or with other covert actors in the camp. These services and the standing he acquired for himself outside his own group rankled some of his own comrades.

He was asked: "Is it true that in 1942, when Warszawski asked you to assist the party organization, that you refused to do so?" "Not true," Eliezer replied. "In 1943 I was constantly in contact with Comrade Warszawski and with Fajnzylber, both from the Sonderkommando, and we spoke of a joint plan for an uprising by the Sonderkommando at the camp. I was the liaison with the Russians in this matter." It was an interesting reply, but it did not answer the question.

"Did you belong to the party organization in 1942–1943?" he was then asked. "To the best of my knowledge at the time there was no party organization," he explained — again not answering the question that had been put to him. But his answer indicates that he was cut off from his Communist associates in the period from the end of 1942 to the beginning of 1943, and that his activity had taken place outside that circle.[51]

His interrogators asked about the proceeding at Buchenwald — how many people had participated, what the charges had been, and how it had been decided. Eliezer replied that there had been two or three examination proceedings. He had been accused of beating and stealing from prisoners. On one occasion he was called on to confront witnesses and had forcefully deflected their claims. Wacek Cherubin, a member of the party from Poland who had been killed during the evacuation of the camp, had told him: "We agreed that in Birkenau you did much positive work, but in certain circumstances you made mistakes." Eliezer said that he had asked Cherubin whether "these were mistakes that anyone could make while doing good work, or were they dishonorable ones? Do you consider me a comrade or not?" According to Eliezer, Cherubin had told him, "Yes, we consider you a comrade." But this, he learned, was not the whole picture, because "Suttor notified me that the decision of the committee of inquiry would be reexamined, since I was not entirely a positive person."

After the Americans liberated Buchenwald, a third commission of inquiry had been established, composed of Kisiel, Stefaniak, and Baruch Goldberg. But, Eliezer said, "it did not convene. Kisiel was supposed to have collected evidence against me. But they told him, Eliezer, 'Let it go, it's not important, and so on,' and Kisiel declared that there was no reason to open an inquiry."

Throughout this time, Eliezer asserted, there had been leaders of the underground cells, some of whom were party members, who had brought him into their plans, preparations, and actions. Among them were Achsen, Shimon Rutkowski, and Jozef Szpilski, although there were others, like Kaminski, who tried to exclude him. He was party to the underground's activity at the end of the Buchenwald period and in the initial days after liberation.[52]

Before asking a series of pointed questions on the crimes he had been accused of, the investigators thought it important to take up the charge of "original sin" that still hung over Eliezer. The question was whether his ideology was consistent with that of the party. In particular, they wanted to hear about the heresy that everyone attributed to him. The wording of their question made it clear that they considered his deviation a grave one. "Is it true," they asked, "that at Beaune-la-Rolande you made a speech suffused with panic, expressing an opinion that made it possible for people to understand that the Soviet Union would be defeated?"

"That is a bald-faced lie," Eliezer retorted. "The lecture I gave was legitimate and focused on war tactics. The source of the rumor is no doubt the fact that when the war broke out I said that it was not impossible that the Germans would win a number of victories at the beginning of the war, but that this would certainly not determine the outcome of the war. In 1941, when the Germans were arrayed near Moscow, I made a speech in which I proved that, despite the defeats, the USSR would win the war."

As a loyal Communist who understood that his fate lay in the hands of orthodox party men, Eliezer knew that he had to demonstrate that, even as the Wehrmacht destroyed one European army after another, he had never lost his faith in the Soviet Union, and certainly not in its leader, the Sun of the Nations.

How, then, the judges asked him, did he explain certain phrases he had used, such as "no one has ever come out of here." All his comrades, he noted, both those who were disturbed by his behavior and the nature of his connections with the Nazis and their agents, and those who had asked him to lead the Polish-French Communist cell in the camp, agreed that he had spoken those words. In this case, Eliezer had a better answer, one firmly grounded in the circumstances of the camp, the tendency of the prisoners to hang on to every rumor, including those spread by the Nazis as part of their campaign to gain control of the prisoners by dividing them through deception and misinformation. Yes, Eliezer acknowledged, he had spoken in that vein from time to time. But that had been a deliberate attempt to combat the counterfeit optimism created by unfounded rumors about battlefield victories, which was producing in his fellow prisoners a dangerous complacency. "I frequently offered the thesis that no one would ever be allowed to leave here. This brought people to the conclusion that a fight of one sort or another was inevitable." He meant not to show pessimism and hopelessness but rather to foster fighting spirit. Activism was a life force, uniting individuals into a group and increasing the chances of survival. He took pains to stress that he had not said this at a moment of despair and collapse. In that context, saying that no one would ever get out alive would have been tantamount to implying that there was no reason not to engage in the vilest of selfish acts because in any case no one would ever have to answer for his crimes. On the contrary, he took this approach when he began to understand that he was fighting for his life.[53]

The investigators then moved on to the more serious charges. They first asked Eliezer why he had beaten Dr. Nedvěd, a leader of the Czech group, and whether he had made a practice of clubbing prisoners for no reason. They asked whether he had kicked an elderly prisoner who had asked for more soup, and if so, how he explained that.

Eliezer admitted beating Dr. Nedvěd, but said that the doctor himself, after coming to understand the circumstances, "never blamed me." There was no truth to the charge that the beating had caused Nedvěd's death. The doctor, Eliezer insisted, had died of typhus some weeks later. He had said as much at the Buchenwald inquiry, and his claim had been confirmed by other testimonies. Yes, he had beaten prisoners, Eliezer admitted, sometimes with a club. The beatings were absolutely necessary, and the claims that he had done so when there was no need for it, simply for his own pleasure, were "nonsense." He had beaten "only to preserve order and discipline, which were in the interest of all the others. . . . I might have made certain mistakes, it could be that sometimes I overreacted. You need to understand here the position of a block chief." He wasn't supposed to beat prisoners — that was the job of the room wardens. But "in Block 20 I had room wardens that were sent from the camp administration, the worst sorts of criminals. In this situation I thought it advisable to assume this function myself." He had done so to save the prisoners from these criminals and for no other reason. After he managed to replace the violent room wardens with people of his own, people like "Comrade Berneman from Spain, Comrade Majcher Langman, Zygmunt Swierdłowski from Austrowitz, a former member of the KPP, and Kędzierski from the PPSW," there was no longer any reason for him to intervene.

He did not remember kicking an old man who asked for more soup and thus could not know if the man died as a result. Such general accusations should not be made against him, he said. He demanded that any charges made against him be specific. "It could be that I beat someone who asked for more soup, but you have to understand in what circumstances the soup was handed out. People were always famished, and hundreds lunged for the remains of the soup in the kettle. To prevent problems in handing out the remaining soup, some block chiefs simply poured it out, which I never did," he explained. But he did not recall any specific incident involving an elderly man.[54]

"Were there block chiefs who did not beat prisoners?" he was asked. Yes, he responded, but their room wardens did the beating for them. In well-run blocks they did not engage in beatings. From the beginning of 1943 there were "no mass beatings at all." A close examination of Eliezer's words shows that he was speaking of beatings in Block 20, between February 1943 and July 1943, after his term as Block 9 chief under Konczal, "the blackest weeks" in his life.

The beating of fellow Communists was unavoidable, Eliezer claimed. He himself had been beaten a short time after his arrival at Buchenwald by a Polish Communist. An order had come at night to send, immediately, five hundred people to Dora-Mittelbau, a Buchenwald sub-camp in the Harz Mountains. Communists with seniority at the camp warned him. He hid, was captured, and the room warden hit him in the teeth. He understood the circumstances, and he did not then or now think it was surprising. He reminded his interrogators that he, in the course of performing his duties, had been beaten more than any other block chief, precisely because he treated the prisoners under his charge with a light hand.[55]

When he was asked about the theft of and commerce in food, he rejected the accusation categorically. Up until March 1943 he had not been a block chief, and therefore he could not set policy. During the period in which he did not serve in that capacity there had been theft and trade in food. But that had stopped when he was appointed block chief. The accusations about stealing twelve cubes of margarine had been demonstrated false in earlier investigations. Dymanski, Blass, and Langman could all confirm that he had not traded in food — that kind of thing had started only after he was transferred to a different block. On top of that, he was the only block chief who ate from the general kettle and did not avail himself of the perquisite of having one of his helpers cook for him. He also saw to it that food was handed out in the block rather than outside. What about murders and severe violence in the block? Nothing of the kind, he replied. During the entire period in which he had been block chief, from March 1943 onward, there had been relative quiet in his blocks. By May 1943 the block contained some five hundred prisoners, and during his tenure only one man had died, of a heart attack. "Under concentration camp conditions these results were a real sensation," he said. His block, he stressed, had been "the only block without murders."[56]

The atmosphere in the room grew heavier as the questioning continued. The investigators asked: "Is it true that during your tenure as block chief you displayed toleration for crimes committed by a man named Frank?" Eliezer acknowledged that Frank (Frantisek) Krasiewicz had been block clerk from May to August 1943. He had been appointed to that post by the camp elder, Frantz Danisch, even though Krasiewicz was illiterate. But Krasiewicz had committed no crime in his block, and when the new camp was set up, Eliezer said, he persuaded Krasiewicz to go there.

"Is it true that Krasiewicz did what was called 'sport,' and what does that mean?" the investigators asked. "Sport," Eliezer told them, was the name given to punitive exercises. He himself had meted out such punishment to prisoners, Eliezer said, to enforce discipline. His practice had been "not to send any report upward." To do so he had to preserve discipline and order autonomously, "to punish ourselves." He went on to explain: "People had dysentery and at night they did their business in the bowls that were used for eating. In the morning I found full bowls under the beds. I didn't know whom they belonged to, so I ordered fifteen minutes of exercise as punishment for all the people who next to their beds the full bowls were found." Others testified that "sport" included hours of kneeling in mud, snow, and puddles, "physical activity" that sapped them of all their remaining strength.

At this point the investigators asked if there was any truth to the charge that he took part, along with another official named Tadek, in the murder of two men. Eliezer's response indicates a reluctant acknowledgment that a murder took place. He had been present and had told Langman about it, and had gone so far as to tell him that he could not oppose it. Because the murder had been committed in his presence, he told Langman, he felt as if he "shared responsibility."

"One of your accusers," the investigators asked, "testifies that you often said things like 'a thousand Jews kicked the bucket, what's the big deal, we'll have less of a black market,' and that you laughed at Jews who were on their way to their deaths. Is that true?"

"When, where, and to whom did I say that?" Eliezer protested. "It's not true, I reject that categorically. A number of times I reiterated to comrades that the fiber of Polish Jewry was of bad quality. Jews in our camp were the remnants of the Polish ghettos. A large number of them were those who had survived thanks to the black market, to trade with the Germans, and so on. I argued that such people were not the normal foundation of Polish Jewry. It was a sordid element. . . . I said that their only response to the danger of death was prayers and singing 'Hatikvah.' I did not laugh about that ever. . . . I frequently blushed in shame . . . it was necessary to explain their behavior. . . . Where did the Jewish Sonderkommando come from, what was the source of those who frequently informed to the Germans, and that kind of thing? I defended the Jews while explaining what element we had in the camp and that not all Jews were like that."

"And how did you treat the Jews?" the investigators asked. "I did not treat them in any special way," Eliezer replied. "Of all the elements in the concentration camp the Jews were the least aggressive. The camp administration even sent the Jews to places where escape was possible, which they would not do with other nationalities. At the end of 1943 the camp commander wrote a letter to Berlin regarding the urgent need to evacuate the camp. In response came an order to evacuate everyone except the Jews. Jewish prisoners began to escape only toward the end of 1943. My opinion was that when it came to organizational work, we needed first to seek support from the most combative elements in the camp, but we did not treat the Jews in any special way."[57]

After liberation Eliezer was accused of having adopted antisemitic stereotypes. He did not understand the situation that most of the Jews were in, his accusers charged, because he saw things from a different angle. He had special rights and as such enjoyed enough food and drink, and wore clean clothes that kept him warm in the cold. He had real shoes, lived in cleaner quarters, and did not work. He was almost never beaten, wasn't taken out for "sport," and did not have to stand in endless inspections. True, he, too, was subject to the camp administration and to the arbitrary whims of his superiors. They could have killed him without blinking an eye or sent him to the gas chamber. Nevertheless, he lived in a world entirely unlike that of the average prisoner.

Another accusation was that he had played a role in sending people to the gas chambers, and that he had made bad use of his power to determine who would remain in the work detail, in the block, and who would be used to meet the next quota. What was his part in the selection?

Eliezer responded that he never chose people for the gas chambers. There was "no real heroism on my part, but that was how things worked out." When he arrived at Auschwitz-Birkenau there were no such quotas. The block commander would make the choice. And in 1942 he had not been a block chief. In 1943 he was a block commander — over Poles and Aryans, "and they did not take those people to the gas chambers." Neither did they take people from the isolation blocks that he had overseen, so that the Jews there were also saved. From March to October 1943 there had been no exterminations by gas. In the autumn of 1943 a large selection for the gas chambers was organized, but it was managed by the SS doctors, and he had no role in it. In fact, he and a few other block chiefs tried to impede the transport and to save whomever they could. In November 1943 the block commanders were told to leave all the unfit Jews in the blocks when the work details set out. "I knew what this meant [and] after consulting with other block commanders I took measures to hide the weak. I frequently replaced the weak men (at the collection points or in inspections) with prisoners from other blocks (Poles and others)." These efforts were not always successful, he related. If the ruse and the identity of the person making the substitutions were discovered, his life would be in danger. Sometimes selections were a total surprise. The Nazis would arrive at Block 7 with a list and take people. "Block 7," Eliezer explained, "was for those who were not fit for work, like an infirmary." When they did not have enough for their quota they took the weakest from that block and others to the gas chambers. If that was not enough, they would take people from the easy work detail (*Kommando Holzhof*), and once they even reached the *Maurerschule* (Block 4, where builders and plasterers were kept). Only young people worked there; they took fifty. Sometimes they would simply surround a barracks and gather up people for the gas chambers. When he could, Eliezer said, he hid people inside the block.[58]

In 1943, party comrades charged, he had failed to save one of their company, a man named Katz. Eliezer said that the charge was baseless. Katz, he said, had been more than fifty years old and had thus been designated to be included in the quota of people over that age to be sent to the gas chambers. There had been no way to rescue him. "Forging a birth date in the block would not have had any results, because [the SS men] would arrive with a list from the office on which the age was marked."[59]

The panel then asked Eliezer about his treatment of *Muselmänner*. There were two types, he responded — those who became *Muselmänner* after contracting typhus, and those who reached this state because of the difficult conditions in the camp, despair, and apathy. He did not hide the typhus cases, because if they stayed in the block they could infect all the prisoners. And, he added, a *Muselmann*'s life could not be saved — he was a lost cause. Even if he were placed in a good work detail, given good shoes, and supplied with an extra liter of soup each day, this would at most put death off by a bit. But these same benefits and goods, when granted to the healthy, could save lives. Many other survivors, he noted, had cited this same logic.

Eisner and Kowalski pressed him further. So what happened when you yourself came down with typhus? Didn't you stay in the block? Yes, Eliezer acknowledged, they left me in the block and saved my life. With Konczal's consent, Langman devotedly cared for him. It took him two months to recover. Throughout this period he was nursed and cared for in the block and was not sent to the infirmary, where he would have been in danger of being taken in a selection. Without going into detail, he admitted that he had been kept in the block despite the danger of infection.[60]

He was then asked if he withheld help at times that he could have extended it. "You stand accused of not having done enough for Sawek Kirszenbaum," the investigators said. Sawek, a member of the Paris group, had been close to Szmulewski, Eliezer, and the other veterans of the Spanish Civil War. Eliezer denied this charge as well. When Kirszenbaum and a friend of his had arrived in the camp, he assigned them "not to the best [*Kommando*], but the best one there was at that time," he said. He spoke with the kapo and foreman and reached an agreement that the two men would not be beaten. Eliezer said that he provided them with supplemental food, extra blankets and clothing, and tried to move them to a different work detail. But he had little influence at the time. Only when he became block chief did he have the power to arrange better conditions — but by that time Sawek had already died.[61]

With the round of questioning approaching its final phase, the investigators turned their attention to one of the most intriguing points in the case — the riddle of the attitude toward him displayed by the leaders of the group that he had been associated with for so long. "What then, is the source of these persistent accusations against you, from people in responsible positions?" they asked.

"I have a hard time answering that," Eliezer said. "I have asked the same question myself, especially in Buchenwald, when six Czechs accused me in what was close to being a libel." The accusations had an objective cause — the thankless position he had filled, which had made him "part of the German machine." In his opening statement he had raised the question of whether it was possible to hold such posts without becoming part of the system.

In an answer he offered at a different point in the inquiry, he noted that many of the Communists from the Paris group had assumed such positions. Blass had been a clerk and later a block commander. Suttor had been a kapo. Dymanski had been a block commander and later camp elder. Karol Bracht had been a kapo. Szmulewski had been a deputy block commander. Fajnzylber and Warszawski had been in the Sonderkommando. One of the women had been the elder in the women's camp. They filled these posts at the behest of the party, on the reasoning that such positions had to be used to save prisoners, or at least to reduce the level of danger. He was not sure that everyone had succeeded.

But there was another reason — his name. "People were hurt more by my actions than they would have been if they had been performed by a person with an unfamiliar name," he suggested. He paid, in other words, the price for being a prince. Even though he went by the name of Leon Berger in the camps, the Jewish prisoners knew that he was Eliezer Gruenbaum, son of Yitzhak Gruenbaum.

The third in his list of explanations he proposed was that perhaps he had "gone too far." He added that "I stress that in Birkenau not one of dozens of comrades took exception to my behavior and none of the accusations are connected to the time in Birkenau." What did he mean by this? Was he retracting his claim that those had been "some of the blackest weeks in my life?" Or did he mean that the accusations were attempts to settle earlier accounts with him, regarding things that had not happened at Birkenau? Or that nothing had been under his control?

Eisner and Kowalski were not satisfied. The riddle remained unsolved. "Maybe no one protested because they feared you?" they asked. Eliezer denied this. "No," he said. "If anyone thought that his life was in my hands — my life was actually in their hands." As a camp official, he served as a buffer between the prisoners on the one side and the Nazis and their senior collaborators on the other. It might have looked like a person in this position lived a protected life, he maintained, but the position also brought with it obligations, and in particular dangers that other prisoners were not exposed to and did not even know about, he asserted. Camp officials were not necessarily collaborators — some of them covertly worked against the system, its goals, and its activities.

How was it, he said sardonically to his interrogators, that those who now referred to him as "alien," unreliable, and as a person who was, because of his sordid behavior, not made party to the underground's secrets — how was it that such a person was assigned some of the most delicate and complex missions in the camp? How was it that Miciol, who had served with him in Spain, had been sent to him, Eliezer, immediately upon arriving in the camp? Who sent him to Eliezer? "I was among the very small number of comrades that Miciol reported to about the establishment and activities of the PPR." When Miciol planned his escape, Eliezer connected him with the Russians who were meant to lead the breakout. Furthermore, Eliezer said, he gave up his own place among the escapees in favor of Miciol. Didn't Miciol ask him to brief him about the situation in the camp and what to expect? Who had brought the whole matter before him and asked him to be involved? Hadn't it been Szmulewski and his associates in the group's leadership who had now, after the war, turned their backs on him? Why had he been in the know with regard to Sliwa? If he was not worthy of trust, why had they asked him to write to Sliwa's brother, a member of the Gwardia Ludowa, in order to establish contact with forces outside the camp? Why had Szmulewski brought him a watch to be used to pay the messenger? "There were dozens" of such cases, he said, "in which people placed their trust in me." How was that consistent with what people were saying now?[62]

He didn't know. Something had broken, but he did not know what. After all, he noted, "the accusers all had the best of relations with me in Birkenau." Furmanski had kissed him when they parted, Szmulewski had welcomed him enthusiastically at one point and invited him to have a drink with him from time to time as a sign of brotherhood. When they had needed to find a hiding place for their friend Alexander when he came down with typhus, Szmulewski asked him to go to Blass and arrange it. Wouldn't Szmulewski have gone to Blass himself if he lacked confidence in Eliezer? He told his questioners that he could not solve that riddle for them. "In Paris there is a psychosis of accusations against me," he said. He was referring to the atmosphere he found in that city when he returned there after the war at the party's behest, when everyone turned their backs on him.

"How do you explain that psychosis to yourself? Why have all those people changed their attitude toward you now?" the panel persisted. "I already told you how I explain it to myself," Eliezer replied as he felt the noose began to tighten around his neck.[63]

The ideological stage of the inquiry contained further explosive material. The panel highlighted both the dense ideological-political context of the affair and the deep disagreements that had cut through the camp. Disputes over principle, disagreements about strategy, tactics, and politics, along with ego and power rivalries, had riven the Communists. They took these tensions, divisions, and personal contentions with them to Auschwitz, and the survivors carried them out of the camps as well. These were exacerbated under horrendous conditions, raising issues of heroism, cowardice, collaboration, and the glory and ignominy that were both the lot of those who were active in the underground.

One of the questions that preoccupied Eliezer's questioners, as well as those who had worked alongside him at the camps, was Poland's postwar fate. The Soviet Communists and their allies viewed the Soviet victory as an opportunity to take control of other European countries and to unite them into a close and secure alliance. They envisioned Poland as a seventeenth member state of the USSR. But other Communists, especially the Polish emigrants in France, took a more nationalist and independent stance. They also wanted a red Poland, and also viewed the victory over Germany as a great opportunity. But they wanted their country to be free and independent. It was in this spirit that Eliezer responded when he was asked about his role in political activity in Auschwitz. He laid it out chronologically: In 1942, "we received three party theses on the situation from France. I translated and distributed them." In 1942 and 1943 he conducted political discussions in the blocks with party members and others he sought to recruit. In 1943 he took part in extensive discussions with the Russian prisoners and other supporters of the Soviet line regarding Poland's future. The Russians, he said, "planned to make Poland the seventeenth Soviet republic. This predatory position was supported by several Jewish comrades. "I fought against this position," he told Kowalski and Eisner — which did not make them like him more.[64]

This was the end of Eliezer's initial testimony. The panel proceeded to hear the witnesses. It is not clear what criteria were used to determine which witnesses to call. Some testimony was given before the investigating judges, but some was submitted in writing. Eliezer was present when some of the witnesses appeared before the panel, and heard of the testimony of others when it was presented to him and his response solicited. We do not know how the witnesses were brought to Warsaw or Paris. Some may have provided testimony a short time after liberation, while still in the vicinity of the camps. The panel may have, at some point, traveled to Paris, where most of the witnesses it had summoned were located. Eliezer prepared questions for those witnesses whose testimony he was present for, which are included in the court documents. Testimony from at least twelve witnesses was considered during this stage. Furmanski was the first, testifying on June 25. When he arrived at Birkenau, Furmanski said, he found Eliezer (who had been deported to Auschwitz three weeks before him) already as a room warden in Block 9. Eliezer, he said, was suffused with "brutality, anger, and 'Jewish antisemitism,' which we paid a high price for because he was considered a party man. I was sometimes forced to make a clear separation between his past history in the party and his actions and behavior in the camp." Furmanski quoted Eliezer as saying things like "Another thousand Jews kicked the bucket, so what? Less black market!" That's how he spoke to the Poles, Furmanski said, as if "he were trying to distinguish himself from the Jews. Sometimes I burned with shame when I heard the things he said to Polish criminals. On that basis you can understand Berger's [Eliezer's] attitude toward people and party members. When comrades spoke to him, because they knew him from the past, instead of raising their spirits he would say pessimistically: 'No one will get out of here,' 'you don't come here to live, you come here to die.' An example of how he treated me? He'd known me for fifteen years. From Warsaw. When I was sick he could come to me and say: '*Muselmann*, how much longer do you want to live? You've got another two days.'"

Despite this, Furmanski said, Eliezer had treated him "better than others. Sometimes he gave me a piece of bread. Sometimes that was the initiative of the block chief [Konczal], who out of professional brotherhood (work in the dairy) treated me specially. His [Eliezer's] behavior and way of talking did more damage than bread could repair."[65]

Furmanski spoke also of the existence of a covert political organization, the compartmentalization of its structure, and of Eliezer's "original sin." In 1942 there was no organization beyond a small leadership cell, he claimed; a larger group was established only in July 1943. "The executive of the party cell included Max Wilner, until July 1943, after that Arnold and Szmulewski. After a discussion of the subject we decided not to include Berger in the executive. We concealed that from him because we did not trust him. Nevertheless, the executive decided to take advantage of his position as block chief to obtain material assistance."

Furmanski complained of the pessimism that Eliezer infused in those around him and the "counterfeit party line" to which, in his view, Eliezer gave voice. His skepticism about the Soviet Union's power to win the war had already roused discontent in Beaune-la-Rolande, as well as in Birkenau. When asked whether Eliezer had ever killed someone with his own hands, Furmanski replied:

> I did not see that he beat or murdered anyone, but people frequently came to me to tell me about such things, to object and ask me to intervene. I am convinced that he killed [people]. . . . Finkelkraut, who was also a room warden, frequently spoke about this. . . . I recall that back at the beginning of 1942 [*sic* — he seems to have meant 1943] Finkelkraut came to me beside himself and said that the previous night Berger and Tadek had killed two people.

Eliezer, Furmanski said, surrounded himself "with Polish lowlifes of the worst kind. . . . I'll explain his behavior in this way: he was convinced that no one would come out of the camp [alive], that there would be no judges, that he would never have to explain his actions. He told me: Who will you have to account to? Scumbag. He instituted a carpe diem tactic — just keep going."

But, Furmanski noted, Eliezer's behavior changed in 1943. He grew less brutal, "and I no longer heard about killings. The grievances against him were only about the vulgar way he treated people and antisemitism."[66]

Furmanski's testimony regarding Eliezer's crude behavior and his disaffection and arrogance toward his former comrades during the initial weeks in Birkenau is consistent with the testimony of other witnesses. Other witnesses also confirmed that Eliezer proclaimed that no one would emerge alive from the camp. Furmanski corroborated Eliezer's claim that there had been no party organizational framework during their first year in the camp, and that this was established only in the summer of 1943. There were contacts, there was activity, but an active party cell took form only then, and they decided to make use of him but not allow him inside.

Finkelkraut was the second witness, testifying on August 9, after he had returned to Paris, where he tried to rebuild his life. He had not been a party member, but despite this had been among those who asked Konczal to appoint Eliezer his deputy. Finkelkraut had been a resident of Block 9, meaning that his testimony is a primary source about Eliezer's behavior.

Eliezer had, Finkelkraut maintained, "killed out of necessity." He had done so at the command of the block chief, but "had he not wanted to do it then he would not have." At the end of 1942, when they arrived in Birkenau, Eliezer had filled in for the block chief. One night a transport of Jews from Holland arrived. One of them had attacked the night guard, and "Gruenbaum and Tadek killed him. Ludwig Konczal, the Block 9 chief, was also present."

According to Finkelkraut, Eliezer beat prisoners "horribly." When he kicked a prisoner, "he aimed at the belly or lower." When asked why he beat people up, he said that "all these people should be killed." He was especially brutal toward Jews, in particular old ones. "They've already lived enough," Finkelkraut quoted Eliezer as saying. When they went to him to ask for help he would say, "What for, they'll all croak," and "If you want to get out of here alive, it'll only be at someone else's expense." When Sawek Kirszenbaum fell ill, he asked Eliezer to care for him. Eliezer didn't want to. Said he couldn't. Sawek had not spoken to Eliezer directly because he didn't have the courage to do so. "If Gruenbaum had wanted to, he might have been able to save him." If anyone asked him "if he were Gruenbaum's son, his response would be a terrible beating." He "gave up, broke, as early as 1942. He looked out for his job. Groveled before Polish reactionary elements. Gathered around him people from a black planet" (the criminal prisoners were marked with black triangles). Finkelkraut offered the investigators the following list: "There are in Poland people who committed murder in Birkenau, like Gruenbaum: Ludwig Konczal — murderer; Czyczakowki, an *Arbeitseinsatz* in the Polish camp, behaved horribly; Alfred Zabilski, commander of Block 10 in 1942, murderer; Bogdan Komranicki — Ukrainian, *Kommando* kapo (*Aufnahmeschreiber*), murderer. Sychbara Kazimiesz — son of the mayor of Nowy Sącz, behaved very well, helped a great deal."[67]

Herman Freilich, a member of the group from Paris, gave his testimony on August 20. He had also been in Block 9 and was one of the men who had asked Konczal to give Eliezer a post in the block. His account also painted an ugly picture of the defendant. In his different capacities at Birkenau in 1942, Freilich told the panel, Berger "did not help, on the contrary, he tormented." As deputy block commander and thus in "control of everything," he had "kissed the ass" of Block Commander Konczal — who was a murderer — and had meticulously carried out his orders. When food was handed out he beat prisoners while using foul language, such as "*gudłaj*" (a derogatory term for Jew) and also "go give up the ghost." He beat prisoners, and had beaten him, Freilich, several times. Freilich related that he came down with typhus and that after he recovered, Konczal, with whom he had good relations, had ordered Berger to give him an extra portion of soup. But after the commander left, Berger had not followed the order. He kicked Freilich, saying, "You son of a bitch, either way you'll die soon." Eliezer kicked mostly in the back, he said. Freilich testified that when he asked Eliezer why he had changed so fast, he answered, "Shut up, son of a bitch, you'll get yours, too." Luckily, Eliezer could not go on beating him once he was transferred to another block and worked in the kitchen. In Beaune-la-Rolande "he behaved OK. He was in the party and did whatever the party told him to," Freilich said. But in Birkenau "Berger broke as a Communist and as a human being. He told me once [after three months in Birkenau]: 'Look just how far a human being can sink.'"[68]

David Szmulewski and Eliezer each had had a very good vantage point from which to get a clear view of the entire range of the other's actions. For this reason, the stock phrases that pervade Szmulewski's testimony are surprising and vexing, compared with testimony that he would give at a later date. His claim that he heard of Eliezer only in November–December 1942 at Birkenau is questionable, as is the choice of subjects he chose to focus on. He opened by asserting that Eliezer had been "a demoralizing factor" in the group. Anyone who went to him seeking encouragement or assistance, Szmulewski recounted, would receive a stock answer: "Either way, three or four days from now you won't be alive." Each time he was asked to join in "organizational work" in the cell he managed to evade it "and did nothing." A good example was his refusal to cooperate with Warszawski, a member of the Sonderkommando and one of the central organizers of the uprising.

Even when Eliezer linked him up with people he thought were worthwhile, they turned out to be "dishonest people." He did this even "when he had correct information about the existence of work in the camp and when he knew people who were involved in that work."[69] In his frugal and spare manner of speaking, Szmulewski explained that Berger had traded on the information and connections he obtained. He was in no rush to share things he knew with his comrades. He did so to an extent, at a pace, and apparently also at a price that he himself set.

Emanuel Mink had been surrounded by a hero's aura since his service in Spain. His behavior at Auschwitz reinforced his image as a courageous and bold man. He took part in underground cells and headed the cell established by Szmulewski and others. At Auschwitz, even respected prisoners, as he was, officers and commanders of men, had to carve out a position for themselves almost from scratch. When he met Eliezer, who had been under his command in Spain, their positions had practically reversed. Mink was the solider and Eliezer the commander. Eliezer's treatment of his former commander, whom everyone respected, was the background to the impression that Mink formed of him in Block 9 and while filling other posts in other blocks. His testimony bore special weight, both because of his standing and the moral stature he had in the movement, but also because of his extensive experience. In particular, the panel listened to him because he spoke from a commander's point of view, that is, as a person who knew how to weigh the variables at hand and examine the question of Eliezer's behavior, taking into account all his responsibilities, the dangers he faced, and the burden he bore.

Mink arrived in Auschwitz in March 1942. At the end of 1943 he was transferred to Birkenau. That was the worst period of all. In Auschwitz there had been a party organization from the end of 1942, but that was not the case in Birkenau, where he found "weak and divided party organization." When he arrived, Szmulewski and Alexander established a Jewish leadership in Birkenau. They aimed to establish ties with the national underground groups. They were able to achieve cooperation with the Russians, Germans, and Poles. He did not state how these relations were established and what Eliezer's role in this had been. Eliezer had repeatedly claimed to be the architect of most of these ties. Rumors about Eliezer's behavior had reached Mink while he was still in Auschwitz. Communication between the two camps was not simple, Mink said, but even then "we had information that Berger had beaten and killed [prisoners]." We, the veterans of Spain, Mink said, believed that it was our duty to teach people how to behave in this situation and to help reinforce them. Berger never did that, he maintained.

According to Mink, during that difficult period, at the beginning of 1943, Warszawski and the others proposed to Berger that he take on the leadership and organize a party cell in the camp. They told him that as a block commander he was the only person who could do this. But, Mink said, he refused. Szmulewski and others visited his room several times in attempts to persuade him, but, in Mink's words, "Berger threw them out." That is why, he said, they all took their distance from him, and "the attitude toward him was very negative."

But, Mink told the investigators, Berger treated him, Mink, "very well, and even gave me sausage." Mink said, however, that he stopped approaching Berger "because of the party's attitude toward him." It was known that as block commander, Berger had helped load *Muselmänner* on trucks headed for the gas chambers. True, he had to do this as part of his job as block commander, Mink said, but he had evinced "no regret. I myself saw how he laughed at Jews who went to their death praying, instead of rebelling." Only when "he himself received the boot from the Germans, who ejected him from his position because he was a Jew and thus he himself was in danger, only then did he begin to think about organizing an escape." Mink summed up his impression: Berger behaved in a way unbefitting a Communist. He rejected calls to organize and refrained from extending help. He did nothing to raise the Jews' spirits. "He treated the Jews horribly, and laughed at them like an antisemite," Mink concluded.

Mink proposed that the defendant's behavior should be judged by comparing it to that of other prisoners who had held positions of power at the camps. The panel should indeed be cognizant that anyone who held such a post had to perform "dirty work." Warszawski, he noted, "had in fact been in the Sonderkommando, which we condemned, but later he acted like a hero. Under the most difficult conditions he pushed for the establishment of an organization, provided much help, and organized nearly the entire Sonderkommando to participate in the resistance. As a result of this the Sonderkommando later set fire to Crematorium 2. Warszawski himself died a heroic death, after they burned the *Oberkapo* [chief kapo] and the entire group broke out of the camp," he explained. Making his key point, he added that "in Auschwitz we had block commanders of our own and people in other posts who took these positions after the party recommended it, and those helped a great deal and before anything else saw to saving the team. They undertook political work at the behest of the executive and *did not beat* [prisoners — the emphasis is in the original]. There were isolated cases of beatings (because of theft, failure to observe rules of hygiene), but these were rare." Had Berger done his job with the needs and best interests of the prisoners as his central concern, Mink said, "you could absolve him in part, but he thought only about himself." He was asked whether other party members who served as block commanders and Birkenau also engaged in beatings. Mink said that he thought they had, but did not know for sure. He had spent only a short time in the camp, he said. It would be better to ask Szmulewski and Alexander.[70]

One of the following witnesses was Simon Laks, a musician. His testimony was recorded on August 6. Eliezer, Laks said, "beat [prisoners] unnecessarily, kicked an old man because he asked for more soup. A few weeks later the old man died. [Eliezer] took the rations of the dead and traded in them."[71]

Victor Majzlik told the panel that he knew that at Jawischowitz, at the beginning of 1944, the party committee imposed a ban on Eliezer. The reasons were "manslaughter, torture, and beatings of his defenseless comrades at Birkenau camp." He seems to have meant to say that he had not been an eyewitness to these events and had only heard of them from others.[72]

The latest testimony in the investigation file was heard on November 7, 1945, from Napieracz, a Polish Communist Party activist in Buchenwald. His presentation focused on the question of Eliezer's standing during the inquiry that had been conducted there, and what his position in the group had been following that investigation. This testimony paints a picture different from that subsequently provided, in a later proceeding, by Eliezer and his counsel. Napieracz had been a member of that earlier party panel and noted that the judges there had accepted the claim of the Czech group that "Berger beat them there and stole (margarine, sausage) from them." The prosecutors had proved that "1. Berger beat the Czechs, one of them until he died; 2. During an inspection [of Berger] at Birkenau, they found eleven cubes of margarine."

On the basis of these findings, Napieracz related, Berger had been removed from his position as an "inspection clerk" (it is not clear what position he was referring to). Furthermore, Napieracz said that he confirmed "with full force that the party court expelled Berger from the party in Buchenwald."[73] This testimony contradicts all that is known of the proceeding at Buchenwald, as recounted by testimonies that do not come from Eliezer and his supporters. It is important to note that Napieracz's testimony was taken some two months after the panel handed down its judgment and the publication of the party's verdict. It is not clear who sought out the testimony and what the purpose of soliciting it was.

Up to this point the witnesses did not favor Eliezer. Most of them offered a picture very different from that he provided to the panel in his opening statement and his initial testimony, in particular his account of the outcome of the first proceeding in Buchenwald. Especially problematic for Eliezer was Mink's testimony. Unlike all other witnesses, Mink explicitly compared Eliezer's actions to those of others who had held posts at the camp. There had been others who had acted differently, this witness maintained — they did not beat prisoners or did so only in exceptional cases, and others were true heroes. The witness supported Eliezer's position only on one point — his close associates had not set up a party cell at the camp until the summer of 1943. One of the major reasons, however, was that Eliezer had not agreed to take charge of setting it up. This explained both the anger and disappointment felt by his comrades — such emotions could have been felt only against someone they took to be a central and influential figure. He had preferred to set his own standards for how to help the group, and put most of his efforts into establishing and reinforcing his contacts with other forces in the camp, among them the prisoner-staffed administration and various other underground forces.

At least three questions remained unresolved. First, how could Eliezer's claim to have played a central role in the camp underground be reconciled with the isolation and interdiction described by his colleagues? Most of them stated that he had displayed his true colors during the first few months in the camp, during his time in Block 9 under Konczal. By the end of 1942, they claimed, life in the camp had brought his worst qualities to the surface and turned him malevolent. Yet, second, if this were the case, why had they nevertheless insisted, during the initial months of 1943, that he should be the point man in organizing their group? Third, how to square the harsh and horrible things they said about him with the emotional partings from these very same people that Eliezer had described, and with later testimonies offered by other witnesses?

Eliezer, or Berger as most of the witnesses called him, did not see these testimonies as closing the case. He ratcheted up his counterattack. His first step was to prepare questions to put to all the principal witnesses, asking that they provide the court with their answers. He then offered his own response, longer and more detailed than his previous testimony. The response offers a more complex picture than that painted by the witnesses. He protested what he claimed was slander by the witnesses and supported his position with a meticulous account of his covert activities.

He submitted nineteen questions to be posed to Langman, among them:

1. Is it true that Block 9 was the only Jewish block in which murder was not methodically practiced?
2. Could [Langman] indicate the differences between people's attitudes toward death, food, and clothing in Block 9 as opposed to what prevailed in Block 8, where he had spent several months?
3. Is it true that in the winter of 1942, thanks to my connections with the Russians who worked in the laundry, that I organized clean clothes for the entire block once or twice?
4. Is it true that the bread, margarine, and soup rations were incomparably larger in Block 9 than in the other Jewish blocks (such as 8, 13, 15, 16, 17, and so on)?
5. Is it true that Block 9 was considered the best Jewish block?
6. Is it true that when the Jews were, in January 1943, transferred from Block 9 to Blocks 8, 27, and elsewhere they found their conditions to be notably worse?
7. Is it true that at the time of the transfer I was beaten by the block commander for not obeying [his order] and leaving people in the block?
8. Does he know of other cases in which I was beaten by the block commander, the kapo, and so on? If so, for what reasons?

He also asked whether Langman knew about the speech he, Eliezer, had made in 1942 to the prisoners in the block about preserving discipline in such a way that would make it possible to do away with beatings. Was it not the case that when he left Block 9 in the autumn of 1942, conditions worsened significantly? Did Langman know about the circumstances under which he was returned to Block 9—this after he had been transferred and had found a better location? Was it true that at the time of the so-called Bloody Star, the anti-Jewish Christmas riots of 1942, he hid many prisoners in the block even though this was forbidden? And what about the comrades whom he placed in better blocks or work details, among them Sznajder, Wikrowiecki, Kalinski, Michrowski, Kirszenbaum, and others? Was it true that in September 1942 he had initiated an unneeded large-scale digging project as a way of saving two hundred *Muselmänner* from Block 13? Surely Langman knew about his contacts with the Russians and men of the Sonderkommando and his attempt, along with Michrowski and Mirecki, to organize an armed uprising and escape? What was Langman's account of his relations with the Czech group, and, of course, what was his opinion of Eliezer's party loyalty, alleged ideological deviations, and in particular the accusation that he had sown demoralization among his fellow prisoners by casting doubt on the chances of a Soviet victory?[74]

He prepared an even tighter set of questions for Szmulewski, because he had been one of the leaders of the Communist underground. If there were any bases for Eliezer's claims regarding his ties to the cell and the actions he had been involved in at its behest, they could be made clear to the investigators by Szmulewski's responses. The questions revolved around four points — escape, Eliezer's connections with underground activists in and outside the camp, aid actions that he organized, and his loyalty to the party and his role in maintaining or weakening morale.

Eliezer sought to force Szmulewski to address issues that Eliezer had raised in his opening statement and initial testimony. He asked Szmulewski if it was true that he, Eliezer, had maintained ongoing contacts with Russian prisoners, with whom he had planned escape operations. Had he not repeatedly urged Szmulewski that they had to concentrate their efforts on organizing the escape of individuals and arming the escapees? Was it not true that he had tried to buy weapons with money he received from Berneman, who worked in "Canada" and served as a pipeline for money from there to the underground? Had Eliezer not done all this with party's sanction and with its knowledge? Was it true that he had taken part in preparing for the aborted attack on the *Blockführerstube*? Was it true that he had maintained contact throughout 1943 with Kostek Jagelo and the PPR that he led, as well as with the Germans Blass and Erich Mitiu, and others? He asked about the groundwork for the Sonderkommando rebellion: "Is it not true that I was in constant contact with Comrades Fajnzylber and Warszawski and that I discussed with them the difficulties of launching the uprising at the time of the night shift?" The point was to show that he had played a role in this heroic action. Had Szmulewski not suggested several times that he accompany him to the women's camp to make contact with Comrade Marie Claude and others? In other parts of his testimony Eliezer said that he had turned down such overtures from Szmulewski so as not to needlessly place the communications channels at risk. His point was that he knew about the leaders of the covert cells and their means of contact with the women's camp.

Eliezer also asked about the assistance that he extended to the underground. Was it not true that he had, at Szmulewski's recommendation, established contact with the warehouse so as to supply the camp with clothing with the help of the cleaning *Kommando*? That he had systematically provided new prisoners with paper, envelopes, and stamps? That he had been the first to allow Croatian prisoners to establish contact with their families? That he had, at the request of his Communist comrades, taken action against the theft of packages and the swindling of prisoners in the *Kommando* group? That weak prisoners close to the Communist group were sent to his block so as to receive better nourishment, because it was generally regarded as offering better conditions? That had he been evaluated "positively, as a good and organized block commander?" Was it true that the percentage of prisoners taken to the gas chambers from his block was much lower than the average? Had the action he had initiated against the SS orders that required block commanders to mark those designated for the gas chambers not subverted the process? That he had lobbied on Szmulewski's behalf with Blass when Aaron, a member of their group, had come down with typhus and it was decided not to send him, as required, to the infirmary?

In the cluster of questions regarding his ideological purity and his contribution to reinforcing the morale of his fellow Communists, he noted that he had been targeted by the non-Communist AK faction in the camp. Its members charged him with being "detrimental to society and the state" as a result of his profound influence over the Poles. Was it true, Eliezer asked Szmulewski, that the person who had informed him of this was Szmulewski himself? Was he not one of the leading speakers about Poland's future after the coming Soviet victory? Had he not promoted the party after the camp commander (*Lagerführer*) had, in the autumn of 1943, given a speech to the Poles promising them liberty in exchange for fighting a common war against the Bolsheviks? Eliezer ended his document with the question: "Does Szmulewski know of a case in which comrades brought improper behavior to my attention?" Had he not acted properly, why did no one tell him?[75]

He posed four questions to Furmanski, regarding how Block 9 compared to other blocks. Eliezer focused in particular on the difference between Block 9 and the one that Furmanski lived in, commanded by Albert Hemmerle. Eliezer claimed that Hemmerle "'ate' several prisoners alive for breakfast and for supper," as Furmanski told him on several occasions. He also composed questions for Léon (Leib) Epstein, the secretary of the foreign printers' section of the Communist Party in Paris, who knew Eliezer from Beaune-la-Rolande. Epstein spent a short time in Block 9 and was active in the Auschwitz underground. In the questions, Eliezer sought to use Epstein as a character witness. He asked Epstein to recount how Eliezer had concealed him in the block to give him time to recover from beatings he received in his work detail. He also asked Epstein to tell about cases in which prisoners in the block were murdered, and about the beatings Eliezer received from the block commander and the reasons for this, and on the ties they had maintained after Epstein was moved to another block. Eliezer also wrote that Freilich's testimony was not free of errors — he had "been expelled from our group on charges of doing business with Germans."[76]

About a month after arriving in Paris, Eliezer felt despondent. His center no longer held — his comrades from the Polish underground, from his Parisian immigrant days, comrades-at-arms from Spain, and even from his months in occupied France had all turned their backs on him. By the beginning of July 1945 he felt as if Paris were casting him out. He hoped that he might still be accepted in Poland. In his plight, lonely and despairing, he wrote an emotional letter to an acquaintance in the Polish Communist Party:

> Andrzej,
>
> I have been in Paris for more than a month and I still do not know anything official about the way the things regarding me are going. On top of that, the atmosphere that surrounds me is enough to give me a sense of what direction they are going. I know that you are occupied with many other things, but I nevertheless ask you to transfer me to Poland as quickly as possible.

Napieracz and Epstein, who were acquainted with the issues, were in Paris. Eliezer sensed that Epstein had "apparently formed a [negative] opinion of me," but he still believed that both men could fill in details that could put his actions in a more favorable light. He estimated that the information his investigators had gathered was sufficient and that it was likely that they had already drawn conclusions. He was well aware that their decision would seal his fate and his future in Poland, and that he faced two principal options: "Either punishment as a war criminal, or acquittal. And neither of these two things can be pronounced here [in Paris]." He thus exhorted them to expedite his return to Poland, no matter what the conditions.

He also reminded his correspondent of the merit he had earned in the party, "Spain and the devil knows what," as he wrote. But he also expressed skepticism about their ability "to grant me something for all that," on top of which he did not know if they would want or be able to take his past into account. He was at peace with himself with regard to all that had transpired. Were he given the chance to open a new leaf in Poland, he would make every effort to succeed, but he doubted whether he would be offered such an opportunity. "For general and personal reasons . . . all that has been enough for me . . . it's already a little too much for my nerves," he wrote, reiterating his request that he be allowed to travel to Poland as soon as possible.

The most important lines in the letter were: "Since I am writing to you in a private capacity, I permit myself to add, without panic or pretense, that the thing that troubles me more than anything else is that I did not have a heart attack in the camp at the right moment. Had there only been an opportunity to break my neck, I would have been very happy."[77]

Two weeks later, on July 21, 1945, he was able to present to himself and to others a much sharper picture of the circumstances of his reception in Paris, as far as he saw it. The most important factor was the change that had occurred in the opinions of some of the most important members of the Jewish-Polish-French underground in Birkenau. The change had occurred, so he believed, under pressure from the public at large there in Paris, and out of fear that they, too, would sink into the quicksand of standing accused of collaboration. This was especially true of those who had, like himself, taken on positions of authority in Auschwitz-Birkenau, and who could thus easily "be pulled into the same morass." The picture became clear to him after two conversations he conducted with people whose names he could not reveal to his interrogators. He learned from these sources that those who had bid him emotional farewells in Birkenau as friends and had even stood by him and supported him during the inquiry at Buchenwald had now been compelled to change their positions. Those who tried to defend him "got yelled at and threatened," and "you need a lot of civil courage to go against the flow." Paris was not the place to examine his case objectively, he maintained, even more so because not all members of the group had gone back there.

He wrote again to the panel in Warsaw, asking that he be brought back there immediately, even if they believed that he was liable for death. He reminded them of the major investigations he had already gotten through. The first was the one that party members had conducted without his knowledge in Jawischowitz: "You can ask Rutkowski, one of the party men in Buchenwald, as well as Henfitz from Paris." He cited the inquiry held at Buchenwald, as well as those conducted by Polish nationalist groups, "who would gladly have taken advantage of the situation to persecute me." In addition there had been the inquiry in the Communist Party cell there. But "the best proof" of his innocence, he maintained, was that the party signaled its confidence in him by, after the arrival of the Americans, appointing him a member of the (Communist) Polish committee at the camp. At the party's behest he even spoke at mass rallies at the liberated camp, and the party signed his name to one of the leaflets it distributed as part of its campaign to gain support among the liberated prisoners. From the camp, the leadership sent him to Paris on party business. Would the party have used him as its public face, he asked, if even a shadow of disgrace hovered over his name? Furthermore, when the Americans began investigating charges against alleged war criminals, there were hundreds in the camp — Poles, Jews, Russians, Czechs, and Germans — who knew him from Birkenau and who could have filed charges against him had they considered him a malefactor. The fact that none did so showed that no one there thought he was guilty of anything.

In other words, Eliezer argued that the position taken by his comrades in Paris was motivated not by what he actually did during his time at Birkenau, but rather by other considerations — grievances, fears, and local pressures. He thus demanded a precise account of the charges against him and to be allowed to return to Poland, where the inquiry would continue. "Even if I am liable for the death penalty, neither of these things should be an obstacle," he wrote. Only in Poland, he maintained, could he receive a proper opportunity "to prove that the motive for my actions was not what I stand accused of here, egotism, cowardice, and fear of death."[78]

His request to receive the charge sheet was honored. But his desperate plea to be allowed to return to Warsaw in order to present his defense was turned down. Like a soldier laying out and organizing his gear on the eve of his last battle, Eliezer gathered up his remaining strength and readied himself to respond to the accusations against him. He tried to understand why his explanations thus far had failed.

He became ever more aware of how many adversaries had ranged themselves against him. It was an unholy alliance of people who had held positions of authority in the camps, apprehensive that poking around in the wreckage left from the camps might have very serious consequences and even crash down on their heads. They sought to deflect the censure they feared onto a victim who could serve as an easy target. Eliezer understood that he was the scapegoat.

Each time he recalled new facts or thought of a more incisive way to present his case, he wrote to his interrogators in the hope that he could persuade them. These missives offer an indication of what kind of atmosphere he faced in Paris and how desperately he was groping for a way to recover from profound trauma and return to the routine of everyday life. He was not alone — all members of the Communist underground cells that had functioned in the camps during the war found themselves facing an impossible situation. Each activist realized that he or she could suddenly be accused of collaboration or disloyalty. It created an atmosphere in which each Communist first fought for his own life. The result was a moral map of a struggle for survival in the lower depths and the contours of the reconceptualization that the questions raised by the war mandated, the beginning of the struggle over the representation of "what really happened there," the differences between history and memory and the politics of both.

Eliezer now sent the panel a summary of his defense, a final attempt to convince the investigators that he had done the best he could under impossible circumstances. He opened with a brief survey of the question of whether a person of leadership abilities, to whom the party had assigned a command, should have accepted positions that were part of the network of self-government in the camps while at the same time being part of the Nazi bureaucratic and command system. He again emphasized a point he had made previously, orally and in writing — every assumption of a position of responsibility was "objectively part of the apparatus that was supported by the SS."

He reiterated that he accepted these positions on orders from the party. He had done so even when he would have rather evaded them, knowing both that they would destroy him and that he had already, like many others, been crushed by the experience of his encounter with Auschwitz-Birkenau.

A single theme ran through his testimony — he insisted that he had been loyal to the party and punctilious in following the true path it laid down. As a loyal Communist — and as one who had learned to appreciate how important loyalty was — he utterly rejected the accusation that he had deviated from the party line and that he had denied that the Soviet Union would win the war. The position attributed to him on this matter was "a libel, pure and simple." Had he deviated, why had the party sought an opportunity to enable him to escape the camp in May 1942, and why had it continued to recognize him as a member of the party committee? After all, just prior to their deportation from Beaune-la-Rolande, he had been briefed on the proper course of action expected of party loyalists at the destination they were being sent to. When they had arrived at Birkenau, it had quickly become clear that the instructions were incommensurate with the conditions at the camp. But he had never done anything that he had not fully coordinated with his comrades, in particular with the "organization secretary," Sznajder, his long-standing partner in the leadership. Sznajder himself had told him "that he had instructed party members to work diligently so as to avoid beatings. That they remain disciplined and not give any reason to murder them." That is how he had acted, his principal goal being "to reduce the number of killings in the block."[79] The same logic and loyalty to the party line had motivated his position that it was important to install party members in positions of responsibility and work details at the camp. This would enable them to provide assistance, to subvert the Nazi system, and to organize escapes. He explained that "the positions in the camp and in particular in the *Kommandos* would be exploited only for assistance and to reduce beatings and terror, but first and foremost as a springboard for establishing contacts with civilians so as to find ways of escape and to carry out sabotage." The Sonderkommando uprising, the flight of the twenty-six, and the escape of Marian and the four Russians were all good examples of what he had preached, he wrote to his interrogators.

He had carried out his orders — he did all that was in his power to work covertly to undermine Nazi economic interests. The minute he understood from Kalinski — the first person who had told them — the economic importance that "Canada" and Birkenau played in funding Hitler's war machine, he had advocated doing everything possible to disrupt its operation. When a transport arrived from Holland, he managed to organize the collection of several hundreds of thousands of dollars from the Jews who had arrived, while they still stood on the railway platform, before they were examined and their property confiscated, and saw to it that the banknotes were burned. (There was no confirmation of this story from other sources.)

Stealing and wasting construction materials were part of these efforts, he claimed. He wrote that it had been his idea to pour cement floors in the blocks, important given the boggy soil at the camp. He had done so in his block, and other block commanders followed suit. In the process, hundreds of sacks of cement were stolen from the construction companies that worked at the camp, while at the same time conditions for the prisoners were improved. At the end of 1943, in the disarray following the German order to dismantle the prisoner blocks so that they could be shipped back to Germany, Eliezer said he had initiated the theft of wooden joists, boards, and other flammable materials be used to heat the barracks, further undermining the Nazi effort. A total of forty barracks went missing, Eliezer claimed. These were all stolen by prisoners, mostly Russians. Eliezer said that he was beaten by *Lagerältester* Ton, and a disciplinary report was filed against him.[80] This claim also lacked corroboration from another source.

The charges about his pessimism and his tendency to sow confusion among his fellow Communists were, he insisted, in error. The eruptions of optimism that overcame the prisoners, especially upon the arrival of newcomers in transports who said that the war was about to end, were impediments for those trying to organize an uprising. It had also been necessary to counter the weakness that resulted from such optimism. That was why he had told prisoners that they needed "to prepare for a long, hard war," and that anyone who thought victory was at hand was fantasizing. His effort to tighten the ranks had turned into an "oracle that turned into an accusation of lack of faith in the Soviet Union's victory."[81] Plenty of other survivors and witnesses, he noted, had maintained that the illusion of victory had weakened the resistance.

He was no antisemite. True, "the Jewish element that reached the camp lacked all its activist and ethical elements — those had retreated with the Red Army. What arrived from Poland in large numbers were the residue of the last Jews to survive in the ghettos, a large percentage of whom had lived this long thanks to wheeling and dealing, connections, and money." They no longer included any "popular" (proletarian) elements, he declared. Eliezer said that the camp administration also viewed the Jews as a "less dangerous element." That is why they were directed to work details and factories from which it was easier to escape — the assumption was that they would not even try to do so. The same logic, Eliezer said, had led the commandant of Auschwitz II to apply to Berlin for permission to replace Polish with Jewish laborers — the Poles would run away, but the Jews would not.

Also baseless were the accusations that he had jeered at those heading for the gas chambers or that he had viewed the annihilation of the Jews as a "means of fighting profiteering." He had been and remained critical, sometimes highly critical, of antisocial phenomena in the Jewish public. But this was no different from Russian prisoners who censured Russian collaborators who arrived in transports or Poles who decried compatriots of theirs who had worked with the Nazis. Yet when he had "criticized Jews who served Hitler and sought to brand them with a mark of disgrace, that made him an antisemite." He, like other members of the movement, had indeed publicly disparaged the behavior of those being taken to the gas chamber. "We declared that we would not go to our deaths without resistance . . . we did not see prayer or the singing of 'Hatikvah' as glorification of heroism. Going toward death without resistance had to be censured," he said, and they censured it.[82] His close relations with the Poles and Russians in the camp and his declaration that they should not all be branded as antisemites made him enemies. True, Eliezer said, there were many antisemites among them, some of them virulently venomous kinds, but there were also many who identified with the plight of the Jews and were willing to help. The generalizations and hurtful stereotypes had no basis in fact, he said, nor any operational logic.[83] It had to be remembered that among those opposed to his close relations to the Poles were some who had forgotten that Auschwitz was located in Poland and that most of the civilians employed there were Poles. Communication with the free world was possible only via Poles from the resistance movements, and any escape plan required contacts with underground activists outside the camp fences — meaning Poles. The Nazis themselves realized that the Poles were in a key position for rebellion in the camp, which is why they got rid of them in the spring of 1943. Only later had new transports of Poles arrived in the camp.

It had been necessary to enlist Poles of goodwill in the common battle against antisemitism. That is why he stressed the Jewish fighting spirit. "I made the Warsaw ghetto uprising very popular among the Poles in the camp," he maintained. But when a transport arrived from Majdanek that included dozens of Jews who had taken part in the rebellion, they joined in the chorus of condemnation against the Poles. They charged the Poles with having avoided contact with the ghetto fighters and with having barely provided any aid. Relations with the Poles were sullied as a result.

He sought cooperation with Polish elements and quickly clarified that this was prior to the severing of relations between the Polish government-in-exile in London and the USSR. Working with the Poles was much harder than working with the Jews. He had done so without having gained any "personal benefit," and at great risk to himself because the Poles were always under the Gestapo's watchful eye. They were the primary focus of the camp's political department (*Politische Abteilung*), and most of the blood that splattered the "bloody wall in Auschwitz's Block 11," where prisoners who had been interrogated were executed, was Polish blood. Anyone who circulated among them took his life in his hands.[84]

Then there was the murder charge. Eliezer offered clarifications to reinforce his previous testimony, admitting to some of the allegations against him. As a rule, he claimed, he had not allowed the killing of *Muselmänner* in the block. But once, when he overheard a conversation between two *Muselmänner* who were waiting to be transferred to Block 7, he learned that one of them intended to tell the authorities about the Communist cell's activities in the hopes that the SS soldiers would reward them with better treatment. "I believed that it was my duty to take action. I do not know if they would have carried out their intentions, but if they had done so, several of our comrades would have been shot dead. It would have been criminal of me not to have prevented that. So I assumed responsibility and prevented their transfer to Block 7, and I did not oppose the block commander's decision to kill them. Otherwise I would have been justifiably held responsible for not having done anything. . . . They are accusing me of not having prevented the killing of a few whiners and informers." Yet, Eliezer continued, " a few comrades, who were present at hundreds of killings and made no attempt to prevent them, now think they have the right to cast such filth at me."[85] The killing of informers and collaborators was part of the routine activity of the underground, he said.

"As long as I was responsible for Block 9 I was compelled to assume the thankless task of keeping the block commander from intervening in the enforcement of order. I was placed between the block commander—a murderer—and a crew of men half-mad with hunger, despair, and close proximity to death," Eliezer explained of the time he served as the top Jewish official in the block under Konczal's reign. When a transport arrived he would speak to its people in Polish, French, or German and explain the camp rules. He stressed the vital importance of obeying the rules and maintaining discipline, and the need to observe at least minimal standards of hygiene. "I wanted to be enabled to manage the block without violence," he declared. But all that was quickly forgotten. "Every display of weakness or a failure to invest sufficient energy" led to "the intervention of the block commander and cost several lives." As a result he had been compelled to take steps to prevent "unnecessary risk to the lives of friends." The claim that the mortality rate in his block was the same as in blocks run by German criminals was a lie, he insisted. During the eleven months in which he ran the block there were fewer than thirty deaths, despite outbreaks of typhus and dysentery.[86] During his time at the head of Block 30 he had had almost no reason to use violence — a fact that, in the autumn of 1943, other block commanders noted in astonishment. Szmulewski could testify to that. He had been the only block commander who had opposed the beating of his men in their work details. Even the Czechs had said that his block was the only one from which complaints about the fair distribution of milk, jam, and other food had not been received by the kitchen. He had, he said, also managed to persuade those of his Polish and Russian contacts who received packages to give up lard, bread, and supplementary rations so that they could be given to Jews. In the summer of 1943 his operation to steal straw to stuff the mattresses of his prisoners was uncovered. Luckily, the camp commander had reacted leniently. Several times a camp doctor had held up to other block commanders the commendable physical condition of the men from his block.[87]

Given that he stood accused of having broken, of having behaved with cowardice, of having been solicitous only of his own life, he wished to list cases "that were fairly well known in the camp and which it would be hard to believe that I invented":

- In August 1942 young German kapos forcibly removed the shoes from Dutch Jews in Block 9. He tried to prevent this and was beaten and was taken to the latrines to be hanged. Russian prisoners who worked there intervened and prevented his hanging.
- In September 1942, at a selection of *Muselmänner* in Block 13 when he was assistant clerk there, he permitted some of them to escape.[88] He was beaten by an SS soldier and barely managed to avoid having a charge filed against him.
- In September 1942 he had saved these same *Muselmänner* from death when he initiated the establishment of a *Kommando* to construct paths in the camp. He inflated the extent of the work by including unnecessary tasks ("Pits we dug lasted until the summer of 1943 and turned into pools in the winter"). This continued until the group was certified as "fit for work," thus saving its members.
- In November 1942 he lodged a complaint at the infirmary about murders being committed in the Weichsel *Kommando*. The carnage ended, and several kapos

were punished. Someone informed on him for having lodged the complaint. For a week the kapos tracked him, seeking revenge.

And there were other such incidents in which he had saved lives, he claimed.

He rejected the charge that he had sent people to the gas chambers, which he termed "a bald-faced slander." He had not treated *Muselmänner* inhumanely, and there was no basis for the charge that he thought they were not worth saving. "In the case of comrades my position was that we should always try to save them, up until their final seconds," he claimed. And others? "I thought that we needed to direct our efforts, and the means at our disposal were never sufficient, to get the best possible results. It was more logical to help the healthy, so that they would not become *Muselmänner*. I advocated caring first for the young."

The accusations regarding sick prisoners were also painful. He had frequently isolated those with infectious diseases and had them cared for in the block. Looking back, he was convinced that he had acted correctly. In this way he had curtailed the typhus epidemic that broke out in the block on May 20, 1943. Yet his policy had produced the slander that he had not helped Kirszenbaum. The comrades in Paris knew the truth very well. He felt, he said, "awful revulsion" against those who were leveling this charge at him.

He enumerated all the times he had been presented with opportunities to take on an easier post. Yet he had always preferred the general good and had acceded to his associates' requests that he take on positions of responsibility. These easier jobs that he had rejected, which had not so far been mentioned in the proceeding, had included serving as an "assistant to a jurist who knew languages in Auschwitz's political department. That offer had come in February or March 1943, and although he was a lawyer and knew languages, he had refused.

His revilers, he charged, were even using his bout with typhus against him, asking how it was that he had remained in the block. Their question, he said, was "Why didn't I die?" To which they supplied an answer — that "I must have been a member of the SS team." But he was not the only prisoner to have been kept in the block with typhus. Blass had been as well. That was the rule regarding all members of the party and others close to it. He had never hidden the fact that Block Commander Konczal had given him special treatment and let him remain in the block — luckily for him. "The SS didn't even know I existed," he declared.

There was no hiding his profound disagreement with his party comrades about Poland's future. "On this subject," Eliezer wrote, "I was at first entirely alone." Most of his Jewish friends maintained, as the Russians did, that Poland should become part of the Union of Soviet Socialist Republics, and conducted their propaganda in accordance with this view. This was a double error, Eliezer maintained. It was not the right solution for Poland, and taking such a position would also divide them from the rest of the Poles in the camp. In any case, it became a moot point following Stalin's declaration regarding Poland's future.[89] Stalin proved him right, but this did not end the charges regarding his "nationalism" and deviation from the party line. The same was true of his advocacy of Polish patriotism and his invocation of Polish heritage. These were perceived as deviations, and "comrades condemned me for this and called me a fanatic." The anti-Polish tone of the Jews increased when Polish right-wing groups like the AK sought to eject Jews from desirable positions and work details. When that happened, his position was considered even more out of line. The divisions within the Paris group regarding their vision of the future also derived from a lack of knowledge regarding the position of the Polish government-in-exile, of the Soviet-aligned Polish Left, and of the military and paramilitary underground movements active on Polish territory. There was also competition for resources, real and imaginary fears, and all this in the framework of a diabolical system that was designed to set people against each other. Eliezer did his best to explain to the investigators the way in which ideological and political tensions had affected how witnesses depicted his actions in the camp.[90]

What, then, lay at the root of the "insistence on accusing me, the course of the laying the blame on me, and this in unison by everyone here in Paris?" He offered three reasons.

First, he said, it was a direct result of his position in Block 9. Among other things, accusers based their charges on unavoidable mistakes he had made, and in particular by "exaggerating certain incidents beyond all proportion."

Second, many people thought that he should have focused only on the good of the Jews. His contacts with non-Jews and his friendships with Poles and Russians were perceived as the warped behavior of "someone with mental retardation."

Third, some of his accusers had been sent from Birkenau to other camps. But their initial months in Block 9 had been a seminal experience for them, the place where they "broke and sank into depression." Those who had been with him only in those early months had not seen what happened in the time that followed. This was evident from information he had received, according to which most of the comrades who had come out against him had spent only a few weeks at Birkenau. Unfortunately, they were joined, when he returned to Paris, by people "who were in Birkenau the whole time and who up until my trip [to Paris at the party's behest] had a different opinion of me."

He regretted that none of his comrades had come out against his slanderers and did not declare that no charges should be filed against him. He was disappointed that none of them had acted to snuff out, from the start, the "atmosphere in which anyone who was ever in contact with me at the camp is madly seeking accusations so as not to be seen as my partner. Everyone who comes to me with regard to opinions on my matter searches for something bad to say about me." These included people for whom this was a way of papering over "their political inaction and their defection from positions of responsibility in 1942 and 1943." Perhaps they wanted to deflect fire from themselves to him.[91]

He summed up by enumerating the seven principles that stood behind his actions during the four years he spent in the camps. He did so "taking a critical approach," he wrote. His conclusions were as follows:

||| In Beaune-la-Rolande he had acted impeccably. Even in cases in which he disagreed with party policy he had accepted it — even though his position was later shown to have been correct.

||| He was not at all sure if his decision in 1942 to take on positions of responsibility had been the correct one. But in doing so he carried out the policy of those who asked him to do so, and did so in a complex situation and under unusual conditions. The more senior posts that he took on in 1943 were entrusted to him on the basis of the work he had done in 1942. Whatever the results, desirable or not, they were the products of that policy. The criteria for appointing people to such positions ought to be investigated, he suggested — perhaps it would have been better to choose someone "less famous."

||| The bottom line was that he had acted in the only way possible. He had made mistakes, but he had not broken at any point, nor had he evinced cowardice. He should, in retrospect, have tried harder to convince his comrades of the logic of his way of thinking, he wrote.

||| The sum total of his political work, along with sabotage operations and escape plans, was not great. But the extent of this activity was dictated by the objective difficulty in establishing and maintaining contacts in the camp, the heavy workload, and the variety of issues that had to be seen to in the block. He himself had little control over that.

||| He acknowledged that he bore more heavy responsibility for not having, in 1943, established a central leadership at Birkenau. Yet, despite this, the sum total of his routine and political work in the camp had been better than those of his comrades at Birkenau.

||| He noted that none of the accusations against him related to his period at

Jawischowitz and Buchenwald. Despite the relatively better conditions at Jawischowitz, however, he had been unsuccessful in establishing contact with the resistance outside the camp and in planning and executing escape operations. Here, he acknowledged, he had not done everything he should have done and could reasonably be criticized.

||| He may well have made mistakes during these four years, he wrote, but he had never lost his confidence in the ultimate victory of the war against Hitler. He had never stopped thinking about the imperative of fighting the enemy, and had never placed his personal comfort and safety above his duty.

A large part of his letter was devoted to the breakouts he had attempted to organize. He viewed these as the apex of his activity in the camps and had never let off trying to plan and carry out such operations. These efforts began with a disaster, the escape of the Russians and the murder of the Sonderkommando rebels, that caused him to sink into depression. His comrades thought he had broken and assumed that he had lost faith in victory. He had asked to be relieved of his responsibilities and to be left alone, to get out of the public eye and devote himself to coping with the pressures of life in the camp. Dymanski and others persuaded him to resume his leadership position. He did so and tried to establish contact with the Russians and Poles. It quite naturally took time to build confidence between these groups and to get them to cooperate. He had established contact with Jagelo, the leader of the PPS group at Auschwitz, and tried to establish contact with forces outside the camp through Franz Kejman and others. At about this time he also began cooperating with Szmulewski, one of the leaders of the underground.

As early as the spring of 1943 he had advocated establishing an overarching underground chain of command for all the members working in the same work detail or living in the same blocks. He fostered some of the contacts himself—between Alexander and Furmanski, and between a member from Plonsk and Dima of the Russian group. Many members of the Paris group knew about this—he had been in regular contact with at least ten of them. Most of them preferred to focus on providing material aid to prisoners and were divided with regard to the importance of pursuing connections outside their own circle, escape plans, and whether the Poles could be trusted. But these had been differences of opinion on policy, not personal feuds. He later discovered that a party organization had been set up at Birkenau. He had not belonged to it, but he provided it with important services throughout this period. Some accused him of not joining that framework because he did not want to be part of the organization. Others claimed he was considered untrustworthy. He had already refuted those charges. He asked whether Blass,

Suttor, Iwanow, Miciol, and others would have maintained contact with him — and through him with the Paris cell — if he had not been considered trustworthy.

His response to those who doubted his contribution was that his activities "during that period [should have] won him a commendation and having his name included in the annals of the 20 most heroic and historic operations in the war against Hitlerism at Birkenau."[92]

||| In September 1945 the Polish Communist Party's commission of inquiry concluded its investigation, issuing a dry report of its findings (the document's grammar and style are unpolished; the translation here reflects the inconsistencies of the original):

> REPORT ON BERGER
>
> On the basis of the attached testimonies as well as Berger's statement, guilt on the following points can be determined:
>
> 1. During the period prior to Stalingrad — the creation of panic. In a lecture he gave in Beaune-la-Rolande he spoke of a possible defeat of the Soviet Union, Furmanski's statement attached. Refused Warszawski's request to organize the party at Birkenau. In this regard, the party's attitude toward him was negative (Mink). Said that "No one will get out of here" (Alexander). There can be no doubt that hundreds of our best comrades fell in Birkenau as a result of this sort of spirit of solidarity and the moral "courage" displayed by Gruenbaum. "He produced the worst sort of panic" (Alexander).
>
> *Murders*
>
> 2. Brutality (1942–43): "In several cases I beat people without good reason" (Berger testimony). "Dr. Niedzwiedz [Nedvěd] was beaten by me when I did not know him and did not know who he was" (Berger testimony). "Gruenbaum is directly responsible for the deaths of hundreds of people, with a club." Sent people to the gas when he could have saved them. Ordered that food be distributed outside, thus causing deaths. The mortality rate in his block was like that in the criminal block" (Marceau). "Beat unnecessarily, once kicked an old man in the belly when he asked to receive an additional portion of soup. The man died a few hours later. He collected the items left by the dead and made commercial use of them" (Laks).
>
> "Berger displayed leniency toward the crimes of his deputy Frank, a true hangman of prisoners, who put prisoners through 'athletic' routines (Szmulewski) and rebuffed people's requests for help" (Mink).
>
> In response to the accusation in the camp that Gruenbaum had killed many comrades with his own hand, he declared to me that "he had not intervened in

many murders, because they involved people *who could have been* murderers or informers" (Alexander).

Beat people viciously, an act that induced hundreds of deaths.

Czechs lodged complaints against him. In Buchenwald the Czechs brought him to trial, accusing him of beatings that on one case caused death, of stealing from prisoners. These charges were proved in the trial (Napieracz).

3. Jewish antisemitism. "Thousands of Jews have kicked the bucket, so what—less black market." He mocked Jews in front of Polish fascists and criminals and spread antisemitic propaganda. He jeered Jews who prayed as they were led to their deaths (Mink).

4. He always carried out the orders of the SS (Wilner). Even though he testified to frequent clashes with the Germans, the fact that he was a block commander (according to the statement he wrote) confirms the opinion of his accusers that he carefully carried out the Germans' orders.

5. At Buchenwald in 1945, thanks to the *personal* intervention of Napieracz and Rutkowski (and without the party's intervention, as Berger claims in his letter of July 21), who knew him from party work, the party took care of him.

[The following is a handwritten addition signed by Napieracz] Following the accusations of beating Czech comrades, Berger was relieved of his post as inspector.[93]

The "party conclusions"—in other words, the verdict—state that "the commission, after examining documents regarding Gruenbaum's unbefitting behavior, has concluded that he placed himself outside the party framework, and can never return to it."

A handwritten note was appended to the decision: "Beyond this, we note that he was banished [from the party] during nearly his entire time in France. [The banishment] was connected to his personal collapse during his incarceration in Łódź (Poland). Toward the end of 1937 or at the beginning of 1938 Berger was in the party for a short period. After that he was banished again, because his case had not been concluded." What was meant by his "collapse" in Łódź? Had he collapsed, why had his Communist comrades accepted him in Lancicia? How could he have been so active in Paris? How had he set out for France with Kaminski's group? The judges offered no explanation.

Had Eliezer not told the truth about anything? Were his scores of pages of testimony, his plethora of claims and the piercing questions he put to the witnesses, all fabrications? Did none of the issues he raised justify his acquittal on at least some of the counts against him?

10 Paris, June 1945– May 1946

ELIEZER ARRIVED IN PARIS at the beginning of June 1945 as an emissary of the Polish Communist Party, tasked with promoting the party's vision of a new Poland. He was just one of the displaced persons who streamed into the country after the war — *les déportés*, as the French called them in admiration, compassion, and fear. Tens of thousands of *déportés* found their way into France in the period between the end of 1944 and the end of the war, people seeking to return to what they saw as their homes in France.

Some of them were resistance fighters that the Gestapo and its accessories in the Vichy regime had arrested and sent to concentration camps. Others had been deported by the Vichy government in 1943 to be slave laborers, and still others had been prisoners of war who had been captured in the French defeat in 1940 and who had been held in any of a variety of locations at the whim of the Third Reich. Still others were Jews or members of other minority groups who had been sent for extermination but who had managed somehow to survive. Like other countries, France had difficulty absorbing wave after wave of returnees. It had the best of intentions, but the aid agencies set up by the Allied command could not keep pace with ever-increasing needs.

At the end of World War I, France had desperately needed working hands to rehabilitate its economy. But this time around most of the returnees constituted a heavy economic and social burden. The presence of these gaunt and traumatized refugees challenged the French to live up to the principles of liberty, equality, and fraternity that were so central to their pride and national identity. Returning citizens were one thing, but by the summer of 1945 there were more than one hundred thousand *déportés* of forty-seven nationalities on French soil. Only a handful of those who had been deported during the war because of their religion or foreign nationality returned. More than 77,000 of the 350,000 Jews living in France on the eve of the war had been murdered.[1] Furthermore, there were internal refugees, people who had been forced by the war to leave their homes in one part of the country and flee to another.[2]

Coping with the refugees required French society to take up the complex challenge of addressing its recent past and of probing still-open wounds. What was to be done with the Vichy regime's officials and supporters? What about those who had served in the "French Gestapo"? What about informers, collaborators, and other traitors to the Free French cause?

Many were charged with treason and brought to trial, most famously Vichy leaders such as Marshal Pétain and Pierre Laval. Their photographs were pasted up on walls and appeared daily on the front pages of the newspapers, and their names were heard endlessly on the radio. The same desire to take revenge against traitors led to accusations against Eliezer and others who had served as concentration camp officials. The air in Paris was dense with charges of betrayal.[3]

Most treason charges were based on article 75 of the French criminal code, which was devoted to "collaboration with the enemy." Some critics warned that the proceedings were summary and that in many cases former resistance fighters and relatives of *déportés* served as jurors. Some maintained that the special courts of justice that had been set up to handle these cases were acting just like the Vichy government's special courts. Under the circumstances, as one of de Gaulle's associates wrote, "it was not possible to do justice in peace and quiet." But the provisional government had to take action, because otherwise citizens would take the law into their own hands and set up revolutionary courts — as had had already occurred when rioters broke into prisons in Dinan and Cusset and carried out lynchings against alleged collaborators. The authorities would quickly lose control.[4]

Pétain's trial opened on July 23, 1945. Following the presiding judge's opening words, Pétain read out a statement in which he claimed that all he had done had been in France's interests. He was not guilty, he said, and the court did not represent the people. If it convicted him, the jurors and judges would face God's judgment in the future. Pétain was convicted and sentenced to death. The jurors recommended mercy. Pétain was imprisoned on the island of Yeu, where he died in 1951.[5]

The situation opened a window of opportunity for France's Communist Party, which had many Jews, as well as prominent artists and intellectuals, in its ranks. The party and its members had played a prominent role in the country's liberation, acting as a proxy of the victorious Red Army and a major combat force within the resistance. Its members were thus undisputed heroes in France. All this made it one of the most significant political organizations in postwar France. The opportunity that this presented was not lost on the party. Perhaps it could even govern France.

The party's power derived from its control of economic, industrial, and commercial concerns, real estate, the publishing industry, and newspapers.[6] Conscious of the esteem in which it and its heroes were held by the public, the party had campaigned energetically to have Pétain brought to trial and had advocated the death penalty for him and other traitors. It also sought to have its new heroes acknowledged and memorialized. It pushed to have its intellectuals admitted to the Académie française, the conservative scholarly institution that had supported Pétain, and to have members appointed to administrative positions in the civil service and as officers in the army.

All this was choreographed by the party's chief, Maurice Thorez, the talented son of a mining family. At this time he pursued a pragmatic line, allying himself with de Gaulle and serving in his provisional government. On July 21, 1945, he surprised his followers by declaring publicly that the time had come to end the witch hunts against collaborators and that there had been too many strikes of late.[7] Such accommodation did not sit well with everyone — some members were disappointed that the war of liberation had not brought on a Communist revolution. Thorez's pragmatism, as evidenced by his acceptance of de Gaulle's positions that workers had to increase production before they could get higher wages, and that the army had to be strengthened, alienated some of the party's supporters in Paris's proletarian Red Belt. But that loss of support was countervailed to some extent by the fact that many intellectuals were declaring themselves Communists.

One of the PCF's major problems was that, in 1945, it based a large part of its propaganda on the Red Army's heroism. But prisoners of war and deportees returning to France told horrifying stories of the rape, plunder, and murder to which they were eyewitnesses in Soviet-occupied Germany. The party leadership reacted angrily to the stories as they spread through France. PCF posters censured the "cynical Hitlerist scoundrels" who had infiltrated France to slander "the soldiers of the magnificent Red Army, who saved the civilized world from the Nazi legions."[8]

Given the PCF's strategy of contrasting itself with the Vichy regime and positioning itself as a party that could take the reins of government, the last thing it needed were members who had blood on their hands and who stood accused of collaboration. It was no time to make fine distinctions. Eliezer and others like him were liabilities. They could drag the party down with them.

For Eliezer the turning point came in August 1945. Although Bronke Gurfinkel was waiting for him when he returned to Paris, he did not move in with her. She helped him in his efforts to readjust, but they soon parted. They had been separated since he left for Spain, but the rumors that Bronke must certainly have heard from her party comrades, some of whom had been key activists in the women's underground at Auschwitz-Birkenau, may well have had something to do with it. She returned to Poland. "We both keep beautiful memories from the past in our hearts, and I retain feelings of gratitude, but we no longer found within us a desire to become close again," Eliezer wrote to his mother. Miriam was disappointed. She had hoped that he would settle down and start a family, and that doing so might moderate him and draw him away from subversive activity. Her husband, Yitzhak, consoled her: "But you know him, my little kitten. It won't be long before he finds another female." The most important thing, Eliezer's father said, was that "the nightmare of his past in Auschwitz should stop afflicting him — and us."[9]

Isolated now that his former friends were keeping a distance from him, and troubled by the investigation being conducted by his party, Eliezer still tried to carry out his mission — to persuade Polish Jewish survivors "to return to a homeland wiped clean of antisemitism and desperately in need of people prepared to build a new life, a life of socialism and social justice." This was the message contained in the pamphlets he always took with him when he descended from his rented apartment. But not all the Jewish immigrants in Paris shared his vision of a new Poland. Even the staunch Communists saw their future in Paris.[10] Some in the Polish party saw this reluctance to return to Poland as subversion.

One day he took the text of a pamphlet he had written to the printer and then went to a small café that served as a hangout for veterans of the Spanish Civil War. He had set up a meeting with a Spanish anarchist who was interested in hearing more about the new regime in Poland. But before he reached his destination, passersby began shouting: "Arrest him! Arrest him! Here's the murderer from Auschwitz!" Someone grabbed him, and before he knew it he was surrounded. "Leave me alone! You're mistaken!" he cried, to no avail. "It's him — the monster from Block 9 at Auschwitz!" shouted one of the men gripping him. Such furious attacks on suspected Nazi collaborators were not at all uncommon in those days. As usual, the police appeared and put out the fire before it got out of control. An official arrest warrant was issued against Eliezer the very next day. The witnesses told the policemen and judge that Eliezer had been "the head of the Birkenau death camp."[11]

Two of the witnesses were a twenty-eight-year-old student, Jacques Gebet, and his neighbor Eliahu Pakin, a thirty-seven-year-old tailor. The two men claimed to have encountered Eliezer in Birkenau. Pakin, scion of a family of Communist activists, said he had accounts to settle with Eliezer. Eliezer's brother Yonatan would later claim that the encounter in the street had not been a coincidence. He maintained that, after hearing that Eliezer had returned to Paris, the two men hunted him down. When they found him, they laid an ambush, called the police, and turned him in.[12]

The French investigation of the charges against Eliezer would last eight months. This time it was an official, systematic, and transparent inquest, with prosecution and defense and presided over by an investigating magistrate. Eliezer's case was one of dozens of similar ones, of varying levels of drama. Some French citizens were critical of the authorities for what they said was a tendency to try to finish off such proceedings as quickly as possible, but other citizens were eager to get them over with. Nevertheless, Eliezer, his attorney, and his family and supporters were allowed to take all measures they needed to respond to the accusations. This time the witnesses could not evade giving answers to questions posed by the defense. Furthermore, his family, led by his father, were permitted to seek out and call in defense witnesses to counter what Eliezer and some of his associates believed was pressure from the Polish and French Communist parties. Eliezer believed that, in the Polish inquiry, the party had deliberately not called up witnesses who would have testified in his favor.

In the summer of 1945, Yitzhak Gruenbaum was serving as the permanent vice chairman of the Zionist Executive. He was a leader of the General Zionist Party and chairman of the Rescue Committee for European Jewry. In this capacity he arrived in London to attend the first postwar Zionist Congress. The congress's aims included laying out the Zionist movement's postwar program; considering the parameters of the diplomatic struggle against Britain's so-called White Paper policy limiting Jewish immigration to Palestine; choosing a new Jewish Agency Executive; discussing and coming to a resolution on a new line of action regarding the impending postwar political settlement; renewing the ties that had been severed during the war between the Yishuv and Jewish communities in Europe; meeting Holocaust survivor representatives; crafting an agenda for dealing with the survivors; and discussing the *Briha* illegal immigration campaign. It was the first opportunity for the most senior Yishuv leadership to meet with Zionist leaders from the lands that had been conquered by the Nazis during the war.[13]

Just as the elder Gruenbaum was listening to some of the leading Jewish anti-Nazi partisan fighters tell him what happened to Poland's Jews during the war, a telegram from his friend Marc Jarblum, who was in Paris, was placed before him, informing him of his son's arrest. Jarblum's cable said "there's no cause for concern," but Yitzhak, understandably distressed, decided to cut short his visit to London. He would go to Paris, meet his son, confront the charges that he hoped were not true, and plan out his next steps. "The bottom line is that Eliezer is my son," he explained. He reached Paris during the first week of September 1945 and took a hotel room near the local Jewish Agency offices, then a busy outpost of Zionist activism.

The first meeting between father and son took place in the prison and lasted all night. Further meetings were limited to once a week, in keeping with the prison's rules. Eliezer convinced his father that he was innocent, Yitzhak later recounted in an article he published in the 1960s, and he wrote to his wife and two other sons to tell them this. What convinced Yitzhak was Eliezer's "tragic confession. He did not hide a thing from me. . . . I listened to his confession in enormous pain, sorrow, and great compassion. I did not hide this from him. I told him, 'How could you raise your rod against Jews? Are you not my son?' "[14] Eliezer told him that when they arrived in Birkenau from Beaune-la-Rolande, they were herded into a block ruled by "a huge Pole, a criminal prisoner." His friends asked him to persuade the Pole to appoint him, Eliezer, as his deputy, so that the Pole "could rest more and would not have to get upset." Eliezer said he got on the Pole's good side with the help of his excellent command of colloquial Polish, which he used to tell him racy stories about Paris life. But then his friends were transferred to other blocks, and Eliezer found himself with people he did not know, who had not chosen him as their leader, and who did not understand how the son of a Jewish leader from Poland could have struck up a friendship with a brutal, ignorant, and violent gentile murderer. Relations with the other prisoners had degenerated, and they became hostile to him.[15]

Yonatan later wrote that his father received the impression that Eliezer had suffered for being his son. Hundreds of Jews had done worse things but had not been pursued, as Eliezer had been, after liberation. Yet "a kapo who is a well-known Communist and the son of Gruenbaum is a sensation. Everyone talks about him." But they don't talk about what he did but rather about what they thought he did, Yonatan wrote. Those who hear the stories elaborate them, and suddenly the public is certain he is a traitor.

The father took comfort in the fact that most of the accusations against his son, and the hostility against him, could be attributed largely not to his actions but to his name.[16] Yitzhak summed up the situation in a letter to his wife: "He told me everything. I believe that he did not do anything bad, but the things look otherwise. Only Jews are accusing him. They cannot forgive him for many things, especially for having grown distant from them and for not having followed in his father's footsteps. That's what one of the prisoners said. He has problems with his friends. They conducted some sort of inquiry and decided to expel him."[17]

Eliezer presented the same picture to his mother: "I know that I was OK. I have the moral right to defend myself and fight for my honor. . . . I do not know if I will win at this stage . . . but I am sure that I will win sooner or later."[18]

To provide Eliezer with every means of defense permitted to him by French law, it was necessary to hire an attorney who could conduct his case professionally, wisely, and fearlessly. Eliezer, his family, and those who supported him settled on André Ballot, a forty-two-year-old lawyer who also held degrees in political science and German linguistics and literature. His dissertation on the Weimar constitution and his other academic achievements won him a citation for excellence. After completing his studies he had served for two years as a lawyer in the French army. He won a Croix de Guerre medal for outstanding service.[19]

The charges contained in Eliezer's file — case 56-37-SN.PJ.SE.4—were heard before Inspectors Vézard Emilien and Renaud and Investigating Magistrate Maurice in Paris's de la Seine courthouse.[20] They took evidence in September, and the first cross-examination was held on October 9. The witnesses who took part were Jacques Gebet, Zylberstein, Isaac Loberstein, and Eliahu Pakin. The four of them first presented their stories. "I was arrested in 1941 in Paris, at the same time as Gruenbaum," Gebet declared. "I escaped and was recaptured in 1942." In 1943 in Birkenau he heard that Eliezer was "the worst block chief, who mistreated prisoners to the point of causing the deaths of some of them." He provided the names of witnesses to these deeds.[21] Zylberstein, thirty-seven years old, had not been in Eliezer's block, but heard prisoners talking about him. This witness said that Eliezer "inflicted real terror on his fellows, many died of the blows he dealt them. One day I asked him for bread and he refused to give me any. He said that the Jews had come here to die."[22]

Isaac Loberstein made serious accusations. "Gruenbaum was the chief of Block 9, where I was," he testified. "He was very evil. Inflicted terror. He had 950 men under his thumb. When I arrived I spoke to him in Yiddish. He displayed displeasure and beat me with a stick. The prisoners went out to work at 3:30 in the morning, and to spur them on he beat them with a pickax handle. Some, the sick and tired, couldn't go out and remained in the camp. In the evening we found them dead from his beatings. Gruenbaum mocked us: 'What good will it do you to eat, you don't have more than half an hour to live anyway.'

"My son was in a neighboring block and tried several times to come see me," Loberstein continued. "He [Eliezer] beat him with his stick and my son died from the blows he received from Gruenbaum and others. My son wept outside the window and pleaded to be allowed to see me. He continued to refuse."

Loberstein said that Gruenbaum always walked around with a stick. When they returned from work there were many bodies in the block. "Gruenbaum killed them. The Germans told him that he had to beat us, but not to death but so that people would fear him, he killed a lot. Every day was like that."[23]

Pakin's testimony was more detailed. Gruenbaum, he related, had been among those who received him in September 1942 and had tattooed his number on his arm. "When I told him he was hurting me, he slapped me and struck me with his hand and foot," Pakin said, adding that the SS appointed Eliezer chief of Block 9 as a reward for his services. He habitually beat people, Pakin recalled, "with a large stick. He caused the death of many Jews." Pakin said he knew two of these victims. When Sawek Kirszenbaum, Gruenbaum's friend, was sick and pleaded to be allowed to remain in the block, "I myself intervened," but Eliezer sent Kirszenbaum out to his work detail anyway. Kirszenbaum returned even sicker and Gruenbaum sent him to Block 7, the "antechamber to the crematoria and the gas chambers." At the beginning of 1943, the SS told the block chiefs to prepare lists of prisoners who could not work so that they could be sent to the gas chambers. Gruenbaum immediately complied, and himself selected prisoners for death a few times a week; "About a hundred went to their deaths after he sent them," Pakin maintained.[24]

At this point Magistrate Maurice called on Eliezer to respond to the accusations. Eliezer laid out his story in the same way he had in the past, responding as well specifically to the new issues that had been raised. He categorically denied Pakin's accusation that he, Eliezer, had tattooed him. The tattoos were done at a different location by a special team. He also denied that he had designated prisoners for the gas chambers and that prisoners had died as a result of his beatings. The SS had not appointed him block chief—that had been done by a criminal prisoner who served in the camp's self-governing apparatus. "Had I turned down the position I would have suffered consequences," Eliezer asserted. But he added that "we had an interest in accepting that post in order to improve the lives of the prisoners."

Here Ballot stopped him and asked him to repeat what he had just said—that he had assumed the post of block chief because it had been in the "general interest," a way of improving the prisoners' lives. Eliezer then offered a detailed account of his service in one capacity after another until liberation. Before he completed this survey of his time at Auschwitz-Birkenau-Jawischowitz and Buchenwald, Ballot asked him to tell the court about the incidents in which his accusers claimed he had acted criminally.[25]

The investigating magistrate now commenced his cross-examination of both Eliezer and his accusers. Eliezer once again denied Pakin's charges, but Pakin stuck to his story. "Gruenbaum was the one who tattooed and beat me," he insisted. "My number in the camp was 613368, as you can see on my forearm. Pinkiert, whom Gruenbaum designated for the gas chambers, bore the number 613369. . . . I was sick in Block 7 when Pinkiert was designated for the gas chambers. . . . These events happened in 1943."[26] Pinkiert was, Pakin said, the second of the two men he knew who had been killed by Eliezer.

Eliezer responded: "In 1942 I was in Block 9 with Pinkiert. In 1943 he was no longer in my block and I could not have designated him for the gas chambers." Pakin lamely responded that "as secretary to the block chief he helped his boss." Zylberstein also stuck to his account. He had heard from a friend that Gruenbaum "beat them and would not listen, not to the French and not to the Jews, just to the Poles and the Germans." But he said that he personally "had never seen Gruenbaum beat anyone or send anyone to the gas chambers, because he was not in his block."[27]

The judge also cross-examined Gebet, who likewise stuck to his story—Gruenbaum's declaration regarding his appointment was a lie, the witness said. "They did not ask Jewish prisoners to choose their leaders. It was a gang of Polish and German convicts, criminal prisoners, chosen by the SS, and they kept order." Gebet declared that he himself would never have taken on himself "to work with a man like that. When the criminal told Gruenbaum to kill people, he did not refuse, so that he wouldn't be killed."[28]

Ballot zeroed in on the question of Eliezer's appointment, and Gebet retreated. "I don't know what the circumstances of his appointment were . . . because I was not in his camp, I can speak about him only on the basis of hearsay," the witness said. "In any case, it wasn't the Jews who appointed him, but rather maybe Ludwig the murderer." Zylberstein came to his aid, calling out: "I was with Gruenbaum, I stand behind everything I said."

Eliezer again rejected the testimony against him. "With regard to the appointment, I stand behind my account," he said. He pointed out that Zylberstein had not made the charge he was now making in his testimony to the police. It was all new. He had known Zylberstein in the camp, but did not remember ever beating him. Furthermore, "Sawek died of dysentery and not in the gas chambers. His body was brought to the morgue by some ten of his friends. When he arrived in the camp I helped him and gave him food."

"Not true!" Pakin shouted. "That's a lie. I was Sawek's best friend, and he [Sawek] did not want to talk to Gruenbaum, because he had changed his spots. I asked him to leave Sawek [in the block] because he was sick. But he refused and sent him to work. He was [then] in Block 7, and from there he was sent to the gas chambers."

Eliezer responded: "Every evening I passed on bread to Sawek and his friends, and I looked for better work for Sawek and his friends, I was not the one who sent him to [that] *Kommando*. I spoke with the foreman so that he would not beat them. A doctor who examined him sent him to Block 7, and I could not do anything for him. I went to intercede for him with the chief of Block 7, and as a result he was able to stay there without being sent to the gas chambers, until he died."

At the end of the interrogation, the judge asked the witnesses whether they still stood by their claims. They answered in the affirmative, but now introduced an entirely new claim. "Gruenbaum, who declares himself a Jewish survivor of a concentration camp," they said, "did not register with the French Federation of Jewish Concentration Camp Survivors, did not request a membership card and did not receive compensation, which demonstrates that he had reason to hide."[29]

Following this stage in the proceeding, three more witnesses — Daniel Finkelkraut, Ijziykléar Oléar, and Haim Idel Goldstein — gave testimony during the first half of October. They were asked about the accusations that had been made against Eliezer. Inspector Emilien summed up the picture as it stood after these testimonies. According to Finkelkraut's testimony, he said, Gruenbaum had used draconian enforcement methods. He beat prisoners in several cases. Several witnesses claimed that this was necessary in order to maintain discipline and hygiene. According to Oléar, Emilien said, forcing the sick to work saved them from the gas chambers. Others, like Goldstein, argued that Eliezer abused prisoners even when SS men were not present. "I could not determine whether Gruenbaum was appointed to decide who would go to the gas chambers, but this does not seem reasonable to me," Emilien remarked. "Likewise, I could not say for certain if the beatings he gave prisoners caused their deaths. It could well be that they caused serious injury, which later had fatal consequences." Emilien stressed that two men who had been summoned as defense witnesses, Langman and Berneman, had not appeared in court to testify. One claimed that he was "always traveling," and the other simply said that he "cannot accede to our summons."[30] Presumably Langman's reason for not testifying was not his travels but his apprehension about testifying in Eliezer's favor. Berneman, in all likelihood, did not show up for similar reasons. It may be that Oléar testified because he no longer had anything to lose.

At this point in the proceedings, Eliezer was in the position of benefiting from the lesser of two evils. Those who had turned him in had admitted that they had not been in his block and had not personally seen him commit the crimes he was accused of. Eliezer's responses presented a much more complex picture than had been presented by his accusers. This enabled the defense to demonstrate that there was "something in the air" that was keeping witnesses from testifying.[31]

So as not to leave matters to chance and to try to neutralize the pressures on witnesses, Eliezer's father sought out good defense witnesses and to meet with influential Jewish figures. These included Adam (Avraham) Rayski, a senior correspondent for the *Neue Presse*. Rayski, originally from Białystok, had joined the Polish Communist Party at a young age. In 1932 he moved to Paris and jointed the PCF. After the fall of France he joined the underground and was sent to Lyon, where he served as a coordinator. His son and wife had remained in Paris. From July 1941 to the end of the war he served as secretary of the PCF's Jewish Department and was among the party's Yiddishists. In an interview conducted for this book, he said that "one day in September 1945, when I came to the office, I was informed that [Yitzhak] Gruenbaum was waiting for me. The purpose of his visit was to obtain my assistance in freeing his son, thinking that the Communist Party could do this! Of course, this was impossible because the decision on the arrest had been made by the police, who received information from Jewish prisoners who returned from the camp." Rayski subsequently offered more details, saying that Gruenbaum had asked him to use his connections to ensure that Pakin and Gebet would withdraw their testimonies.

Yitzhak Gruenbaum's approach, Rayski later wrote to the author and his research assistants, "was that 'I forget that the person standing before me is not a political person but, quite simply, a wretched father.' I related to him in detail about the meeting with Henri Bulawko, the responsible person in the prisoners' organization, who had been the head of HaShomer haTza'ir. Bulawko reported to me regularly about the situation, because he had frequent meetings with Y. Gruenbaum, who had been given a room in the French offices of the Jewish Agency."

Bulawko had not mentioned Eliezer in his memoirs, Rayski added, nor was he willing to speak about him. Bulawko indeed refused to respond to the author's questions, and like others said not a word about Eliezer in his memoirs.[32] Rayski added that Eliezer had been a member of the Kampf organization, which had been founded in 1933 for Jewish students who had come to Paris from Poland. But he had left the organization because he objected to its use of Yiddish.[33] Rayski wrote, in response to our question, that "Eliezer was not one of the volunteers for Spain. He certainly was not in the Botwin Company or in the Dombrowski Brigade. Had he been there, we would have known about it."[34] But the documents presented to the French court contradicted this claim. Eliezer appears on a list of volunteers published by independent researchers. A significant number of fighters in the civil war also testified to his involvement. But none of this convinced Rayski, who refused to retract his claim even after we sent him the documents that had been presented in court and reminded him of the testimony of Charles Liblau, an old friend of Eliezer's, and others. Could it be that someone wanted to strip Eliezer of a part of his biography? Could it be that that desire remains a living force in Paris even today?

Yitzhak Gruenbaum himself sought out Liblau, as the latter related in his memoirs.[35] Liblau wrote that he saw a notice in a newsletter put out by former Auschwitz prisoners about the arrest of a man named Berger; readers who were acquainted with the story were invited to assist the investigation. Liblau responded. He met with a police inspector who asked him to relate everything he knew about Berger. Even though his testimony was "confused," Liblau wrote, it included all the information he provides in his memoirs. His impression was that by the time he spoke to the inspector, a great deal of testimony had already been collected. The inspector, Liblau wrote, even tried to help him put some order into his "chaotic" story.[36] A few days later an elderly man "with a noble and pleasant face" knocked on his door.

> "Am I in the presence of Mr. Liblau?" he asked in French.
>
> I did not respond to his question and offered him a seat. The stranger surveyed my modest room with his wise gaze and then examined me for a moment.
>
> "Is it true?" he suddenly asked me in Polish, in a broken voice. . . .
>
> A long, tense silence . . . followed that question. The father's heart guessed the answer . . . two tears flowed from the corners of his eyes along his impressive and agonized face.

Liblau's memoirs continued:

> I reminded him of a centuries-old Jewish custom: when a family member dies, all the mirrors in the house are covered as a sign of mourning. For seven days the members of the family sit on upturned chairs, and the men wear clothes that have been cut with scissors. I added that such a learned man, full of understanding of human tribulations, one who had before the war been a shining defender of the interests of the Jewish community in Poland, who had for so many symbolized human dignity and human rights, ought to expunge forever the memory of such a son. In any case, I added, justice would soon be done [to Eliezer] for his crimes and shameful collaboration with the Hiterlist forces in Birkenau.
>
> Another long silence pervaded the room.
>
> "But he's still my son," he finally murmured in a voice full of despair and bitterness.
>
> He left without even having the strength to say goodbye and I never again had to see this respectable and miserable old man.[37]

Liblau's memoir offers a long account of his acquaintance with Eliezer. He "always wanted to shine," to impress people, to lead. "He impressed us, simple workers with little education," both with his powers of discernment and analytical ability about Polish politics, society, and economics. He attacked amoral merchants, the petite bourgeoisie from which he had come, and condemned the Piłsudski regime, which he believed was acting in the interests of Polish and Vatican reactionary forces. He won over everyone with his willingness to speak out against his own important and respectable family. For him, the Soviet Union was a miracle — only that country had succeeded in providing a democratic solution to the problem of national minorities, while ensuring the equal rights of all its citizens.

He also, Liblau wrote, analyzed the state of the Polish Communist Party for them.

> He explained the internal rivalry between the "rightist" majority led by Comrade [Adolf] Warski and the "leftist" minority led by [Julian] Leszczyński and offered his judgment of who was leading the party in the right direction. When the trials of Bolshevik theoreticians and members of the old guard began in Moscow, Eliezer interpreted the situation for us and offered an effusive account of the courage, devotion, and loyalty of Stalin and the prosecutor, [Andrey] Vyshinsky, to the Communist Party, Soviet people, and the interests of the international proletariat. Thanks to their efforts and leadership, Eliezer said, the forces of evil would be uprooted. The struggle had to be a merciless one and there was no room for sentimentality.

Liblau praised Eliezer's explanations as being "clear, logical, and bold in expression, and they captivated us."[38] When he was arrested for underground activity and then sentenced to a long prison term, he gained "the halo of a martyr," Liblau recalled. "It seemed to us that he was fated to be the leader of the party." But, according to Liblau, he lost interest in Eliezer. Despite Eliezer's popularity, Liblau said, he and his friends were sometimes "taken aback by his arrogance" and his desire to stand out. He hated to lose arguments, and when he did he turned hostile and resentful. "More than anything else, he had a passion for being in charge," Liblau wrote. As a consequence, "he often seemed repellent to us."[39]

Liblau also ended up in Block 9. "How surprised I was when I noticed that the man with the club in his hand, who ruled over the block's 700 prisoners, was Comrade Berger! He bore the official title of *Blockschreiber* [clerk] and, along with others, wielded all the powers that the Hitlerist authorities agreed to place in the hands of prisoners." Now he was "his majesty the kapo, with his shaven head, eyes full of hatred, foaming at the mouth, his face disproportionately long. He constantly waved his club, synonymous with his power in the camp. When I saw him I was paralyzed with fear; what could I do so that he would not identify me? I had nowhere to hide."

Only a few days later, Liblau wrote, did he begin to comprehend "the full significance of the hell" he had landed in "and the criminal role played by Comrade Berger in the assortment of inspectors and kapos who had been enlisted from among the lowest of the criminals." During inspections, the prisoners of these two blocks stood close by each other and could watch Eliezer.

> I was ashamed for him, I felt I was somehow an indirect partner in his actions. It was as if the mire he wallowed in sprayed on me, too. Nothing remained of the scornful attitude, which was so evident in his speeches at party meetings. . . . He groveled in the most humiliating way before his new leaders. To satisfy his pride, which grew out of his desire to command and rule, he tortured and killed prisoners who had the bad luck to find themselves under his authority.

Eliezer took advantage of every opportunity to abuse people who were malnourished and defenseless, according to Liblau. "This creature, lacking in all morals . . . [who was] naturally weak, became a notorious monster prepared to carry out every cruelty."[40]

Liblau's account of his encounter with Eliezer's father has the ring of authenticity. But he was not called as a witness before the investigating magistrate and did not undergo cross-examination. He did not see the nefarious deeds that he attributed to Eliezer, but rather based his account largely on hearsay, even those events from Eliezer's and Liblau's initial period in Birkenau, what Eliezer variously called his black weeks or months.[41]

If Liblau and Yitzhak Gruenbaum indeed met and had the conversation that Liblau recounted, it must have been a heavy blow for the father, and not the first one that he incurred. Despite his sense that things were going less badly than he originally supposed, he did his best to bring in more witnesses and support. At the London Congress he met Haika Grossman, a leading figure in Poland's HaShomer haTza'ir movement, and Antek Zuckerman, a native of Vilna who moved to Poland in 1936 and was a leading member of the Dror Zionist youth movement. The two of them stopped in Paris on their way home from London. Grossman later related that Yitzhak asked "that we testify that it could be that a kapo would have filled the position at the behest of the underground." She said that she could not say that in court "because I had not had such an experience; I had not been in a concentration camp, and it was Auschwitz, it was horrifying."[42] Ballot and the inspectors also collected testimonies and presented documents that could cast light on the case. Six more witnesses were summoned.

Léon (Leib) Epstein, forty-two years old, related that he made Eliezer's acquaintance at Beaune-la-Rolande. Eliezer's behavior had been "unexceptionable." At Birkenau, toward the end of 1942, Epstein was placed in Block 9, where he met Eliezer, whom he described as "chief of the prisoners." He spent about three weeks in there before being transferred to Block 2 (or, according to another transcription of the testimony, Block 11). Epstein said that he spoke with Eliezer several times. He had never seen him beat prisoners. He left Block 9 at the time Gruenbaum came down with typhus. In December 1942 Epstein was sent to Auschwitz and cut off from his friends. Epstein said that he had never heard of Eliezer killing prisoners or beating anyone to death. It was only when he returned to Paris the previous May that "I again saw friends from the camp and heard that he behaved in a reprehensible way."

"Block 9 was a special block for Jews," Epstein testified. "The discipline there was not stricter than in other blocks. I know that there was a shoe repair workshop there, but I did not remain long enough to become acquainted with the details. . . . The diet in Block 9 was identical to that in other blocks — very bad." He spoke of the language issue as well. "Gruenbaum knew very little Yiddish," Epstein recalled, "and I never had an opportunity to hear him speak that language."[43]

When the Communist Party commenced its inquiry, Eliezer had listed Epstein, who then served as secretary of the PCF's foreign print workers' section in Paris, among those who could testify about his actions in the camp. He prepared five questions for Epstein, believing that the answers would support his innocence. He had hoped that Epstein would tell the inquiry how Eliezer had hid him in the block to allow him to recover from a beating he had been given in his work detail. He also wanted Epstein to testify about whether he knew of the beatings that Eliezer had received from the block commander and what the circumstances of those beatings had been, and whether the two of them had remained in contact after Epstein was transferred to another block. Epstein either did not respond to these questions in the Polish inquiry, or his replies have not survived in the documentation of the trial that has come down to us. In any case, they would not have changed the party's decision. In that proceeding, Eliezer told the judges that he feared that Epstein had been caught up in the general atmosphere and had changed his opinion of him.[44]

Finkelkraut was called to testify again. He had arrived in Birkenau along with Eliezer just prior to July 1942 and had been sent to Block 9. Unlike most of the witnesses and those who had been involved, he was not a party member and thus presumably felt he could speak freely. On the basis of their acquaintance with Eliezer from Beaune-la-Rolande and with the consent of other prisoners, he and Freilich had gone to Konczal and proposed that he give Eliezer a position. Eliezer had not been involved, and not known about it, and his fellow prisoners had told him about it only after Konczal had agreed. After Eliezer was transferred to another post in Block 4, Finkelkraut said that they had asked him to return, "so as to avert Konczal's lethal intervention." Eliezer, Finkelkraut testified, "acceded to his friends' proposal, even though he could have instead taken the role of block clerk without bearing any special responsibility."

Finkelkraut said that Eliezer began using violence against his fellow prisoners after being named to the post, "but perhaps he was compelled to carry out these actions because he was subordinate to Konczal, who was very violent with us." He added that Eliezer was himself brutally beaten by Konczal several times because the block was too noisy and too dirty. But Eliezer had never tattooed prisoners, he testified. There was a special team that did that. Furthermore, to the best of his knowledge, Eliezer had never sent anyone to the gas chambers. Block 9 offered better living conditions than any of the other blocks, he maintained. Mortality was lower, food rations were relatively reasonable, and the prisoners there received clean laundry via Russians who knew Eliezer. The block was heated in the winter, and there was a shoe-repair workshop. Sometimes it was necessary to slap prisoners, for their own good and to avert abuse, but that had to be done on a reasonable level. It might well have been that Eliezer forced sick prisoners to go out to work, but this may have been to keep them from being sent to the gas chambers. But he did not remember for sure.

According to Finkelkraut, he had never seen Eliezer ladle out soup or beat sick prisoners, nor could he name any victims of such abuse. Block 20, where Eliezer served as block chief after leaving Block 9, had been an isolation block where there had been no selections for the gas chambers. He did not know if Eliezer had cooperated with the Russians and Poles in underground activities against the Germans. Sawek Kirszenbaum, he said, had unquestionably died because of illness. He knew no one named Loberstein or his son, and had no idea how the son had died. Gruenbaum, Finkelkraut added, did not speak Yiddish fluently.[45]

Finkelkraut's testimony is also important because of the differences between what he said in his repeat testimony and what he had told the investigating magistrate two months previously. Then he had said that even if Eliezer had killed out of necessity, he could have avoided doing so had he wanted to. He had also accused Eliezer of involvement in killing a Dutch prisoner, of having habitually beat prisoners horribly, and of having aimed his kicks "at the belly or lower." In his earlier testimony, Finkelkraut had said that when Eliezer was asked why he beat prisoners, he would say that "all these people should be killed." He had been especially cruel toward Jews (and most of the prisoners, and those who were beaten, were Jews), and in particular toward the elderly, Finkelkraut had testified earlier. In the French proceeding,

Finkelkraut testified that once appointed to his block post Eliezer had begun to use violence against his fellow prisoners, but qualified this by saying that he may have had no choice because he served under Konczal, "who was very violent with us." But he made no mention of the brutalities he had cited in his previous testimony.

During his initial testimony, he had claimed that Kirszenbaum had gone to Eliezer and asked to be treated for his illness, and that Eliezer had refused. "Had he wanted to, he could have saved Sawek," he maintained. But the second time around he said unequivocally that "he unquestionably died because of illness." At first he had said that Eliezer had done all he could to keep his position and that he had toadied to the reactionary forces. Now he offered a full account of how Eliezer had been chosen for the position by his friends.[46] These were hardly fine details that could be ignored. What had happened to Finkelkraut in the two months that intervened between the two court appearances?

David Szmulewski, a central figure in the Communist underground at the camp, was also summoned to appear before the investigating magistrate. During the Polish Communist proceeding he had offered very tight, cautious, and measured testimony, dodging the questions Eliezer had prepared for him. In France, he offered an altogether different sort of testimony. He told the magistrate that he had never been in Block 9 and that he thus "did not know what happened there." There were block chiefs and prisoner chiefs (kapos) who had beaten prisoners so as to prevent theft, but he did not know if Eliezer imposed such measures. Neither did he know if Eliezer had killed prisoners or designated them for the gas chambers. Sawek had died of typhus, he maintained, and he had no memory of a man named Pinkiert who had died at Birkenau. In response to a query from Ballot, Szmulewski said that Pakin had "indeed experienced a passing attack of insanity, which led to his transfer from Block 5 to Block 7." In the previous inquiry, he had stressed that Eliezer had been "a demoralizing factor" among the members of the groups, and stressed that Eliezer had evaded cooperation with his comrades in the underground. Even when Eliezer had placed his contacts at the disposal of his comrades, Szmulewski had testified then, he sent them to marginal figures rather than to the really important ones.[47] All in all, Szmulewski's testimony in Paris was much more favorable to Eliezer than his Polish testimony had been. Why?

Ijziyklėar Olėar first testified that he himself had been known as a harsh and brutal block chief. Then he had established ties with the underground, and cooperated with the plan to dig an escape tunnel. When someone told the Nazis, Olėar told the court, he had been interrogated and tortured but had not informed on his partners and friends. When he returned to Paris he, like Eliezer, had been brought up before his comrades, and had also been banned. Oléar realized that in this regard he and Eliezer were in the same boat.

From time to time he clandestinely visited his friends in Block 9, especially Gruenbaum, who would give him soup and bread. He had not been a resident of the block, so he had no way of knowing what the conditions there were. He could say, however, that the prisoners in Block 9 were not compelled to stand outside for two or three hours in all weather, at the whim of the block chief. The block chief did not steal the prisoners' food and give it to Polish civilians in exchange for alcohol — the prisoners received their rations. Oléar responded in the negative to questions about whether Gruenbaum designated prisoners for the gas chambers and had dealt them mortal blows. He confirmed that, to the best of his knowledge, prisoners were tattooed by a special team.

"In the concentration camp there were people of all sorts of types," he remarked. There were, he said, evil people who behaved badly and people of bad will who did things at the expense of other prisoners. For that reason, a block chief sometimes had to use force. No block chief was innocent of that. Block discipline had to be very strict, both because the SS was always watching and because of the urgent need to impose the rules of hygiene.[48] Oléar's testimony clearly did not accord with the malevolence that Eliezer had been accused of.

Two other witnesses who appeared at this stage were Haim Idel Goldstein, of Block 8, and Martin Steg, who had spent a short time in Block 9. They told the court that the conditions in Block 9 were better than average. Goldstein added that Eliezer had beaten prisoners with a stick even when this was not called for, but that he did not know whether any of his beatings had been fatal, nor did he know anything about Eliezer being involved in sending prisoners to the gas chambers or in tattooing them.

According to Steg, Gruenbaum was a prisoner just like all the other prisoners. The first time he heard of Eliezer's brutality was when he, Steg, returned to Paris. He did complain, however, that Eliezer had not set aside a room for prayer services, perhaps because he was a Communist. Steg promised his questioners that he would convene the board of the prisoners' organization "so that the members could learn of the accusations being made against him. . . . I will ask at an assembly if prisoners from Birkenau have grievances regarding brutality on his part." Since Goldstein and Steg had not spent much time in Block 9, the testimony they could offer was limited, both in Eliezer's favor and against him.[49] This round of testimony thus left Eliezer, his family, and his attorney hoping for the best.

Ballot tried to reinforce the defense's arguments by presenting documents showing that Eliezer was not the "monster" described to the policemen who arrested him and to the judge who ordered his detention. On the contrary, he was an underground fighter who did all he could, even putting his life on the line time after time, in the antifascist struggle in which he was no mean partner. Eliezer's attorney asked the court for permission to add to the investigation file a translation, which the Polish consul in Paris confirmed as being a faithful rendition of the original, of an article that appeared in October 1945 in *Pioner*, a newspaper in Wrocław. In it, a former inmate of Buchenwald and a member of the Polish Workers Party offered an account of underground activity in the camp. He named Eliezer as a member of the Polish cell's leadership.

According to the article, the cell's leaders were Josef Tripola, Henrik Mikołajczyk from Poznań, Vaclaw Jablonski, Josef Regliszyn, and Leon Gruenbaum, all of Warsaw.[50] If Gruenbaum had indeed sold his soul to the Nazis, Ballot argued, presumably he would not have been included in the underground leadership. Its members would have been well aware that an informer in their ranks would have put the lives of many people in danger.

Ballot also submitted a letter from the Association of Spanish Republican Volunteers, Polish Section, stating that Eliezer Gruenbaum, going under the name of Leon Berger, had fought in their ranks. Inspector Marchesseaux, one of the case's managers for the court, presented the magistrate with a document outlining Eliezer's doings in France. He wrote that "on March 3, 1938 . . . [Eliezer] left France temporarily in order to enlist in the International Brigades in the service of Republican Spain. . . . At the end of the war he returned to France, as has been confirmed with his exit permit (military 'pass') from the Pyrénées-Orientales department, Saint-Cyprien camp of March 10, 1939, copy attached." Marchesseaux further noted that Eliezer had been conscripted for a short while into the Polish army, before it withdrew from France to Britain.[51]

Yitzhak Gruenbaum traveled to Brussels, where he considered going on to Poland to locate other witnesses, to try to counteract what seemed like the Polish Communist Party's intention of ostracizing Eliezer, and to use whatever influence he still had there, as a former Polish political leader, to lobby on his son's behalf. In Brussels he met a female acquaintance of his son's. He related Eliezer's story to her, and together they analyzed the situation. She promised to use her connections to find important witnesses, and help Yitzhak in both Poland and France. She seems to have carried out her mission successfully, because several former prisoners contacted the father, asked after his son, and "told him that there was no basis to any of the accusations and that they wanted to help."

Yitzhak returned to Paris at the end of October 1945 in much better spirits. He told Eliezer about these recent developments, and "Itche, the poor guy, was very happy, because he had become accustomed to having his best friends turn their back on him, people who owed him a great deal." Yitzhak told his family and his assistant and friend Apollinary Hartglas that "one of our most important witnesses" (he may have meant Langman) "who had doubts about whether to testify, has finally decided to say everything he knows. He spent two years with Itche, and for a time even shared a bed with him. He knows everything and can invalidate or explain all the charges." Langman, Eliezer's friend, about forty years old, indeed overcame his misgivings and agreed to tell what he knew:

> Gruenbaum was named room warden by one of the comrades, while he himself slept. He was transferred to Block 4, but the comrades demanded his return. Gruenbaum did not tattoo. There was a specialist who did that. Gruenbaum never once decided which people went to the gas chamber. I don't know that he killed, but he beat [prisoners] because there were some who got into fights. . . . He was always okay with me and I do not know anything bad [about him]. Several times I asked for bread to help friends and he did not refuse.[52]

Another development, the father related, was that "a lot of the accusations have been eliminated. It has turned out that they are without foundation." One witness in particular — he did not mention Pakin by name — persisted, "because he thought that Itche was guilty of the death of his closest friend." But when the matter was examined using the medical records from Auschwitz, and the testimony of members of the Polish underground led by Józef Cyrankiewicz, which he had managed to obtain, "it turned out that his friend died of dysentery following on typhus."

All that remained were accusations "about beatings that once indirectly caused a death." Ballot had successfully refuted the testimony of Eliezer's accusers during his first cross-examination. "I, too, am now more optimistic," the elder Gruenbaum wrote. "If I am able to find a member of the court at Buchenwald it might be that Itche's case won't even go to trial."[53] In a letter to Hartglas he added information about events in Paris, assuming that he would share the information with other members inside and outside the party and in so doing rebut the rumors that were rife in the Yishuv. Itche, he wrote, had taken on "a very difficult and very dangerous job, to be the deputy of the chief of Block number nine, a criminal." He had done so at the behest of his friends, who knew his talents from his service as their leader in the French camp.[54] To do this job he had needed "a strong grip on the unruly Jewish masses who knew that he was my son, and it required him to offer himself as a sacrifice in order to defend them . . . in accordance with the legend that they created about me." In other words, the prisoners had expected that Yitzhak Gruenbaum's son would be able to protect them in the camps just as the father had looked after their interests in Poland. Eliezer had to live up to those expectations.

He, as Eliezer's father, could not have acted in any other way, Yitzhak explained to his friend. "Without my presence, Itche would have remained alone, because the party turned its back on him out of fear of Jewish public opinion," he wrote. "Now it is neutral, but at the start it was entirely under the influence of the accusers." You have to understand, he urged, that "I have to be in Paris to defend my son's life and honor, which is also the family's honor. I am convinced that he is absolutely innocent of any crime, and the additional inquiries only confirm that opinion." Had he himself not come to Paris, he concluded, his son would have been lost—it would have been standard for a death sentence to have been handed down in such a case.[55]

On November 29 the court held a session in which Ballot offered Eliezer's lengthy response to his accusers. His opening statement at this stage in the proceeding traced Eliezer's life from his enlistment in the Spanish war through his liberation from Buchenwald, and placed his antifascist activity front and center.[56]

He ended with an account of Eliezer's time in Buchenwald: The underground there had established a commission of inquiry into his actions and, "after collecting about a dozen testimonies, ruled in Gruenbaum's favor, emphasizing the great work he had accomplished at Birkenau." Gruenbaum had taken part in underground activity, and when the Wehrmacht collapsed he was one of the leaders of the uprising at the camp. On April 11, 1945, he had taken part in cutting through the barbed wire during the liberation of the camp. That day he headed the Polish unit that scoured the area around the camp in search of fleeing SS personnel. The uprising, Ballot asserted, saved the lives of thirty thousand prisoners. While this number was an exaggeration, Ballot did not overstate the events. After liberation, he told the court, Eliezer had been chosen as a member of the committee representing the Poles. Ballot ended his presentation before the investigating magistrate with the following defense of Eliezer:

> There are few people who have to their credit a similar number of operations against the Germans, of heroism, of consistent resistance. Gruenbaum sought to aid his friends and save them, this in a situation in which so many, in the oppressive circumstances they found themselves, did not have the strength to think even about themselves. The limited number of beatings and blows . . . were necessary actions that saved human lives. [The following sentences was inserted in handwriting.] Gruenbaum did not select or kill prisoners. He acted ceaselessly in

> the interests of his friends against the Germans. [Here the typescript resumes.] Gruenbaum is innocent. It is inconceivable to see him in a French prison after years of incarceration and anti-Nazi fighting. He should thus be freed at once and the accusations of abetting the enemy dismissed.[57]

Even if it looked as if they had managed to stem the tide of accusations and that the French justice system was attentive to the counter-testimonies, Yitzhak did not cease his efforts to enlist more witnesses. He sought out in particular people who could testify about Eliezer's role in the underground. If he could obtain such evidence, he estimated at the beginning of December 1945, the case would be closed. On January 8, 1946, he again wrote to his family that, while there had been no breakthrough, the Polish embassy in Paris had obtained testimony from a member of the underground at Jawischowitz and from the man that Eliezer had "carried on his back [during the death march], so saving his life." Eliezer had mentioned this incident during his defense in the previous proceedings as well, but had never specified who that person was.[58]

At the end of 1945 and the beginning of 1946, more than four months after Eliezer's arrest, Marc Jarblum, himself a lawyer, and another lawyer who was offering advice, proposed a new idea. Perhaps it would be worth trying to persuade the Poles to transfer the trial to their country, where the milieu would be friendlier to Eliezer. After all, he was a well-known and long-standing Communist, and perhaps this would make it easier for them to prove that all he had done had been in the service of the party, Roman Frister writes in his book that the two attorneys pleaded with Yitzhak Gruenbaum to call the Polish embassy and to persuade its staff to request Eliezer's extradition. "The French will not want to refuse," they told him. "The request will only help rid them of a nuisance they don't need," Jarblum said. "And I know the process in Poland. The Communist Party Central Committee will never consent to the conviction of a longtime party member for offenses of this sort. It will not be comfortable for them to admit that the party placed its people as kapos and block chiefs in Auschwitz. They will prefer to acquit your son without a public trial." Furthermore, Jarblum said, Eliezer "wants to return to Poland. He has a great political career in front of him there."[59]

But their predictions did not come to pass. The Poles preferred to stymie any attribution of collaboration with the Nazis at Auschwitz to anyone associated with their party. The consul received Eliezer's father warmly and agreed to issue Eliezer a Polish passport that he could use to enter any country but Poland, but he said that extradition "is not in my power" and that an application should be made directly to Warsaw.[60] The Polish Communist Party had already expelled Eliezer from its ranks. It wished to wash its hands of him and others like him. The decision would not change later, when the idea of his return to Poland was again proposed.

On January 16, Yitzhak reported a new development, but opinions about its significance were mixed. The investigating magistrate and his staff had taken up the subject of whether the French legal system was authorized to hear Eliezer's case. Was France the proper place to examine the accusations against him? The reasons given were that Eliezer was not a French citizen, that the crimes he was accused of had not been committed on French territory, and that most of them, if they had indeed taken place, had been committed against people who were themselves not French citizens. What, then, was the legal basis for a French proceeding? But there was an unstated reason as well, a much simpler one — why should France and the French people, who had enough collaboration cases of their own to deal with, many of them much more severe than Eliezer's, volunteer or be volunteered to deal with Eliezer's case? In other words, the question was how his case could best be placed at some other country's doorstep. Perhaps, the legal authorities told Ballot, "the matter should be handed over to the [international] courts for war criminals that were then operating in Europe — the most famous being that in Nuremberg."[61]

That possibility alarmed the father. He was concerned on two counts. The practical meaning of such a step would be, at best, dragging out Eliezer's matter still further, with many more months of preparation and waiting for the results, not to mention considerable legal expenses. In the worse case, the nature and powers of the international courts were such that a trial could end in a severe verdict and sentence, up to and including death. Yet he was anxious about another consequence — moving Eliezer's case to such a court would, even in the case of acquittal, place him in infamous company that included senior Nazis and war criminals. "But our lawyers have already notified us that this idea was rejected already by the French authorities themselves," he wrote to his wife. Furthermore, "Itche's matter is close to its conclusion." The previous day, he reported, the lawyers had spoken with the attorney responsible for the proceeding, who had said that "he is leaning to ordering the case closed." A special committee would make the decision, but everyone was promising "that the decision will be made soon and will be to our liking," Jarblum promised. "Prepare champagne and a passport. Itche is on his way out."[62] This time, too, he turned out to be wrong.

The father's mood rose, but mostly fell, during his time in Paris. With all his love for his son, and even though he believed Eliezer's claims, he had heard him charged with horrible crimes. Among other things, he had learned that his son had an aversion to the name Gruenbaum and had made every effort to expunge any connection he had to his father and family and the bourgeois Zionism they typified. According to Frister, Yitzhak Gruenbaum's "mental strength eroded, his physical strength waned. His money was exhausted and his clothes wore out. His beard looked unkempt. He turned down invitations from Jarblum and other friends. He was infuriated by the sympathetic glances in his direction and the words of encouragement which, while they may have been sincere, were not persuasive."[63] He was outraged by the feeling that even his good friends were treating him like a leper and avoiding his company. Taking into his confidence his friend and former student Moshe Sneh, then commander of the national staff of the Haganah, the Jewish defense militia, Yitzhak later wrote that he felt

> a strange sense of emptiness around me, as if my friends, even those closest to me, are avoiding talking to me. I did not understand what happened. Now I know and I think that all of you, you in particular, chose the worst possible path when you did not tell me the things that everyone was talking about [regarding Eliezer] when I was not listening. I understand that it is difficult to speak with a father about a son who has gone so bad according to the stories, every single one of which has been disproven in my investigation, but you also need to think about the feelings of the person who walks among his friends and acquaintances as if everyone knows except him that someone from his family has died. I write this because I have been told that people spoke to you about revealing the secret and you could not, and I learned of it a few days after the beginning of the Congress [in London] from [Yaakov] Hazan and Jarblum, and I myself did not reveal the secret even to you.[64]

During his long, lonely evenings Yitzhak completed the manuscript of his book *In Times of Destruction and Holocaust*, his account of his own doings during the war, including what he viewed as the achievements and the failures of the Rescue Committee that he had headed.[65] He and his son were now being called to account for his actions and omissions.[66] He sent the pages to his assistant Hartman, who sent it on to the publisher. Yitzhak periodically updated Hartman, Hartglas, and sometimes Sneh as well, all of whom had been his students, assistants, and associates since his time in Poland, and also asked them to update him on the how Eliezer's case was being discussed in the Yishuv.[67]

While Yitzhak habitually concluded his letters by writing: "I do not want these things to become publicly known so I request that you not tell anyone," both he and his correspondents knew that this really meant the opposite. He wanted them to pass the information on to others who knew him and wanted to hear how they reacted, and in so doing about the public response. He knew that rumors were already spreading through the Yishuv.[68] He admonished his eldest son, Binyamin (Benio), of Kibbutz Gan Shmuel, to pay no attention to what people were saying, but then had second thoughts: "Perhaps there needs to be a response to the story." In another letter he shared his thoughts about his decision not, in the meantime, to visit DP (displaced persons) camps in Germany out of fear that "the Jews there are liable to take advantage of my appearance to demonstrate against Itche and that could worsen his legal situation." He scoured the replies of his three friends for indications of how people who were important to him were reacting. Being far from Jerusalem, caught up in complex and tragic personal and family circumstances, he could presume that some people would revel in schadenfreude and take advantage of the opportunity to get him out of politics. He had been in this position before, when Eliezer was first arrested for Communist activity in Poland.

He was incensed by those who called on him, explicitly or implicitly, to abandon his son and return to his public life in the Yishuv. A family friend traveled to Jerusalem to offer solace to Miriam, but also tried to persuade her to ask her husband to come home. Yitzhak was furious. "Who sent Mrs. Temkin to my wife regarding my return?" he caviled in a letter to Sneh:

> Why did she do such a thing, which is liable to cause a real catastrophe for my wife, in her condition? I cannot believe that any of you told her to go to Jerusalem to convince my wife to demand that I return, with the justification that if I don't come back I will not be able to continue to work in the Jewish Agency and Rescue Committee. Are they really talking about that as well? I do not understand what could have come over her to speak to my wife about all the accusations that are being falsely made against my son.[69]

Writing to his close friend Hartman, he sardonically remarked that

> following Mrs. Temkin's visit you also came to upset my ill wife? I never imagined that you would not understand. Do you think like Mrs. Temkin that I ought to abandon my son to his fate if I do not want to leave the Jewish Agency, or that they will compel me to leave it? I imagine that some people are saying that the father of such a son should not be a member of the executive. I never thought it possible that you and my friends would lend a hand to such an idea or that you would panic because that was being said. I would find the courage to do something even more serious were there any truth in the false accusations against my son. After investigating and conducting many conversations I have learned that everything that they have said about him, even the most serious people, especially them, is nothing but hearsay, is nothing but defamation and slander.

> I repeat my wife's request: if you believe me, you must help me search out witnesses who saw things with their own eyes and who know what happened at Birkenau. If not that, do not interfere, and especially do not speak to my wife about this regretful matter.[70]

Gruenbaum wanted to find out just how deep the cracks were in his public image. He had an opportunity to do so in September 1945, when Ben-Gurion and his wife came through Paris on their way to London. Gruenbaum asked Ben-Gurion to update him about the political situation. "Don't worry, everything is going as it should," Ben-Gurion said. "Do your work in Paris and return safely. I saw Miriam. She looks very well and her Hebrew is excellent." But he did not ask Yitzhak a single question about his son.[71]

Ben-Gurion again passed through Paris the following February, distraught and upset following a visit to two DP camps.[72] He had witnessed the lynching of a Jew suspected of having been a kapo.[73] Yitzhak wanted to share his dilemma with Ben-Gurion. He once again hoped that the leader would offer words of encouragement. He asked whether Ben-Gurion thought he had acted properly when he abandoned his public duties and devoted himself over many months largely to his son's defense. He asked whether it might be possible to establish a committee to determine whether he had acted properly. After all, he said, his case was not at all like that of Leopold Amery, the former British cabinet minister whose son had defected to the Nazis and was executed after the war for treason. He had looked into the case and found that his son was innocent. Ben-Gurion's reply, Yitzhak reported, was unequivocal: "He rejected me and demanded that I bring my son to trial before Jews. I refused." Two trials, by the Communist Party of Poland and the French, were enough, he bitterly told Hartman.

Ruth Kluger (Kliger) Aliav, a Ben-Gurion loyalist, was part of the European network of the Mossad LeAliyah Bet, the body that brought Jewish refugees from Europe into Palestine illegally, and the Department of Special Operations of the Jewish Agency's Political Department. She served as a staff soldier in the latter's so-called "parallel system," the covert special operations and intelligence effort to create and arm an army for the new Jewish state.[74] She did not like the way Yitzhak Gruenbaum conducted himself in his son's case. As she accompanied Ben-Gurion on his visit to the DP camps, traveling in the same train and car that took them from one camp to another, she was able to tell him what she had seen in the office in Paris.[75]

She had been unsure about whether to tell Ben-Gurion that Gruenbaum was in Paris in connection with his son's trial, she told her interviewers years later. She worried that it would burden Ben-Gurion unnecessarily, especially if he were to tell her to share with him the thing that she thought was unpardonable — the use of the Jewish Agency letterhead stationery for letters he sent on his son's behalf, and the use of Jewish Agency funds to purchase food that he had his Jewish Agency driver take to his son. She had the stationery hidden from Yitzhak, and when the Jewish Agency treasurer, Eliezer Kaplan, went over Yitzhak's expense account and asked about the outlays for food for Gruenbaum's son, she told him: "If you want answers, ask the members of the Agency Executive . . . or instruct them to pay out of their own pockets." She realized that, given Gruenbaum's state at the time, "ill and emotional," no one wanted to raise the issue with him.[76]

Aliav spoke of an incident that occurred during one of Ben-Gurion's DP camp visits:

> We arrived in Munich. . . . We sat in a room. . . . Suddenly there was a deafening noise. It was horrible . . . someone had apprehended a kapo — there were people like that, and began to beat him until he was bloody. And Ben-Gurion just sat there . . . and I got up and ran outside . . . and they caught another kapo and started meting out justice to him as well. It was an awful thing.
>
> Q: And he didn't emerge from the room?
>
> A: He sat there the whole time.
>
> Q: With his head in his hands? . . .
>
> A: I thought he might collapse. It lasted about two hours. He tried [to pull himself together], and I didn't know if he was alive or not. . . . He didn't move. . . . Then they fell silent [outside]. . . .
>
> And suddenly he got up and spoke about a fair trial. That only the Jewish people had the authority to do that. About trials in courts, with judges, not by everyone. I felt that he was choking and then — if you know this — his voice would somehow break. With a sort of falsetto. . . . I felt that he had been witness to a tragedy, of what Jews were capable of, and of what we had come to, or not come to.[77]

Yitzhak Gruenbaum carried on. Along with Ballot and friends and advisers in Brussels, Paris, and Warsaw, they tried to locate witnesses who would offer a different picture of Eliezer's actions. They found Julian Gottfried, Phillip Woutka, and Egon Isaak Ochshorn (Okshorn).

Gottfried testified that he had spent six months with Eliezer at Birkenau and had visited him frequently. He told the court that Eliezer's friends had asked the block commander to appoint Eliezer as room warden, so that he could prevent the theft of food, ensure fair distribution, and maintain solidarity. At that point no organized underground groups had been set up.

Eliezer moved to Block 4 and then returned. He established contacts with the Poles and Russians, organized a shoe repair workshop, and saw to it that the prisoners had clean laundry. His block was better heated than the other. When Kirszenbaum had come down with typhus, Eliezer took care of him in Block 9, although he died later, in Block 7. Eliezer, Gottfried maintained, had beaten prisoners only to maintain discipline and for the good of all the prisoners. No one had been sent by him to the gas chambers, nor did he have any authority to send people there. He had not tattooed prisoners — that was done by a group of experts. In March 1943, Gottfried was sent to Auschwitz, returning to Birkenau two months later. He and Eliezer maintained steady contact, and Eliezer gave him a pair of shoes when he saw him barefoot in the snow. He also gave him bread.[78]

Phillip Woutka testified next. He claimed that Eliezer had never sent anyone to the gas chambers and had never dealt mortal blows to anyone, only moderate beatings as needed to maintain discipline and to prevent more-brutal intervention by Konczal. Under his direction, Block 9 became the best block in the camp. Thanks to Eliezer prisoners had been spared having to stand outside for long periods in the rain and snow. The block was clean and heated. Food was carefully distributed. Prisoners repaired shoes and received undergarments, unlike in any of the other Jewish blocks. Eliezer had been beaten by the block commander and had also been punished with ten nights in the "standing bunker" when a wire cutter was found on him. He helped prisoners, especially those who had come with him from Beaune-la-Rolande. For example, he had Alex Gravinage transferred from a worse block into his own.

The third witness was Ochshorn, a Vienna-born Communist who had been imprisoned at Buchenwald, Dachau, Birkenau, and Gross-Rosen. He had testified at the Nuremberg trials. His deposition arrived from Brussels in the second half of February 1946. Through his contact with prisoners who had been there before him and his position as block clerk, he had amassed much information about events at Auschwitz-Birkenau,[79] where he spent the period from October 1942 to October 1943. He had met Eliezer at the beginning of February 1943, and they were in touch for eight months. He had never seen him beat a prisoner, nor had he heard of any such thing, and certainly not killing prisoners or sending them to the gas chambers. He knew that Eliezer had been active in the underground and in planning an uprising, and that he had been punished in the standing cell when he had been discovered with a wire cutter. Members of the underground did not put their trust in anyone who was not above all suspicion.

In February 1943 he and several other members of the underground asked

Eliezer to find a hiding place for Blass, the editor of a German Communist newspaper, who had been assigned to Block 7, from where he was to be sent to the gas chambers. A hiding place was found, and Blass was saved. At the time, there had been forbidden pamphlets and Polish underground newspapers in the room that Ochshorn occupied as block clerk. Eliezer visited him on a daily basis and regularly worked on manuscripts that were spirited out of the camp. Ochshorn had had full confidence in him.[80]

For obvious reasons, members of the underground made a great effort to cover their tracks. Some witnesses did not know about other aspects of Eliezer's "professional" identity in the camp. Ochshorn's testimony reinforced the impression that Szmulewski and Mink, who were well informed about the underground and Eliezer's role in it, had testified against Eliezer out of ulterior motives. Had they not had ulterior motives, they could have attested to his extensive underground activity at the camp, in addition to what they saw as his deviant character and actions they took exception to.

Despite all the ups and downs, it looked by the end of February and beginning of March 1946 that the chances were increasing that Eliezer would be released. Ballot took advantage of the defense counsel's right to sum up. He offered a detailed account of the evidence, in particular seeking to topple the foundation of the testimonies of Pakin and Gebet. He also sought to demolish the most serious of the charges — murder, homicide, and aggravated injury. He had to undermine the trustworthiness of the accusers — Pakin's testimony that Eliezer was responsible for the deaths of Kirszenbaum and Pinkiert, and Loberstein's testimony that Eliezer had killed his son and was responsible for the deaths of many others. The accusation that he took part, along with Tadek, in the murder of Dutch Jews, dissipated. Apparently the court accepted Eliezer's claim that the prisoner in question had planned to inform on the underground. That being the case, his killing was in line with the spirit of the underground's activity. We may presume that, had there been more solid evidence about this case, it would have been brought before the court.

After this opening, Ballot declared that the three major prosecution witnesses, Pakin, Gebet, and Zylberstein, all admitted that they had not themselves seen Eliezer commit any of the crimes they accused him of. On top of that, Loberstein's allegations were "confused." Pakin and his neighbor Gebet had offered only hearsay they had obtained from Zylberstein, who himself had not been an eyewitness, while Loberstein's testimony was full of inaccuracies. Goldstein, who played a key role in the stories told by Pakin and Gebet, completely contradicted their claims. Pakin himself, Ballot said, was "a miserable man who had suffered an attack of temporary insanity at Birkenau."[81] There was no basis for Pakin's accusation that Eliezer had tattooed him, and

Eliezer thus certainly could not have slapped him when he objected. Neither were there any grounds for the claim that Eliezer had designated people for the gas chambers. In Block 9, after all, he had been only a deputy of the block chief, whereas prisoners were not sent to the gas chambers from Blocks 20 and 30. Kirszenbaum had died of dysentery after recovering from typhus and had not been sent to the gas chambers, and at the time that Pakin placed Pinkiert's death, Pakin had no longer been in Eliezer's block.

Ballot put a great deal of effort into a methodical presentation of the falsity of specific statements made by Pakin. He passed up no opportunity to remind the investigating magistrate that Pakin had lost his mind in the camp and that his testimony "should not be given even the slightest credibility, given that his brain is subject to hallucinations and pathological fantasies." His accusations, Ballot stressed, were nothing but "a sorry fabric of contradictions." They were without validity, and they should not be considered in the verdict.[82]

Ballot shattered the claim that Eliezer had designated prisoners for the gas chambers, presenting every shred of relevant testimony to demonstrate the contradictions and inconsistencies in the prosecution testimonies. He cited Oléar, Szmulewski, Finkelkraut, Woutka, and Langman and referred the judge to the specific places in the court record in which their testimony showed Pakin's to be false. Even Goldstein, on whom Pakin and Gebet based their claims, had declared that he "knew nothing about Gruenbaum designating prisoners for the gas chamber." The accusation that Eliezer had done so was thus without foundation.[83]

In the same way he pulled the rug out from under the testimony given by Gebet, who had read out to the judge, under cross-examination, a composition on the appointments of camp officials. When the witness had been asked to be more precise, "there was a withdrawal of testimony," and he seemed not to know anything about Eliezer's appointment as "head of the prisoners," that is, block chief. Gebet had not been in Eliezer's block, and his entire testimony was hearsay. "The fact is," Ballot pointed out, "he knows nothing."[84] The same was true of Zylberstein, who had declared under questioning that "I never saw Gruenbaum beat anyone, or designate a man for the gas chambers, because I wasn't in his block." That being the case, "Gebet and Zylberstein, when pushed into a corner, had to acknowledge that their initial accusations were baseless."[85]

Loberstein's testimony was central. He had accused Eliezer of beating his son to death, and Ballot knew that he had to neutralize this testimony with great caution. He noted that Loberstein had made no mention of this accusation during his initial testimony to the police. Was it not odd that when he filed his complaint against Eliezer with the police, he had seen no reason, or had not remembered, to accuse Eliezer of killing his son? Loberstein had first made that accusation against Eliezer, Ballot noted, only a month later, during the hearing itself. Yet it was hardly a marginal matter that might simply have slipped Loberstein's mind. When he remembered to mention it, he had stated that his son had died of a beating administered by "Gruenbaum and others." But it turned out that Loberstein had been away with his work detail at the time and had not been an eyewitness to his son's beating. And Loberstein himself had said that his son had lived in a nearby block, not Eleizer's, meaning that there would have been no contact between the two.

Loberstein, Ballot continued, had testified that his son died of blows inflicted by a club, but not that the blows dealt by Eliezer had killed him. He had not mentioned how long after the beating his son had died, or whether he had not in the end, like others, been sent to the gas chambers. "It is certain that the younger Loberstein was not in Block 9, and there is not a single witness who recalls his death there, nor any incident in which he was dealt mortal blows." Ballot reminded the judge that none of the other witnesses had ever seen Eliezer beat a prisoner to death. The vague accusation regarding Loberstein's son, he concluded, had not a leg to stand on.[86]

"Gruenbaum can without a doubt state that the Jews, the group to which he belonged, had been brought to Auschwitz-Birkenau to die there," Ballot said. "That is the unfortunate truth, given that hundreds of thousands of prisoners could not withstand disease, or were sent to the gas chambers." But, he stressed, "Gruenbaum did not say to his friends, 'what good is it for you to eat, after all you don't have more than half an hour to live.' According to most of the testimonies, he worked hard to divide up food equally and prevent its theft. He denies that he used such words. Or it may be that they were nothing but an expression of the futility of all effort to survive in the face of Nazi brutality and the unceasing threat of the gas chambers."[87]

Most of the witnesses, Ballot noted, had said that prisoners were better off in the blocks in which Eliezer served, and that in this sense he had been "very effective." The fundamental question was "Was it a mistake to accept the position of head of the prisoners and clerk in Block 9 and later in Blocks 20 and 30?" French prisoners of war, he explained, had been held under the provisions of the relevant international treaties, living and operating under the command of fellow prisoners. A decisive part of the hierarchy to which they were subordinate was their own. The status of the other prisoners was different. "These positions were assigned, unfortunately, to criminals." It was "in the interests of the prisoners that their associates accept these positions wherever possible."

He quoted Paul Tilliard, a member of the left-wing underground who had been interred for two years at Mauthausen, from an article he had published, under the title "I Lived in the Nazi Hell," in *Ce Soir* on August 31, 1945: "The prisoners had an interest that political prisoners become kapos, that is supervisors over their comrades in the camp." In this way they could prevent prisoners from being assigned to work that was too harsh, could obtain additional rations, allow rest periods at work when there was no danger that overseers would see, help smuggle food in the barracks, and see to it that a volunteer was beaten instead of a friend whose physical condition meant that he was liable to die if he received such a punishment. The prisoners in Birkenau, Ballot declared, had preferred to have their friends in positions of responsibility, and Eliezer acted accordingly. His Jewish friends had persuaded him to be head of the prisoners, and he had not been the only one.[88] Ballot went on at length about the relatively good conditions in Block 9, using the prosecution witness Goldstein to buttress his claims. Goldstein had said that the block was heated in the winter, clean, that prisoners did not have to stand out in the cold for long inspections, that laundry was done, and that shoes were repaired.[89]

When he "gave mild blows and slaps," he did so to prevent theft, Ballot maintained. He noted Goldstein's testimony that he could avoid beatings when SS men were not around, and because there was no theft in Block 9. But Goldstein had confused cause and effect — the infrequency of thefts in Block 9 was not a natural situation but a result of Eliezer's actions. He forcibly prevented sick prisoners who had no strength to go to the latrines "from soiling with their urine and excrement the common food pot and the living quarters." He thus prevented the rest of the prisoners from infection and "the collapse of the weak ones." He mitigated "the deadly intervention of Konczal and his deputies, criminal prisoners," and prevented fights. As a result, the mortality rate in Block 9 was less than in other blocks. "He never gave beatings with a club on the orders of an SS man or criminal prisoners who were chosen for this purpose. They were the ones who imposed such punishments and other killings," Ballot stressed. Eliezer had compelled prisoners, including those who were ill, to report for work only when he had information that prisoners were to be collected for the gas chambers. He could not share this information with his comrades and fellow prisoners for fear that the Nazis would find out that he was sabotaging their plans, so they did not understand why he was forcing them to work. The depictions and analysis provided in most of the testimonies were consistent with what Eliezer had testified to previously.[90]

Ballot also offered a summary of all the times Eliezer himself had been beaten, in order to prove that he had not enjoyed any special consideration and to show that his life, just like the lives of the other Jews, had constantly been on the line. "In short, Gruenbaum was not a Nazi accomplice," he maintained. “He received the same treatment as that meted out to other prisoners.” Even as Konczal’s deputy, he had been compelled to take a night shift and stand outside in the cold, even immediately after his bout with typhus, before he had recovered completely.[91] The only possible conclusion, Ballot said, was that

> interventions by the head of the prisoners and block clerk on behalf of the prisoners were legitimate and in fact a duty. . . . Slaps and blows . . . that many witnesses believe were needed and even obligatory for the sake of the prisoners cannot be turned into an accusation of abetting the enemy. His attitude the entire time was anti-German, he was a fervent opponent of them and their actions. The men of the SS are those who need to pay for their crimes, not the martyrs who survived.[92]

There was no basis for the accusations of arrogance, or an unwillingness to speak Yiddish, which had been perceived as rejection of his own Judaism and contempt for the prisoners as Jews. He spoke Polish, Russian, and French, had studied Hebrew as a child, and knew German well, but he simply did not know Yiddish. Here and there he made use of German, which is close to Yiddish, in order to respond to those who addressed him in the Jewish language. He was indeed a secular Communist. In that he differed from some of the other prisoners, but when he did not speak Yiddish it was not because he scorned the Jewish religion or wanted to butter up the Germans and Poles. He simply did not know the language.[93]

Ballot wanted to end on a high note, so he saved his account of Eliezer’s underground activity and the Buchenwald proceeding for the end. “To conclude the rejection of the claims against Gruenbaum, we should remember that, because of the charges raised against him by several prisoners from Birkenau, a commission of inquiry was established by prisoners in Buchenwald camp,” he told the court. This commission heard the accusers and Gruenbaum, and “his position won their almost unanimous sympathy.” He “was cleared of all guilt and was permitted to take part in the covert work in the camp.” This was corroborated by an affidavit from Dr. David Landau, a prisoner at Buchenwald, who made his declaration at the health clinic at the settlement of Kinneret, Palestine, on October 16, 1945, and whose testimony was included in the defense’s documents and attached to the record of the proceedings in the preparatory court:[94]

> In December 1944, thousands of prisoners who were evacuated from Birkenau and Oświęcim and sent to Buchenwald. I worked for two years as a doctor in Buchenwald. I met Eliezer Gruenbaum among the prisoners who were evacuated

> from Birkenau and Oświęcim. . . . Some of his friends from Birkenau accused him of brutal behavior during the time he served as block chief. The underground committee of Buchenwald prisoners set up a special court to examine the case. They heard several witnesses and the accused, whose attitude won over nearly everyone's sympathy. The testimonies did not prove the charges and Gruenbaum was permitted to take part in underground work.

During the evacuation of Buchenwald, Gruenbaum helped prisoners change their identities and supplied them with refuge so that the SS and Gestapo could not find them, Landau had testified; Eliezer had been one of the commanders of the uprising aimed at saving thirty thousand prisoners. After liberation he conducted propaganda among the Polish prisoners so as to persuade them to return to Poland. He was a representative of Polish prisoners when officers in the Warsaw government's auxiliary paid their first visit to Poland. During his short stay there, Gruenbaum gained many friends, thanks to the trust in which he was held and his brave advocacy of the prisoners.[95]

Beyond being innocent of aiding the enemy in any way, Ballot said, Eliezer had done his duty by dealing out light slaps and blows at times. He had aided friends who lacked the strength and energy to think about themselves and had engaged in ongoing anti-German and anti-Nazi activities. He had fought in the Spanish Civil War alongside the Republican forces. Under German occupation in France, he had served in the underground, distributing anti-German leaflets in the Thirteenth Arrondissement in Paris. On April 1, 1941, he had been arrested for this activity and for his participation in the war in Spain.

He had continued to engage in "patient and persistent resistance" in Birkenau, Jawischowitz, and Buchenwald, and "witnesses know about Gruenbaum's efforts on behalf of his friends the prisoners in Block 9, but know less about his underground activity." The reason was that "the principal underground activists with whom Gruenbaum maintained contact were Poles and Russians who were, at present, after surviving, residing in Poland, Russia, and other countries, but not in France." Nevertheless, the defense had proved, with Finkelkraut's testimony, that Gruenbaum had attempted, along with Russian prisoners of war and the Polish-Socialist group in the camp, to organize breakouts. He continued to be active in Buchenwald, as testified by Dr. Landau and in the affidavits of a Polish party member, Michel Nazim, cited in an article he, Nazim, wrote, the translation of which had been certified by the Polish consul general. Had Gruenbaum acted dishonorably, "he would not have been one of the representatives of the Poles in the central underground organization in Buchenwald," Ballot emphasized.

"Gruenbaum did not volunteer of his own free will to serve the SS, which ran the Birkenau camp," Ballot wrote. "His actions did not in any way aid the enemy. On the contrary, it was a prisoner's struggle *against* [emphasis in the original] the enemy. Gruenbaum had been a prisoner who had carried on his anti-Nazi activity within Birkenau itself, as well as at Jawischowitz and Buchenwald, with consistent heroism." He had been under arrest in France since September 4, 1945. "It is time to stop and put an end to the detention of a person who was an innocent victim of the Nazis." Furthermore, it was improper for a French court to take up an accusation against a Polish citizen by another Polish citizen regarding actions that occurred on Polish territory. "I thus have the honor to request a firm verdict in this matter: Gruenbaum has committed no crime of aiding the enemy," he concluded.[96]

||| AT THE BEGINNING OF MARCH, Yitzhak Gruenbaum was starting to feel that the legal proceeding was winding up to his satisfaction, and that the only remaining open question was not whether Eliezer would be released but rather when he would be released and under what conditions. He thought that "when they free Itche and it will not be possible to go home immediately, Itche will go for a while to Switzerland, and I will quietly visit the camps." But by March 14, Yitzhak had lost patience. He wrote to his family that he wanted to bring his eldest son, Binyamin (Benio), to Paris and to return himself to Palestine, "but he [Yitzhak] felt sorry for Itche" because "he knew that Benio would not be able to do for him all the things that he [Yitzhak] has been doing."[97]

On March 20, 1946, the director of the War Crimes Investigation Authority in France issued a laconic legal notification to the Treatment Centers, citing sections of the French legal code, that it found no authority "to continue to pursue the Gruenbaum Eliezer case. French military courts that have the authority to judge war crimes cannot consider actions performed outside the country by a foreign citizen against other aliens."[98] This brought the French proceeding to an end. Ballot could close down the case with satisfaction and add Eliezer to the list of defendants whom he had saved from what seemed at first like certain conviction.

With Eliezer's release impending, it was understood that the quicker he could be gotten out of France the better. The longer he stayed, the more chance someone would appeal the ruling and thus delay his departure and even return him to jail. But, since Eliezer was a stateless man, getting him out of France was easier said than done, in particular after it transpired that the Polish consul general did not plan to keep his promise to issue Eliezer a passport. Another option was to obtain an immigration certificate from the quota held by the Jewish Agency. Eliezer qualified because the process of locating him and assigning him a certificate to rescue him from Europe had begun during the war, and this technicality could be used to answer any questions that might be raised. Yitzhak, with his senior position, could also cut through red tape. But putting Eliezer at the head of the line at a time when so many Jewish refugees were waiting to receive such certificates, and given the bad reputation that still pursued him, was liable to be condemned by the public. People could already be heard saying that "a certificate should not be wasted on Gruenbaum's kapo son." On top of that, there were persistent rumors that Ben-Gurion himself was opposed. He may have felt that allowing Eliezer to receive a certificate would be a blow to his integrity, since "he had never ever taken advantage of his position to obtain benefits for himself or his family, and he was determined not to violate that sacred principle now," Frister wrote.[99]

According to Frister, the first to document this story, Hillel Seidman, then the representative of Agudat Israel, the ultra-Orthodox party, in the Palestine Office in Paris, remembered Yitzhak Gruenbaum from his days as a Jewish leader in Poland. He heard the rumors about Eliezer in Paris, and while Gruenbaum was hardly a favorite of the ultra-Orthodox leadership, Seidman was touched by the tragedy of Eliezer's story. By chance, Seidman bumped into Yitzhak at a nearby café. Yitzhak was sitting alone, leaning on his table "like a man bearing the whole world's suffering on his shoulders. At one point it looked to Seidman as if he were crying." Seidman greeted Yitzhak in Yiddish, asking "Don't you recognize me? I'm Hillel Seidman from Warsaw." He asked Yitzhak if he could keep him company, and Yitzhak answered in the affirmative. Seidman spoke about Warsaw and shared with Yitzhak his estimation that Yitzhak's struggle against Agudat Israel had actually strengthened it. "Until you showed up, the rabbis never even dreamed about having representatives in the Sjem and the Senate," he said. Gruenbaum smiled and said: "You used that power to fight me and Zionism."[100]

Eliezer's case did not come up in this conversation, but Seidman suggested to Yitzhak that they meet again. "How about if we eat at Katz's restaurant tomorrow?" he asked. Gruenbaum agreed. The kosher establishment was located near the Pletzel, Paris's old Jewish quarter. Frister relates that the waiter brought Yitzhak a skullcap with his menu but that Yitzhak, loyal to his principles, turned it down. At the end of the meal Seidman asked if he could help Yitzhak or his son. Gruenbaum said he needed a certificate for his son. He presumed that Agudat Israel, like all other parties, had received a share of the certificates and that, like the others, it always kept a few to use in cases of emergency. Seidman realized that it was not at all easy for Gruenbaum, his sworn political enemy, to make such a request of him. He promised to bring the matter before his party's leaders and get back to him soon.[101]

Seidman went quickly to present the issue to Matthew Miller, the leader of Agudat Israel in France. Miller brought it up before his party's leadership. Felicia, daughter of Rabbi Moshe Schor from Warsaw, reacted angrily to the suggestion that a certificate be given to a "heretic." She handed out a leaflet signed by Eliezer, one of the ones that warned camp survivors not to be taken in by Zionist propaganda and called on them to return to Poland. "You want to allow such a man into Palestine?" she asked. But Miller exerted the full force of his office, and the proposal was approved. A certificate that had been assigned to Agudat Israel was put at Eliezer's disposal.[102]

Eliezer departed France with his father at the end of April 1946. He wanted to go to Poland, but Poland did not want him. His second choice was to remain in France, but France would not allow it. He had no other choice but to fly to Egypt and proceed from there by ship and train to Palestine. On May Day the Zionist leader and his anti-Zionist Communist son arrived in Jerusalem, the undeclared capital of the Zionist state-to-be.[103] Yet the rumors and accusations continued to pursue him and his family.

11 Jerusalem, May 1946–May 1948

WHEN THEY ARRIVED IN Jerusalem, Yitzhak asked his close friends to come to hear Eliezer tell his story directly. Sneh and Hartman accepted and arrived the next day, May 2. "[Yitzhak] Gruenbaum looked like a shadow of his former self, bent, pale, gaunt," Hartman recounted.

> Itche sat down with us and Gruenbaum said, "I want you to listen to him." He explained that he had accepted the position of kapo in Auschwitz on orders of the Communist Party, in order to save comrades. Jews who heard the name Gruenbaum in the camp thought of him as "Lord" Gruenbaum. They thought that if it was Gruenbaum's son, that he was their "rabbi." He didn't even understand what they were saying to him, because he barely spoke Yiddish. Sometimes he had to hit [prisoners] to save lives. Ironically he saved the life of Pakin, who assailed him in Paris, when he beat him before the Germans. They saw the blows and left him alone, otherwise he would have gone to the furnaces. He spoke of his attitude to the Jews who went to the furnaces without resisting, and that he tried to organize an uprising, but was not able to. We sat there for eight hours and listened. The upshot of what he said was that he had acted in accordance with the principle "I did what I did to save people, because had I acted otherwise there would have been many victims, so I hit people."[1]

Yitzhak then spoke with Jewish Agency treasurer Eliezer Kaplan. He told him Eliezer's story and about the Paris inquiry. Yitzhak asked Kaplan's opinion about whether he, Yitzhak, should resign from the Jewish Agency Executive. Kaplan did not venture to give an answer to this difficult question, suggesting that it be brought up before an unofficial meeting of several members of the Executive, who could discuss the issue and reach a resolution. Kaplan stressed the importance of making a decision in an "authoritative" forum. Otherwise, he said, "you'll never be able to remove this stain from the story of your life."[2]

The meeting took place the next morning at ten o'clock at Kaplan's house in Jerusalem. Participating, in addition to Kaplan, were Rabbi Yehuda Leib Fishman-Maimon and Dov Yosef. There is no record of other participants, and we have no way of knowing whether others were invited and chose not to attend because of the subject of the meeting. One hardly needed a special political sense to understand that the issue at hand was, in the context of the spirit of those times, a ticking bomb. Yitzhak Gruenbaum offered an account of the meeting to Natan Cohen:

> When I arrived with my son I already knew of all the rumors about him. I knew from my own investigations what was true and what not. The French did the same thing. They investigated and ruled: there is no crime in anything we have uncovered. If there are things that have not been discovered, a man cannot be held in jail until a new investigation begins. They freed him. I brought him to Palestine. . . . I asked my colleagues to convene and wanted to tell them about my son, how and why he had been freed, and to ask: if you say that it's not all right, I will resign. I could not remain on the Jewish Agency Executive if my son were to be found guilty. . . . Ben-Gurion did not come. I knew he wouldn't, and it made a bad impression on me. . . . Dov Yosef, Kaplan, and Fishman seem to have treated the whole matter seriously and listened to what I said. When I told them everything, Fishman was the one who said: "There's nothing that would justify your resignation in relation to your son's matter." So I remained.

On Frister's account, Kaplan advised against recording minutes of the meeting or listing it among the Executive's official sessions. Those present accepted the judgment of Rabbi Fishman, the principal if not the only speaker, that there was no cause for Gruenbaum to leave his post.[3] Frister presumes that Yitzhak turned to Kaplan largely because they shared moderate political views, but also because he thought that the treasurer was more likely than Ben-Gurion to evince understanding for his plight. Ben-Gurion did not attend because, just a few days previously, on April 20, he had set out for Cairo and London to prepare for the convening of the Anglo-American Committee of Inquiry on Palestine.[4] There is no way of knowing whether Ben-Gurion would have come to the meeting at Kaplan's apartment had he been in the country.

Yitzhak hoped to keep the meeting out of the public eye. While still in Paris he had given thought to the best way to do this, sharing his ideas with Hartman. When he arrived in Palestine and began his consultations with the members of the Executive, he learned that rumors about his son's actions in Birkenau and of the inquiries into his behavior were snowballing. The subject of Eliezer came up at a gathering of Jews from Białystok, and news of this was published in the press. Further stories about Eliezer were in preparation, Yitzhak discovered. He was told that, at the gathering, a new immigrant named Galchinsky had told about his experiences in the camps, including "the behavior of Gruenbaum's son." The chairman of the meeting asked him not to do so, on the grounds that "a special committee is looking into the matter and we should not address it until it announces its findings." Following this incident, Eliezer Leder, one of Gruenbaum's representatives on the Rescue Committee in Istanbul, and Zvi Kalmantinovsky, a leader of the Białystok group, spoke with Galchinsky to see if he had any evidence to support his claims. They concluded that "at best, he repeated only what he had heard from others, or made things up himself, no more than that."[5]

HaMashkif, the Revisionist Zionist newspaper, had received a letter about the accusations made against Eliezer at the Białystok meeting. It notified Yitzhak that it planned to publish the letter as well as an article about the charges it raised, and asked for Yitzhak's response. Yitzhak replied, asking the newspaper not to publish the letter and article. He told them about the inquiry in Paris that had cleared his son of guilt. The editors turned him down and asked again for a response from him to be included in their article. "Since here [in Palestine] there are *additional witnesses* who were *not* interrogated in Paris," they wrote (emphasis in the original), "we request that you forward us your comments as soon as possible."[6] They included a copy of the letter they had received:

> WHERE DOES JUSTICE LIE? A LETTER TO THE EDITOR.
>
> Yitzhak Gruenbaum has recently returned from eight months in Paris. Immediately upon his arrival a uniform communiqué was published in all the newspapers, saying that his son had been acquitted on all counts of murder and torture of Jews at Oświęcim.
>
> The writer of these lines was a refugee from Białystok who at the time printed a "letter to the editor" about a meeting that took place in the Keren Kayemet LeYisrael hall, in which a survivor of Oświęcim, Mr. Galchinsky of Białystok, spoke of the exploits of Eliezer Gruenbaum.
>
> The meeting was well-attended, and one person who was there was a man from our city, the author Z[usman] Segalovitsh. He listened to all the shocking descriptions that Galchinsky presented to the meeting. The extent of the shock made by Eliezer Gruenbaum's exploits can be gauged by the fountain of tears that flowed from the eyes of this writer. Suddenly — it turns out that he is ostensibly innocent, and as such that everything Galchinsky described is false. Just a blood libel against a pure and innocent soul. In this light, all the other survivors of Oświęcim who have confirmed what Galchinsky said are also fabricators. And poor me, who felt it my duty to denounce this scandal before

all Israel, am guilty, in this light, of making accusations of things that never happened.

So that I can confess my sin with a full heart, I hereby call urgently on his father, Mr. Yitzhak Gruenbaum, to bring a civil suit against all those who libeled his son.

According to Galchinsky, he is the man who has seen affliction by the rod of Eliezer Gruenbaum's wrath. By his account, thousands of Jews were tortured and killed by Gruenbaum. Such testimony was taken also from other survivors of Oświęcim. If all these survivors are fabricators and slanderers, they should be punished.

The Hebrew public in Palestine and in the world has no interest in having anyone suffer from false accusations, but it also has no interest that a person, even if the son of a good family and the son of saints[,] benefit from the merit of his father when his hands are stained with innocent blood.

Justice, justice pursue! Purge the evil from among you! These two principles are from our moral code.

The letter was signed "Sh. Levin, a refugee from Białystok."[7] We do not know if Yitzhak responded to the newspaper's second request. If he did, his answer did not persuade the editors. A few days later they printed Levin's letter verbatim. *HaMashkif*'s readers thus learned about the entire affair.

A few days later the response of the chairman and secretary of the Committee to Aid the Jews of Białystok wrote to Yitzhak Gruenbaum in response to the latter's inquiry. According to the letter, the organization did not have a man named Sh. Levin listed among its members. An inquiry had shown that the "refugee from Białystok" was Yitzhak Weiner, a longtime member of the Yishuv. "If we may believe him," the chairman wrote, "he wrote his letter out of a sincere feeling of 'justice, justice pursue,' but we are astonished by his lack of the courage to reveal his name and not to fire his arrows from behind the fence." The chairman and secretary further reported that "we do not have the power to take a position with regard to his [Yitzhak Gruenbaum's] son, but with regard to Galinchsky's testimony in general, we must note that in several matters regarding people from our city about whose fate we are very interested in learning, we took testimony from him [Galinchsky] that was later found to be baseless. There may have been no deliberate lie here but rather quite understandable imaginary delusions deriving from the hardships he has endured."[8]

But there was no stopping the surge of forged letters, signed with false names, being sent to the newspapers. Apparently fearing that the situation was likely to get out of hand and hurt his son and his family, Gruenbaum made another bad decision—he approached the Editors' Committee of the Journalists' Association and asked to be allowed to present the story from his point of view, to share with them the results of the French investigation, and to ask them not to cover the story. The editors considered his request and rejected it.[9]

The Gruenbaum family lived in an apartment at 7 Abrabanel Street in Jerusalem's Rehaviah neighborhood. It was a quiet, green side street a short walk from the buildings that housed the offices of the Jewish Agency and other Yishuv institutions. The apartment was one of many the Agency owned and rented out to its senior officials.[10] Yitzhak and Miriam suggested that he live with them, at least until he decided what to do. They made the same offer to Rivka, the wife of Eliezer's brother Yonatan, who was pregnant with their first child—Yonatan was still in Europe, serving in the Jewish Brigade, and Rivka was living on her own in Tel Aviv. Rivka was well-acquainted with Eliezer's story from the reports Yitzhak had sent to Miriam, but now she met Eliezer for the first time.[11]

Yitzhak hoped that Eliezer would undergo a transformation once he saw Palestine and became acquainted with the Yishuv, and that he would eventually decide to settle there. But he evinced no interest in Jerusalem or its society. He spent most of his days shut up in his room, working assiduously on Marxist studies of Jewish history—a continuation, as it were, of his graduate studies in history, in keeping with his ideological predilections. In the evenings he went out to walk his dog around the neighborhood. From time to time he visited the home of Berl Locker, a neighbor, friend of the family, and colleague of Yitzhak's on the Jewish Agency Executive. He liked to tell Locker's young son Dani bedtime stories. When the British evacuated Palestine in May 1948 and the bombardment of Jerusalem began, the Lockers' apartment was within range of the shells, and they moved in with the Gruenbaums. Dani Locker, who was five or six years old at the time, later recalled that Eliezer loved him very much and liked to seat him on his lap. Dani liked to stroke Eliezer's shiny bald spot.[12]

Despite the pall that hung over the family and its sense that Eliezer was not inclined to change his plans to return to the place he saw as his homeland, Poland, there were moments of joy, hope, and contentment. Eliezer had returned to his family, and, no matter that they had chosen different paths and ideologies, they were together. Rivka later recalled that the change in the father's face, bearing, and body language was palpable. His countenance had previously been tough, tense, and anxious. With Eliezer home, he became gentle and easygoing. The three brothers, she recalled, evinced great love for each other despite their differences of opinion, and the two others clearly admired the charismatic, intelligent, perceptive, and charming Eliezer. Furthermore, all three loved their parents deeply.

Binyamin, the eldest, and his wife, Ami (her full first name was Bat-Ami), had a daughter named Nurit, who was nine years old when Eliezer arrived in Rehaviah. Today she retains vivid memories of how much warmth pervaded her grandparents' house. She also remembers the many cats that the family kept. Nurit and her family lived outside Jerusalem, at Kibbutz Gan Shmuel. Eliezer wrote her letters in Hebrew — but in Latin script. He remembered the Hebrew he learned as a boy and was speaking the language fluently soon after arriving in Palestine, but he never learned how to write it.

At one stage, Rivka related, it was suggested that Eliezer join Gan Shmuel, the kibbutz where his older brother lived and then a bulwark of the Left. But neither Nurit, other family members, or members of the kibbutz recall any formal proposal of that sort being brought before any kibbutz forum. Neither do they recall Eliezer visiting the kibbutz.

Eliezer followed the Yishuv's political issues from the conversations he heard in his father's house, from news he heard from his father's friends and colleagues at work and in the General Zionist party, dinner table talk, and people he encountered on weekends. He could also hear his father's criticism of Ben-Gurion's policies, and as Ben-Gurion's position as leader of the Yishuv grew ever more beyond challenge, Yitzhak grew more frustrated.

A month or so after arriving, Eliezer saw his father arrested with most of the rest of the Yishuv's leaders during Operation Agatha, also called Black Saturday — an event that changed the Yishuv's view of the British. He also witnessed the debate within the leadership over the proper response to this drastic British move.[13] Furthermore, Eliezer could see that relations between the Yishuv and Palestine's Arabs were growing ever more hostile. But he chose not to get involved. There is no indication that he tried to make contact with any of the Yishuv's political forces, even the Communists. Perhaps he did not approach the latter because he realized that the local party would not see him as an asset, just as the Polish one did not. Or it might have been his certainty that he would never of his own volition make this place his home.[14]

One childhood friend, Sarah Stefania Poznański, managed to break through the social cordon that Eliezer had placed around himself. Stefa, as she was called, had also arrived in Palestine at the end of a long, difficult, and convoluted journey. She was the daughter of Shmuel Abraham Poznański, a historian and one of the world's leading figures in the study of the Karaite sect. He had also served as the senior rabbi of Warsaw's Great Synagogue.[15] She was now officially Stefa Rosenzweig, widow of Jozef Rosenzweig, scion of a wealthy Warsaw family; her husband had studied law before the war and worked as an attorney afterward. Young and pretty, Stefa was of independent mind and mismatched to the milieu in which she had grown up. At the age of seventeen she had fallen in love with a Polish officer and had planned to elope with him. Rumors of the romance reached her father, and he confined her to their home. Undeterred, she leapt out of a second-story window, but in doing so hit her head and thus aborted the elopement. She married Rosenzweig when she was twenty-one, and the two of them lived for twelve years between the two great wars as an aristocratic couple among the bohemians of Warsaw and Lwów. Their son was born when she was thirty-three. They called him Shmuel, after her father.

When World War II broke out, Stefa and Jozef joined the Polish underground. Rivka Gruenbaum related that they hid on the Aryan side of Warsaw and that Jozef smuggled arms into the ghetto. In 1943 they handed their young son over to a Polish peasant woman who had worked as a servant in the family home. Jozef died of tuberculosis at Bergen-Belsen. Stefa survived, ended up at a DP camp, where she asked to join her brother and sister in Palestine. She also began looking for her son. She arrived in Palestine in the summer of 1945 and carried on with her efforts to locate the boy in Poland and reunite with him.[16]

Yitzhak Gruenbaum and Stefa's mother were both from Plonsk, and the two families met again when they both lived on Tłomackie Street in Warsaw. Their children played together. When Stefa arrived in Jerusalem in 1945, she visited the Gruenbaum family. Yitzhak was in Paris at the time, trying to rescue his son. Stefa and Miriam together tried to understand Eliezer's condition from the reports Miriam had received.

When Eliezer arrived in Jerusalem in May 1946 and moved in with his parents, he met Stefa at their home. A friendship developed between these two lonely people, a friendship that metamorphosed into love. Rivka said that the two of them would tell each other of their lives late into the night. Gradually but steadily Stefa's spirits improved, and her feelings for Eliezer grew stronger. "She was happy, glowed with happiness," Rivka said. Stefa's sister-in-law, wife of her brother Adek, later related that "She was really blooming, she began a new life, it looked as if everything was going to work out." Miriam, Rivka recalled, viewed Stefa "as tantamount to a daughter-in-law, she loved her so much."[17]

Stefa had, upon her arrival, given her brother Adek the address of the servant with whom she had placed her son and asked him to obtain assistance in finding the boy and bringing him to Palestine. Yishuv officials indeed located him in a Polish village, living with the same faithful peasant woman. But she had become attached to the boy and refused to give him up. This was not an uncommon occurrence at the time. When the people handling the case finally managed to overcome her resistance, Shmuel, now eleven years old, was reunited with his mother. But three months later it became clear that Stefa was unable, both physically and mentally, to care for him, and after some hesitation she sent him to live on a kibbutz in the north. This third parting was one many children of survivors experienced after the war. She went to visit him from time to time, but then the War of Independence broke out and she was unable to get to the kibbutz. Eliezer and Stefa began to talk of marriage, and were determined that after their wedding they would bring Shmuel back and establish a family. Stefa was almost forty-four years old, while Eliezer would soon turn forty.[18]

||| ELIEZER KEPT A DIARY during the time he spent in prison in France and afterward when he lived with his parents. It is an unusual document. Few people who served in official positions in the concentration camps wrote about their pasts. Even fewer did so this soon after the war and this directly. He used his diary to struggle, piercingly, with the dilemmas he had faced. He (or those who edited parts of it for publication) called the diaries *In the Death Zone*.

> All of us must have seen, at the cinema, the scene of a passenger ship sinking at sea. There is panic on deck; women and children first; a crowd of people mad with fear, pouncing on the lifeboats; the ability to think vanishes. Only one desire remains — to live! And standing by the lifeboats are officers, pistols in hand, holding back the mob, and shots are heard.
>
> We lived for days, weeks, and years on the deck of a sinking ship. The convoys arrived each day and dumped huge numbers of new people on deck, all imbued with one ambition — to live! Panic would break out at every opportunity — rescue, life. Perhaps an extra bowl of soup would serve as a lifeboat, or a better shoe, or another shirt.
>
> And we, the officials, would stand by the cauldron of soup as if by a fountain of life. . . . Otherwise there would have been famine in the camp. You could feel hunger on a full stomach as well. It did not gnaw away at the stomach but at the entire human being, at all the thoughts and feelings of a man who stands face to face with the risk of dying of hunger. People died of hunger on a daily basis, in front of everyone. Each person knew that he, too, would die of hunger. Therefore, eat at any price! We did not dole out milk — we doled out life. Another liter of milk meant another two or three days of life, additional strength for work, and therefore fewer beatings. It can provide strength during a selection for the gas chambers, a sense that tomorrow might come — who knows? Perhaps tomorrow people will be chosen for a better *Kommando* and will search for experts. Anything but to be a *Muselmann*.[19]

In such circumstances the kapo or other concentration camp official played the role of the captain in a sinking ship. It was his responsibility to maintain order, to give prisoners a sense of security against the arbitrary whims of the strong. Once, Eliezer related, when rain began falling at about 10 a.m., the *Kommando* teams were sent back to the camp in the early afternoon. But the kitchen had already divvied up the soup according to the work details, not according to blocks. The details assembled in front of the blocks and began to hand out soup to their members, as if they were still out at work. Among the smaller group, those that had twenty to thirty members, the food was distributed quietly and in good order. But in the larger groups it went out of control — prisoners who had already received their rations pushed into line to get an extra portion, while those who had not yet eaten feared that they would be left hungry. Soon all hell broke loose.

> Everyone jumped on the cauldrons — those who had not received their rations out of fear that if they waited quietly there would be no soup left for them, and those who had already received theirs in order to take advantage of this rare opportunity to get a double portion! They massed around the kettles. . . . People collected spilt soup from the ground, in which hundreds of feet had stomped, and slurped it. One man was toppled into the pot, and when he emerged soaked in soup, with pieces of potato and beet stuck to his coat, 700 crazed people ran after him and licked the food off him. Only a few stood aside. Half of them did not receive their meal that day.

Frequently, Eliezer wrote, "those assigned to bring the cauldrons from the kitchen would spill soup on the ground so as to be able to lick it up and for once eat their fill." Another dilemma was to whom to give second portions when something remained at the bottom of the pot.

> The worst was the matter of second portions. A thousand hungry people! Just 30–50 liters to dole out. A line? You today and him tomorrow? And can you be sure that you'll be alive three days from now? Today vegetable soup with gruel and tomorrow fodder beets. Today, only today!
>
> The dishing out of the soup went quietly, but now the battle over the remainder begins. Who will get seconds? . . .
>
> I tried different methods. Distributing the soup according to a list of young people, also choosing just by looking who needed it most. I also tried using a line. It didn't work. You could make speeches, shout, plead. But, as the French say, "a hungry man's ears are blocked."[20]

Once, while seconds were being handed out, a commotion broke out and Eliezer slapped a young man who was pressing forward toward the pot with all his might.

He looked at me with such sorrow and despair, without anger or resentment, so that I didn't know where to hide. I ladled soup into his bowl. His eyes brightened with absolutely stellar joy. But twenty empty bowls were immediately presented to me. . . . I put the ladle in a friend's hand and fled.

Have you ever seen people whose final thought and last word before dying is "food?" Have you ever seen dying people, expiring with a happy smile on their faces when you put a chunk of bread in their hands that they no longer have the strength to lift to their mouths?[21]

In the end, he wrote, "The extra portions had to be handed out with a stick in hand. Jesus managed to divide two loaves of bread among thousands. Two loaves and five fish without a stick, but they were satiated, the evangelist writes."[22]

The apologetic effort involved in writing these entries, write Galia Glasner-Heled and Dan Bar-On, show what a profound need Eliezer had to justify his actions, quite beyond his need to escape punishment and the legal authorities. He wanted to restore his legitimacy, his place in society. He wanted people to believe that he had done only what was necessary to ensure that not all the people getting on the lifeboats would die simply because no one was willing to stand by the rope ladder and keep order.

Once I was ordered to do a job in the camp. I had to collect people to work. The SS man who ordered me to do the work went with me to the famous Block 7, in front of which more than two hundred *Muselmänner* lay, sat, and kneeled in the mud, a listless clump of human beings drained of all their strength and cast aside by the Hitlerist machine. They were waiting to be sent into the block. "Choose 20," the SS man said. "But they can't move," I tried to protest. "What? They can't move? Take a look!" A sentry brought, at the SS man's command, several pieces of bread and the SS man began throwing them into the crowd. It's impossible to describe what happened then. No one who hasn't seen such a thing could believe or imagine it. Had a film director staged such a scene, you would say that it was a tactless, unpleasant exaggeration. What is stuck in my mind is a supine human skeleton. He didn't have the strength to move, he didn't have the strength to open his eyes. He simply extended the bones of his hand upward and wiggled his fingers in the air as if he were waiting for a miracle, for a piece of bread to fall into them. Have you ever seen how one dying man strangles another dying man and tears from his mouth half-chewed bread mixed with spittle? I have seen it, and not just then.[23]

The diary returns again and again to hunger, shoes, clothing, hygiene, and the way the Jews went to the ovens like lambs to the slaughter. For a long time he could not understand this, Eliezer wrote. After all, "no one can comprehend it. Why? Why doesn't a single person rebel? After all, he'll die either way!" People tried to explain it to him: "One reason was the Jews' natural cowardice." But Eliezer found that unconvincing: "Aryans," he asserted, "would behave exactly the same way." Another explanation that he heard was that those designated for death were too weak to resist. But that could not be the case: "In 1943–1944 all a man needed to be selected for death was a rash or a pimple." So that was no explanation for why, at that time, when the people being sent to the gas chambers were not feeble, when they were not scarecrows with no life left in them, merely empty shells, as Primo Levi and other survivors would later term the *Muselmänner*, they did not rise up against their oppressors. The truth was, he wrote, that going quietly to one's death can be an expression of self-respect. Sometimes he heard, from the trucks taking prisoners to the gas chambers and crematoria, the sounds of the "Internationale" and "Hatikvah." In general, however, prisoners went to their deaths passively, in "apathy and despair." It was something he never succeeded in understanding. He was making the same claim he had made earlier in the party inquiry, if in a more temperate way.[24] He wrote that in January 1944 some eight hundred Jews were selected for the gas chamber. They were put together in two formerly empty blocks. Two unarmed sentries, prisoners like themselves, were stationed in each block. There they waited for two days for the Gestapo's political department to sign off on the death list. True, each of the men knew that he was forbidden to leave the block. Each one knew that a breakout would not accomplish anything. After all, there was still the electrified barbed-wire fence, the guard towers, and the rest of the warning and reinforcement system. But there had been successful attempts to break through those defenses. Storming out of the block and over the fence would have been a desperate act, but there was at least a tiny chance of succeeding. Waiting for the trucks meant certain death.

> I went in among the doomed men. Some of them were lying on their beds—sleeping or too weak to move. In the corners and the spaces between the beds groups of worshippers stood. Some of them approached me, asked that I notify their friends. They deluded themselves into thinking that some sort of intervention could still save them. Some of them asked to now be repaid for the portions of food that they had at various times given to friends. Some approached me and cursed me . . . others shouted: "We wish you success, you'll be our avenger!" A group of children, about fifteen or sixteen years old, stood in a corner bawling. An elder French man came up to me and said: "Say something to the children, lie, but calm them down, for God's sake!"

> I don't know what happened to me. My nerves reached a breaking point. Unconsciously, apparently, I was resentful, intensely resentful of those people who were going to their deaths without any thought of resistance. I burst into a speech or shouts, I don't remember exactly what I said, but I know that I shouted that I would not lie, that I would not deceive them about their fate, that I wouldn't calm them. "You want to delude yourselves up to the last minute! You don't want to look your bitter fate directly in the eye! Who is guarding you here? Why are you sitting quietly? Am I or that kid [one of the four prisoners who were guarding the two blocks] stopping you? Don't you know what you should be doing?" At the beginning of this speech of mine, they gathered around me and listened attentively. Heads rose from the beds. But when they realized what I was talking about they took their distance from me, each one to his own corner. In a minute I remained alone in the middle of the block. A cold, listless quiet prevailed. I stopped in the middle of a sentence and took out a cigarette. A head rose from a nearby bed. "Leave me a bit." I tossed him the cigarette and went out into the hallway. No one informed on me.[25]

Hope had a paralyzing power, Eliezer maintained. The illusion that things would work out eradicated any chance of rebellion. It also divided those who believed that their fate was sealed and they had nothing to lose from those who thought that hope of surviving the war was not lost. "Why did they go that way to their deaths?" Eliezer wrote. "After all, they knew where they were going, why did they go without resisting? After all, they had nothing to lose!"

The Nazis understood very well the value of illusion, Eliezer wrote. From time to time the Gestapo would start false rumors, especially just before a selection, or when their informers sensed subversive tension in the camp. They would tell the prisoners about German defeats at the front, about Italy's expected capitulation, about the Allied invasion of Europe, and so on. On the eve of mass executions or during times of breakouts, the camp leaders would speak before the Poles and Russians, imbuing them with hope, or would suddenly distribute to the Jews letters from Belgium or France indicating that immigration certificates to Palestine could be obtained for prisoners in the camps, or letters from relatives full of encouragement and optimism. The rumors were intended to give hope to those who remained after a section, to widen the gulf that separated them from those destined for the gas chambers, and thus to make it easier for the killers to continue to carry out the exterminations in peace and quiet.[26]

In this way, he added in his diary, the camp administration undercut what little chance there was for the success of the escape operations that he had been involved in. In 1942 he and his collaborators — he did not name them —

made contact with a Polish prisoner and a Polish civilian who worked in the camp who were prepared to help organize a breakout. The prisoner came from the same town as the civilian, and everything was ready. But at the last minute the contact prisoner pulled out. "It's not worth the risk," he said. "The war will be over in six weeks, and we'll somehow get through that period." Two months later he was sent to the gas chambers, another "victim of hope."[27] What stands out here is how difficult it was for Eliezer, who viewed himself as a fighter, an underground operative, an activist, a man who took his fate in his own hands, for better or worse, to understand the paralyzing passivity and debility that he described. He offered his readers a complex range of explanations, but fundamentally he disparaged and condemned them all.

He explained the rationale for his own actions in his diary just as he had done in the legal proceedings. But in his diary entries he had more time to order his thoughts, to analyze, polish, and sharpen his points. He did not hesitate to acknowledge that he had made mistakes, that he had behaved in some of the ways he had been accused of, but he rejected any suggestion of criminal culpability. In this he was consistent. That had been his position in both the Polish and French proceedings, in the latter with the help and advice of legal counsel. In the diary he offered a more appalling account of the dilemmas he faced and of the hell of the camp, as if to counter those who would judge him, to say, let's see you judge a person who lived and acted in that nightmare world. As far as he was concerned, his time in the camps was just one segment of a life devoted to fighting for justice on the side of the weak. Even at Birkenau, he wrote, he had had the audacity to do his duty to the prisoners, in the face of their tormenters.

We don't know what he wrote in the rest of the diary, but the passages that were published make it clear that despite some inconsistencies and incongruities in his line of argument and his explanations, he defended himself ably and fluently. This was not apologetics. He wrote defiantly and candidly and clearly believed his entire story, even its weak parts. Glasner-Heled and Bar-On argue that writing the diary enabled him to unburden his heart and free himself of the weight he carried, to try to gain justification and legitimacy, to help readers break through the obstacles that prevented others from understanding his world. They also claim that the diary reveals a range of his ways of coping with the horror he had lived through. His style varies as he attempts to grapple with sometimes contradictory dilemmas. The diary, they write, contains "complex emotional ambiguity — strength along with weakness. Openness and honesty alongside denial. Vulnerability and surprising sensitivity alongside toughness and rigidity. Refinement along with truculence toward his readers. This complexity of course reflects the situation," they write. But, they add, it also reflects his personality: "A man in which all these oppositions live together, a man of extremes, a man of poles."[28] These contradictions make the fundamental question all more acute: Who were you, Leon Berger?

Despite his romance with Stefa and his family's descriptions of the closeness they felt to him, Eliezer continued to feel that the Yishuv was not his society, Palestine not his country, Zionism not his dream. This may explain his father's efforts on his behalf during two emotional visits he, Yitzhak, made to Poland in 1947, the first from February 24 through March 7, the second from September 22 to October 12. News of his arrival spread quickly through the Jewish community, and he received an emotional welcome at gatherings organized in places where many Jews lived.

Some 150,000 Jews resided in Poland at the time, most of them repatriates who had returned after fleeing to the Soviet Union. A minority were survivors of the Holocaust. Immediately upon his arrival in Warsaw, Yitzhak asked to be taken to the remains of the ghetto. He had met some of the leaders of the uprising for the first time in London in 1945. He spoke to the Jews about their lives in the Diaspora, about the Land of Israel, about what had happened to Jews around the world during the war. He disputed those who accused the Zionists of profiting from the catastrophe. Despite all that had happened, he proclaimed, the world remained unwilling to recognize the right of the Jewish people to their homeland. The emancipation of the nineteenth century had solved the problem of the individual Jew, he said; the Jews of the twentieth century had to fight for a national solution. He always concluded his speeches with an emotional call for *aliyah*, immigration to Palestine.

His agenda included meetings with members of the Polish cabinet and the leaders of the Polish Workers Party, the official name of the Communists. Among other things, he used these talks to lobby for Polish support for the establishment of a Jewish state. The pro-Zionist speech later made by Ksawery Pruszyński, a member of the Polish delegation to the United Nations during its discussions of the future of Palestine at the UN's temporary home in Lake Success, New York, was the outcome of two developments. Poland first had to be instructed to make such a speech by its "big sister," the Soviet Union. Second, the Polish government had to be convinced that it was in its own interests to do so. The enthusiasm of Pruszyński's eventual speech is attributable in part to Yitzhak's efforts during his trips to Poland.[29]

But Yitzhak did not just engage in the Yishuv's public affairs. He also lobbied for his son. He continued to seek out witnesses who had known Eliezer in the camps and who could offer a positive account of his actions there, testimonies that could challenge the conclusions of the earlier party inquiry and its decision to expel Eliezer.[30] In parallel, he spoke with senior Communists who had served with Eliezer in the party and the underground. There had been many Jews in the party leadership before the war, and those who remained alive following Stalin's purge of its leadership and ranks now held key positions in the Polish party apparatus and government.

Yitzhak told them of his ongoing efforts to obtain testimonies that would clear his son of turpitude. He probably informed them of the outcome of the French investigation, but what he stressed was Eliezer's wish to return to Poland and participate in the "building of socialism." Abraham Rosenman relates that Gruenbaum was received respectfully and politely by Polish leaders, who asked him to convey their greetings to Eliezer, but when it came to the possibility of Eliezer returning to Poland as a rank-and-file member of the party, the answer was no.[31]

The fact that he needed the goodwill of Poland's Communists did not mitigate Yitzhak's penchant for saying exactly what he thought, even if in doing so he angered his hosts. At one of the receptions organized during his trips he told a member of the Bund that he, Yitzhak, had been the only person who had dared to write in *Ha'olam*, the official newspaper of the World Zionist Organization, about the murders of Heinrich Ehrlich and Victor Alter. The two victims were members of the Bund who were executed on the charge of being counterrevolutionaries during the purges that Stalin conducted during World War II.[32] No one in Poland dared pronounce the names of these two men in public. At a meeting of representatives of local and district Jewish organizations, Yitzhak told of the attempts to rescue Jews from the Holocaust, and their meager success. In the course of doing so he told of a last-minute appeal he made to Roosevelt, Churchill, and Stalin just before the Yalta Conference of February 4–11, 1945, in which he demanded that they bomb the death camps and their access roads. He related that the American and British leaders had sent him hypocritical and evasive responses, adding that "the third one did not deign to answer."[33] But the Communists' refusal to allow Eliezer to return had nothing to do with Yitzhak's behavior. It was a product of their view of his actions and the fear that any association with him and what he represented would mar the party's image. The documents that Yitzhak showed them, both during his visit along with others he later sent, were brought before a party oversight committee. Eliezer remained a persona non grata in Poland.[34]

Gruenbaum thus returned empty-handed. It seems improbable that he had intervened on his son's behalf at his own initiative. Presumably he agreed to do so, with all the personal and public implications it had — only in response to repeated pleas from Eliezer, and after the father became convinced that his son had no intention of remaining in Palestine. Eliezer's determination indicated great alienation from the cause to which his father and the rest of the family's enthusiastic Zionists had devoted their lives. Even the chilly and humiliating treatment he was receiving from his Polish homeland and its Communist leadership did not moderate that alienation nor his zeal for resuming his life in the country of his birth.[35]

By the autumn of 1947 it was no longer possible to ignore the growing suspense surrounding the upcoming debate over the future of Palestine in the UN General Assembly. Jerusalem was already under siege. As a professional revolutionary, Eliezer was especially sensitive to the tension in the air, and as a veteran soldier he could catch the scent of gunpowder. He had always believed that when war came no one should sit on the sidelines. Even though he had no intention of making his home in Palestine, at the beginning of 1948 Eliezer began, apparently with encouragement from his father (whether that encouragement was mild or vigorous, we do not know) to look into enlisting in the Yishuv's armed forces. There may have been another reason as well — living up to an unwritten agreement with his father. His father had promised to do all he could to enable Eliezer to return to Poland, but on condition that if he did not succeed, Eliezer resign himself to giving up that dream. A revolutionary through and through, living in a proud and pedigreed Zionist home, as part of mobilized young Yishuv society, Eliezer could not do otherwise but join the fight.[36]

But the enlistment authorities turned him down. Rumors that spread through the Yishuv in the months that followed indicated that the military did not want in its ranks a man who bore the stigma of having been a hated kapo in Auschwitz. Following World War II, many refugees and survivors from the Holocaust had arrived in Palestine, and such people constituted a large part of the Yishuv's fighting forces. But the Yishuv ethos could not accept that kapos who had helped run the German camps could be heroes. Eliezer did not make the grade, and it is hardly surprising that no one had time to listen to him or others like him.[37]

But he did not take no for an answer. Yitzhak realized that he would have to pull some strings. Only an order from high up would enable his son to enlist. He spoke to Shimon Koch (Avidan), who had commanded the Palmach's German Platoon (made up of Jews of Aryan appearance who could penetrate behind enemy lines) during World War II, commander of the Palmach's First Battalion and from December 1947 the commander of the Givati Brigade. When

Koch did not help he tried another contact, one that was more embarrassing for him. Frister relates that, just as Yitzhak set aside his self-respect in Paris to plead for the assistance of Hillel Seidman of Agudat Israel in getting an immigration certificate for Eliezer, he approached Ben-Gurion and asked him to order Eliezer's enlistment. This time Ben-Gurion acceded. At the beginning of May 1948, Eliezer joined the Jerusalem People's Guard as a private.[38]

12 Ramat Rachel, May 21–22, 1948

THE PEOPLE'S GUARD RESERVE, to which Eliezer was attached, was one of the units that took part in the battles of southern Jerusalem.[1] The force was called up on May 15, the day British rule came to an end and the armies of Iraq, Egypt, Syria, and Transjordan invaded Palestine. Over the course of the next seven days the unit performed guard duty in the city. On May 22, when the situation worsened at Ramat Rachel, a kibbutz on Jerusalem's southern boundary, the IDF command decided that a People's Guard detachment under the command of Menachem Richman would relieve a force that had retreated from the settlement.

Ramat Rachel stood on a hill that overlooked the Jerusalem–Bethlehem road. When hostilities broke out, it found itself at the tip of an enclave, surrounded on three sides by Arab settlements and forces. To the south lay Bethlehem, to the east the village of Sur Baher, and to the west the village of Beit Safafa and the Mar Elias monastery, which served as a forward position for the Egyptian army. Only a narrow corridor connected the kibbutz to the Jewish neighborhood of Arnona and, beyond it, to Talpiot. This corridor would, within hours of the commencement of hostilities in the area on May 15, turn into the battlefield on which the force led by Richman — "Richie" to his soldiers — would fight.

On Saturday, May 15, a day after Israel proclaimed its independence, Arab forces began shelling Ramat Rachel. The shelling continued for the rest of the week that followed, alternating with attacks by ground forces. At 4 p.m. on Friday, May 21, heavier bombardment began.[2] Residential structures, the food supply warehouse, the school's dining hall, the bakery, the hayloft, and the livestock enclosures were badly damaged. Large numbers of cows and chickens were killed, their bloody and twisted carcasses scattered around the barn and the rest of the settlement.

Under cover of the barrage, an Arab force of 250 approached the kibbutz and prepared to attack. The kibbutz's defenders — its residents and the military unit that had been sent there to reinforce them, returned fire, and the Arab force retreated. By 10 p.m. the defending force reported twelve dead, major damage to the kibbutz, and fires. Some of the men defending the settlement — inexperienced reservists with little training and no combat experience — were suffering from shell shock. They were not communicating and were unable to fight.[3]

The attacking force consisted of three separate units. One was an Egyptian army detachment of eight hundred soldiers that had arrived from the south. It had separated from its mother unit that had advanced along the coast, attacking Ashkelon, the kibbutzim of Negba and Nitzanim, and reaching Ashdod. The second component was a company from the Sixth Battalion of the Arab Legion, the army of the kingdom of Transjordan. This force had been called in to secure the British retreat from Jerusalem but had not returned to its base in its home country. The third component was a collection of five hundred irregulars, some of them from the nearby Arab towns and villages, which had received arms and training from Arab Legion officers. In addition to rifles, this combined force was equipped with heavy weapons, including 3-inch mortars, four 3.7-inch cannon, and armored personnel carriers, including two that had just recently been captured from the Jewish defenders of the Etzion Block. The force also had two antitank guns and several tanks.[4] The commander of the Egyptian detachment, Colonel 'Abd al-'Aziz, headed the combined force. That the irregulars and the Arab Legion men were willing to accept the authority of an Egyptian commander was unusual in this war. Without first coordinating with the Arab Legion command in Ramallah, to which he was hostile, the Egyptian commander resolved to attack Jerusalem from the south. The first objective was to take Ramat Rachel.

On Saturday, May 22, at first light, the bombardment resumed and intensified, lasting until 8 a.m. The kibbutz's internal and external communications lines, as well as its electrical system, were damaged. At 11 the Arab force began shelling again, densely and continuously. Some of the charges were incendiaries. At 12:30 it stopped, allowing the defenders to see that, under the cover of the bombing, Arab troops had been able to position themselves just one hundred yards from the fence. On the south and southwestern sides the outlook was even worse — two Arab squads had penetrated the kibbutz itself. The defenders threw grenades that hit the attackers and forced them to retreat, but the general feeling was that the situation was deteriorating. The local commander tried to regroup his forces but discovered that the fighters on the western sector had abandoned their positions and gathered in the dining hall, while the untrained and unequipped squad had retreated to Talpiot.[5]

Even before the retreat from the western sector, the bombardments and the injury and damage they caused sapped the morale of the eighty kibbutz members who were defending the settlement. They called for urgent aid and reinforcements from the Jerusalem command. Some of the defenders talked of abandoning the kibbutz. The staff's operations log is full of both kinds of messages. The regional commander wanted to send a runner to Jerusalem headquarters to describe to the officers there how the situation was worsening. Under the conditions of battle, no one was willing to volunteer for the mission. He thus decided to go himself, ordering his deputy, a man who lacked the proper training to lead troops, to execute an orderly retreat if the ground offensive renewed. Once he arrived at headquarters, the regional commander was able to impress on his superiors just how grave the situation was. They began to organize reinforcements without yet knowing that western-sector defenders had given way and retreated to Talpiot without informing their comrades fighting on the eastern side. They learned of this only once the reinforcing force was ready to set out.[6]

At 2:50 in the afternoon the shelling turned heavy again. The remaining defenders were able to make out dozens of Arab troops preparing, under cover of the bombardment, for an attack from the west, from the direction of the Mar Elias monastery, while others were advancing from Beit Safafa under cover of the terraces that lined the hill below the kibbutz. Under the circumstances, and after learning that the defenders of the western sector had retreated, the remaining Jewish fighters retreated in the direction of Arnona and Talpiot.[7] In their dash through open territory they were easy targets for Arab snipers, machine guns, and the armored vehicle, all deployed at strategic locations. The fleeing defenders dodged one source of fire only to encounter another.[8] An entry in the operations log of the regional command at 3:25 p.m. states that the Arabs had broken through into the kibbutz. Another entry at 4:02 p.m. states laconically, "They have taken Ramat Rachel." Further entries say that Arab forces entered the kibbutz and that villagers from Sur Baher and Beit Safafa entered the kibbutz and looted it, taking whatever they could find, including the cows and chickens that had survived the shelling.[9]

The Road to Ramat Rachel, May 22, 1948: 1400 Hours

Ramat Rachel was a point of vital importance, located on the top of a hill overlooking the road that ran from Hebron through Bethlehem to Jerusalem. But its fall was more than a strategic loss — it was a blow to the morale of the Jewish fighters defending Jerusalem and to the fortitude of its besieged population.[10]

Today, our picture of the battle is deficient. We have soldier testimonies, memoirs, and a few newspaper reports written at the time, as well as studies covering the events of the days surrounding the action at Ramat Rachel. But these do not provide a precise account of what happened. Attempts by combatants and the families of those who fell to find out more about what their comrades and sons experienced in the battle, along with the efforts of scholars and journalists, have failed to produce unambiguous answers to the many questions the battle raises. While there is, in fact, documentation that could cast light on the stories of the defenders killed that day and fill in the gaps about what happened, the Israel Defense Forces Archives make these papers available only to the families of the fallen and to their designated representatives. Despite the unique moral and public significance of Eliezer's story, the archive refused to make an exception to this policy for the purposes of the present study.[11]

To the best of our knowledge, the Moriah Battalion's regional reserve, the force that assembled that morning outside the Ta'amon Café, was called up to help defend Ramat Rachel when the situation there grew grave. There was no better-trained force to call in. The soldiers were taken by bus to the southern edge of Talpiot, where they conducted observations of the terrain they expected to cross. The soldiers were briefed, their gear checked, and they prepared to set out.

They began to move south toward the kibbutz in the late afternoon, through the wadi below Arnona. They could see Jerusalem on its hilltop to their north, billows of smoke rising from buildings that were in flames. The force was led by a "sandwich," an armored pickup truck of Haganah manufacture. According to another account, the soldiers covered this territory in the bus that had taken them to Talpiot, which does not seem logical. Eliezer and some twenty other soldiers rode in the armored vehicle, along with Company Commander Richman and the driver. Everyone in the armored truck, even those who were not seasoned fighters, knew very well that the vehicle was an ideal target for the enemy as it trundled slowly, in full daylight, through terrain covered by enemy forces. The rest of the force proceeded on foot.[12]

Before long, the Arab troops, dug in at commanding points over the Israeli force's path, commenced rifle and machine gun fire. Antitank cannon and ballistic shells were also fired at the advancing men. Soon there were casualties. One shell scored a direct hit on the armored truck, halting it in its tracks and wounding some of its passengers as well as some of the men walking alongside and behind it. The regional reserve had been virtually destroyed.[13] The battle report stated that Richman was among the twelve men killed by a shell. Another source states that a bullet penetrated the vehicle and hit Richman in the heart. Shlomo Havilio, the battalion's deputy commander, said in an interview with a researcher for this book that "the truck took a direct hit by a shell, and when the force got out Richie was killed." Ya'akov Nitzan told us that Richie, his brother, had been hit in the abdomen inside the armored car; his intestines came out and he held them in his hand until he was evacuated to the home of Hugo and Elisheva Boyko, agronomists and pioneers in the field of ecology, on the southern reaches of Talpiot. He died there. Eli Vald and Ze'ev Rivlin, who both also rode in the armored truck, also spoke of how Richman and the driver were hit.[14] The authors of the battle report wrote that some twenty-five to thirty soldiers were wounded that day, and that at the time of the report's composition some of the dead and wounded were still in the field because it was impossible to send in men to retrieve them.[15]

A report written sometime later was more generous. It states that Richman's force set out toward Ramat Rachel in the late afternoon, by bus. Along the way it was hit by a shell. Men were injured and the force could not proceed. At that same location a truck used by the People's Guard that had abandoned Ramat Rachel's eastern sector and was making its way toward the city was also hit. Most of its passengers were killed or wounded.[16] Eliezer was the force's machine gunner, a position he received after he told Richman that he had combat experience from Spain. Compared to the rest of the soldiers in the force, he was an experienced veteran.

The Road to Ramat Rachel, May 22, 1948: Late Afternoon, Evening

That Saturday morning, Eliezer had stood with the group of soldiers waiting on the sidewalk outside the Ta'amon Café. He and his companions had then been driven to the edge of Arnona and Talpiot, from which point they had set out for Ramat Rachel. Their armored truck was hit a short time later. Richman, their commander, was mortally wounded. Other soldiers were also injured, among them machine-gunner Gruenbaum.[17] He took a piece of shrapnel in his jaw; Ben-Hanan, a journalist who wrote an account of the battle, said that Eliezer's face was covered in blood. After being evacuated from the damaged vehicle, Eliezer took cover and returned fire. The Arab attackers were at a distance that only the machine gun could reach in an attempt to silence the sources of the offensive barrage.[18]

One of the accounts of the incident states that someone grabbed the back of his shirt and called out "It's over, we need to retreat." Because of his injury, Eliezer lost consciousness, and "when he woke up from his faint the sun was already setting. Quickly looking around, he realized that he had been left alone in the open field. With his remaining strength he turned and began to crawl northward on all fours, toward the first row of houses, about 500 meters [about a third of a mile] away. Suddenly his bare head rose, glistening in the sunlight, the drone of the bullets from the southeast intensified, and it sounded to him as if wasps were seeking to make a nest on the back of his neck. He could make out the edge of Rehaviah [*sic*],[19] with its red-roofed houses. A bullet lodged in his neck and cast his body forward. His Via Dolorosa came to an end."[20]

It is a vivid account, but it is not clear on what sources it is based.[21] Were the soldiers in Eliezer's force equipped with helmets? If they had helmets, how would Eliezer's bald pate have glistened in the sun? At what angle was the sun during the battle and in the afternoon, and how was Eliezer's body oriented toward the sun? These are exasperating questions that could be ignored, were the answers to them not likely to disperse some of the cloud over the causes of his death.

On the Israeli Ministry of Defense's official memorial website, the text on the page devoted to Eliezer is based on material from the 1950s. It tells of his brief service in the Israel Defense Forces and the circumstances of his death. The material posted there is written in close cooperation with the families of the fallen soldiers and thus must be read as an official account agreed on by these two parties, the family and the ministry:

> At the beginning of the War of Independence, he reported for service in the People's Guard, and when the fighting intensified he volunteered for active service. His military experience, sound judgment as an older man among younger ones, his friendliness, and his self-discipline, his justification of the inadequacies in supplies caused by the conditions of the emerging country's army in formation, and the good humor with which he made his comments all did much to raise his company's morale. For the most part he served as a machine gunner, and also served temporarily as a deputy squad commander. . . .
>
> On May 22, 1948 a concerted attack was made on Ramat Rachel and the defenders were desperate. Eliezer volunteered to set out with the reinforcement platoon and took his machine gun with him. On their way from Talpiot to Ramat Rachel in an armored vehicle, the vehicle was hit and the company commander was killed. Eliezer was the first to jump out, covering his comrades' retreat with his machine gun. He was hit in the cheek by shrapnel and continued to shoot and to cover them. He refused to be carried by his fellows and continued to move back at a crawl, rose up, took a bullet in his head, and fell.[22]

In an account he wrote in 1964, Yitzhak Gruenbaum claimed that Eliezer had also taken part in the battle of Katamon, that he had done guard duty at various points in the city, and that he raised the spirits of his fellow-soldiers:

> When an armored car was sent to Ramat Rachel he asked to go along. Another soldier also wanted to go, so they drew lots and my son won. He was very

pleased. In the approach to Ramat Rachel they encountered an Arab ambush, which opened fire and hit the armored car. The commander was killed. My son was also wounded as he covered the group with his automatic weapon. During the retreat, toward an abandoned house in the area, my son suddenly reared up and at that moment a bullet hit him in the head and he fell.[23]

Yitzhak offered a similar story to an interviewer. His son, he said, had been sent with a group of soldiers to relieve Ramat Rachel, which was under heavy attack. "The armored car was only a few hundred meters from the kibbutz. When the Arabs noticed it they opened fire. The commander was killed and progress was impossible. The soldiers exited the armored car and my son operated his machine gun. He was wounded a few minutes later and the entire group, along with him, began to approach, at a crawl, a house that stood nearby. But they could not remain there either so they went out and crawled again, to a more distant house. Along the way my son got up, for some unknown reason, and was immediately hit by a deadly bullet."[24]

According to Roman Frister, Yitzhak Gruenbaum's biographer, Eliezer fell in battle after sustaining two wounds. He first took a hit in the cheek, and was then hit again as he crawled away from the damaged armored vehicle. Frister does not say what caused the injuries. He tells his readers that he was permitted to view Eliezer's personal file, in which an entry for May 22 states:

> Armed with a machine gun, he went to support the Israeli forces at Ramat Rachel. On his way from Talpiot to Ramat Rachel, the convoy of armored vehicles was shelled. The company commander fell in battle. Eliezer covered the retreat of his comrades with machine gun fire and continued to fight even after being wounded in the cheek by shrapnel. When he tried to withdraw at a crawl, he was hit again and died on the spot.

Frister makes no mention of a bullet in the head, nor does he say whether Eliezer's file contains an injury and death report.[25] The entries on Eliezer in two memorial books put out by the Ministry of Defense, *Yizkor* and *Gevilei Esh*, as well as later interviews from the 1960s, cite no source for the circumstances of Eliezer's death or of the additional information they contain — that he was the first to jump from the damaged vehicle, that he refused to allow his comrades to carry him, or the reason he got up when he very well knew, as a battle-tested soldier, what the consequences of standing erect under fire would be.

We thus have at least two versions of what happened. In one he was killed when hit by a shell, while in the other he was shot in the head (or, according to some accounts, in the back of the neck). What is the significance of these differences, and what are their sources? Could it be that they are not accidental variations?

Rumors soon spread that Eliezer had been shot by Jews in revenge for his crimes as a block chief at Auschwitz-Birkenau. The battlefield, in these accounts, was just a way of covering up the fact. A survivor serving in the same contingent and who recognized him found an opportunity to take revenge—perhaps with the help of others. It was said that the rumors first appeared at the time of his death, and that similar claims were made in broadsides pasted up in Jerusalem's ultra-Orthodox neighborhoods, as well as in the tabloid *Iton Meyuhad*.[26]

Glasner-Heled spoke with Frister, with the journalist Gershon Hendel, and with an official at the IDF Archive. All of them claimed that the rumors were baseless.[27] According to Uriel Ben-Hanan, a journalist who wrote about Eliezer,

> The people who were there in the Ramat Rachel battle all testify that the story is malicious and fabricated. They stated this categorically. . . . A reconstruction of the battle leaves no doubt as to the way Itche died. Shlomo Havilio, later a member of Israel's foreign service and then deputy commander of the southern sector of "Operation Pitchfork" [also known as Operation Kilshon, the joint effort by the Haganah and IZL to capture British facilities and to connect isolated Jewish neighborhoods in southern Jerusalem], the man who sent Richie and Eliezer on their mission, said: "That kid should have received a medal. What bravery! What spiteful gossip. If such a thing had happened, wouldn't I have heard? What do they want from him, they should be ashamed of themselves, they are spilling blood."[28]

Eran Turbiner, who produced a comprehensive study of the battle, spoke with Ya'akov Nitzan, Richie's brother, who said "I have dealt with the subject for years, examined the material in the IDF Archive, and have found no reference [to such a story]." Nitzan told Turbiner that he had a hard time believing that "under conditions of battle and the dispatch of the armored vehicle that someone would think of doing such a thing." Reinforcing Ramat Rachel was a suicide mission, he said, and he wondered how his brother, a very level-headed person, had agreed to it. He said that the armored vehicle was made of tin and that several men, Gruenbaum among them, were killed when a shell hit it. "There was no radio set in the armored car," he said. "The platoon commander disappeared. There was total chaos."[29]

Nitzan told us that Richie did not even know the soldiers who set out for Ramat Rachel on May 22, and that he was assigned to the mission only at that moment. Nitzan said that he did not know who took command of the force after his brother fell. He supposed that the rumors that Eliezer had been "liquidated" were "nonsense spread by the ultra-Orthodox, who wanted to get back at the father, Yitzhak."[30]

Turbiner also spoke with Havilio, deputy commander of the southern Jerusalem sector. While Havilio arrived at the site of the battle only late in the day, he knew that "it's nonsense, who could think about such things." In battle conditions "there was no way . . . no one could have planned something."[31]

Gavriel Tsifroni, then a correspondent for the newspaper *Haboqer*, told Turbiner that he visited the battlefield that same day. "All the rumors about a Jew killing him are baloney," he said. "At the time of the incident no one said anything [like that]." Ze'ev Rivlin, who was in the armored vehicle with Eliezer, said that in his opinion Eliezer was hit by the artillery shell. "We had met each other a week, ten days before it happened, there were really brave boys there. Eliezer was a very serious guy and I admired him a great deal. I remember that he read all the time, that he spoke about Spain where he had fought with the Brigade, but he didn't say anything about Auschwitz and I'm hearing from you for the first time that he had been a kapo."[32] Shalom Dror, Richie's battalion commander, also said that he never heard the rumor surrounding Eliezer's death and that in any case "it doesn't make sense that there would be an assassination — the attitude toward kapos was negative, but they didn't carry out assassinations."

Eli Vald, who also rode in the armored vehicle, told us that he, like Eliezer, had only been in the unit for two weeks. Itche, he said, was an introverted type who did not speak much with people, perhaps because he didn't know Hebrew well. On their way to Ramat Rachel they "took a shell. Richie, the company commander, was killed, and the leg of the driver flew off. Everyone who was still alive jumped out of the car and was called to take a position." He didn't remember if they returned fire, perhaps "because they were in an inferior position," and "there was chaos after the death of the company commander and there was no one to impose order." Itche "got out of the armored car with his machine gun (after the shell hit) and even though they told him to stay down and crawl (so as not to get hit), he continued to advance erect. Then he was hit and died."[33] Yehuda Lapidot, who commanded an IZL force that fought at Ramat Rachel at a later stage, and who afterward studied the battles, said, "That whole story is rumors. No one could confirm it. It was known that they didn't like him."[34]

Some years after his son's death, Yitzhak sought out Eliezer's fellow soldiers and asked them to recount the battle and disprove the spiteful rumors. Yosef Ami, commander of Region 4 at the time of the battle, came to his aid. He located some of the men and inquired about the rumors.[35] Ami also met with Ya'akov Eshed, who had served as commander of the southern Jerusalem region.[36] Eshed, Ami said,

> went to Talpiot a few days after your son fell. Your son's company belonged to the battalion that Eshed commanded. I asked him if he ever, during the fighting, had heard a comment from anyone, or any sort of rumor, snide remark, or gossip regarding the circumstances under which your son fell, and his response was that throughout the period of the battles he had heard nothing. He knows that your son fell in the battles at Ramat Rachel inside an armored car hit by enemy artillery. I asked him if he would be prepared to confirm this testimony in writing, and he said that he would do so eagerly if you ask him.

Ami took this testimony very seriously, principally because Eshed had become acquainted with the story of the battle as a member of the team that wrote the IDF's history of the War of Independence in Jerusalem.

The studies indicate that the force prepared for battle hastily. They note that the force's commander was brought in at the last minute, that he had no acquaintance with the unit, and that the unit itself had been cobbled together from men who were not fit for such a battle. They also indicate that evaluations of the risk to the force, moving as it would by light of day in a targeted area, was mistaken. Neither was the vehicle they were assigned appropriate for the mission. Similar situations were common on other fronts as well. The testimonies also show that the first strike at the relief force for all intents and purposes destroyed it. The nature of the unit, with its inexperienced men, its inability to function after the loss of its commander in the first volley, and the dysfunction of its other commanders led to a state of total disarray.

The resulting confusion could have stymied any premeditated plan to strike at Eliezer, but it could also have served as the perfect cover for such an act. The hurried manning of the force, just before it set out for battle, could have made it difficult for a person who planned to shoot Eliezer to have an opportunity to do so, but it certainly does not rule out the possibility that a man who knew him from the camps, one who by chance encountered him in these circumstances, might resolve to kill him at the first opportunity. Such a coincidence might be unlikely, but it is hardly fantastical.

If a man did indeed take advantage of this unique set of circumstances to get rid of Eliezer, he would not necessarily have advertised what he had done. Yet given the ideological and emotional charge of such an action, he might in fact have done so. The spirit of a standard fighting unit would not tolerate one of its members shooting another in the back, but if such a thing were to happen, the unit's men would have good reason to keep the matter a secret until their dying days. But it would be very difficult to keep such a secret for so long, especially in an improvised unit in which the men did not have long-standing ties. So such a secret might well come out in the end.

On the one hand, it seems illogical that a soldier in the unit would deliberately kill his unit's machine gunner, the one man who could respond to the strafing that the force was receiving from the enemy. On the other hand, it may well be that logic would not be in play when a former concentration camp prisoner had a chance to take revenge on a man he viewed as one of his oppressors. The testimonies are not sufficient to decide the question of how Eliezer was killed. Even after all that has been said and written about the case, no one can prove whether or not he was liquidated under cover of battle. What we have are four possible and contradictory stories.

According to the first, Eliezer fell in battle, killed by enemy fire. In the second, he was murdered by one of his fellow soldiers in his unit. In the third, he behaved suicidally because he could no longer take the pressure he had been living under. He had in fact hinted at such a possibility in letters he wrote to Polish Communist friends involved in the Polish party inquiry. Perhaps he decided that he had nothing more to live for, given that no one seemed ready to accept him. He was astute enough to understand that, given the atmosphere he had felt in the Yishuv — an atmosphere that would continue in the newborn State of Israel — no one would accept him for the foreseeable future. He might have preferred a hero's death to a life of mortification.[37] A fourth version combines the previous two. Just before setting out for battle, his comrades may have placed the proverbial pistol on the table — that is, they may have indicated to Eliezer that his end was near and that he could take advantage of the opportunity to die as a hero and clear his name. Eliezer may have taken advantage of the battle to meet his death.

||| ELIEZER FELL IN BATTLE in the late afternoon of Saturday, May 22, 1948. His father spent that morning at an improvised airstrip in the Valley of the Cross in Jerusalem, waiting for a light aircraft to take him to Tel Aviv. He was scheduled that evening to sign Israel's Declaration of Independence, after the fact and along with other important figures who had been unable to take part in the official signing. But when the plane finally arrived it was unable to take him, and he was assured that he could board another plane that was scheduled to land minutes later. That plane never showed up. He would later say that it turned out for the best that he missed his trip to Tel Aviv. Instead, he went home, and was there that evening when emissaries arrived with the news of his son's death.

Yitzhak and Miriam were told that their son had fallen on the way to Ramat Rachel.[38] No one else was in the house at the time, and the emissaries went on their way once they had done their duty, as protocol dictated. Frister relates that the couple sat in silence. Yitzhak tried to write something but set it aside, and Miriam, according to Frister, told him, as if reading his mind: "Don't think that, Took [her pet name for her husband]. It's not your fault." Yitzhak did not respond; "And what could he say?" Frister asks. "How could he pass judgment on the vagaries of fate? Was he supposed to believe that it was written in heaven? What might have happened had he not moved heaven and earth to get Itche out of jail in France? Maybe he would still be in prison but alive?"[39]

Keta Kol, wife of their neighbor, friend, and Yitzhak's party colleague Moshe Kol, told Turbiner that her husband and Yitzhak went to the hospital to identify the body. They easily found him among a large number of bodies of men killed in the day's fighting, thanks to his signature bald head. She did not remember Moshe telling her anything special about the wounds Eliezer had incurred. Perhaps he had not said anything, not wanting to trouble her any more than necessary. A bullet wound to the back of the neck could have destroyed part of the face. In researching the present work, we were unable to gain access to Eliezer's death certificate and thus to find out whether it includes any details about the nature of the wound.

Frister relates that, as soon as news of Eliezer's death began to spread, the telephone in the Gruenbaum home did not stop ringing. Friends wished to offer their condolences. Because of the battles, and the blackout ordered for security reasons, people did not go out on the street at this hour.

Rivka and Yonatan, who were living in Tel Aviv, received the news by telephone. Rivka related that her father-in-law told her that, after receiving the news, "they closed up the apartment. They didn't want to see anyone. They spent three days alone in the house, fasting, they barely ate, crying on one another's shoulders. The only person they allowed in was Stefa."[40]

The rumors reached Stefa while she was doing the evening shift at the hospital where she worked as a substitute nurse. She ran to the Gruenbaum home. It was close to 8 p.m. when she got there. She knocked on the door, and Miriam opened it. The two women fell into each other's arms. Yitzhak sat in the living room. When he heard the voices he got up, approached, and invited Stefa to sit with them, to mourn and be consoled. Stefa refused.

Other details about what happened at that time come from fragments of things that other members of the family later heard from Yitzhak and Miriam. What is certain is that Stefa returned to her apartment on Ben-Yehuda Street, about a ten-minute walk from the Gruenbaum apartment on Abrabanel Street. Her brother Adek was waiting for her there—he had heard about Eliezer and knew that his sister would be frantic and in need of support. Third- and fourth-hand reports offer some indication of what they said to each other, and indicate that, like Eliezer's parents, Adek did his best to calm Stefa. Stefa, according to these accounts, felt that she had no strength to begin again and that nothing could console her. Brother and sister agreed that they would attend the funeral together, once they learned when it would be held.[41]

A short while after Adek left her, Stefa Rosenzweig killed herself.[42]

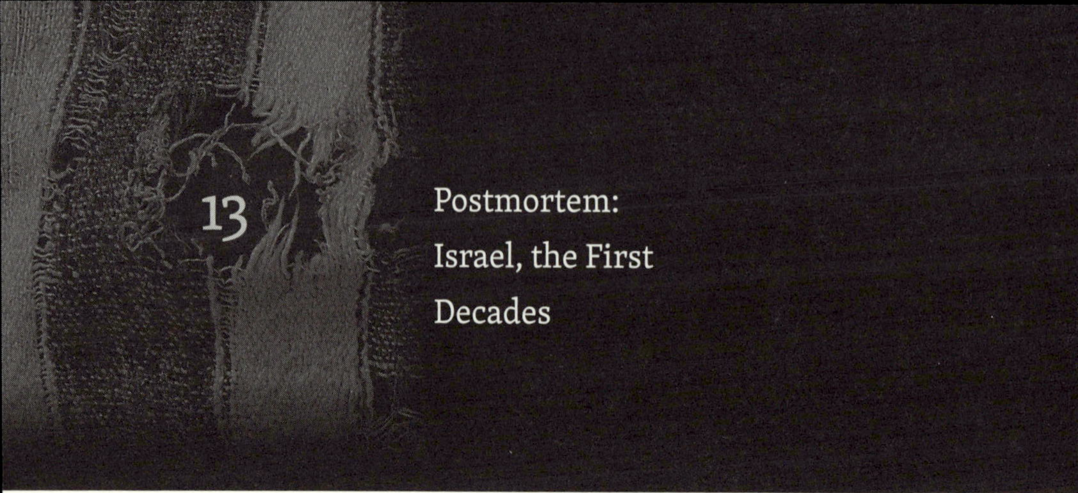

13 Postmortem: Israel, the First Decades

FOLLOWING ELIEZER'S DEATH, his family sought a way to honor his memory. The family of every fallen soldier feels this need — creating a memorial to a son who fell in battle is an integral part of how parents and siblings cope with their overwhelming sorrow. It is also an important part of the way that the society that sent the soldier into battle constructs its communal ethos. This was especially the case for the new State of Israel. Its people viewed themselves as reliving the divine command to Abraham: "Get you out of your country . . . to the land that I will show you, and I will make of you a great nation." They saw what they believed as the great promise of their future as inextricably linked to their history in their ancestral land, to which they were now returning and settling following a bloody War of Independence with its myriad acts of personal and collective heroism.

The Israelis who took up the question of how the nation should honor its fallen looked both to Jewish tradition and to the ways other countries memorialized their soldiers. It was an especially difficult task because Israelis were still mourning their dead from "there," from the Holocaust and World War, when they suffered new losses "here," in their new home. The task was also complicated by the fact that the fallen came from a multiplicity of ethnic groups, cultures, traditions, and languages. The new country had to rapidly forge a consensus about an issue that was laden with profound pain. It needed a concept of the proper way to establish physical memorials — headstones for individuals in cemeteries and monuments to groups of soldiers on battlefields. And ways needed to be found to provide for the spiritual side of memorialization — for example writings about the fallen and memorial anthologies. These discussions took place both on the level of the government and in civil institutions, such as the kibbutz movements, among local authorities, and as part of spontaneous initiatives by writers and intellectuals.

When Eliezer's body was moved from the temporary cemetery at Sheikh

Bader to the official military cemetery in Jerusalem,[1] his new resting place was marked with the standard headstone. But the family sought a further way to perpetuate his memory. Three national and literary projects to memorialize soldiers had taken form while the war was still being fought. The most important was the book *Yizkor* (Remember) — the name is that of the traditional memorial service for the dead. It contained biographies and photographs of 4,797 of the approximately 6,000 Israelis who fell in battle. The first volume was published in 1955 by the Ministry of Defense.[2]

The second literary project was *Gevilei Esh* (Scrolls of fire), an anthology of works written by 455 of the fallen, published in three volumes between 1952 and 1961. Of the men and women memorialized in the book, 367 were either native-born or had come to Palestine prior to 1939. Another 77 had arrived between 1940 and 1947; only 11 had arrived in 1948. Many were officers, and only 37 of them had less than an eighth-grade education.[3]

Gevilei Esh received much more attention than did *Yizkor*. It style was more vivid and captivating, and it was, by nature, less repetitive than the other work. Some of the soldiers included were excellent writers. The overall impression was that they were the best of the best.

A third project was *Levavot Dovevim: Avot ʿal Banim sheNaflu* (Speaking hearts: Fathers on sons who fell), an anthology of pieces written by the fathers of the fallen, published by the IDF publishing arm *Maʿarachot* in 1957. The writers were largely men who had long lived in the Yishuv, including the fathers of some of the most prominent figures memorialized in *Gevilei Esh*.[4]

Private memorial projects produced a literature that formulated what has been called "the melting pot of Israeli collective memory," an authentic and spontaneous expression emerging from civil society, voicing its agonies, doubts, and aspirations.[5] As with *Gevilei Esh*, this genre was devoted by and large to the Sabra, as native-born Israelis were called. One example was *BeHayeihem: Klil Demuyot miMilhemet haShihrur* (In their lives: A wreath of figures from the War of Independence), a work devoted to the native-born, edited by the poet Anda Amir and illustrated by an artist and beloved author of Hebrew children's books, Nahum Gutman.[6] Another example is the memorial erected at Netaʿim, a *moshav* (semi-collective farming village), emblazoned with the motto "To our sons! Your heroism is seen as a legend and the people sing your glory."[7] Memorials such as these well expressed the public mood and the Israeli populace's feelings about the generation of warriors who had fallen in battle. It was a society that appreciated and admired the heroism of its fighting men and their contribution to the establishment of the Jewish state.

This was the context in which the Gruenbaums sought a way to memorialize Eliezer — that is, they wished to integrate their private mourning with their country's collective memory. Yitzhak maintained that, in addition to Eliezer's inclusion in the *Yizkor* project, his writings should be published. When he heard about the plans for *Gevilei Esh*, he asked its editorial board to include Eliezer, offering them his son's article "The 'Colonial' Commercial Network of the Ancient Jews," as well as selections from Eliezer's diary *BeHatzerot haMavet*, in which he wrote about his experiences in Auschwitz and Birkenau.

We can only conjecture how the editors reacted to Yitzhak's suggestion, given that they must have heard both the rumors about his actions in the camps and about the circumstances of his death. What could they have thought when Yitzhak offered them passages in which Eliezer explained his conduct in that hell? The IDF and Defense Ministry archives say that their files do not include the correspondence between Yitzhak and the editorial board. The literary archive Genazim's file on Reuven Avinoam, the chief editor, contains nothing relating to his work on *Gevilei Esh*.

But a small group of people were aware of the behind-the-scenes struggle between Yitzhak and the book's editors. In the end, Eliezer's writings were included in the volume, but only, according to journalist Nahum Barnea, following "nerve-wracking lobbying by the father" and the pressure he, Yitzhak, put on Ben-Gurion.[8]

Yitzhak's plea initially faced resistance because of the feeling that people like Eliezer should not be allowed into the elitist, mythical pantheon of the fallen, which was rightfully a place for the clean and pure. But there were also convoluted personal issues involved, in which Avinoam, to his misfortune, played a major role.

Avinoam himself was the bereaved father of a soldier, Noam Grossman. After his son fell, in the battle of Atarot north of Jerusalem, Reuven Grossman changed his name to Avinoam, meaning "father of Noam." The soldiers memorialized in *Gevilei Esh* appeared in alphabetical order, such that Noam Grossman would have appeared in the book beside Eliezer Gruenbaum. It was more than Reuven Avinoam, the book's editor, could bear. He did not want Eliezer the kapo in the book, and certainly not side by side with his hero son.[9]

But this time Yitzhak won his battle and got his son's biography and writings included in the first volume of *Gevilei Esh*. It may well be that Ben-Gurion made his position clear to Defense Ministry officials, who passed the message on to the book's editors.[10] On August 6, 1952, a short time after the first volume appeared, Gruenbaum wrote a letter to its editors.

> *To the Department for Memorializing Soldiers in the Ministry of Defense,*
> Dear Friends!
> You have erected a fine monument to our sons and daughters who have, with

their blood, granted us independence and freedom — an eternal monument. Future generations will know about the lives, thoughts, and aspirations of those who sacrificed themselves on the altar of the nation and homeland.

I was especially happy that you included in this monument-book not only my son's article but also his writing about the death camp, which he survived as if so that he could die for his people in their war of independence.

I am truly grateful to the department, and especially to the editor of *Gevilei Esh*, R. Avinoam.

Only the father of a son who fell in battle could produce an eternal monument-book of this sort.

Sincerely,
Y. Gruenbaum[11]

The letter makes no reference to the controversy. However, addressing Avinoam directly, referring to his tragedy, and thanking him explicitly for including passages from Eliezer's diary in the book can be seen, if only barely, as an acknowledgment of the difficulties the editor had to cope with, in particular his decision to leave Noam next to Eliezer. But Gruenbaum seems to have been incapable of comprehending the disparity between his conception of the right thing to do and what others thought.

In 1961, Auschwitz survivor Yehiel De-Nur, writing under the pen name Ka-Tzetnik, published his novel *They Called Him Piepl*, the third installment in a trilogy that included two other books, *Sunrise over Hell* (*Salamandrah* in Hebrew) and *House of Dolls*. That same year he testified at the trial of Adolf Eichmann in Jerusalem, where he referred to Auschwitz as "another planet" before fainting on the witness stand.[12] Originally named Yehiel Feiner, De-Nur had been a pious boy at the Chochmei Lublin Yeshiva before being sent to Auschwitz-Birkenau in 1943. He stayed there through liberation in February 1945. He wrote *Sunrise over Hell* in a displaced persons camp in Italy. When he arrived in Israel the book was translated from Yiddish into Hebrew and shocked readers with its graphic and explicit depictions of the horrors of the camps. His pseudonym, which means "prisoner" or "camp inmate," was meant to indicate his faceless new identity, just one of millions of prisoners. He continued to write, producing a series of books that were no less provocative and titillating.[13]

They Called Him Piepl tells the story of a prisoner named Prochtenbaum from his arrival at Auschwitz-Birkenau through his appointment to the position of assistant block chief and his accession to the position of block chief. De-Nur portrays him through the eyes of several other prisoners, focusing on his horrible deeds and, in particular, his brutalization of pious Jews. The language is direct and physically explicit. Like Eliezer in his diary, he did not omit a single detail and had no mercy on his readers. (While the story takes place largely in Birkenau, the characters often speak of "Auschwitz" as a generic term for the entire complex of camps.)

> Prochtenbaum would have a great career here in Auschwitz, Mony considered.[14] When they brought Prochtenbaum to the camp, he himself was already the *piepl* [sex slave] in block 82. Immediately upon arrival, on the first day, Prochtenbaum wept copiously: "Outside I was a famous person." Everyone in the camp says that outside he had been a big millionaire or a famous man. "If you can say that you helped me, all doors will open for you after the war," Prochtenbaum promised him. Mony quickly brought him his portion of soup from his little room. Not because doors would open for him after the war, but simply because he could not bear Prochtenbaum's tears. They moved but also disgusted him. Because what prisoner at Auschwitz cried on the first day because of an extra portion of soup? Then Prochtenbaum began to suck up to the block chief—he beat weak prisoners. At his own initiative, he imposed order while soup was being passed out without anyone asking him to do so. The block chief immediately saw that he was a born block orderly. Prochtenbaum rose to the rank of chief orderly, but that still wasn't enough for him. At every opportunity he did his best to display to Ludwig Tin, the camp elder, his talents and aptitude for being a block chief himself. He'd without a doubt get there, but on the day they made Prochtenbaum a block chief, this camp would be inundated with more blood than all the circles of Auschwitz taken together. Because who knows if he would not want to prove to the Germans that he was capable of serving them as camp elder? It was obvious that Prochtenbaum had decided to make himself a great career at Auschwitz, at any price, and it was evident with what resolve his polished boots were marching toward that goal of his.[15]

At Birkenau, Prochtenbaum served as chief assistant to Bruno, the chief of Block 10. Mony was one of Bruno's *piepls*, giving him an opportunity to become acquainted with Prochtenbaum, take stock of his character, and show the reader that even the "traders[16] can't stand him, and justifiably so." According to Mony, "he is an inflated toady, a nauseatingly smooth-talking ass-licker of his superiors and a trampler with his boots of those subordinate to him."[17]

He harbored a special hatred of religious Jews, Mony wrote. His eyes "blazed with a strange, distinctive fire when a religious Jew fell into his hands. All the more so if it were a rabbi!" Anytime anyone reminded him that he was the son of Prochtenbaum, the important Zionist leader, "he was overwhelmed, to the loss of his senses, with a murderous fury. . . . Prochtenbaum would be struck with madness when anyone pronounced his family name. He sought to uproot everyone who knew who he was." It was difficult to understand why he craved "to immerse his name in a river of blood . . . perhaps he feared that his pedigree would be an obstacle to his career at Auschwitz, and maybe he did not want a single person who could tell of his exploits at Auschwitz to survive. At any rate, the name Prochtenbaum provoked his rage just like a red cloth incites a wild beast. 'Mr. Chief Orderly' was what he would be called—nothing else!"[18] In almost every transport that arrived in Auschwitz there was someone "who was dazzled by sparkle of the Prochtenbaum name, and they fell victim to him like flies to honeyed poison. From each transport Prochtenbaum chose a victim as an example, so that all the others would see and know that he was not to be called Prochtenbaum but rather 'Mr. Chief Servant!'"

Mony goes on to tell how Prochtenbaum abused a rabbi with "sport":

> On the other side of the main road, Prochtenbaum recited a selection of the rules of "sport" to a group of prisoners. No doubt a new transport. One of them may well have again fallen happily into his hands, having known him "outside." . . . Every "prominent" [prisoner with seniority] in Auschwitz had his own personal obsession. Prochtenbaum had no sooner been made a "prominent" than he got the compulsion to shout "Rrrrrebitzin! Rrrrebitzin! What have you done all your life?" He'd grind his teeth. "I'm sure you haven't had any exercise. Now we'll have you do some calisthenics. It's healthy. Skip-jump, skip-jump."[19]

Another of the book's characters imagines how Prochtenbaum's father would feel when he learned what his son had done:

> He'll probably be the first to come to Auschwitz at the end of the war to wallow in the dust, and the first to stone his son's hung carcass. And his son is himself. Poor Prochtenbaum! For the rest of his life he will believe that he fashioned his son's club with his own hands. He will not know how he should eulogize and mourn. To the end of his days he will no doubt roam, dressed in sackcloth and with ashes on his forehead, ashes from the furnace, of Jews his son murdered before their time. A son, after all, is an organ of his father's body, just like fruit is an organ of a tree. All the more so when those he killed became his victims largely because they pronounced the name of his father. How many Jews might still be alive had the father of chief orderly Prochtenbaum been a small businessman, a cobbler, or the beadle of a synagogue. Who knows how many Jews might still be alive had Prochtenbaum, the Zionist leader, been childless?[20]

Articles in the daily press mediated between De-Nur and his readers, drawing the latter's attention to the boldest, sharpest, and juiciest parts of his texts, telling the public whom this horrifying character, son of a Zionist leader, was based on.

Who is Prochtenbaum? The religious weekly newspaper *Panim el Panim* asked the question in an article headlined "The Son of the Zionist Leader, Who Sent Jews to the Furnaces." Was he a fictional character, simply a generic kapo?

> A few days later [following the book's publication] we sat with Ka-Tzetnik. We spoke about his character Prochtenbaum and he said, "No, I don't manufacture characters, symbols. I try to present the facts as they were. Very frequently, when I read what I have written, it seems to me that the text is still insipid, that it's still not what it ought to be."
>
> "Let's say it: Prochtenbaum is a man who lived and acted and did what he did. Prochtenbaum junior is the son of Prochtenbaum senior. Both the father, the eminent Zionist leader, and the son as well, are part of factual reality."[21]
>
> And then we recalled—it was in the final days of the war. The crematory smoke spread until it reached us. Those who spent months calming the winds, those who demanded that we not latch on to rumors had to confess. They did not, of course, confess to their horrible error of trying to keep the Holocaust silent. All they did was convene mass meetings and condemn with literary language those who went to the furnaces with a prayer on their lips [rather than rebel]. They began to turn the greatest atrocity of all generations into a myth.

The reference in the last paragraph is to the statement released by the Jewish Agency Executive on November 24, 1942, which declared that a systematic and large-scale project to murder the Jews was under way. A debate ensued in the Yishuv, and various officials charged that the community's leaders, Yitzhak Gruenbaum among them, had known about what was going on and had maliciously concealed that information from the public.[22]

The greatest of these silencers, and the greatest of the speakers at such protest and mourning rallies, the newspaper explained to its readers, was the man that the book named Prochtenbaum senior. After the war, the newspaper added, a rumor spread that "Prochtenbaum" had been captured and arrested as a war criminal and would be hanged. What did the father do?

> "Prochtenbaum" senior, a man with excellent connections in the "Jewish Agency Executive in Jerusalem," did not don sackcloth and ashes. He put on diplomatic garb and set out on a special plane to save his son. He saved him and brought him here. Some say that the son fell in one of the difficult battles of the War of Independence. The father hung a picture of him over his work desk. There were those who saw to it that a "literary work" by the son would be included in the book *Gevilei Esh*, which collected the works of the holy and pure martyrs who fell in the War of Independence.[23]

Panim el Panim also told its readers about the backstory to *Gevilei Esh*. Some had tried to conceal the affair, and others thought it should be disregarded on the grounds that Eliezer's death had atoned for his sins. But "a writer, a grieving father, who found his martyr son's literary testament placed next to the 'work' of 'the leader's son,' was so distressed that he fainted. Since then he has not touched *Gevilei Esh*.[24]

"Everyone acknowledges that every detail, every special revelation of the days of horror, requires learning a lesson, reaching conclusions," the newspaper wrote, and of course the "Prochtenbaum atrocities" were no exception. It was vital to find out "how it happened that a son who grew up in such a Zionist, national home became what he became? How could it be that the father and national leader carried on his fatherly connection to this son?"[25]

The weekly asked a famous rabbi — whose name it did not give — to explain the phenomenon. He, the paper reported, had been

> as white as a sheet, his hands trembling, when he said: "There is much discussion among us today about the problem of the attitude of patriotic young people in Israel to the Jews of the Diaspora, to the Jews of the Exile. It is no secret that many young people do not like these Jews, especially those who look outwardly like Diaspora Jews. It is known that there are "Sabras" who use the term "Soap" to refer to Diaspora types. Have we given any thought to the fact that we ourselves are bringing up, God forbid, such "Prochtenbaums"?[26]

It would be wrong to join a "conspiracy of silence," the newspaper asserted. Holocaust researchers should take a close look at the incident and ask "what will such a phenomenon lead to?" The ancient Jewish sages explicated the verse from Leviticus "She shall profane her father," saying that the root of a child's wickedness lies in his father's house, in the way he was brought up. Prochtenbaum had been the son of "the leader," not just a kapo. "He was a phenomenon, a phenomenon that demands investigation."[27] A kapo who had grown up in a secular Zionist family. Now, in our young country, the newspaper asked, with the kind of education and environment the Sabras were growing up in, who will put us on the right path?

The newspaper cited further passages from the book, categorized by atrocity, with explanatory subheads. It concluded the article with an imputed, chilling, baseless, and not at all accidental link to current events:

> The big trial that opened this week [the Eichmann trial] may recount the atrocities committed by the gentiles in the Holocaust. But it is our duty to relate — with all the piercing pain it causes — those same bloody and wounding phenomena. We must do so for our own sake and for our future.

> The attempt to cover up these revelations is like the attempt to keep the Holocaust under wraps in the years 1940–1943.
>
> Intellectuals, educators, and scholars must address this phenomenon called "Prochtenbaum." Was the *procht* [fruit] really an offspring of the *baum* [tree]?[28]

Herut, the daily newspaper of the Revisionist party of the same name, led by Menachem Begin, also waded into the storm. Its editor, Isaac Rembah, ended the mystery. He headlined his article with a reversal of the famous verse from Jeremiah 28 about how the sins of fathers are visited on their children. His piece, which appeared in the issue of September 10, 1961, was entitled "When Not Fathers but Sons Eat Sour Fruit." It addressed "Ka-Tzetnik's shocking and wonderful" book, published not long ago. Anyone who had not yet read it "indubitably lacks something for the deepening of his Jewish awareness, and should quickly make up for this deficit."

Rembah wrote that he "found himself facing in astonishment one of the book's most repugnant characters, that of a Jewish block chief by the name of Prochtenbaum."[29] We cringe, he wrote, each time that Ka-Tzetnik opens a window through which one of the chambers of the inferno could be viewed.

> But Prochtenbaum, the brutal block chief who beat his racial brethren over their heads, who battered a saintly rabbi, took joy not only in doing the will of his sadistic Nazi commanders, but also in anticipating their wishes, in going above and beyond and multiplying his schemes to extract what little life remained in the body of a Jewish boy, who took masochistic [*sic*] pleasure from all kinds of agonies that he added those on their final marches to the gas chambers. This Prochtenbaum infinitely nauseates and infuriates us.
>
> Were we to encounter him now, we would tear him to shreds, we would cut off pieces of his impure body and throw them to the dogs. There is no end to, no measure of the bitterness in our souls, to the anger confined within us against this cruel man, who we view as 77 times worse that the lowest of the Nazi carnivores.

Could it really be, Rembah asked, "that this reprobate emerged from the womb of a Jewish mother?" He did not leave his question unanswered:

> The more we read about this Prochtenbaum and his exploits, the more we suddenly feel as if the earth were opening up before us and we are falling into it and losing consciousness — after all, most of us know who this Prochtenbaum is. We know his parents, his father, his relatives, the members of his family. He is the son of a great Zionist leader, famed throughout the Jewish world. And you do not know what is greater, the pain or the disgrace. Sorrow or fury. Lord of the Universe, Lord of all Souls! Why are you so cruel to your children?

In the second half of his piece, Rembah surveyed a series of cases in which sons and daughters shamed their parents and families. These are offspring and heirs "who dishonor the names of their fathers, who wallow in moral offal, who desecrate all that is sacred to the rock from which they are hewn, who knock down with abandon all fences, who cast off all restraints and even leap into the enemy camp in order to exacerbate the agonies of the nation from which they came." Where did "such errant children [get] all this rampant evil and corruption?" They clearly, Rembah maintained, "did not inherit these horrible deviances from their fathers." If so, then "how did this cancerous venom get into their blood and poison their bodies, penetrate the most hidden cells in their souls and spread into every vein and muscle, into the brain and heart?"

What is the connection between all this rampant evil and corruption and what the errant child received from his parents? Rembah asked. What did he take from his home and his school and the street? Who knows "what alleys he wandered through and what he took in and absorbed from there?" How, then, might it be possible to explain "the horrifying tragedy that befell a man beloved by the entire nation, Theodor Herzl?" Why was fate so cruel to him "in taking from him and from his nation all three of his children, that led all of them on twisted paths, that cast them down into cesspools outside the bounds of society, that violently shook their souls and dumped them into the maw of contradictions and mental tortures and even compelled them to peer beyond the normal world, to the point that the Devil came and put an end to the miserable and depressing lives of all three? But Satan even pursued the daughter's son and took his senses from him and led him to suicide."

But then was there any lack of orphans who grew up into whole and ideal adults, good and honest, beneficial to society and loyal to their people and homeland? Was there any shortage of children from broken homes who grew up "in an atmosphere of hatred and poverty and filth, but nevertheless successfully and unfailingly battled with all their strength against the forces of destruction and defeated them?" Herzl was not the only man to suffer such a catastrophe, that his own issue brought disgrace on him. There were also two great Jewish authors, "of enormous talent, both of them with their feet planted firmly on the land of the Jewish nation, who gave the nation the best of their work, from the gift that God bestowed on them," Rembah continued, laying the foundation of his thesis. Nevertheless, the sons of Mendele Mocher Sforim and I. L. Peretz, "two young men who grew up in Jewish homes and absorbed a Jewish atmosphere rejected their origins, turned their backs on their people and religion, cast off the faith of their race as if it were a repulsive and overly-heavy load, and took refuge in the religion of Jesus." Herzl's son Hans did the same. Moreover, the families of Mendele Mocher Sforim in Odessa and I. L. Peretz in Warsaw, unlike Herzl's, were not broken ones.

But such troubles were not only the lot of Jews. It happened to "the best of the gentiles" and "caused their families painful tragedies." There was no easy answer to the "caprices of fate," Rembah explained. For example, Winston Churchill's daughter, Sarah, had not been an honor and a glory to her parents. She was a chronic alcoholic who misbehaved on the street and in bars, shattering bottles of whiskey and throwing glasses at the patrons of nightclubs. She tottered through the streets of London drunk and caused public scandals. From time to time policemen arrested her as she rained blows on their heads. That was the daughter of Churchill, "for whom the world was his footstool, who had done so much for his people and country and all of humanity. A statesman and writer and educator of his people, a man of many talents, by the grace of heaven endowed with faculties. One of the first, perhaps the very first, of the world's great men that has been crowned by all." Yet he, too, saw his personal life crash down before his eyes. He, "discerning and wise, charming and active, perceptive and farsighted, who trampled millions of enemies under his feet, who led the world in days of crisis with determination and genius, failed utterly in his own home." Had he kept anything from his daughter? Had he not given her the most advanced education? Had he not imbued her with his spirit, sent her to fine schools, ensured that she live among the good and noble? Rembah asked questions to which the answers were evident.

He offered his readers another example. Some of Franklin Delano Roosevelt's sons kept him up at night and caused his wife, the no less honorable Eleanor, pain and agony. Roosevelt, too, was a great man, one of the pillars of human society of the last generation.

The most awful example, Rembah wrote, as he continued his nightmare journey, was the accomplished and celebrated British statesman Leopold Amery, one of the architects of the British Empire and a member of many cabinets. Yet his son, a scion of the nobility and one of the most famous figures of the interwar period, had brought disaster and disgrace on his father and his family. At the start of World War II, "when Hitler rose up to conquer the world and to destroy Britain and its Empire," the son defected and went to serve the führer in Germany, working in the Nazi propaganda effort. After the war he was captured by the Allies, brought to trial for treason in England, and executed. No less. "How did Leopold Amery's son come to such convolutions?" Rembah asked. All these fathers, he said, certainly asked, "What sin have I committed for a son like that to be born to me?" Here Rembah completed his list of famous figures whose children had brought ignominy and disaster on their peoples.

As harsh and shocking as the Prochtenbaum case might be, as yet no "honest man, who is not consumed by resentment and a desire for revenge," would attribute "the abominations committed by the son to his parents." Such parents deserve "pity and consolation. And some say that in such cases silence is fitting. Why probe the unhealed wounds of parents who have been afflicted by heaven while they still bleed?" Rembah, too, imposed an obligation of silence on himself. True, "a number of things happened with this kapo, who survived the valley of death, after the curtain fell on the horrifying drama of the annihilation. Something that does not give even me any rest. There is no choice but to speak of it in public," he promised his readers.

Two weeks passed before Rembah brought before his readers, on September 24, 1961, the matter that disturbed his sleep. Its headline was "What Is the Connection between Prochtenbaum and *Gevilei Esh*?" Rembah informed his readers that on the eve of the Yom Kippur fast three men — Yisrael Amir, head of the Defense Ministry's Personnel Division; Lieutenant Colonel Moshe Averbuch, head of the Commemoration Department; and the poet Reuven Avinoam, editor of the ministry's literary projects — visited Israel's president, Yitzhak Ben-Zvi, and his wife, Rachel Yanait. The three presented the first couple with a copy of the third volume of *Gevilei Esh*. The president and his wife were the parents of a fallen soldier — their son Eli had been killed in the War of Independence, and writing by him had been included in these volumes.

While he did not want, God forbid, to say anything bad about the project, Rembah noted that not every fallen soldier who had left behind literary or artistic works had been included in these volumes. It seemed suspicious to him that so few of the young men and women who had fallen in the war and who had belonged to IZL and LEHI (two right-wing underground forces, the former headed by Menachem Begin, the veterans of which formed the backbone of the Herut Party) had been included in *Gevilei Esh*. Could it be that "only a few, who can be counted on the fingers of two hands, among the many hundreds of heroes who had been members of IZL and LEHI, had left behind diaries or letters of the quality necessary to serve as an example for future generations?"[30]

"I took the two previous volumes of *Gevilei Esh*, published by the Israeli government, off my bookshelf," he wrote, and

> with awe and reverence we leafed through the pages of these two thick volumes, reading the names and diaries and letters and writings of all sorts of fallen soldiers, all of them pure heroes and martyrs who in life belonged to various movements — but in the hearts of all beat an unbridled love for their Hebrew nation

> and homeland. In the name of this love, which burned in their souls, they set out to fight, knowingly putting their lives in danger, marched with their weapons to places where they knew for certain that death lay in wait for them.

The Ministry of Defense was right to labor to commemorate them with *Gevilei Esh*, Rembah wrote, in keeping with the intentions of those who had initiated the project, who wrote: "to shape the image of the generation as a whole, the moral and spiritual image of the fighters."

As Rembah perused the three volumes before him,

> suddenly, as if a lightning bolt had struck me, you read the biographical note of one of them, and your mouth opens wide in astonishment and anger — what is this one doing here? Such a biography has no parallel in these 1,200 pages. It's entirely exceptional and as you read each line your astonishment grows. How did such a biography end up here? No, this is not its place, someone was engaging in black humor, making a bad joke by bringing "an idol into the sanctuary."

Who decided "to include this one among our wonderful young people, who not only died heroically but also lived purely, loyally, loving their homeland?" Rembah urged his readers also to take a look at Prochtenbaum — as he decided to call Eliezer in this article as well — and decide for themselves. He went on to summarize Eliezer's story.

While the Communists were allies of the Nazis, following the Molotov-Ribbentrop Pact and the partition of Poland between Germany and the USSR, "the war against the Nazis was not Prochtenbaum's war." While he was a member of the Jewish people, the fate of his fellow Jews who were rotting in the ghettos that the Nazis set up did not interest him. Afterward he was deported to Auschwitz, but "there, seeing the suffering of the members of his people, their agonies, there too the Jewish spark did not light up within him."

After citing several passages from Ka-Tzetnik's book, Rembah returned to *Gevilei Esh* and "Prochtenbaum's" biography. He recounted his brutal deeds and his story until "his father, the great Zionist leader" brought him to Jerusalem. He told of Prochtenbaum's enlistment in the army and how he fell in the battle of Ramat Rachel. "Take note," he wrote, "of an interesting detail in the biography, as we read in *Gevilei Esh* — he did not take advantage of his family connections for his own gain." What a great deed Prochtenbaum performed at the end of his life, Rembah marveled. What exactly was the meaning of this declarative gesture? he taunted the father, who had helped write the biography. "There are many versions of the way he died running around. But we will accept the official version of the biographer — he was felled by an Arab bullet," Rembah declared, while at the same time making a reference to the rumor that Eliezer had been killed by his comrades-in-arms.[31] "Had it been proper to include selections from Prochtenbaum's diary among the writings of these gifted people?"

In one passage, which Rembah quoted in such an abbreviated form as to be nearly incomprehensible, he asked whether the book's editors thought that this was a fitting message to convey to future generations: "There, too, in the face of the deaths of his brethren, the members of his own people," [Prochtenbaum was first of all a Communist]. "His heroes and friends were the Russians, and when he heard the anthems that people sang on their final journeys he gave priority to the 'Internationale' and only afterward heard 'Hatikvah.'" Characterizing the Jews, Prochtenbaum explained that there were no rebellions because of "the Jews' natural cowardice." Was there a more natural place for him to voice his opinions on the Jews' natural cowardice, Rembah asked sarcastically, than in "these scrolls, in which every line testifies that the opposite is true"? Was his way of coping with that horrifying place something to brag about, to bring before the public as a means of education and as an example for future generations?[32]

Prochtenbuam was a traitor and a disgrace to his people, Rembah declared. He had caused his parents great sorrow, and "the soil that covered him is the only atonement for his sins." Yet he, Rembah, would not have written about him, would not have said a word even after the harsh things Ka-Tzetnik had written that revealed who he really was. But Rembah asserted that he could not remain silent when Prochtenbaum's father had not done the same. "Has the rot of favoritism eaten so deeply into the bones and the soul," Rembah asked, "that the editor had not dared to reject these manuscripts that desecrate *Gevilei Esh* and the nation's heroes and the eternal aura that surrounds them?"[33]

Ka-Tzetnik's book, and the charge that the editors of *Gevilei Esh* had been compelled to include Eliezer's story in their project, led to a new round of public vilification of Yitzhak Gruenbaum, Eliezer, and everything that the connection between father and son was seen as exemplifying. Previously published pamphlets that had not before gained wide readerships, such as Moshe Shonfeld's *Serufe haKivshanim Ma'ashimim* (Those burned in the furnaces accuse), M. Wuzelman's *Ot Cain* (The mark of Cain), and Sh. Shalmon's *Pishae haZionot beHashmadat yehude haGolah* (The crimes of Zionism in the annihilation of the Jews of the exile), now gained new currency. From time to time, in particular in the days leading up to Israel's Holocaust and Heroism Memorial Day each spring, newspaper articles revived the affair. After the publication of *They Called Him Piepl*, the Gruenbaums sought to stem the tide by suing De-Nur for libel. Their attorney sent a letter to De-Nur, who responded — also on the advice of counsel — that the character of Prochtenbaum was a literary creation and that the author would not enter into the question of the character's likeness to any real person. The similarities were, however, clear for all to see, and according to *Panim el Panim* at least, De-Nur had confirmed that Prochtenbaum was based on Eliezer. Neither the newspaper nor De-Nur denied it. But in the end the family did not file suit. It would not have been an easy matter for a court to decide; a trial would have been long and expensive; and it could backfire on the family.[34] They had seen themselves that such a thing could happen. The libel suit that the State of Israel pursued against Malkhiel Gruenwald in 1954 after the latter wrote a pamphlet charging Israel Kastner, the press secretary for the Ministry of Commerce and Industry, with collaboration with the Nazis, had been fixed in the mind of the public as the Kastner trial, not the Gruenwald trial.[35]

The members of the family did what they could, each in his or her own way, to reject any connection between the two figures. In newspaper interviews, and Yonatan in the unpublished book manuscript he authored, claimed that De-Nur had never met Eliezer at Birkenau, and that like others he had based his charges on malicious rumors, out of hatred for all that Yitzhak and Eliezer stood for, and because of his own difficulties in coping with the scars left by his own experience.[36]

But the affair did not lose its attraction. Eliezer's story remained a subject of polemic and of research on the Yishuv and the Holocaust. Later, the public and scholarly debate over the so-called New Historians and Post-Zionists and their writings about Zionism and the Holocaust[37] kept drawing the family and Eliezer's story into the eye of the storm. Menachem Gerlik and Rabbi Mordekhai Noigershel, two of Eliezer's most prominent Haredi accusers, related that a book by one of the New Historians, Tom Segev, on the Holocaust's impact on Israeli society, *The Seventh Million*, served them as an inexhaustible source of information. Eliezer's case was taken up by Israel's state and commercial television stations, which produced two documentaries that breathed new life into the story. Matti Regev, a grandson of Yitzhak Gruenbaum, threatened a lawsuit against one of writers, setting off a wave of reactions and new testimonies.[38] Also feeding the debate was the public and private activity of Holocaust survivors or their agents, or those who claimed to be such, who had been unable to forget Eliezer and what he represented. A son of Rivka and Yonatan, who bore his late uncle's name, became religious as a result of the involvement and activity of Gerlik, one of the most vocal slanderers of the family, further fanning the flames.[39]

Some survivor testimonies had been recorded after the war, but many date from the State of Israel's first decades. Still others were recorded as late as the

1980s and 1990s, at a time when one might have expected the controversy to have faded away. Most of these have the same deficiency of those presented in the French proceeding—many of the witnesses had not actually seen Eliezer commit the deeds that they attributed to him. Their accusations were based on hearsay, rumors, possibly hazy memories, and judgments. Some of them quoted shreds of information provided or adopted by one or another source, usually without checking their accuracy. They then augmented this and passed it on to others. Most of the testimonies painted a harsh picture. Few survivors or colleagues of Eliezer's from the party or underground who provided testimony displayed the same determination to present a different picture or to present Eliezer's story in its broader context.

Hilary Strauweiss, a member of the Łódź Jewish Committee and a member of the central committee of the Marxist-Zionist Po'alei Zion movement in Poland, testified in December 1945 that he had been, during 1943, an inmate of Block 22 at Auschwitz-Birkenau. At work, he met Jews from Block 30. He testified that "the Jews in this block commonly said that whoever wanted a quick death should go to Block 30," where Gruenbaum—he did not remember the first name—the block chief was one of the biggest sadists in the camp. "More Catholic than the pope," he went beyond the Germans' orders and beat the Jews lethally. His condition "was better than that of all the other prisoners, he had a lot of food at the expense of his prisoners, that he stole. No Jew wanted anything to do with him except in emergencies. For his part, he did not want contact with Jews. All his social connections were with the block chiefs and the camp administration. He was one of the greatest skunks."[40]

Avraham Berl Skakal gave testimony in 1947 to the Jewish History Committee. He related that at Auschwitz he had met the son of Yitzhak Gruenbaum, who was a "kapo and block chief, and wanted to curry the favor of the Germans at the expense of the Jews, whom he beat to death, and the bread and margarine remained with him."[41] Henoch Rajcher, originally from Kraków and an inmate at Birkenau, testified in 1958 that "the SS treated the Jews no different than they treated the members of other nations. Just that the Jews they sent to the fire. The worst were the Jews who were called *Ordner* [warden, in the camp self-government], among them the son of Yitzhak Gruenbaum. . . . The worst of them was the young Gruenbaum. He abused us and showed the Germans who to send to the gas."[42]

In 1964, as part of his effort to clear his son's name, Yitzhak published an article in *Heint*, a newspaper published in Montevideo, Uruguay. The piece aroused the ire of Charles Papiernik. In an article entitled "The Truth about Eliezer Gruenbaum," Papiernik offered his impressions of Eliezer. He and his three brothers had met Eliezer at Beaune-la-Rolande, where he was "head of the camp." "We voted for him because of his name," Papiernik said, "for being the son of Gruenbaum. The Spanish Civil War also added something, and he had been a leader of the Polish Communists in northern France." On June 27, 1942, the four brothers had been sent to Auschwitz. Upon their arrival, an SS soldier declared to them: "Miserable Jews, you have not come here to live." But he was more hurt by what Eliezer said afterward, in German: "You parasites, you lived off the blood and sweat of other nations. You worked only in commerce and [unclear word]. Now a new Reich is being built and Germany will know to benefit those who are productive." He demanded productivity and "gave us deadly blows over the heads with a club, trod on old men, shouted and went wild. That is how he intended to be useful to the Third Reich."

Papiernik's brother Yitzhak remained in Auschwitz as part of the tailor *Kommando*. Charles and his two other brothers, Mottel and Feivel, were sent to Eliezer's block in Birkenau, but a day later Feivel was sent back to Auschwitz to another work detail. Charles was placed at the camp construction trades school, under reasonable conditions. He had this good luck, he related, because "apparently they needed us to build blocks and structures for the gas chambers. They also gave us relatively better hygienic conditions." The kapo and block chief also treated them well. A few days later he went to visit his brother Mottel and found him

> lying by the block with his arm swollen. He couldn't lift it or put it down. He was crying. To go to work like that meant certain death. Maybe he could stay in the block? He looked at me. His eyes pleaded. You're after all in better condition, with a green ribbon on your arm [the ribbon marked Charles as a preferential worker].
>
> I went to Ludwig [Konczal], the brutal Polish block chief. He sent me to the room warden, Gruenbaum. I told him about our tragedy—we had been seven brothers, one had been killed at the front [as a French soldier], there were four of us in Auschwitz, the others must be imprisoned in France. I tried to persuade him to let my sick brother stay in the block for a few days, until the swelling in his arm went down. I wept, asked for mercy. He could have done it if he had wanted to. But he answered me in Polish: "So many Jews have bit the dust, so big deal if another does."
>
> The next day my brother signed up as sick. Maybe despite everything . . .

But, according to Papiernik, Gruenbaum saw him and beat him on his swollen arm until he collapsed. Then he kicked him like a crazy man and commanded that he be transferred to Block 7. Everyone knew that that meant being sent to the gas chambers. "The next day my brother was taken, before my eyes, with a hundred others to the gas chambers."

It is easy enough to understand Eliezer's father, his pain at his son's deeds, his efforts to free him, Papiernik said. But he could not understand and could not accept the father's attempts to rehabilitate his son's reputation. He could not accept it when Yitzhak Gruenbaum wrote that

> the starving prisoners at the camp could not understand what his son's intentions were, that he had placed himself in the balance between the block chief and the starving masses, that someone else had done the killing, not his son. I [Papiernik] want to declare with full responsibility (and I am prepared to appear before any court) that Eliezer Gruenbaum, the all-powerful room warden at Birkenau, with his block chief Ludwig, were murderers, sadists, and torturers. I accuse him directly of sending my brother to the gas chambers after beating him; of torturing Jews to death, of being a collaborator with the SS at Auschwitz-Birkenau.

There were block chiefs and room wardens who, Papiernik maintained, "did not cooperate with the SS. There were kapos who saved [prisoners] from beatings and also from being sent to the gas chambers." They also tried to make life better for the prisoners, he said. No one forced them to behave like Nazi beasts. Eliezer had done so because he had resolved to play along with the Nazis, even at the price of murdering his Jewish brothers. "Only in 1943, after the defeat at Stalingrad and the [opening] of the second front, [when] he was sent to Buchenwald, did [Eliezer] seek ties to the underground and become active in it."

Eliezer's father probably didn't know, Papiernik continued, that his son "would go berserk every time someone at Birkenau called him by his name or mentioned his father. Anyone who did that was a candidate for the next world. The fact that his son confessed to this and asked for forgiveness does not change anything. The father cannot forgive or rehabilitate the actions of a person who worked directly for the SS, who tortured, killed, and sent hundreds of Jews to the gas chambers.

The organization of former Auschwitz inmates in Paris that Papiernik headed was aware of Yitzhak Gruenbaum's arrival in the French capital in 1945 and his desire to dismiss the charges against Eliezer. They also knew when Eliezer was released from prison and taken out of France in a closed vehicle. But they did not know that French law stipulated that French courts could only hear cases against French nationals or non-French citizens who had committed crimes on French soil or against French citizens. Had they known this, they would not have turned him over to the French authorities, Papiernik testified. "We wanted to understand a father whose heart was bleeding, so we did not react. We forgave him, he is after all a father." But it was not appropriate for a former leader of Polish Jewry to try to cleanse his son's name, Papiernik maintained. He signed his testimony with his full name and as "Former Prisoner no. 43422."

Papiernik did not appear on the list of prosecution witnesses in the French proceeding. He did not add his testimony, which charged Eliezer with responsibility for the death of his brother, to the testimonies on Eliezer's complicity in murder. The testimony was recorded later, a long time after the war and in response to Yitzhak's article in *Heint*. Similarly, Loberstein had testified that Eliezer was culpable for killing his son only when he was called in for a second round of testimony. Yet a fact like that could hardly have been forgotten and is not the kind of thing a witness would postpone telling. The question of why Papiernik did not speak up at one of the postwar legal proceedings was answered by Papiernik himself.

He claimed that he had not done so because of decisions made by his organization and similar ones. It was direct testimony not from Oléar, who had himself been ostracized by the underground at one point, but from one of the chairpersons of the postwar organization in Paris of former Auschwitz inmates. Papiernik said that the resistance had resolved to pursue a deliberate policy of shunning suspected collaborators, who were to be "vaporized" and "expunged" from the collective memory. Eliezer had seen this as a "psychosis" directed against him, a "psychosis" that after Papiernik read Yitzhak's article might indeed erupt again. He, Papiernik, could no longer bear not to publish his story. His testimony implies that Eliezer was not turned over to the French authorities by happenstance. There had been a decision to turn him in, at least before counterpressure was put on the group to silence the voices coming from the street, before the fear grew that a public and open discussion about collaborators would also hurt them, the Communists, and in particular the Communist parties of Poland and France.

Was Papiernik describing things he had seen himself? He and his brother Mottel had been assigned to different blocks and a different *Kommando*. With regard to exactly when Eliezer first established ties with the underground, the testimonies contradict one another. Did Papiernik make up the story about asking Eliezer to help his injured brother, a request Eliezer allegedly rejected roughly and violently? Yad Vashem's database of names shows four Papiernik brothers in shipment 5 to Auschwitz, just as Eliezer himself was. Charles Papiernik's three brothers are all listed in the Auschwitz death register within the space of a few days — Mottel on August 10, 1942, Yitzhak on August 18, and Feivel on August 22. All survived less than two months at Auschwitz. A fifth brother, Ya'akov, arrived in a transport the next month and also died at the camp.

In other words, the Papiernik brothers reached Auschwitz *together* with Eliezer. That being the case, when would Eliezer have had time to get into a position to be the man who received them at the camp and in his block? Eliezer was asked at the time of the transport's arrival to serve as an interpreter, which he did, but some witnesses reported that he had been beaten because he tried to pursue an independent line, to the benefit of the prisoners, during his first three days at the camp. These facts are largely corroborated by the testimony of other prisoners who were there at the time. The rejoinder Papiernik attributed to him, "So many Jews have bit the dust, so big deal if another does," was attested to, sometimes using the same precise words, in other testimonies. When Mottel Papiernik died on August 10, Eliezer was Konczal's deputy. The claim that addressing him by his real name or referring to his relationship to his father sent him into a rage is supported by other testimonies. Was Papiernik's account of his conversation with Eliezer, and of Eliezer's hostile response, untrue? This behavior matches that which Eliezer himself testified to as having occurred during his "black period."[43]

Yeshayahu Lichtenstein testified in 1995 to Yad Vashem that he was placed in Eliezer's block on November 7, 1942, at the age of fourteen. As he lay on his ledge he heard a kapo shouting. Afterward he was told that the voice had been that of "the son of Yitzhak Gruenbaum, who had been a member of the Polish parliament and was a member of the Jewish Agency [Executive] in Palestine. . . . I was in shock. A Communist journalist from before the war who had turned into a kapo crueler than the Germans themselves." His interviewer asked him if he was certain of this, and he replied:

> One hundred percent . . . there was no doubt that it was the son of Yitzhak Gruenbaum, who also had a son at a kibbutz. I did not see it with my own eyes, but they said that on that evening he murdered one of the rabbis who was at the Basel Congress with his father, so that he wouldn't identify him. . . . He was a sadist from birth [who took out] all his weaknesses on the Jews. . . . He was the kapo of the block. . . . I heard about Yitzhak Gruenbaum in Israel, I heard this story from a few people and it was in the newspapers as well. In 1945 the Americans captured him and his father took money from the Jewish Agency and paid it as bail.[44]

Charles Liblau, who had known Eliezer in Poland, offered an account of how they met again under miserable circumstances in Birkenau, and of the difficult time he had when Eliezer's father spoke to him imploringly in Paris. "As for his end, there are several versions, and there is no way of ascertaining how accurate they are," he said. "Some say that he was imprisoned, others that an avenger killed him, and still others that he was killed in 1947 at Ramat Rachel in the War of Independence. The last days of Comrade Berger, son of

Yitzhak, a delegate to the Polish Sjem and chairman of the Jewish caucus, remain shrouded in mystery. In any case, his death was not a loss to the Jewish community nor to mankind. May the stone that I throw on his coffin serve as a memorial."[45]

A central source for the accusations was publications by Haredi Jews. One such was the pamphlet by Moshe Shonfeld *Serufe haKivshanim Ma'ashimim* (Those burned in the furnaces accuse), published toward the end of 1974 by an organization that called itself "The Bnei Torah Circle of Ze'irei Agudas Israel." Shonfeld noted that he based his information also on "Ka-Tzetnik's book." The latter ends its grim account with the author's prediction that Prochtenbaum's father would be the first to cast "stones at his son's hanged carcass."

But the facts differed from what Ka-Tzetnik had forecast, Shonfeld wrote: "Gruenbaum walks erect among us, surrounded by respect and admiration as a prominent Zionist leader. He spirited his son the murderer into Israel, and even though it was not an Arab bullet but a Jewish avenger who ended his life, his name was included in *Gevilei Esh*, the memorial book for the fallen soldiers of the War of Independence." All this because the father knew of his son's "hatred, potent as death, for the observers of the Torah and those who raise its banner . . . and why should he condemn rather than shield him?"

The "Yevsektsis" (members of the Soviet Communist Party's Jewish Section) in Russia and the kapos in the ghettos and camps, Sholfeld claimed, were all nourished by the same "mad loathing of Jewish heritage and its heirs." Eliezer was like Chaim Rumkowski, "who served for decades as chairman of the Zionist Organization in Łódź . . . and crowned himself 'king of the ghetto' under Nazi patronage . . . and abused his miserable 'subjects' with mad dictatorial brutality, added further persecutions to the persecutions of the Nazis, carefully and precisely organized the death transports without mercy . . . [and] even appointed himself the sole person who could marry young couples," and "Alfred Nossig, the elderly Zionist leader, Herzl's personal friend, [who] tarnished his old age in the Warsaw Ghetto as an informer and spy for the Nazis and was sentenced to death by the Jewish underground." They were all traitors, and they all drank from the same well.

The father was party to the original sin of bringing Agudat Israel into the Yishuv's Rescue Committee, Shonfeld continued: "Unfortunately . . . he did not see fit to break off cooperation with Agudat Israel in Palestine in the Jewish Agency's Rescue Committee. He understood that leaving Agudat Israel outside was more dangerous to his plots than having it inside. The result was that while all the national Agudat Israel organizations in the world did great things to rescue Jews, operating independently, Agudat Israel in Palestine was bound in the chains of the Jewish Agency and did nothing."

The Rescue Committee, he wrote, "took the name of rescue in vain, and it would have been more correct to call it the Concealment, Silencing, Distracting, and Braking the Energy Committee." Agudat Israel's representatives were full of burning desire to save Jewish lives, whereas the Zionist representatives, and Chairman Gruenbaum in particular, were preoccupied with the question of how to take advantage of the Holocaust and its horrors to fortify the National Home and to justify the demand to found a Jewish state. The decision of Agudat Israel in Palestine to join the Jewish Agency's Rescue Committee was "the original, first sin," but not the last sin of collaboration with militant secularism within a secular framework. "The collaboration was disastrous at its time as well as subsequently," Shonfeld wrote, apparently alluding to the "Status Quo Agreement," in which Ben-Gurion laid out the contours of the relation between the new Jewish state and the Jewish religion, and which Yitzhak had played a role in drafting.[46] In fact, recent studies show that Shonfeld was correct in saying that, less than two months after it was founded, the Rescue Committee was doing little except talk. But he was wrong as to the reason. The real problem was conflicting pressures from representatives from all segments of the Yishuv political spectrum who had had demanded to join the committee, Agudat Israel included. Gruenbaum could not hold his own under the circumstances.[47]

Another such book was *Ot Cain* (The mark of Cain) by M. Wuzelman (together, the initial and last name can be read as *Muselmann*), edited by Menachem Gerlik. One of the book's chapters, written by M. H. Friedman, opens by recounting Gruenbaum's failures and his profound alienation from European Jewry.[48] After presenting their views, the contributors to the book take up the subject of "The Apple [that] Doesn't Fall Far from the Tree," as one chapter subheading puts it. Readers are referred to books by Ka-Tzetnik and a Communist historian, Bar Mark. This section of the chapter compares the behavior of religious and nonreligious Jews under the same harsh conditions. The former are described as "simple Jews, believing Jews and observers of the Torah and its commandments, who even in the terrible conditions that prevailed in the death camps did not sell their souls to Satan." The chapter quotes an article by Elie Wiesel that appeared in the holiday supplement to the *Yediot Aharonoth* newspaper on Rosh Hashanah 1982,[49] in reference to the wonderful fortitude of religious Jews and their rabbis in the camps, in support of the all-embracing thesis presented at the end of the chapter: "Adzheke [Eliezer] Gruenbaum was not the only Jew to collaborate with the Nazis. Unfortunately, many of our people, nearly all of whom belonged to the *maskil* secular Zionist cohort and left-wing groups, committed the sin of collaboration and did the Nazis' bidding no less and even more serious away when they served in the *Judenrat* councils, the Jewish police in the ghettos, in the concentration camps, and in the extermination camps."[50]

The researchers for Dov Kroytoro's documentary film *HaBen shel Gruenbaum* (Gruenbaum's son)[51] were told by Gerlik, whom they termed "a Haredi historian," that he heard "from a friend that his father had witnessed an incident in which Gruenbaum ordered prisoners [sitting on the back of an open truck] to take off their shirts and then sprayed them with cold water until they froze to death." The truck went back and circled around the camp, and when it reached him he sprayed them with water, and after each circle there were fewer living Jews left."[52] Zvi Blumprucht told the filmmakers that "Eliezer would beat prisoners. He told them: Do you see that chimney? You'll go [through it], or do you see the furnace? You'll go there. He just wanted to humiliate them." Jacques Klinger said that "Itche was a handsome, big, intelligent guy. It was known in the block that he had killed several people. He had a system — he'd lay the man on the ground, put a stick to his neck, and do a 'seesaw.' . . . I asked him, 'How can you do that?' He said, 'Look, this man is already dead, just that he's breathing.'" Other testimonies refer to other block chiefs using this killing method.[53] Simon Gutman recounted that his father had been in Gruenbaum's block and that he went there every evening. Gruenbaum was very wicked, and Simon warned him against doing anything bad to his father.

Elie Garbarz, a member of the Communist Party from Paris,[54] related that he had heard that Eliezer made a habit of using the epithet "dirty Jews." But even so he was no worse than others, and a myth had grown up around him because "his father was a public figure." Palshemko Lampka painted a nicer picture: "He was 100 percent a good guy. He didn't beat, didn't do anything. I didn't hear."[55] As far as can be discerned from the film itself, these testimonies were included without any effort on the part of the filmmakers to verify them.

Gerlik told Turbiner, one of the researchers for the film, that when he edited *Ot Cain* he had in his possession "really horrifying testimonies about Eliezer and Yitzhak Gruenbaum," but that he had toned them down because he had not wanted to impinge on the chances of Eliezer's nephew, who had become religious, to find a good match. He also claimed that Ka-Tzetnik had told him that he had chosen the name Prochtenbaum ("fruit tree") for the character he based on Eliezer to imply that the apple had indeed not fallen far from the tree:[56] "Yitzhak was a terrible antisemite," he asserted, and with regard to Eliezer, there was plenty of testimony that he was the same. "It's unbelievable what a beast he was," Gerlik said. One example was that he had ordered the leader of a Hasidic sect to crawl on all fours at the door to the block.

Turbiner also spoke with Rabbi Mordecai Noigershel, who told him that most of what he knew about Eliezer came from Ka-Tzetnik's book, and that what he knew about Yitzhak Gruenbaum's roles during the war he knew from reading *The Seventh Million*, a history of the impact of the Holocaust on Israeli society written by Tom Segev. "Rivka, Eliezer's sister-in-law, demanded that Ka-Tzetnik declare that Prochtenbaum was not Gruenbaum, and she knew why. I didn't ask him to say that Prochtenbaum was not Noigershel. Even if Ka-Tzetnik had added literary imagery to the character, it still leaves him a man who sold his brothers to gain his status at Auschwitz," the rabbi declared. Rabbi Menachem Porush, a leader of Agudat Israel, told Turbiner, in contrast, that "Yitzhak was hostile to Haredi Judaism and to Agudat Israel, and his son, well, his son fell in the battle of Ramat Rachel, was a martyr, and in such a case I have nothing to say."[57]

The members of the family consistently sought to portray the story using the testimony Eliezer offered during the proceedings in Poland and France, using the questions and notes he had drafted then, as well as the writings from which the selections included in *Gevilei Esh* were taken. They also used Yitzhak's version of events. Yonatan Gruenbaum wrote a book on the affair during the 1980s but never published it; parts of it were given to academic researchers. A fourth source was Matti Regev-Gruenbaum, Yonatan's son.

Yonatan, the youngest of the three brothers, sought to highlight the logical and factual flaws in the written and oral allegations made about Eliezer. In particular, he directed the shafts of his critique at the book written by the Communist historian Bar Mark on the one hand and on several of the Haredi writers on the other. The atmosphere of a lynch mob had grown up around Itche, he wrote. The reason was that he was the son of Yitzhak Gruenbaum: "No other Jewish kapo was persecuted the way Itche was."[58]

He invested great effort in understanding the context of the attacks on his brother, his father, and the relationship between them. He also examined their positions within larger milieus that impinged on issues such as post-Emancipation Jewish identity, the challenges that Zionism presented to other identities and movements, Haredi infighting, and to the agonizing question of God's presence during the Holocaust. In an attempt to add depth to his manuscript, he pointed out the anti-Zionist and Haredi sources of the accusations and their impact on the family story. While Yonatan did a good job of grappling with the charges made by Mark and by Eliezer's Communist comrades, the opinions and positions voiced in Haredi texts were beyond his professional and rhetorical abilities to withstand.[59]

His son, Matti Regev, tried to complete his father's project. In the interviews with him that appear in the documentary film that he took part in making, *HaBen shel Gruenbaum* (Gruenbaum's son), and in a newspaper article he authored, he did his best to score a success where his grandfather and father had only gone hoarse in failure. Along with the film's producers and researchers, he searched out witnesses and testimonies in Poland, and documents in France that would prove that the accusations against Eliezer were a malevolent conspiracy aimed at his uncle and family. During the process, Regev fell out with the creators of the movie, and they parted ways. Some of those involved came to view Regev as a propagandist in his family's service. He came to see them as sensationalists and yellow journalists. The two sides threatened to sue each other, eventually reaching a compromise according to which the film would include a segment in which Regev would stand by his uncle's grave and give his version of the story. When the film came out, viewers and critics wrote that the genre the filmmakers had chosen did not do justice to the gravity of its subject. Film is a rhythmic medium, they argued, that requires drama and is dependent on hunting up cinematic material that can create a convincing and suspenseful narrative. One of the critics, Tamar Rotem, wrote in *Ha'aretz*:

> A gangling man strides in the dark. His hand, hanging by his side, holds a yellowing photograph. The outsized photograph, which looks as if it has been taken off a wall, shows a vigorous man with a smoothly-shaved head looking straight into the camera. His gaze is resolute but not menacing. The man's face is clean-shaven, round, and clear, but at the same time bold in expression, of the type that remains in one's memory. This brief scene from the film *Gruenbaum's Son*, which will be screened on the night of Holocaust Memorial Day on Channel 2, shows Matti Gruenbaum [*sic*] on a quest to reveal the enigmatic figure of his uncle, Eliezer Gruenbaum (seen in the photograph), a quest that is the focal point of the film.
>
> The photograph seems to attract the viewer's gaze like a magnet. It is difficult not to ponder the relaxed expression of the man in the picture, a man who was accused of being a sadistic kapo in Auschwitz, so vicious that the Jews killed him in the War of Independence (even though the accusations were never properly adjudicated). In the end, the natural expectation — even if it may be somewhat childish — is to receive some sort of confirmation about the accusations, or a proper answer to the question marks raised by this figure. The photograph, in any case, does not show the face of a human monster.[60]

Kroytoro's film documents the nephew's journey to Poland and Paris to seek out people who had known his uncle. The filmmaker tries to dispel the fog around the mysterious subject of his film and to uncover the truth behind the stories about Eliezer's life and death. It also examines the claim that Eliezer was not killed by enemy fire at Ramat Rachel during the War of Independence but was rather murdered as revenge or killed himself in battle. In Rotem's account, the film refutes the first claim, but not the second.

Rotem wrote that Eliezer's character and family background turned him, to his disadvantage, into a symbol, "a symbol of betrayal of his brethren. And from the moment he became a symbol the facts became less important, and he became an easier target for anger and frustration. How does a symbol come into being? The film does not occupy itself with explanations, but according to Matti Gruenbaum [Matti Regev], Itche's personality, so full of contradictions, and the position held by his father [Yitzhak] were no mean factors." The family, represented by the nephew, developed a "mythology" around Eliezer. Matti Gruenbaum, a playwright, "bears this family cross and ardently defends his uncle."

Regev's trip to Poland and Paris is problematic, she wrote, because "he does not seek to uncover the facts. On the contrary. The impression one receives is that Gruenbaum [Regev] is seeking to take advantage of his trip to shore up the facts he has in hand and that he is not prepared to accept every conclusion with an open mind. Gruenbaum [Regev] himself sees no problem with this."[61]

In 1989 Matti Regev responded to the recurring attacks on his grandfather, without making any mention of his uncle.[62] He wrote in the daily newspaper *Hadashot* that, a few weeks earlier, the same paper had, in its weekend supplement, allowed Haredi writers to again slander his grandfather, who was described as

> a Holocaust criminal, pure and simple. . . . Why should they accuse God? It's easier to blame Yitzhak Gruenbaum for not saving the children that God had decided to exterminate. . . .
>
> They take half-truths, facts from here and there, and bind them together the same way that they tie defective *mezuzot* to train accidents. For the average Israeli, contemporary history begins when Ben-Gurion pissed for the first time in the Holy Land.

The Haredim, for their part, have a longer historical memory, and they had hated Yitzhak Gruenbaum long before the Holocaust.

> They hated him because their policy was that the anger of the gentiles should not be aroused. And when faced with Auschwitz's crematoria, their policy was that angering the Germans was forbidden, and if one had to die then one should die a martyr's death. Yitzhak Gruenbaum was not afraid to arouse the fury of the gentiles. The Warsaw ghetto rebels were his disciples. That is the fundamental difference and the source of their hatred, and everything else is lies and slanders.

Past and present, the Haredim, Regev maintained, made use of the Holocaust in their effort to obliterate the Zionist enterprise, and his grandfather "was the only Zionist leader who had the courage to come out against them openly." He was not deterred by their threats and pressure, "and that is why there is a torrent of libels against Yitzhak Gruenbaum."[63]

His grandfather's name, he wrote, "has been forgotten and obliterated. Ben-Gurion stars as a prima donna in contemporary history. . . . The reason is that Gruenbaum has no party, no people to preserve his heritage. The Jews who knew him, who knew who he was and what he did, went up to heaven in the smoke of the crematoria of Auschwitz and Treblinka."[64]

||| THE STORIES OF SOME of the Gruenbaum family's third and fourth generation may be viewed as a response to the heavy burden that their family history imposed on them. The daughter of Bat-Ami and Binyamin, Eliezer's older brother, left Israel and lives in the United States with her children. Eliezer, son of Yonatan and Rivka, became religious and studies in a yeshiva. He underwent this metamorphosis while he was a teenage member of the socialist-Zionist youth movement HaShomer haTza'ir. The trigger was his reading of *Emunah u-biṭaḥon* (Faith and trust), a work by the Hazon Ish, Rabbi Avraham Yeshayahu Karelitz, who had been the leader of the Haredi community in Palestine and the early State of Israel. He later began attending classes at the Na'aseh veNishma Yeshiva in Tel Aviv. His teacher there was Rabbi Menachem Gerlik, a man that the family considered one of the most prominent slanderers of its good name. Gerlik also opened his house to Eliezer, and Eliezer decided to become a student at the yeshiva and to live an observant life. He first studied at the Or Sameach Yeshiva in Jerusalem, then went on to the Ponivetz, Tifrah, and Slobodka yeshivot, where he obtained most of his Torah education.[65]

Rivka tried hard to fight his return to religion, but without result. He had an arranged marriage with a young Haredi woman and has lived in that community ever since. Apparently, however, he inherited his family's political genes — he was later elected a city councilman. According to his mother, who has been active in organizations that fight efforts to persuade Jews to become religious, her son was ensnared in a premeditated operation. She is convinced that the Haredim wanted him in particular — after turning the atheistic Zionist leader Gruenbaum into a demonic figure, they wanted revenge as well. They wanted Eliezer so that they would have the upper hand in a horrifying struggle to prove that they had been right all along.[66]

14 History, Politics, and Memory

Realm of Memory 1

A great outpouring of retribution and revenge began while the prisoners were still in the camps. Isaiah Trunk has noted that hundreds of copies of a "blacklist" of perceived collaborators circulated at the time. It provided personal details and an account of the crimes committed by each suspect, along with a call for revenge. Cells of resistance movements and independent local organizations liquidated prisoners who collaborated with the Germans or other oppressors. On the eve of liberation and immediately thereafter, prisoners hunted down their nemeses among former camp officials, seeking an outlet for their pain and frustration. This was the background to the accounts of Eliezer being beaten at Buchenwald by a detachment of prisoners. Fearing that lynchings and other acts of vengeance would multiply, the Central Committee of Liberated Jews in the American Zone issued a memorandum declaring that collaborators should be punished only through proper and institutionalized procedures. They advocated a centralized, rapid, and thorough examination of suspected collaborators and, in cases where it was called for, punishment according to law (they did not specify which law). The urge to capture and punish collaborators was a way for liberated prisoners to cope with their trauma:

> During the war there was a sharp distinction between the German rulers and the Jews, who were condemned to pain and suffering. An elite sprang up, under different names. And under a variety of circumstances it more or less consciously placed itself in a preferential position between the two worlds. The world of the tormentors and the world of the victims. It is only natural that, following liberation, the Jewish world needs to demand that the role of these "notables" of the years of the catastrophe be investigated and that verdicts be reached as to whether they are fit to take a place in our society, or whether they are to be swept out of our camp.[1]

Trunk describes how "courts of honor" set up in the camps and the occupation zones dealt with this painful and complex task. The members of these panels took up each case on its merits, without judging anyone in advance. They did not absolve those who claimed that they had merely followed orders handed down by a higher authority. The fate of the accused would be determined by their actions. At least two witnesses were required for the courts to launch an investigation; the courts guaranteed that those accused could, on their own or via a surrogate, appeal the verdict if new evidence or witnesses came to light.[2] But the mood at the time was such that victims wanted to find and punish their tormentors, and this could not but impinge on how these decisions were implemented. Given that parties and movements were also seeking to settle scores with each other, neither was it easy to keep proceedings free of politics.

The Yishuv also grappled with the questions of how, given that it lacked any official police or judicial authority, to "institutionalize" the examination and judgment of those suspected of collaboration. Furthermore, like the rest of the world, it had no experience in, and no moral and legal categories and language for, considering and judging the actions of people who had participated in an unprecedented mass murder machine. The Yishuv had to decide what the relevant moral and legal proceedings were, and what institutions and procedures could best see that justice was done, while also providing the victims of the Holocaust with psychological balm for their still-open wounds. At the beginning of September 1945, right after his return from a visit to the DP camps and from the Zionist convention in London, one of the leaders of Mapai and a member of the Jewish Agency Executive, Eliyahu Dobkin, told his colleagues on the Histadrut's Executive Committee:

> Here I wish to say some things that I am afraid to speak about, even here, but I am greatly troubled and somehow I have to share these things with my comrades. . . . It is something I would not believe had I not seen it with my own eyes. . . . Among the Jews who survived are . . . people that the surviving remnants view as criminals . . . [and] they treat them even worse than they do the Nazi Germans. . . . There are lynchings.[3]

In Munich he was told about hundreds of Jews who had filled posts at various levels in the Nazi system and who had been murdered by fellow Jews immediately after liberation. One of the liquidators told him: "Three million Jews were killed in Poland, 70,000 Jews remain, and it will be no disaster if a few thousand less are left." He presumed that that was an exaggeration and that the real number killed amounted to a few hundred. He himself saw Jews who got rid of another Jew who, they claimed, was "a most terrible sadist."[4]

But who could be a judge, he asked? It seemed to Dobkin "that here, more than anywhere else, we must attend to what our Sages said: Do not judge your fellow until you have been in his place. . . . On the other hand, it is inconceivable that there not be justice."[5] How could one judge the men of the Sonderkommando? How was it possible to hand down a verdict on a man who bore his own mother's body to the crematorium and who defended himself by saying that "many good Jews performed all sorts of jobs of that sort, it's not so horrible." How should one treat a man who served on the Judenrat of a ghetto? After all, not every Judenrat member took the path of Adam Czerniaków, the chairman of the Warsaw Ghetto Jewish Council, who committed suicide when he learned that he would have to oversee the deportation of the ghetto's inhabitants to the death camps. There had been many "who helped the Germans make up lists and turned over their brethren, and some say that those who served in a Judenrat should not be left alive, and one of these men [who thought this] was a member of our delegation to London."[6]

"It seems to me that it is no secret," Dobkin told his colleagues, "that the son of one of our good Zionists has been accused of this same crime. I feel the pain of the tragedy of this elderly father."[7] Eliezer's story had just started making the rounds in Paris, but his Histadrut colleagues knew very well who the son and the "elderly father" were.

Dobkin reported that, at the London Congress, "it was decided to establish a court, at the very least in Palestine, to prevent all sorts of lynch cases. The court should hand down verdicts at least with regard to those Jews who come to the country."[8]

As time went by and more immigrants arrived in Israel, the number of such cases rose. For example, "M," a member of the Workers Council in a city in northern Palestine, was walking down a street in Haifa when passersby identified him as a collaborator. In Tivon, another northern settlement, a man designated as "Z" was arrested, accused of beating his underlings in a German camp. The man who oversaw the synagogue at the Dan Carmel Hotel in Haifa charged a Jewish tourist who was honored by being called up to the Torah of being a brutal kapo from the Landsberg camp in Germany. He started shouting, frightening the tourist. The other worshippers grabbed the accused man and hauled him off to the nearest police station. Another tourist, from the United States, found in the Nahariyya telephone book the name of the man who had beaten his grandfather to death in the Łódź ghetto. At an ice cream stand in Tel Aviv a woman identified a woman designated as "AT," who she said had been her overseer in Block 7 in Auschwitz. In Pardes Hannah a woman identified her kapo from the same camp's Block 3. The accused woman, who was working as a nurse, was pregnant. In February 1951 a man accused of being "Brutal Harry" from the Dąbrowa Górnicza Camp was arrested, as was "Blinder Max" from the Jaworzno concentration camp, both of them identified by people who were under their charge.[9]

Most of them were in their late twenties or early thirties; a small number were older. One example of the latter was "YS," a fifty-two-year-old doctor from Hadera who had been at Fünf Teichen, or "MT," a sixty-one-year-old attorney who had been at the Sharhorod camp.[10] Many officials from the camps and ghettos blended in with the masses of refugees that made their way through Europe to the DP camps and to other places where refugees gathered. Some of them unsuccessfully sought to emigrate to countries overseas — the immigration laws and quotas of the most popular destinations did not make this easy. Others attached themselves to groups of Jews waiting to gain entrance to Palestine, hoping that when they arrived and the refugees were spread among Palestine's cities and rural settlements, they would escape recognition and be able to start new lives. But in no few cases inmates from the ghettos and camps where they had been officials identified them and sought vengeance. According to Tom Segev, one newspaper demanded that all such collaborators be "liquidated." But, the newspaper cautioned, it was not enough that a person point to another person in the street and shout "kapo!" The suspects' guilt had to be established with certainty, and even then the guilty men and women should not be subject to popular justice — sentences should be handed down and carried out by "authorized institutions."[11]

In the autumn of 1945 the Yishuv leadership decided to establish such an authorized institution, but nothing actually was done. The Jewish Agency Executive was reluctant to take up such an emotional and difficult issue, especially at a time when it had many other urgent matters demanding its full attention. Neither were the British Mandate authorities included to address the subject. They had their hands full with trying to block illegal Jewish immigration, suppress the Jewish rebellion, keeping the Jews and Arabs from each other's throats, and later with preparing for their evacuation of Palestine. When the state was established, however, it was no longer possible to shunt the issue off to someone else. The new country's police force was overwhelmed with complaints filed by citizens who claimed to have identified Nazi collaborators and who demanded their punishment.[12]

The law did not permit the police to arrest these suspects. It could only detain them, record their names, and sometimes save them from an angry crowd — no more. The police called on the Ministry of Justice to draft a law against Jewish war criminals, and in the autumn of 1949 the press reported an exchange of communications between the two institutions on this matter.[13] Segev wrote that "the Ministry of Justice, like the Jewish Agency before it, did not rush. It was reluctant to take on such a delicate issue and preferred to deal with other things first." Rabbi Mordechai Nurock of the United Religious Front, the most prominent of the members of the Knesset active on the issue, and himself a Holocaust survivor from Riga who lost his wife and two sons in the Holocaust, did not let up. Minister of Justice Pinhas Rosen assured Nurock that his office was working on it, but needed more time. Half a year went by, after which Nurock charged that "the State of Israel is the only country in the world in which there is no way of arraigning and judging Nazi murderers and their abettors. Were Goebbels and Goering, may they rot in hell, here among us, the hand of the law would not reach them."[14]

Public pressure eventually worked — experts at the Ministry of Justice and the Ministry of the Police together drafted an appropriate law against war criminals, and on March 27, 1950, Rosen submitted the "Nazis and Nazi Collaborators — Punishment — Law" to the Knesset. It was passed half a year later. Its goal was laid out in the explanation attached to the bill: "Closing accounts with the past, we will not forget and not forgive." The law, it was stressed, reflected the profound change in the status of the Jewish people. Up to this point, the Jews as a nation had had no authority to bring Nazi criminals and their helpers to justice, to demand their extradition, and to bring them to trial in the Jews' own courts. The Yishuv had claimed to speak for the entire Jewish people, even if it had never received any formal mandate to do so, but had no means of enforcing that claim. The State of Israel now asserted its right to act as the people's tribune in addressing the horrors of World War II and its perpetrators. It reiterated this claim in its reparations agreement with Germany and in its moral defense of arresting and bringing Adolf Eichmann to trial in Israel.[15] But some Jews objected, seeing it as a nationalization and appropriation of Jewish leadership by the Zionists.[16]

The law included a retroactivity clause, granting Israeli courts the power to hand down punishments for actions that had not been defined as crimes at the time they were committed. It also authorized these courts to hear cases involving crimes committed outside Israel's borders, and to try people who had already been judged on the same charges in another country. It also established less stringent rules of evidence and procedure and stipulated that the courts could accept any piece of evidence that would aid in uncovering the truth and in the performance of justice. Furthermore, it permitted courts to judge actions alone and not to require proof of criminal intent. Several of its provisions also abrogated the principle of limitations, and the general amnesty that had been promulgated by the Provisional State Council was declared to be without force with regard to these crimes. The law would soon be the subject of pointed criticism.[17]

At the end of the Knesset debate, it was resolved that the law would distinguish between war criminals whose criminal acts were committed during World War II but outside the camps, who would be punished in accordance with international law, and those accused of abuse, exploitation, and persecution of camp inmates. This latter group would be judged in accordance with the moral standards of the Jewish and Israeli people, as codified in the new law.[18]

Trials of alleged collaborators began as soon as the law was passed. Hanna Yablonka counts some forty such trials, most of them conducted during the first half of the 1950s, the rest in the early 1960s. One of them was conducted in parallel with the Eichmann trial. The final person to be brought to trial under the provisions of this law seems to have been "LG,"[19] a woman who had served as a kapo in a camp in Germany at the end of the war. Her case was heard in 1971, two years prior to the Yom Kippur War.

The verdicts ranged from complete acquittal to the death penalty. A total of thirty-three trials were conducted in the 1950s. Yablonka was able to obtain documentation of twenty-one of these, of which thirteen ended in conviction and prison sentences and eight in acquittals. By the mid-1960s five more trials had been held, three of which ended in acquittal and two in conviction and jail sentences. But more than two hundred complaints were filed with the police under the law during these two decades.[20]

The only case in which a death penalty was handed down against a Jew was that of "YA," a kapo from the Karditz and Faulbrück forced labor camps. The sentence was imposed by two of the three judges, Pinhas Avishar and a judge named Lein, against the minority opinion of Judge Yosef Michael Lamm, himself a survivor of Dachau and, as a member of the Knesset before being appointed judge, involved in shepherding the bill through the parliament. Lamm's opinion was that the appropriate sentence was ten years' imprisonment. All three judges recommended to YA that he apply to the country's president to have the death penalty commuted to a prison term. YA did so, and out of consideration for his bad health and the fact that he had had a leg amputated, the request was granted. He died a short time later.[21]

The law would later come to be seen as problematic because of its "accusation and punishment of the victim."[22] It took a place at the center of a historic and painful debate about cowardice and heroism, resistance and collaboration, as well as in political confrontations over history, memory, and the past's relationship to present, and its trajectory into the future.

Two members of the Knesset who were Holocaust survivors, Mordechai Nurock and Aryeh Sheftel (of Mapai — a workers' party — and a survivor of the Vilna ghetto), opened the debate. Both viewed the law as a means of memorialization. It provided only moral succor — no one could bring back the six million murdered Jews, but it was nevertheless important, Nurock said, that "we esteem and sanctify their memory at least in this law." Sheftel said that "we have erected no memorial and no name to the Holocaust and the Jewry that was killed," but this would be the first time that the "Knesset of Israel" (with all that that expression implied in terms of the people's independence and sovereignty) would speak up on the subject, "mandating the performance of justice against the Nazis and their helpers." Nahum Nir-Rafalkes (of the Mapam party), chairman of the Knesset's Constitution, Law, and Justice Committee, said that "this law expresses our remonstration, and that of the entire Jewish people, against these said crimes, and especially against the crimes committed by the Nazis and their helpers during World War II. Our protest receives expression in this law, to the extent that a dry law can express that."[23]

The Knesset debate, on the floor and in committee, quickly turned to the difficult and painful subject of the Jewish Councils — the *Judenräte* — that the Nazis set up in the ghettos, and the fundamental question that troubled so many people. How should such a complex issue be addressed? Would passing judgment on the Judenräte not be a display of arrogance and proof of the inability to comprehend the circumstances in which these people acted? How could the vantage point of the Knesset in Jerusalem not provide a simplistic view of the position in which the heroes of that time and place had to live and act?[24] Yisrael Bar-Yehuda (Idelson), a Mapam parliamentarian from Kibbutz Yagur who was one of the leaders of the United Kibbutz Movement, having arrived in Palestine from Ukraine in the 1920s, took exception to section 10 of the law. That section stated that a defendant who had been a "persecuted person" could claim in his defense that he had committed the acts attributed to him because he had been threatened with death. I know, Bar-Yehuda said

> that this matter is linked, by some Jews, to a number of harsh memories, and we all know that the Judenräte were, unfortunately, a fact and that many hundreds of Jews stumbled in this matter, including Jews who previously had been respected public figures, from nearly all parties and circles. But I think that we would be leading others astray, both in terms of education and of justice, if we were to say that these people should be absolved of responsibility because they did what they did out of fear. I say that every member of a Judenrat who sat there because he was sent there is a criminal, a helper of the Nazis. Because he did this out of the specific animal instinct every person has to defend his life. Because one of the things that separates man and beast is that a man knows that sometimes he needs to accept death rather than to commit a transgression.[25]

Bar-Yehuda maintained that Adam Czerniaków, the chairman of the Warsaw Ghetto Jewish Council, found a way to resolve the ethical dilemma he faced: "Had he not committed suicide, he would have to have been put on trial for helping send tens of thousands of Jews to extermination." Total absolution, he argued, should be granted only to members of the anti-Nazi underground, even if they had committed acts "as the Nazis did," so long as they had done so with the purpose of "destroying Nazism from within."[26]

Judge Lamm (Mapai), a Holocaust survivor himself, was inclined to go easy on Jews who had served as kapos. "I know of many cases in which such people, who were themselves persecuted, did all they could to avert crimes." If two men were in a room with hundreds of other people and they did not keep order — which happened in many cases — there was a danger that the Nazi superior would impose collective punishment on everyone "and would march them barefoot for many hours outside, in the winter cold, less than 17 or 18 degrees." To prevent that, Lamm said, "to forestall a mortal danger to the entire group," it was necessary to punish people who did not toe the line.[27] Sheftel called out, "Who compelled them to accept these positions?" Lamm replied: "I inform you that there were people who held the post of kapo at the request and behest of the prisoners. Member of the Knesset Aryeh Sheftel may have had experience at one or another camp, but I know that there were such prisoners who performed a sacred service as kapo." A person's membership in a Judenrat was not in and of itself proof that a man was a criminal, Lamm said: "It may well be that he did all he could to prevent crimes and it may well be that other Jews were actually interested in having him rather than another person on the Council [Judenrat]. . . . We should not demand of a persecuted man, solely to prove to history that the Jewish people were clean and proper, that he behave in a manner different from what any one of us would have done."[28]

Knesset members Hans Rubin (Mapam) and Eliezer Preminger (Hebrew Communist) backed Bar-Yehuda's position. The Knesset could not ignore, the latter said, "that collaboration is what helped the Nazis carry out their schemes. Collaboration meant when someone took a position on a Judenrat or as a kapo thinking that in this way he could save himself. Furthermore, no one denied that a kapo had to prove his loyalty to the Germans. . . . If he were a kapo for two or three years he would necessarily be a criminal." Moreover, he did not understand what had been called passivity, acceptance of fate, going "like lambs to the slaughter": "I asked Jews how they went in such an organized, German way, such that it was possible to murder 7,000 people each day."[29]

Moshe Ben-Ami (Sephardim) proposed to his colleagues that they keep in mind at least two principles in their discussion of the issue. First, "Do not judge your fellow until you have been in his place." Second, most humans are simple folk: "We are not talking about exceptional people,"[30] who are rare. The debate and the law should address the experience of the average person acting in history, since they are the overwhelming majority.

Zerach Warhaftig (United Religious Front), who had experienced Nazi rule firsthand, opposed the generalizations about Jewish officeholders. He called on his colleagues to study the facts. "There were cases in which a Jew was compelled to accept an appointment and he accepted it with the intention of doing all he could to alleviate matters, and did all he could to alleviate matters," he said, "and they do not view themselves as culpable." It was also possible to separate the question of acquittal or conviction in court, which in his opinion was the principal question, and the question of punishment. "There are situations in which conviction in court with the lightest possible punishment," he suggested, "is much more harsh than a heavy punishment in another situation, because what is important here is the fact of conviction itself."[31]

The debate quickly descended into political jockeying. Members invoked the Holocaust and its horrors to skewer political enemies. They also realized that they were not just judging the past but establishing standards of behavior for the future. Bar-Yehuda's inclination to grant clemency only to members of the underground, under the conditions he laid out, was not disinterested — as a member of Mapam, he had an interest in distinguishing between the "parties of resistance" and the "parties of collaboration." After all, many members of the resistance had come from HaShomer haTza'ir and similar movements, or had been members of left-wing Zionist parties and their associated settlement movements, most of which had ties to Mapam. Those who held up select participants in the ghetto rebellions as paragons also stressed the ideological connection between the rebels and the members of pioneering youth movements like Dror and HaShomer haTza'ir, associated with Ahdut haAvodah and Mapam, two socialist-Zionist parties founded after the Holocaust. Notably, and with clear political intent, they did not include in this pantheon of heroes the ghetto rebels who belonged to other movements, such as the right-wing Revisionist Betar youth movement, the religious Zionist Bnei Akiva movement, or Gordonia, a youth movement associated with Mapai, the nonsocialist HaNoar haTzioni, and the anti-Zionist Bund.[32]

The connection between the Holocaust and both local and international politics was most clearly evident in the speeches made by Eri Jabotinsky (Herut) and Meir Vilner (Communist), who put everything on the table. Vilner called for a war against the new fascists, saying that "the new Anglo-American imperialists are being assisted by German Nazi criminals." He viewed the law through the prism of the Cold War, and as a result declared that the fight was not only against the Nazis of the past, but also against the current incarnation of fascism — Western capitalism:

> One of the defects in the wording of this law is that it is a law only about Nazis. Nazism is just one of the manifestations of fascism, racism, and war-mongering. Nazism can return in other places as well. Fascism and Nazism are returned and reorganizing in Germany and in other places. . . . Fascism and Nazism were forms of government by capital finance groups, which prepared for war, sought to conquer other countries, to gain markets. To divert the masses from the real enemy, they set one nation against another. They disseminated Nazi and fascist racial theory and exterminated the Jews and members of other nations.[33]

Eri Jabotinsky, the son of the founder of Revisionist Zionism, Ze'ev Jabotinsky, demanded the establishment of a special court "to investigate the entire history of the Holocaust and to determine the measure of primary and secondary responsibility that lies on one or another nation, on one or another political party, or one or another person." One of the court's tasks would be "to investigate the behavior of our various institutions, among them and principally the behavior of the Jewish Agency. And when I say 'investigate,' I do not mean that assuming that misdeeds or crimes were committed," he said. "But it behooves us to determine for future generations whether we really did all we could. We must establish that with certainty."[34]

Minister of Labor Golda Meyerson retorted that Jabotinsky's demand was "sacrilege" and asked how he dared "to mention, in the same breath with the Jewish Agency, those . . . whose hands ran with the blood of Jewish babies." Shmuel Merlin, a member of the Knesset for Herut and leader of that party's radical Lamerhav faction, then published an article that intensified the offensive:

> Each of us — including Mrs. Meyerson — should commune with his soul and conscience and place his hand on his heart and say: our hands did not spill the blood of the six million. . . . Did we do everything that we could? Did we exhaust all the possibilities for influence, the connections, public opinion, pressure, threats, diplomatic activity, effective protest operations, and "irresponsible" actions or even desperate ones? There is no point in casting down our eyes.[35]

Everyone who read this knew that Merlin had been one of the leaders of a group led by Hillel Kook (under the alias "Peter Bergson") that had been active in the United States and called for forceful, open, and strident protests that would force the American leadership to do more to save the Jews. Kook's group had stridently opposed the Jewish Agency leadership, controlled by Mapai, and its actions were admired for their creativity and boldness, but also aroused a great deal of opposition from the Zionist establishment and other Jewish organizations in the United States.[36] The Nazis and Nazi Collaborators (Punishment) Law, 1950, thus served as a means of settling other political accounts and honing polemics. It was another example of the difficulty of removing the discussion of the Holocaust from its political contexts of the past and present.

During the early 1950s the Holocaust became the subject of an increasing number of events and debates. A prime example was the controversy over the acceptance of reparations from Germany and the agreement Israel signed with that country in September 1952. The Herut party organized violent protests against accepting German money. On the other side of the political spectrum, Mapam also opposed the agreement, and its spokesmen likened their fight against it to the ghetto rebellions. The Israeli government's readiness to sign an agreement with Germany, they claimed, made it the equivalent of a Judenrat.[37] The same happened during the debate over the Yad Vashem law, which was introduced in the Knesset close to the tenth anniversary of the Warsaw ghetto uprising.

These debates assumed polarities between the ghetto fighters and the Judenräte. A part of the Israeli public viewed the former as the only possible model of heroism and the latter as the acme of cowardice, Jewish supplication, and collaboration with the Nazis. Another part of the public believed that Judenrat members could also be heroes, doing all they could under impossible circumstances to save what Jews they could and maintain Jewish communal life under Nazi rule. Mapam's Knesset members sought to stress armed resistance and to place it at the center of the way the nation would memorialize the Holocaust. Articles written by central figures in the ghetto resistance movements who were identified in Israel with Mapam and by other important party figures reiterated the three points that were at the center of the storm: the moral importance of the ghetto uprisings; the decisive role played by the members of youth movements in the uprisings, and in particular members of left-wing Zionist youth movements, in contrast with the helplessness displayed by the Jewish public at large; and the criminal collaboration with the Germans engaged in by ghetto leaders, Judenräte, and the Jewish police forces.[38]

Although the left wing tried to present a unified front, its different groups and factions jockeyed over who "owned" the uprisings, who had directed the fighting, and which of the fighters had been most courageous. Mapam, HaShomer haTza'ir, and their associated kibbutz movement, HaKibbutz haArtzi, adopted the figure of Mordechai Anielewicz, leader of the Warsaw ghetto's Jewish Combat Organization and a member of HaShomer haTza'ir, who was killed during the rebellion. They established a memorial to him at Kibbutz Yad Mordechai. The rival United Kibbutz Movement and its associated political party, Ahdut haAvodah, chose as its heroes two other leaders of the same uprising, Yitzhak "Antek" Zuckerman and Zivia Lubetkin, both of whom helped found one of that movement's kibbutzim, Lohamei haGeta'ot, the name of which means "the Ghetto Fighters."[39]

Angry retorts were not long in coming, as Roni Stauber and others have shown. True, proclaimed an article in *Herut*, the newspaper of the party of the same name, led by Menachem Begin, the ghetto uprisings put an end to Jews going to their deaths like "lambs to the slaughter." Most of these fighters "fell in this heroic war, but they saved their honor and the honor of their nation." But, the article cautioned, the words and actions of former members of the resistance who were now part of Israel's Left placed themselves at the heart of the rebellion, undervaluing and even ignoring the role played by other movements — in particular the youth movement associated with the Herut party, Betar.

In other words, Yitzhak Gruenbaum had successfully compelled the publication of his son's story in *Gevilei Esh* at a time of avid, varied, and anxious preoccupation with the Holocaust. The pain that led him to do so is understandable. It is harder to take in the considerations and assumptions that led him to believe that the public atmosphere was amenable to a discussion of what his son had done as an official at Auschwitz-Birkenau and that he could place Eliezer in the national pantheon as part of the collective national memory that was then in formation. We can only be astounded at his capacity for taking advantage of every platform that came his way to speak about heroism, collaboration, and the Judenräte, and to point out proper modes of action, as if he had no personal stake in the matter.[40]

It is difficult to understand why Mapam and its newspaper, *Al haMishmar*, so sensitive to symbols and symbolization, hosted Yitzhak Gruenbaum, with all the baggage he brought, as a pundit and columnist. For his part, how could this political leader, journalist, and intellectual have failed to comprehend the extent to which the Holocaust discourse had been politicized? How could he not have been aware of the connection between history and politics in his young country, the transformation of the Holocaust, throughout the political spectrum, to a tool to be used in advancing other agendas? How could he not have understood that he and his family could fall into the hands of people who would have difficulty coping with what Primo Levi called the Manichean tendency to divide between black and white, us and them, friend and enemy?[41] Years would go by before the embryonic society would no longer feel compelled to flee from gray areas and complex situations regarding that terrifying world that did not fit any known model. Perhaps the opposite is true — maybe he thought, in his frustration and pain, that precisely because of this he could add something of his own to the varied mosaic of Israeli society that every interested party was trying to mold as it wished.

Realm of Memory 2

The vehemence of the war that Shonfeld, Gerlik, Noigershel, Shalmon, and their like-minded associates waged against Yitzhak Gruenbaum and his son went deeper than adolescent willfulness or simple political confrontation and debate among adherents of different parties or ideologies. It also touched on other agendas, such as the clarification of identity and the serious theological questions that were fired in their direction. These questions preoccupied those members of the Haredi society who understood that the trauma of the Holocaust could have a destructive impact on their camp if it could not be fit into traditional views of redemption and divine providence. And if Haredi Judaism were to be annihilated by the impact of the Holocaust, that, in their view, would grant Hitler another victory.

The attack on the Gruenbaums was motivated principally by the imperative of coping with painful questions, which historian Ya'akov Talmon combined into a single one when he spoke at conferences at Yad Vashem: "Did these millions die to sanctify God's name? I imagine that many of them were killed without feeling that at all. They died for nothing, like uncountable numbers have done throughout history when humanity's animal nature has burst forth, nothing more." The attacks on Yitzhak and Eliezer were part of a larger process of grappling with questions of identity and part of Haredi society's consolidation of its collective memory in the face of two severe blows: the Holocaust and the establishment of a secular Zionist state. The process included denial, suppression, repression, and simplification. As with others, this process enabled them to live, even if uncomfortably and on borrowed time, with the troubling, bewildering, and clashing challenges that the Holocaust presented. Yitzhak and Eliezer Gruenbaum were easy prey — little effort was required to use the father, son, and their alleged transgressions to accuse the Zionists of responsibility for the Holocaust and what they viewed as despicable treatment of their community during the war. They viewed Zionism as the embodiment of rebellion against God, leading to the Holocaust as divine punishment. Zionism, in their view, violated the rabbinic injunctions against *dehiqat haketz*, seeking to hurry redemption, and *la'alot behomah*, rebelling against the rule of the gentiles. These were precisely the sins that they had accused Yitzhak Gruenbaum of committing during his service in the Polish Sjem.

Yitzhak's role in establishing the Bloc of National Minorities and other initiatives of his to improve the lot of the Jews were viewed by the Haredim as insubordination against the gentiles that would result in violence and legal impositions on the Jews. Events, as they saw it, bore out their interpretation — the elder Gruenbaum's political activity, like that of Chaim Weizmann and other Zionist leaders, exacerbated antisemitism, led to Nazism, and caused the Holocaust. Yitzhak, having headed the Jewish hierarchy in Poland, was the prime suspect in this offense.

In their view, as a central figure in the Yishuv leadership and a committed Zionist, he was one of those responsible for what they viewed as the divine wrath that Zionism brought on the Jewish people. He was guilty in part because of everything the Jewish national movement did to establish a state, actions that provoked the hostility of the world's nations. Zionism was the mother of all sins, responsible for World War II and the Holocaust. When had Hitler's staff made the fateful decision to exterminate Europe's Jews? According to the rebbe of the Satmar Hasidim, it happened when Weizmann, the president of the Zionist Organization, took it upon himself to speak for the entire Jewish people and to accede to the declaration of war against Nazi Germany. Doing so had been a deliberate Zionist attempt to strike out at the Jewish people, "and the nemesis responded in kind that he accepted their declaration and would make war against all of Israel." Shalmon seconded this accusation: "There can be no doubt that this was what Weizmann intended, to put the Jews in danger as much as that was possible." Shonfeld, for his part, referred to Dieter Wisliceny, Eichmann's representative in Slovakia and the man with whom Rabbi Chaim Dov Ber Weissmandel negotiated a halt to the deportation of Jews from that country. Shonfeld claimed Wisliceny had said that the German ambassador in Washington had conveyed to Hitler a report on a convention of Zionist leaders and the Jewish Congress in New York in which the American Jewish leader Stephen Wise had declared war on Germany in the name of the Jewish people. Upon reading this report, Hitler went berserk, fell to the ground, gnashed at the carpet, and shouted "Now I will annihilate them, now I will annihilate them!" Wise was a Reform rabbi and leader of the Zionist Organization of America, as well as, in 1922, one the founders of the Jewish Institute of Religion in New York. This center of liberal Judaism was a thorn in the side of the Haredi community. The combination of Reform Judaism and Zionism was a fatal one for the Haredim.

It was the Zionist movement that had wakened the Nazi beast and was thus responsible for the Holocaust, Haredim claimed. The same Zionist movement abandoned the Jews of Europe to the Nazis, they said, and in doing so confirmed that the Zionists were, in their view, the central actors in the history and fate of modern Jewry. Just as every worthwhile revolutionary movement needs to have its axles oiled, Rabbi Moshe Shonfeld said, the Zionists viewed "the Jewish blood spilled during the Holocaust as oil for the axles of the Jewish state . . . what the Zionists did to European Jewry during World War II can only be defined as murder." As such, the Zionist leaders were "Holocaust criminals who contributed their part to the extermination."[42] According to this way of thinking, the Zionist leadership operated out of a deep malevolence for Diaspora Jewry, and religious Judaism in particular: "For the first time in our history, a wild antisemitism like the Nazi movement arose . . . and for the first time a movement arose from among the Jews that did not lag far behind them in its hatred for the Diaspora."[43] But the Nazis, he wrote, at least voiced their hatred openly. In contrast "these [other] criminals disguised themselves as loving the Jews, with love of the nation in their speech and Hitlerist hatred in their hearts. And in this way they succeeded, in their wickedness, to interfere with every rescue operation that appeared."[44] Ben-Gurion was "consumed by hatred of Judaism . . . it was irrational with him. . . . Many historians also testify that Hitler's hatred of Judaism was irrational."[45]

Yitzhak Gruenbaum, they explained, had said and written things that demonstrated that he privileged the Zionist enterprise and the imperative — irreproachable, in his view — to sacrifice other Jewish interests to the needs of building and advancing the Yishuv. From the moment that the Zionist movement focused its gaze, strength, and resources on the Yishuv, it forfeited the Jews who lived elsewhere. Gruenbaum was one of the architects of this policy and the worldview on which it was based. The secular Zionist leadership cruelly abandoned the Diaspora "out of political motives and astonishing irresponsibility," with a "deliberate method and ideological approach" and its leaders' "hands filled with blood and they interred the exterminated Jewish children of the Exile in the fortifications of [the Yishuv's] defenses. . . . Not only did they not lift a finger, but actually actively sought to block rescue attempts," wrote Rabbi Yisrael Eichler, a Belz Hassid and the editor of the weekly newspaper *haMahaneh haHaredi*.[46]

The focus on the Zionist project led its adherents to disregard the information about the extermination of the Jews that was coming in from Europe, claimed Shonfeld, Gerlik, Wuzelman, and Shalmon during the war and for years thereafter. This accusation contained more than just an echo of elements that penetrated Haredi discourse from the secular anti-Zionist critique of Zionism. But the facts flatly contradict their unequivocal allegations.

A few members of the Haredi community were courageous enough to acknowledge that, at the beginning of the war, they had had the same information at their disposal as did the Zionists and that they were no less responsible for the silence on the issue. No less courageously, they argued that the long time that elapsed before their own society correctly discerned what was happening in Europe was due not to paralysis or incapacity, but to a lack of empathy for their brethren in Europe. Rabbi Moshe Glickman-Porush, another activist, not a low-level one, in Agudat Israel, as well as one of the owners of the newspaper *Kol Yisrael*, admitted that he and his colleagues had not properly understood their previous reportage: "At times we thought that perhaps there was deliberate exaggeration . . . but today we are witness . . . and horrified by the spectacle of mass murder, and especially of the methods they used, God forbid."

A sharp observer who looks at how Haredi groups reacted to the information they possessed during the war, and especially in the final months before word of the Nazi annihilation machine became public, will see that they went through more or less the same psychological process that the Zionists did. They had the same apprehensions about the real meaning of the news, and had the same tendencies to repress their fears. So, for example, when shocking information reached Rabbi Meir Levin, chairman of Agudat Israel's World Executive Committee, the movement's most powerful body, he wrote a letter to Yitzhak Gruenbaum on August 27, 1942. Gruenbaum at the time headed a body called the Committee of Four (along with Eliyahu Dobkin, Emil Schmork, and Moshe Shapira), responsible for Polish Jewry. Levin pleaded with Gruenbaum to establish a "unitary central committee to help save our brethren in Poland." But it was only two months later, on October 23, 1942, that Rabbi Levin presented to his Executive Committee the material he had in his possession about the extent of the extermination program. A member of that body, Rabbi Isaac Breuer, doubted the reliability of the reports, but added that even if they were only partly true, the situation was terrible. Rabbi Moshe Blau, who would, just a month later, beat his chest and confess to responsibility for remaining silent, said that the news was unreasonable and the product of a sick mind. He opposed even holding public prayers for the Jews in Europe.

Yet, as time went by, Haredi circles increasingly felt that they had to change the nature of their engagement with the issue. At the meeting where Levin presented his information, the Executive Committee resolved to issue a wakeup call to members of Agudat Israel in Palestine and to appoint a committee to organize public prayer and supplications. It also resolved to ask to meet with the British high commissioner and to present him with their fears. Members of the Executive Committee criticized the Jewish Agency for not sharing information in its possession with Agudat Israel and for not including representatives of the movement in its discussions of the plight of Polish Jewry. But the information that Rabbi Levin had was sufficient for him to approach Gruenbaum. No new information was presented to the Agudat Israel Executive Committee when it met again a week later, on October 30, 1942, but the discussions were sharper, and it now decided to publish a public statement on the situation of the Jews in Europe and an urgent call for the Jews of the Yishuv and the Diaspora to close ranks.

Rabbi Blau, who just a short time earlier had said that the reports from Poland were the product of a sick mind, now wrote in *Kol Yisrael* that "even if we do not believe in the absolute accuracy of the [reports of the] barbaric malevolent acts against the Jews by the Nazis or at their orders, such as the use of Jews in experimental stations of poison gas, that their bodies are being handed over to the fat production industry and their bones are being used to fertilize fields, that thousands of Jews are being transported in cattle cars so as to reduce their numbers, it is still clear to us that Hitler has resolved . . . to physically annihilate all the Jews in Europe." He could hardly have been more explicit, and within a month all these facts would prove to be true.

Then why did the Agudat Israel leadership not appeal unequivocally and stridently to the Yishuv and the world? Hayim Shalem argues that a partial explanation can be found in the minutes of the October 30 Executive Committee meeting. Rabbi Levin reported then that he had met with the rebbe of the Gur Hasidic sect and with Rabbis Yosef Zvi Dushinsky, Avraham Yeshyahu Karelitz (the Hazon Ish), and Yosef Kahaneman. The rabbis had agreed to the decisions made at the previous meeting, "but asked that we proceed cautiously." He did not say what they meant by caution or why they thought it was important. Perhaps Mordechai Buksbaum offered an explanation when he said that a public campaign would be useless and possibly detrimental. "It may well be that the members of the Executive Committee sensed that they were still alone in comprehending the significance of the news, and that incautious action could make them look like eccentric doomsayers," Shalem suggests. The same mind-set can be seen in the proceedings of the Agudat Israel Central Committee at its meeting on November 18, 1942, and its subsequent actions. The meeting was held just two days before the return of a group of Jews from Palestine who had gotten stuck in Poland when the war had broken out. Its members told their leaders what they had seen in various parts of Poland. Scholars now view these testimonies as the ones that transformed the way the Yishuv leadership understood what was going on in Europe and which led them to publicize the information.

Despite the unambiguous statements made within Haredi institutions, and despite their growing understanding of the true nature of what was happening in Europe, Agudat Israel, like other parts of Haredi society and like other organizations in the Yishuv and the world, in the end wanted the Zionists to make the first move. True, Agudat Israel was not the Jewish Agency and lacked its network of information. It had no official standing as a representative of the Jews and did not have access to all the information that was being received by the Jewish Agency Executive in its capacity as the official and representative governing body of the Yishuv. Nevertheless, Shonfeld and others knew that this had never prevented Agudat Israel from taking independent action when it saw fit to do so. Agudat Israel had added its voice to the outcry only a few days after the official publication of the news of the Holocaust. In contradiction of the charges later made by Shonfeld and his colleagues, there were top-level figures in Agudat Israel who publicly acknowledged their wrongdoing and said that they, too, were guilty of keeping the news under wraps, of silence, of making the political calculation that it would be better, at least for the time being, to proceed "cautiously." In this the Haredim — their leaders, rabbis, and officials — were no different from the Zionists they abhorred. Even when they used terms like "catastrophe," it was a term that only went skin deep. In essence, deep down, they assumed that this catastrophe was much along the same lines as the "normal" familiar persecutions of the Jews known from time immemorial, not a mass, mechanized genocide.

Contemporary audiences may have missed the piercing and unambiguous words of some senior Haredim about the Holocaust, from which it clearly emerges that there were very different voices on the subject within the community, including those who preferred to roll their eyes to heaven and to wash their hands of the matter. But they could have found a more explicit statement of Haredi self-accusation voiced by Moshe Prager, a Haredi writer and scholar who fled Warsaw with the group of Hasidim who accompanied the rebbe of Gur and who reached Palestine in 1940. Prager was closely associated with the Gur Hasidic sect, the largest and most dominant of the groups that made up Agudat Israel. He was the moving spirit behind its monthly journal, *Digleinu*. Immediately after arriving in Palestine, Prager wrote a book called *Yiven haMetzulah haHadash* (the New *Yiven haMetzulah*, referring to a chronicle of the pogroms of 1648–1649 in Ukraine), in which he told of contemporary persecutions in Poland. Immediately following the Jewish Agency's official statement about the Nazi extermination program, Prager confessed "before the entire community on the sin I committed because I did not believe, and I also enticed others not to believe the tidings of Job that have reached us recently." Prager, who continued, after arriving in Palestine, to collect news on events in Europe and thus served as a significant source of information, was invited in October 1942 by Ben-Gurion to offer his assessment of the information that the Zionist leader had received about Nazi atrocities against the Jews. Ben-Gurion wrote in his diary that "Prager receives material from the

Polish government on the situation — on homelessness, the confiscation of property (there is no information about physical annihilation)." This was the final stretch in the process that Ben-Gurion himself underwent before he and the rest of the Zionist leadership decided to make an official public statement. It is interesting that, as a part of that process, Ben-Gurion thought it worthwhile to consult a Haredi expert from the rebbe of Gur's court.

Shonfeld and others stated that, as chairman of the Rescue Committee, set up by the Yishuv and Jewish Agency during the war, Yitzhak Gruenbaum bore responsibility for the feebleness and failures of that body. Most of all, Gruenbaum was to blame for the "deception" it perpetrated. But this was just another version of the charge that the Zionist movement had forsaken the Jews of Europe, in particular those Jews who did not fit their image of the "new Jew." This could be seen, they said, in the allocation of immigration certificates even before the war, the "selection" of immigrants that the Zionists made, and the criteria they used to determine which Jews to save.

Shonfeld had witnessed, as a young journalist, the debate within Agudat Israel about whether to join the Rescue Committee, ending in a decision in the affirmative. He had not been pleased with the decision. One of the most articulate writers in the Haredi community, he had protested, before the decision was made, Agudat Israel's willingness to participate in a Jewish Agency body. Toward the end of the negotiations between the two organizations over the Haredi faction's involvement in the committee, Shonfeld, in a vituperative article, termed Gruenbaum "a wolf in the role of shepherd" and accused him of negligence in the rescue efforts. This was about a month and a half after the official statement on the annihilation of European Jewry, and came in response to a statement by Gruenbaum about the efforts and resources that the Yishuv needed to devote to the rescue operation. It should be kept in mind that the Rescue Committee, which even at its height was not an important body, had only just begun to organize at the time.[47]

There was constant criticism of the Rescue Committee and of Gruenbaum's opinions and actions. Gruenbaum himself objected to the meager powers and budget the committee was granted, as well as its unwieldy structure. At many junctures he threatened to resign and sometimes did so. Because of pressures from the public, all parts of which wanted to be involved in the rescue efforts, the committee rapidly grew too large to be able to operate efficiently. This was the same Zionist Yishuv that, according to Shonfeld and others, disregarded what was going on in Europe and permitted its leadership deliberately and maliciously to forsake the Jews there.[48]

Haredi writers criticized Gruenbaum for his opposition to allowing the parties represented on the committee to raise money separately for rescue operations. Gruenbaum feared that such multiplicity and decentralization of campaigns would reduce the amount of money donated. In accordance with professional advice he forbade such separate fund-raising efforts across the board. He was also apprehensive about launching a new fund-raising campaign, as important as it might be, before the Jewish Agency had found funds to pay off existing obligations, such as financial support for members of the Yishuv who had volunteered for the British army.[49]

In the autumn of 1943, Binyamin Mintz, the representative of Po'alei Agudat Israel (a Haredi labor party) on the Rescue Committee's presidium, sent a pointed letter to Gruenbaum in which he asserted that the committee's operations were "one of the most horrible disappointments of my life." The committee, he said, was a "fiction." Mintz asked for an urgent meeting with Gruenbaum so that he could tender his resignation. Mintz was right, and Gruenbaum in fact agreed with him — but also knew something about other parallel efforts.[50] But he could not tell Mintz, or anyone else, about these other efforts without sabotaging their already faint chances for success — among them a plan to save Jewish children, or three ransom offers to trade money and goods for Jews — that were on the Jewish Agency leadership's table.[51]

As far as Shonfeld and company were concerned, the secular Zionist leaders had rushed to abandon the religious Jewish community. In their view, it was thus hardly surprising that nonreligious Jews filled the most execrable positions in the camps and ghettos. Religious Jews, they claimed, did not accept such positions and had not been party to decisions about the deportation of Jews to the camps and from there to the gas chambers. Two Gruenbaums, father and son, had been key decision makers in those areas, the Haredi writers claimed, performing these despicable tasks without batting an eyelash.

Like the Judenräte, which according to Shonfeld included only secular Jews and which handed over Jews from their communities without delay, the Gruenbaums, father and son, had had the power to determine who would live and who would die. They held such power by virtue of the positions they filled, the father as chairman of the Rescue Committee in Jerusalem and the son in his comfortable and secure position as a block chief in Birkenau — like father, like son. The two of them, like other secular leaders, were "like sworn enemies of our nation." The burden of their sins was unbearable, and they needed to be placed "in the dock." Shonfeld and company wrote that "Hitler had two partners without which he could not have almost finished his work . . . Jewish collaborators in the occupied lands and Jewish leaders who abused their positions and bled their fellow Jews." Only "the Jewish underworld and secularist circles" could produce people like Eliezer.

The attack on the younger Gruenbaum focused principally on the crimes he was accused of committing as a horrifying, bloodthirsty kapo who hated religious Jews in particular. It should be emphasized that this is also what emerges from the testimony of people who did not belong to Shonfeld's group. Eliezer himself acknowledged that he had experienced "black weeks" there, and there may have been more than the one such period he admitted to, when he was in Block 9. At such times he may have let his frustration and rage out on religious Jews, and on their rabbis in particular. By his own account, and according to the testimony of others, he imitated his superiors, and may have enjoyed his power and even have internalized some of their values and antisemitic modes of behavior.

According to Shonfeld and his fellows, Eliezer's brutality was a result of his antagonism to religion. While this was, they admitted, hardly a necessary condition for a man to behave like an animal — that could have other causes — it was important for them to link the secularism inculcated in him by his parents and his profound malevolence toward Judaism to his abuse of his fellow Jews. "Where did such weeds grow? On whose knees did they grow?" Yehezkel Salomon asked:

> He imbibed the hatred of Haredi Judaism and observant Jews in the house of his father, the Zionist leader Yitzhak Gruenbaum, who emblazoned his banner with the slogan "Death to Haredi Judaism." His sons heard his venomous speeches about Judaism from infancy, and well remembered his incitement in the Polish Sjem. They took his slogan, "Death to Haredi Judaism," literally. One of the brothers was sentenced to death by hanging, as a collaborator with the Nazis, escaped, and reached Palestine, where his father had influence, and his father got him into HaShomer haTza'ir's Kibbutz Gan Shmuel (the kibbutz that was home to Udi Adiv, who spied on Israel for Syria).[52]

Eliezer hated Jews and Yiddish, Salomon wrote. Any word that connected him to his parents' home made him go berserk. For Salomon and his associates, he was the very embodiment of Amalek, that biblical nemesis of the Jewish people. Only that could explain what they described as the horrible fate of the sainted rabbi and his students who fell into Eliezer's hands. As they saw it, the Holocaust was thus just one more of many manifestations of the eternal religious battle between Israel, God's chosen people, and the gentile nations, led by the mythical Amalek and his emissaries. This view provided the justification and foundation for the thinking of a part of Haredi society. Father and son, with their shared blood and genes, personified secular Jewish identity, communism, Zionism, and a common antipathy toward religion that could serve as cornerstones of the structure they wished to erect.[53]

Another religious category was linked to the battle against this "Amalek."

That was *kiddush hashem* (sanctification of the Holy Name), the traditional term for martyrdom for refusing to violate God's commandments or to betray the Jewish religion. This term could easily be applied to any kind of religious persecution in which the victims had the power to make a choice. But in the Holocaust, what made a Jew liable for death, in the Nazi view, was not his religion but his race. As such, Jews were not given the choice to save their lives by abandoning or violating their faith. Jews went to the furnaces whether or not they chose to do so while reciting *Shema' Yisrael*. As such, the category of *kiddush hashem* could not easily be used as an exegetical category for explaining what had happened to Haredi Jews.

Despite this problem of explication, such an important stone for the structure could not be abandoned on the side of the road. To resolve the tension that this involved, an attempt was made to imbue the concept with new meanings. The first of these was acceptance and justification of the divine will while struggling to stay alive within the horror and in the shadow of death. The second was the vital nature of the struggle to maintain a religious life within the ghettos and camps. These innovations enabled Haredim as individuals to grapple with questions of faith, and the Haredi community to respond to the irksome questions they were being asked by secular Israeli society. It enabled them to explain why Jews went to the gas chambers in a way that the secularists described as being "like lambs to the slaughter" while reciting the confession of faith, *Shema' Yisrael*. It presented the attempt to observe the commandments of the Torah within the hell of the ghettos and camps, despite the price of doing so, as the truest form of Jewish heroism.

Furthermore, while Zionism glorified the ghetto rebels and resistance and dismissed the victims as "Jews of the Exile" and "lambs led to the slaughter," Haredi society could offer an alternative mythos, a spiritual one. On a hero's pedestal opposite that of the Warsaw ghetto fighter it placed Haredi spiritual resistance in the camps. Hero versus hero.

This model of *kiddush hashem* had another advantage. It offered a definition of who was deviant, abnormal, those who were outside the pale. Jews who served as kapos, members of Judenräte, and other officeholders in the ghettos and camps were such deviants. They had been secular Jews or gentiles; they were "the other side," the direct opposite of Haredi behavior. Observant Jews had braved cold, hunger, scarcity, capriciousness, uncertainty, fear, and clear and present death, and they had not broken. Religious Jews had not been among those who pushed others aside to receive more food. Pious Jews wanted to save themselves, too, but never at the expense of others. They had produced no kapos. Their primary concern was to observe the precepts and commandments of the Torah and to sanctify the Holy Name.

In this narrative there had been no Haredim who were frightened, who found it difficult to withstand that horrible pressure, who collapsed, who informed on other Jews, or who collaborated. They had all been heroes, they had all been holy martyrs, and they had all done this with devotion and great joy. While "the yeshiva students were fortified by faith and raised up above all the horrors of the inferno and sanctified God's name in their lives and in their deaths," and were "the only ones who preserved the human dignity that had been trampled into the dust by the demons," nonreligious Jews had turned into animals, filled posts in the Judenräte, and had abused yeshiva students because they "envied their spiritual fortitude." They did not help the Haredim, nor did they even engage in mutual assistance among themselves.

Religious Jews, it should be kept in mind, were angry at Eliezer Gruenbaum not only because they thought he had been a horrible kapo, but also because he did not listen to their call to exchange his list of "rabbis" for theirs. But not all the Haredi Jews who came his way — nor Czech or Greek or Dutch or Polish or French Jews — died because of him or his actions. They died because they found themselves in a place in which a satanic order pursued a totalitarian program that had been dredged up from the depths of indescribable evil and brutality, imposed in a way the world had never before seen. There were occasions, as survivors and scholars noted, when there was an opportunity to save some people or, for the most part, postpone their deaths — no more. Sometimes, if they were not put on the right list or did not have the right connections, even this faint chance was denied them. A hairsbreadth separated the opportunity to continue to struggle to survive and the next truck to the gas chambers. It is a simple explanation of a horrifying reality. It demonstrated the banality of evil, and it could lead any person who searched for God there to lose his faith.

Those of Eliezer's Communist comrades who charged that he had not done enough to benefit their friends found a simple solution — they accused him of being a villain. The reward due to him for his good deeds, if there were any such, was far outweighed by his evil. That being the case, he could no longer belong to their world. A true Communist would never act that way, they said, nor could a veteran of Spain. They thus ostracized him from their company and expunged him from their common history. In this they followed the precedent of the Soviet Encyclopedia during the Stalin period, in which successive editions blacked out the faces of leaders who had fallen from grace or been eliminated. Eliezer, too, was eliminated from the group portraits of his cohort. Adam (Avraham) Rayski told researchers for this book point blank that Eliezer had not been in Spain. This happened not long ago. In the case of Rayski and, apparently, Henri Bulawko, both brave men with many great deeds to their credit, intelligent and impressive people, Eliezer remains expunged. Nothing will change that. In the final analysis, both camps, the Haredi and the Communist, treated him the same — they erased him.

Ambiguities, contradictions, and evolution are evident in the Haredi attitude toward armed resistance against the Nazis. It was a pressing question for them in part because the answer had implications for another nagging question — did the Haredim in fact go to their deaths like lambs to the slaughter? Those Haredim for whom the answer was no — that is, those who sought to prove that Haredim in fact took part in the fighting — had a problem reconciling their support for rebellion with the halakhic prohibitions against rising up against the gentiles. They could not, like those Haredim who rejected the act of rebellion, charge the Zionists with claiming all the glory for the rebels. They could hardly accede to the charges of their fellow Haredim regarding the "false propaganda" of the heroism of the secularist Zionists who fomented the ghetto rebellions and "the unbridled incitement against others . . . the weak, the exilic, the pathetic who did not have the spirit to fight." This dilemma, along with the unease it caused, could also explain the huge quantity of texts that different groups within the Haredi world have produced on this issue, as well as the convoluted nature of the explanations and responses they contain. Whatever the case, it is necessary to distinguish between questions that came up and were debated in real time, or a short time after the events, and questions and representations of the Holocaust that appeared considerably later. This is true regarding religious Jewish society as a whole and the Haredi camp in particular.

Less than a week after the Yishuv received the first information about the Warsaw ghetto rebellion, two positions took form within the Haredi community. One glorified and extolled the rebellion and saw it as a new incarnation of spiritual religious assistance. The other viewed rebellion as the suicidal act of nationalist groups, unequivocally opposed to the spirit of the Torah.

Hayim Shalem relates that the first Haredim to react to the news of the rebellion and the evidence that Haredi Jews were taking part were Binyamin Mintz of Po'alei Agudat Israel and Rabbi Moshe Blau of Agudat Israel. They did not coordinate their reactions, nor did they speak in the names of their movements, but they were trailblazers because they were, according to Shalem, the first to respond. In May 1943 Mintz published an article in the Haredi newspaper *Haderekh* in which he endorsed the rebellion and commended its fighters. They demonstrated "lofty heroism" that "did not cease throughout the years of anguish." Mintz and those who thought as he did sought to anchor the Warsaw ghetto rebellion in "the popular rootedness of Polish Haredi Torah Judaism . . . in the devoutness of God's Torah and commandments, in the sanctification of God's name . . . in astonishing mutual aid." He thus linked two forms of heroism, that of fighting against the Nazis with force of arms, and the "passive" combat of spiritual resistance.

A week later, when the rumors of the rebellion had yet to be confirmed, Rabbi Blau termed it irresponsible behavior on the part of extremist nationalist elements and stressed that he was certain that no Haredi Jew in the ghetto would take part in such an action that was clearly opposed by Jewish law. "The nationalist press has made delicacies out of this rumor and has lionized the heroism and courage of those who choose to die heroes' deaths and compare this to the rebellion of the Maccabees." If that had indeed been the nature of the rebellion, Blau wrote, then clearly "it did not come from among those loyal to the Jewish faith." It was a clear case of suicide, opposed to religious faith. "Dying a hero's death only for the sake of dying a hero's death has no place in the Jewish religion . . . believing Jews do not pursue their own deaths and certainly not the deaths of others, simply because their situation is dire," he concluded.

A few days later, in another article, he called the rebellion "an act of desperation on the part of a few young people in Poland," whose actions had caused "several thousand Jews to be burned alive." He also stressed the connection between these actions and the nationalist education on offer in the Yishuv, based on demeaning the value of life and on a lack of faith. But Agudat Israel's official institutions did not take a stand.

In the early summer of 1943, Chaim Yisroel Eiss, Agudat Israel's rescue representative in Switzerland, reported to Mintz about "a list of the leadership of the Warsaw ghetto [rebellion]," and noted it included the names of three members of Agudat Israel's youth movement, Tze'irei Agudat Israel. Mintz was unable to obtain the list, but did manage to confirm that members of the movement had participated in the rebellion. As one of Agudat Israel's representatives on the Rescue Committee, Mintz requested that Gruenbaum "notify the public at large that religious youth also stood at head of the defense." Gruenbaum did not respond. Mintz's anger at what he saw as a deliberate attempt to deny religious fighters the glory due them redoubled when, in April 1944, "representatives of Polish Jewry" published in the Yishuv press the names of the men and women who had fallen in the rebellion, along with their political party affiliations. The names of members of Agudat Israel were not included. Mintz protested to the representatives and announced that if they did not find a way to correct this distortion, his party would have no choice but to issue a statement. No correction was made, and no statement appeared in the newspapers. But the incident showed that a part of the Haredi community was not ashamed that its members had taken part in the rebellion, and that it even viewed this as something they could and should be proud of.

In April 1944 Mintz again extolled the heroes of the ghetto, who, he wrote, had drawn their strength from their "Jewish roots." He persisted in trying to gather information about the rebellion and the part played by the religious and Haredi public. That summer, when the Rescue Committee again published a list, this time of the fallen fighters that once more left out the members of Agudat Israel, Mintz was livid. This time he saw it as a double distortion—he maintained that the categorization of the fallen by political affiliation was itself improper, and the omission of the names of the members of his movement all the more so. He had no illusions that this was a mere error. Then, on September 6, came the final straw: most of the Yishuv's newspapers published the text of a statement issued by the Jewish Agency's official news agency, Palcor, which included the names of all the fighters and forces that had participated in the Warsaw ghetto uprising. Each company of fighters was identified by the political or youth movement to which it belonged. The statement made no mention of the members of Agudat Israel (the religious-Zionist party), or Betar.

Mintz lost all patience and, on September 7, issued this statement to the press:

> Having looked into the matter thoroughly, I have true, unimpeachable testimonies to the effect that all the Jewish people's remnants in Warsaw, all parts and political movements, took part in the great battle at Warsaw . . . and now I have unimpeachable testimonies of people who left the Warsaw ghetto after the terrible expulsions, when the Jews prepared for battle. I also have testimonies from people who left Warsaw after the end of the battles and who themselves took part in the ghetto uprising. They all state without exception: there was no distinction between parties in the Warsaw ghetto. Everyone fought against the Nazi filth, as one and with one heart. . . . I have on file the names of Warsaw ghetto fighters that cannot for the time being be publicized, among them prominent members of all the tendencies in Haredi Judaism.[54]

This statement should have made it clear, to anyone who still had any doubts, that there were Haredim who, rather than condemning armed resistance, insisted that their fighters should be included in the narrative of the uprising. Nevertheless, this was not the official position taken by Haredi society and its elected bodies, but rather the position of a member of Po'alei Agudat Israel, a small faction within Agudat Israel that represented that part of the Haredi community that stood closest to the Zionist enterprise. As if to remove all doubts, Rabbi Blau again spoke out, condemning Mintz and his efforts to honor the religious fighters who had been left out of the secular Zionist pantheon of heroes.

The Haredi weekly *Hayesod* responded sharply against Rabbi Blau's attack on the fighters, whereas Neturei Karta, an extremist Haredi faction, lauded him. Agudat Israel's World Executive Committee, its strongest and most important institution, headed by Rabbi Levin, made no public statement about the uprising, its fighters, and the values that motivated them.

This attempt to straddle both sides of the debate continued to characterize the Haredi camp during the State of Israel's early decades. In the period leading up to 27 Nissan (May 3) in 1951, which the Knesset had declared as Holocaust and Ghetto Rebellion Memorial Day, Agudat Israel's daily newspaper *HaModia'* published an editorial, reports, and articles praising the rebels. Similar material appeared in another Haredi newspaper, *She'arim*. One of them stated that "the ghetto rebellion is great for those [Holocaust survivors] who have all their lives had a debt of gratitude to the partisans and rebels who unburden them of shame and disgrace and allowed them to walk with their heads held high." These pieces also protested the ongoing attempt to exclude their community and its members from the narrative of armed resistance: "No distinction should be made between blood and blood and no one should be exalted or demeaned in accordance with anyone's limited and unprescient estimation." They stressed that "the victims of the Holocaust, without exception and without discrimination between blood and blood, were ghetto rebels in their lives as in their deaths." This was a clear and immediate reference to the struggle between HaShomer haTza'ir, Mapam, and Ahdut haAvodah on the one hand and Herut and other secular groups on the other over the glory of the uprisings. Haredi publications continually stressed that the importance of the other form of resistance, spiritual resistance, should not be diminished. This spiritual attitude was the chosen path of Haredi society. Now, a decade after the rebellion, it was wrong to perpetuate the memories of "only specific individuals from among the large Jewish Diaspora" and to obliterate "the pure memories of millions of anonymous heroes whose heroism was not expressed in a stormy eruption of revenge, but whose bold spirit and courage is in no way inferior to that of their brethren, not even by a hair." The uprising, they explained, belonged to the entire Jewish public and was an extension of the Jewish people's daily and spiritual struggle against the plot to destroy them. The claim that the uprising had been organized and carried out by a select few, especially the members of the left-wing movements, was not only a malicious distortion of the truth, but was motivated by political interest. The ghetto fighters were all the Jews who remained after the Nazi deportations, and "they did not fight and fall as Communists or socialists . . . they shouted '*Shema' Yisrael*' and they died as Jews."

Haredi society, or at least part of it, also had to grapple with other challenges it faced at that time. These challenges had no direct connection to Yitzhak and Eliezer Gruenbaum, but they fell on the symbolic and ethical spectrum over which individuals, operations, and projects were then judged, for better or worse.[55] The Haredim were in the arena whether or not they wanted to be. The growing acuteness of the theological questions raised by the Holocaust, the contradictory voices within the Haredi community, and the community's need to defend its "soft underbelly," its theological zone of vulnerability, all prompted the members of this extreme Haredi community to redouble their attack on what they saw as Zionism's own weak defenses. They sought, as it were, to move the battle into enemy territory. Yitzhak and Eliezer Gruenbaum were part of what the Haredi community viewed not just as the Zionist movement's soft underbelly, but the even more sensitive area under the belt. But this was not the only Haredi response. Other Haredi writers and leaders faced these issues directly without trying to sweep them under the rug with simplistic theological concepts or by demonizing the Zionists. These Haredim came up with profound and creative ideas that, while not offering an open-and-shut solution to the problem, offered a way forward that elicited interest and even respect even from those who were not persuaded by them.

Accusing Zionism of responsibility for the Holocaust and the enlistment of every possible argument to prove that charge were the kernel of this means of coping with the catastrophe. For better or worse, the Zionist movement was the mirror of the Haredi world, the place the Haredim gaze was directed at and in which they saw their mirror image. Despite their abjuration of Zionism, it was central to their world and the bedrock of their identity, much in the same way that Christianity's definition of itself is built on the Jewish Other. Zionism's claim to be the true representative of Jewish peoplehood and history, like the Christian claim to be the True Israel, required traditional Judaism to fashion itself as a response to the very claims it rejected. Those Haredim who rejected the Zionist narrative and Zionist categories of heroism and nationhood wrote their story and constructed their memory while peering into the Zionist mirror and grappling with the questions and challenges they found there. The Gruenbaums' story was assigned this context. Yitzhak and Eliezer each played an important role in the Haredi drama. Father and son, they shared a spiritual world—they were both outspoken secularists, one Zionist and one Communist. Both were distant and arrogant, both had strong gazes, and both supplied texts that could be used against them. One had been a famous Zionist leader and one the leader of his group and a block chief at Auschwitz-Birkenau. The space they occupied, and which yawned between them, provided almost everything the Haredim needed for their battle against Zionism and what it represented. A playwright could hardly have fashioned better antagonists than history had.

In this context, the charge that Zionism was to blame for the catastrophe was principally an attempt to divert attention from the need, recognized by some members of the Haredi community, to grapple with the serious questions the Holocaust raised. In the end, the accusation was only one expression of "spiritual poverty and superficiality, and an insult to historical truth and the Jewish people," as Dina Porat has so well put it, as well as "an insult to the Creator and his believers."[56] Shonfeld and his group played a central role in carrying out the mission of implicating the Gruenbaum family in this narrative. The leading figures in this effort, Shonfeld and Gerlik, were almost certainly cognizant of every link in the ideological-theological chain of propositions that they served. Others may perhaps have rather been inspired by a sense of historical mission without intimate knowledge of the details and their ramifications. Like simple Hasidim who value scraps from their rebbe's table as spiritual nourishment without needing or wanting to delve deep into theology and doctrine, the average Haredi was willing to accept on authority, when told by his spiritual and community leaders, that Zionism, as personified by the Gruenbaums, father and son, was the ultimate perpetrator of the Holocaust.

Who gave Shonfeld his orders? Most scholars have fingered the school of Rabbi Avraham Yeshyahu Karelitz (the Hazon Ish) and the Satmer Rebbe as the principal sources from which Shonfeld and his group drew their inspiration. Some claim that Shonfeld was "a disciple and member of the household of Rabbi Yitzhak Ze'ev Soloveitchik (the Gryz), the rabbi of Brisk, [who] later became the head of the Brisk Yeshiva in Jerusalem, who was also a fierce opponent of Zionism. This Rabbi Soloveitchik was also a great admirer of Rabbi Elazar Menachem Shach, the Hazon Ish's successor as the acknowledged leader of a large part of the Israeli Haredi community, who was also apparently an important backer of Shonfeld's group."[57] According to Menachem Friedman, a scholar and expert on the Haredi society, Shonfeld took the view that Zionism had been an "ally" of the Nazis from the Hazon Ish. The latter invoked a story told by Rabbi Yisrael Meir Kagan (the Chafetz Chayim), an earlier important leader of Haredi Judaism and opponent of Zionism, about a man who expended all his money and energy to rescue an inhabitant of his town who had fallen into a pit and won plaudits from everyone who knew him. But then it turned out that he himself had dug the pit into which his unfortunate neighbor had fallen.[58]

Shonfeld grew into the role. His rhetorical gifts, extremism, and certitude had early on made him a spokesman for the Haredi community. In the early 1940s he found a place for himself as a fierce ideological opponent of Zionism.

Friedman writes that Shonfeld "was one of the most prominent, interesting, and talented" members of his group, and was a major influence on the Haredi way of thinking that developed in the "new yeshiva world" in the years 1945–1948. He was unparalleled among the critics of Agudat Israel within the Haredi community itself. The members and officials of his own community did not escape the barbs of his violent and unbridled language.[59]

His political environment was the area between Tze'irei Agudat Israel, a movement he had helped found and in which he was a central figure and ideologue, and Neturei Karta. The latter movement, which grew ever more extreme and split into a number of factions that sought to outdo each other in their extremism and activism, sparked his imagination.[60] He liked to demonstrate his independence of opinion, his antiestablishment position, and especially how ready he was to vacate his titles and positions in his community's official organizations. He seems to have become addicted to liminality. Even though he permitted himself a wide scope for his writing, he never became an advocate for freedom of thought in his community. On the contrary, he demanded rigorous censorship in *Haderekh* against articles likely "to grant desirable material to our opponents"; despite his being the embodiment of a brutal and heated writer, he insisted that articles for the newspaper be "edited for taste and style."[61]

While still an integral part of Agudat Israel, he feared that that party's participation in Yishuv politics would lead it to conformism and that its participation in Yishuv elections could turn it into a Yishuv institution and produce a pragmatic and conciliatory approach. He was not mistaken. He thus opposed the participation of his own organization, Tze'irei Agudat Israel, in Agudat Israel's internal elections. Participation in the elections presented "the painful choice of betraying one's conscience or party discipline. . . . The fact that Agudat Israel has turned into a political party has made it into a party that is guided by interest, and that is the explanation for the moral decline it has experienced," he explained to anyone who would listen.[62] Mintz and Po'alei Agudat Israel were, in his opinion, symbols of a creep toward Zionism. Their ideology had been contaminated by the *Haskalah* and materialism, he claimed, or perhaps they had simply lost their reason. Their connections with the Zionist establishment, the benefits they gained from this, and their pragmatism made that faction into "a Zionist snake in the bosom of Agudat Israel." The party's "contribution" to Haredi society, he wrote, was like "the injection into the Agudah body of the Zionist bacterium, in which they have multiplied and spread."[63] A Jew who read European newspapers of that decade might well think that expressions such as "Zionist snake" and "bacterium" had been taken from the rhetoric of a strident foreign press.

His long-running critique of Agudat Israel finally led him to resign his membership in its Executive Committee and National Central Committee and to continue to censure the party from outside. As a principled combatant and a man who was proud of his modesty, he did not cease to proclaim that he had been right to give up office and honor in the name of his opinions. Despite his central role in shaping the policies of Tze'irei Agudat Israel, and even though the faction did not identify with Agudat Israel and its leader, Meir Levin, the faction did not follow Shonfeld into the wilderness. It remained within the party and was represented in its institutions.[64]

Shonfeld was concerned about the messianic atmosphere that had taken hold of a part of the Haredi community during Israel's first years, "to the point that even in yeshivot and in some Hasidic homes they did not refrain from saying *Hallel* [a set of psalms recited on holidays] on Independence Day." He mocked the "Jews with seniority and position in the home of Agudat Israel" who were swept up by this enthusiasm and "cast eyes shut with devotion at the 'beginning of the redemption' that they prepared as a compensation and payment for the Holocaust."[65] Not only was the State of Israel not "the beginning of the redemption," he maintained—it would actually delay the Messiah's arrival. The state was "the unchallenged legal daughter of Zionism," and the final goal of Zionism was "the normalization of the Jewish people." That being the case, Zionism had rebelled against the very "secret of the endurance of the Jewish people, it has rejected and taken away the rationale for its suffering and agonies, has not sought only to hasten the messianic end of days, but has also had the temerity to entirely displace and depose it."[66] For those who did not yet understand, he reminded his readers that Rabbi Karelitz had ruled that "the state is not the beginning of redemption but rather the end of the Exile. It may well be that the distance in time between the *Iqveta deMeshiha* [the tribulations preceding the arrival of the Messiah] and the *Athalta deGe'ulah* [beginning of the redemption] is very small, this ends and that begins, but the qualitative difference is polar."[67]

Yet he maintained that Haredim should move to the Holy Land without regard to the regime there, and to try to influence its character from within. "Just as it is impossible to defend the borders of the State of Israel at a distance, so it is impossible to defend its sanctity at a distance," he wrote. Nevertheless, a clear boundary had to be preserved between this mission and making "a peace compact with Zionism." Care had to be taken to avoid a situation in which participation in Yishuv institutions, or in those of the young state, could turn into a slippery slope of alliance. "The two conceptions and two world organizations will remain opposed to each other . . . like a thing and its opposite. There can be no compromise between the principle of the Torah's sovereignty and the principle of the nation's sovereignty. An ideological abyss with no bridge or passage."[68]

Among the gentiles, he explained, there was a separation: "Render unto God the things that are God's and to Caesar the things that are Caesar's." In Judaism, however, no such distinction can be made. There is only one way and one alternative: "A state of the Torah or a state that rebels against the Torah . . . the spiritual freedom of Torah-faithful Judaism versus the enslavement of the secular regime of the State of Israel." The Haredim had to remember that a Torah state would not come to them "as a gift from on high." They had to avoid being misled, and "to think that the political independence of the State of Israel has made us free." Sovereignty over this stretch of land belongs to "God and the Torah," not to the state and its institutions.[69]

According to Friedman, Shonfeld "was also a 'Zionist,' in the sense that he incessantly stressed the profound and obligatory connection between every religious Jew and the Land of Israel. He and those who thought as he did "were not anti-Israeli in the crude and simplistic sense" of the word. To a certain extent, they were and remain patriots, perhaps even extreme patriots." Perhaps the best term for their position would be "Jewish patriotism." In other words, "to the same extent that they reject on principle the political framework defined as the State of Israel and the ideals that it represents ('Zionism'), they feel a sense of responsibility to Israeli society as a necessarily Jewish society, with all that implies."[70]

The smoking pistol and the energy to activate the move to blame the Holocaust on Zionism and to make the Gruenbaums its type specimens were provided to Shonfeld by Rabbi Weismandel, a central figure in the "Working Group," the emergency leadership of Slovakian Jewry and one of the initiators of the Europa Plan, which proposed to bribe the Nazis through Dieter Wisliceny, Eichmann's agent in Bratislava, to stop the deportations. Rabbi Weismandel maintained to his dying day that the plan had not been put into action not because of the Nazis or because of political, logistical, or other contingencies imposed by the war, but solely because of the position taken by the Zionist leadership, in which Yitzhak Gruenbaum was central. His claim does not sit well with the facts, but he would not be dissuaded.[71]

After the war, Weismandel became a bitter opponent of Israel and Zionism. The material relating to the Europa Plan was edited and published by his sons and students under the title *Min haMetzar* (Out of my straits). The book served as material for a series of articles written and edited by Shonfeld and his disciples that appeared in 1961–1962 in *Digleinu*, a periodical published by Tze'irei Agudat Israel. The title of the series was *Ani Ma'ashim — Min ha-Metzar* (I accuse — Out of my straits), and the hint was clear enough: Shonfeld was Émile Zola, and the horrible injustice committed against Dreyfus was, in essence, the same crime that Zionism had committed in obstructing Weismandel's rescue plan.[72] Both were conspiracies, and the task of Shonfeld and his associates, in their view, was to frustrate the Zionist attempt to cover up its complicity and to lead the Jewish people. This series of outspoken articles presented "the broad context"; a series of additional "crimes" committed by the Zionists were presented to the readers. The articles also laid out Zionism's "ideological basis," which led to its opposition and hatred of Weismandel. Clearly, the rescue operation planned by the Haredi Weismandel was maliciously suppressed.

The series was published in pamphlet form as *Serufe haKivshanim Ma'ashimim* (Those burned in the furnaces accuse) at the end of 1974, and several further editions have since been issued. Porat adds that Hug Bnei Torah, the organization that produced the book, also put out, between 1977 and 1985, five volumes entitled *Hashqafateinu beAspaklariah shel Dorot* (Our ideology in the mirror of generations), which anthologized many of the pieces written by Shonfeld and his associates. The editor of this series, Aharon Yeshaya Roter, was viewed as Shonfeld's heir — he shared his inclination toward Neturei Karta — and as enjoying close relations with Rabbi Shach. Hug Bnei Torah gradually affiliated itself with Rabbi Shach.[73] *Serufe haKivshanim Ma'ashimim* (Those burned in the furnaces accuse) became their Magna Carta, a book they gave as a gift to people who joined their circle.

We do not know who spread the rumors that Eliezer was executed by his comrades-in-arms during the Ramat Rachel battle. We can only guess. But those who started the rumor were certainly people who had little concern for the evidence. In their brutal determination to circumvent the faith questions the Holocaust raised by blaming the annihilation of European Jewry on Zionism, they were willing to sacrifice not only sworn enemies like Yitzhak and Eliezer Gruenbaum but even members of their own community, such as Mintz and his associates, who were willing to engage in a dialogue with the Zionists and to seek to understand the complexities of the dilemmas that Jews faced in the ghettos and the camps. Shonfeld represents a society in which truth is absolute and brooks no compromise or understanding, a society riven by internal divisions over rabbinic authority and fine points of observance. It is not uncommon for one Haredi court or community to post notices announcing the death of a rival rabbi who is very much alive, as a way of vilifying him and marking him out as deserving of divine punishment. In doing so, they insist, they are glorifying God. Such people will hardly raise an eyebrow about spreading rumors about a soldier being killed by his comrades-at-arms. These are not mere thugs — they are thugs on a transcendental mission.

These contexts and patterns of action constructed a necessary and ethical connection between what was presented as the world of the father and what was presented as the world of the son. Out of this grew a diversion operation that laid out the principal lines of the Haredi narrative about Eliezer Gruenbaum.

Realm of Memory 3

So run the principal lines of the four main retrospective narratives examined in this book — the Communist narrative, the Haredi narrative, the Zionist narrative, and the personal and family narrative. These distinct and central narratives all emerge from a single convoluted life. They cover twenty years of turbulent and varied activity by Itche, Eliezer, Ezriel Gruenbaum, and Leon Berger, all the many names he bore as part of his complex personality. They are also the product of another fifty years of polemic over his memory, heroism, or shame. His life spanned five countries — Poland, France, Spain, Germany, and the Yishuv-Israel, where it, but not the story, ended. There is a narrative for each group, tailored to its needs, written explicitly or implied with shreds and shards. These narratives all seek to blame someone and are less concerned with the roots, reasons, and circumstances of his actions. Like a wretched *Rashomon*, they to this day struggle with each other for hegemony over a collective memory that is in any case shattered.

The Communist narrative embodied an emanation of the fear felt by the French and Polish parties (and the expatriate Polish Communists in France). They were apprehensive that continuing preoccupation with Eliezer, and others who had been in the same position, could reverse the growth in political support they were enjoying and thus harm their chances of becoming the ruling party. The narrative was also shaped by the desire of senior operatives to return, as quickly as possible, to their tranquil routines in Paris and Poland. Eliezer's story threatened to drag them, too, into the abyss. That seemed so menacing that they simply expunged Eliezer, not only from their recent past in the camps, but also from the Spanish Civil War.

The Haredi narrative grew out of that community's need to link the father to the son. It used smoke screens and verbal pyrotechnics to make an easy escape from weighty and agonizing theological questions. This community included many who viewed the Zionist state as the wellspring of all pollution, and who refused to recognize its army, its soldiers, and its officers — yet took to the ramparts to prevent a man they saw as a rotten apple from taking a place in that state's pantheon. These people and their sons did not serve in the Israeli army or place their lives on the line for the Jewish state, but nevertheless took to themselves the right to declare that it was unbefitting for Eliezer to have fought for the country they did not want and did not recognize. They did all they could to ensure that he would not get any of the honor accorded to the fallen soldiers of Israel's War of Independence.

The Zionist narrative emerged from a primal and embryonic society undergoing the complex process of constructing a nation and a society. It had fought a bloody War of Independence and needed heroes and symbols quite different from those embodied by a balding Polish Communist lawyer who had not wanted to come to the new Jewish state and did not want to stay there. Yet this man had not only served as a controversial block chief in Birkenau — he had also, in dying in battle, inevitably become part of the Israeli national ethos.

And, finally, there was a personal and family narrative, belonging to just a handful. For them, even though Eliezer had been their clan's black sheep, they believed in him and to this day maintain his innocence.

||| WAS ELIEZER GRUENBAUM a Shakespearean hero? Macbeth, perhaps? Both evil and tragic? A hero and a villain?

And what motivated him? Was it the pursuit of power? Fanaticism? Communist ideology? Sectorial, almost religious loyalty to his party? His almost utter identification of himself with his movement? Could that be true of a man who was so independent, such an individualist, so critical and insubordinate? Maybe he wanted simply to help others? Or did he want social esteem? Perhaps he wanted to emulate his father — perhaps he felt himself in competition with such a prominent parent?

Could it be that he was arrogant and brutal, but also brave? Having assumed the bearing of a ruler, perhaps he became addicted to power? Was he an active member of the underground? Did he deliberately place his own life in mortal danger? Beyond the mortal danger in which every life at the death camps by definition found itself in?

Could it he have taken the positions he was asked to take, and reach the standing that he reached, without these character traits? Could he have survived those horrible positions without being that kind of person? Did he do it only for himself or also for those close to him? Did he serve himself most of the time, or did he generally serve both himself and his comrades? Could charisma, natural leadership, and charm coexist within him with more dismal and despicable characteristics? Could he have been both brave and cowardly at the same time? Was he also defeated by the horrifying pressure he was under at the camps — was he a victim?

Does the character of Eliezer contain those things that are, as Chateaubriand put it, the soul of history, those nuances that express the uniqueness of a historical event "as it happened" and as it was experienced? Must we attend to these details here, here in particular, in the complex and many-layered story of Eliezer? And what in the words of Eliezer and his associates was fictional, untruthful, refurbished, but less painful than the truth? What was the truth that they, too, whether as individuals or as a collective, had such a hard time accepting?

To what extent does the outcome of this line of thought depend on the tough question of what percentage of Holocaust survivors were those who had enjoyed privileges in the camps and ghettos?

Was Eliezer given an opportunity to make his voice heard? Was there even a chance, among all those circles that overlapped in his life and story, that his voice would be heard? Was he correct when he claimed that he had been deprived of his glory and left only with blood on his hands?

Would his fate have been different — even if he did all that he did — had his name not been Gruenbaum?

RESEARCH NOTES:
FROM CLIO'S ELUSIVE WORLD

I asked F___n about the significance of the name Leon Berger. In French, *berger* means "shepherd." But does it have another, more exalted meaning in French culture? She told me that it is a very common name in France, and many Jews adopted it as a replacement for a previous name that sounded too Jewish. It was a good name for assimilating into French society. Her own uncle, she told me, had done just this when he moved to France. But, no, she said, the name has no other meaning in French culture.

But what about "Leon"? I sought an answer.

The simple meaning of the word is "lion," a symbol of boldness, heroism, courage, kingship. That is clear. Perhaps he also took the name Leon because that was the name of the first Jew to fall in the Spanish Civil War. Perhaps it also referred to that important Parisian Jew, statesman, and former prime minister, Léon Blum? Leon was a good choice. It offered a good and worthy semantic field.

Did he adopt this name because he saw himself, or his friends saw him, as a shepherd, a leader who looks after and protects his flock?

I continued to search, and found the following about Leon Berger:

> In the late 1830s and early 1840s, Heinrich Essig, a town councilor in Leonberg, near Stuttgart, crossed a black and white Newfoundland bitch with a male of the Barry breed from the monastery hospice Grand St. Bernhard. Later a Pyrenean Mountain dog was added. The result was very large dogs with predominantly long, white coats. Essig sought to produce a lion-like animal, a lion being depicted on the Leonberger coat of arms. The first dogs that can be called real Leonbergers were whelped in 1846. They combined the excellent qualities of the breeds from which they stemmed. In short order, dogs from Leonberg were bought up around the world and became status symbols. At the end of the 19th century, the Leonberger became the preferred farm dog in Baden-Württemberg. His watch and draft abilities were much praised. But the breeding stock shrank dramatically during both World Wars and in needy postwar times. Today the Leonberger is considered an excellent family dog that answers to all modern needs.
>
> Due to the purpose for which it was originally bred, the Leonberger is a strong,

> muscular, yet elegant dog. It is distinguished by its balanced build and its calm and confident, yet lively, temperament. Males, in particular, are powerful and strong.[1]

I continued a search for other possible sources of the name, and discovered this:

> The new guillotine apparatus was composed of two wooden slots through which a sharp and diagonal blade traveled. The new form of the blade was meant to cut the head easily and quickly, rather than strike at it hard like the old apparatus, in order to cut it off.
>
> Prior to his execution, the nape of the convict was shaven and he arrived at the killing site in a closed carriage. The convict ascended to the guillotine face forward, his hands tied behind his back and his eyes bare. He was tied with a strap to a vertical wooden board that reached up to his chest. The board turned on a hinge and passed from a horizontal position, when the convict's head entered the *lunette*, a circle the diameter of a man's neck, which held his head in place. The sharp blade would descend rapidly and quickly and cleanly slice off the head, which fell into a basket, ironically called the "picnic basket." Since the heart was still beating, a powerful jet of blood would spurt out. The execution team would be covered with blood from head to toe, and according to testimonies the place stand and dogs would gather there at night to lick up the blood.
>
> The operator of the guillotine would grasp the hair or ears of the convict and present him to the public.
>
> In 1870–1872 the guillotine structure was improved by Leon Berger, but remained very similar.
>
> Leon Berger was an assistant executioner and carpenter. He improved the guillotine by adding auxiliary mechanism, such as a handle to release the blade, a collapsible base for the body, and a shield meant to prevent blood from spraying on the executioner and his assistant. The blade, with its screws, weighed 40 kilograms [88 pounds] and the height of the poles was 4 meters.[2]

"A good name is better than precious ointment; and the day of death is better than the day of one's birth" (Ecclesiastes 7:1). And a name, perhaps, is not chosen or given by chance.

So who are you, Leon Berger?

ELIEZER GRUENBAUM: CHRONOLOGY

Eliezer spent a total of approximately two years and seven months in the Auschwitz network of camps and approximately four months in Buchenwald after being transported from Beaune-la-Rolande on June 27, 1942.

Auschwitz

End of June or beginning of July 1942: arrives at Auschwitz.

Beginning of July: first three days at Auschwitz I.

Birkenau

July 1942: arrives at Birkenau.

July–August 1942: Block 9, "chief of prisoners," deputy to Block Chief Konczal.

End of August 1942: transferred to Block 4. Sent to course at Block Officer School, but the school was shut down before he completed the course. Eliezer appointed clerk in Block 4, a post that granted him relative anonymity.

September 1942: Falls ill with typhus, rides out illness in Block 9.

October 1942: Returns to his post as Konczal's deputy.

January 1943: Transferred to Block 39 (or, according to another version, Block 25). Serves as block chief for five days, charged with preparing it to take in prisoners. A week later he managed to receive a transfer and resume his position in Block 9.

End of February–July 1943: Serves as chief of Block 20.

July 1943–January 1944: Block 20 is moved to the new camp and redesignated Block 30. Eliezer continues to serve as block chief.

January 1944: Removed from position as block chief.

January 20, 1944: Placed as laborer in a *Kommando* assigned to divert the Vistula River.

Buna-Monowitz, Jawischowitz

March–April 1944 to January 1945: Sent to Buna-Monowitz, and then a few days later to the mining camp at Jawischowitz, where he served as a laborer in a work detail.

January 17 or 18, 1945: Evacuated from Jawischowitz.

Buchenwald

End of January through May 1945 (the end of the war): In Buchenwald.

March 1945: First inquiry, spurred by charges made by Czech prisoners.

April 6–7, 1945: Evacuation of Buchenwald; Eliezer active in planning uprising.

April 11, 1945: Liberation of Buchenwald. Eliezer takes part in cutting the fences. During the days that followed, Eliezer serves as pursuer of SS personnel fleeing the camp and hiding in the area.

Inquiries following Liberation

May 25, 1945–Sept. 7, 1945: Second inquiry, sponsored by the Polish Communist Party.

September 1945–March 20, 1946: Third inquiry, by French authorities.

May 1, 1946: Arrival in Palestine.

May 22, 1948: Killed in the battle of Ramat Rachel.

NOTES

1. *Jerusalem, May 22, 1948, Morning*

1. For criticism of Shaltiel, to the point of lack of confidence in him, see, for example, the testimony of Lt. Col. Yeshoshafat Harkabi, "Gold," March 16, 1953, IDFA 922/78/290, pp. 3–4. See also JIA 38/9-473/168, Ramat Rachel Battles, "The Battle that Saved Jerusalem," p. 2. See also Levi (Levitseh) 1986, 364.

2. Ben-Hanan 1989, 4–7.

3. From the time hostilities broke out following the UN General Assembly vote on November 29, 1947, that approved the partition of Palestine through the end of the War of Independence, more than two hundred Israelis were buried in the temporary cemetery.

4. Elath 1979; Melman 1987; Schueftan 1986; al-Tal 1960; Pappé 1995.

5. BGHA, BGD, May 14, 1948.

6. Richman 1996, 102; Glasner-Heled and Bar-On 2004, n. 68.

2. *Poland, Lancicia, District Prison, 1929*

1. The party's Historical Institute, part of the KC PZPR, Duracz Archive, Legal Matter: J. Gutner et al., 1929, 105/1454, Hoover Institution, Stanford, CA.

2. Frister 1987, 267–277; Glasner-Heled and Bar-On 2004, 111–146.

3. The first version appears in Frister 1987, 270–272. The second comes from Yonatan Gruenbaum, unpublished manuscript, chapter on Eliezer Gruenbaum.

4. A company of Jewish volunteers in the Spanish Civil War also bore his name. See Geshur 2000, 502.

5. Frister 1987, 270–276.

6. M. Zertal 1980, 278–288.

7. Yonatan Gruenbaum, unpublished manuscript, chapter on Eliezer.

8. The Comintern, or the Third Communist International, was a union of the world's Communist parties founded by Lenin's left-wing faction of the Russian Social Democrats. Lenin's faction opposed the participation of the working class in World War I and called in 1915 for the establishment of a new international socialist organization, to replace the existing Second International. The Comintern was founded in Moscow in 1919.

9. Yonatan Gruenbaum, unpublished manuscript, chapter on Eliezer. On Eliezer the womanizer see Meir Hartman's comments in Ben-Hanan 1989, 4–7.

10. See, for example, the remarks made by his close disciple Moshe Sneh (Kleinbaum), in Melzer 1995, 1:3. On the fiftieth birthday celebration see Rozenman 1988, 205–206; Frister 1987, 270–276.

11. On Piłsudski see Ference 1994, 469.

12. Guterman 1997, 181–182.

13. For details see Guterman 1997, 358–371.

14. Modern-day Jewish autonomy had its roots in the period of the German occupation during World War I. The Germans allowed the Jews to join free confessional organizations headed by elected committees. The very first law promulgated by independent Poland reaffirmed this arrangement.

15. See Gutman and Bartal 2001, 430–431; Rozenman 1988, 205–218; Shaary 1983, 11–51; ibid., 21–58; Zait 2002, 278–280.

16. Yitzhak Gruenbaum 1963, 156–161; Levinson 1953, 255. On Polish government evasions of the minorities charter see also Zait 2002, 276.

17. Netzer 1980, 115–116; Guterman 1997, 188, 199–206, 370. On the depth of Polish anti-semitism see, for example, Gruenbaum's speech in the Sjem: Yitzhak Gruenbaum 1963, 40–43.

18. Frister 1987, 276–277; Yonatan Gruenbaum, unpublished manuscript; Ben-Hanan 1989, 4–7.

19. Roos 1966; "Piłsudski, Józef Klemens," in Lerski 1996, 439–442.

20. Yonatan Gruenbaum, unpublished manuscript; Frister 1987.

21. Yitzhak took his younger son with him to attend the Sixteenth Zionist Congress in Zurich, and from there passed him on to relatives in France. Frister 1987, 272–273.

22. Frister 1987, 276–277.

3. *Paris, Fifth Arrondissement, 5 Rue Linné, 1931*

1. Poznanski 2001; Poznanski 2000.

2. For obvious reasons, the word "Foreign" was later changed to "Immigrant," and it became the Main d'Oeuvre Immigré. See, for example, Boyarin 1986, 47–48; Zaagsma 2006.

3. Beevor and Cooper 1994, 260–267.

4. Frister 1987, 278; Ben-Hanan 1989, 4–7.

5. Glasner-Heled and Bar-On 2004, 39–40.

6. Boyarin 1991, 46–47.

7. Yonatan Gruenbaum, unpublished manuscript, chapter on Itche, p. 6, n. 12.

8. Paris Inquiry, M. (Monsieur) Marchesseaux, Jan. 20, 1946.

9. Frister 1987, 307.

10. Paczkowski 1988, 49–56; N. Cohen 2001, 301–326; Frister 1987, 307–310.

11. Frister 1987, 307–310; Ben-Hanan 1989, 4–7.

4. *Spain, March 1938–1939*

1. Paris Inquiry, document from archive file, 165–166; Paris Inquiry, M. Marchesseaux, Jan. 20, 1946, 13.735. Compare with Frister 1987, 284.

2. Nov. 8, 1936, in Levin 1987, 76. For a systematic and comprehensive account of the war's background, progress, and outcome, see Brome 1965; Crossman 1950; Hopkins 1998.

3. Negev 2006b, 108–112.

4. Aviv 1991a, 103–114.

5. Levin 1987, 78.

6. Geshur 2000, 502.

7. Shneiderman 2001.

8. On the sins of the Republican camp see Dotan 1991.

9. See Aviv 1991b, 116–123.

10. Zaagsma 2001; Lustiger 2001; Brenner 1983.

11. Zaagsma 2001, 6; Sugarman undated cites fifty-three countries; Levin 1987.

12. S. L. Shneiderman, a senior Jewish correspondent who covered the war for a number of newspapers, quoted in Zaagsma 2001, 20.

13. See Geshur 2000, 502.

14. Geshur 2000. On the claim that they served as cannon fodder, see Shmuel Segel, quoted in Levin 1987. According to Levin, some ten thousand of the forty thousand volunteers fell in battle. See also Zaagsma 2001.

15. Levin 1987, 78; Sugarman undated.

16. Sugarman undated; Williams, Alexander, and Gorman 1996.

17. Sugarman undated; Levin 1987.

18. Yonatan Gruenbaum, unpublished manuscript; Ben-Hanan 1989, 4–7; Barnea 1986, 24–31; Lustiger 2001. On Parisian Communist participation in the company as a way of constructing their identities as Jews and Communists and to place themselves within the immigrant community see Zaagsma 2001. Zaagsma writes of the role the Parisians played in the establishment of a Jewish company, 13–15.

19. Frister 1987, 284. Ben-Hanan also accepts this version. See also Glasner-Heled and Bar-On 2004, 111–146.

20. At the beginning of the war, the Communist volunteers also had to overcome the opposition of the anarchists. See Aviv 1991b. On the international restrictions see Aviv 1991a, Frank 1992; Shneiderman 2001, and Lustiger 2001.

21. Levin 1987.

22. Paris Inquiry, André Ballot. Also, Paris Inquiry, letter of the Volunteer Association in Republican France, Polish Section, Dec. 14, 1945 (document from p. 136 of the archive file), 79 boulevard Beaumarché [*sic*], to Advocate André Ballot, Paris. See also Paris Inquiry, M. Marchesseaux, Jan. 20, 1946, 13.735.

23. The establishment of a Jewish company was first proposed by Albert Nahumi (whose original name was Aryeh Weitz), a Communist activist in Paris who arrived in Spain at the beginning of the war. He gained the support of André Marty, commander of the International Brigades' basic training camp and chief of the Communist delegation

in the Brigades. See also the account of a discussion between supporters and opponents in Zaagsma 2001, 12–13.

24. Ludwig Renn was the main character in the 1928 novel *Krieg* (War). The novel's author, Arnold Friedrich Vieth von Golssenau, adopted his character's name as his nom de guerre.

25. See Shneiderman 2001.

26. See Diamant 1979, 144–145.

27. Sugarman undated; Zaagsma 2001, 16; Lustiger 2001; Frank 1992.

28. Frank 1992; Shneiderman 2001; Zaagsma 2001, 16.

29. See, among others, Zaagsma 2001, 17–18.

30. Lustiger 2001; Frank 1992; Zaagsma 2001, 17–18. Stein 1961 inventories the rifles, p. 230.

31. Stein offers the most detailed testimony about the company's battles, as presented at length in Zaagsma 2001, 17–18.

32. See the detailed account in Stein 1961, which is quoted by Zaagsma 2001, 18–19, 21.

33. Lustiger 2001; Frank 1992; Zaagsma 2001. Stein 1961 inventories the number of rifles.

34. Lustiger 2001; Frank 1992; Zaagsma 2001, 22.

35. Geshur 2000; Levin 1987.

36. Frister 1987, 284; see also the quote from Shmuel Segel that appears in Levin 1987.

37. Paris Inquiry, André Ballot. See also Paris Inquiry, letter of the Volunteer Association in Republican France, Polish Section, Dec. 14, 1945 (document from p. 136 of the archive file), to Advocate André Ballot, Paris; and Paris Inquiry, M. Marchesseaux, Jan. 20, 1946, 13.735. See also Sugarman undated.

5. *Saint-Cyprien, Paris, Les Tourelles, Beaune-la-Rolande, France, 1939–1942*

1. Paris Inquiry, 165–166; Paris Inquiry, M. Marchesseaux, Jan. 20, 1946, 13.735.

2. Sperber 2003.

3. On the Jews in these camps during the war see Poznanski 2001, inter alia 36–42, 228–232.

4. Yonatan Gruenbaum, unpublished manuscript, chapter on Itche; Paris Inquiry, 165–166; Paris Inquiry, M. Marchesseaux, Jan. 20, 1946, 13.735; Ben-Hanan 1989, 4–7; Barnea 1986, 24–31.

5. Ben-Hanan 1989, 4–7; Glasner-Heled and Bar-On 2004, 120–121.

6. Pinkus 2005, 44–45.

7. In the wake of the pact with Germany, the Soviet leadership dictated a new policy to the Comintern, which in turn instructed Communist parties around the world to adopt the new Soviet doctrine. This included branding Britain and France as aggressors that were menaces to "peaceful" Germany and Italy.

8. Yonatan Gruenbaum, unpublished manuscript; Paris Inquiry, M. Marchesseaux, Jan. 20, 1946, and André Ballot comments, Jan. 20, 1946; Paris Inquiry, 165–166.

9. Porath 2001. On France's Jews during the Vichy regime see Marrus and Paxton 1995.

10. Porath 2001.

11. See Jäckel 1981; Marrus and Paxton 1995; Porath 2001.

12. Porath 2001.

13. Ibid.; Poznanski 2001, 305–306.

14. Porath 2001.

15. Poznanski 2001, 48–60. On the way life changed for Paris's Jews, through the eyes of a Jewish journalist, see Poznanski 2000.

16. The Pithiviers camp was set up on German orders in 1940 and designated for French prisoners of war. From May 1941 it held French and foreign Jews.

17. The Beaune-la-Rolande camp was built in the winter of 1939–1940 to take in Canadian troops, but was then refitted as a German prison camp for French prisoners. In March 1941 it turned into a camp for Parisian Jews. See Marrus and Paxton 1995, 166, 170, 203, 223, 249, 252–253; Poznanski 2001, 48–60, 250, 264–265, 319.

18. Paris Inquiry, André Ballot, Nov. 29, 1945, 101–108; also Paris Inquiry, 72–86, Emilien to department commissioner et al., SN.PJ.SE. 4-37-56, Oct. 12, 1945. Emilien's memo is based on an examination by Inspector Renaud, carried out in accordance with the instructions of his superiors and as a continuation of the committee of inquiry of Oct. 19, 1945, headed by M. Maurice, judge in the de la Seine preliminary panel.

19. The fort earlier served as a women's prison.

20. Yonatan Gruenbaum, unpublished manuscript; Paris Inquiry, M. Marchesseaux, 165–166. See also Paris Inquiry, André Ballot, Jan. 20, 1946.

21. Poznanski 2001, 48–60.

22. Eliezer Gruenbaum, AAN 15087, Berger-Gruenbaum file; AAN, Berger testimony, Aug. 13, 1945, before Kowalski and Eisner.

23. See Boyarin 1991, 48–51. Boyarin writes that for all intents and purposes the Jewish section was dismantled, and that the entire Left was dealt a blow when Léon Blum's government fell.

24. November 7 according to the Gregorian calendar, October 25 according to the Julian calendar.

25. Paris Inquiry, André Ballot, Nov. 29, 1945, 101–108 in the file. See also Paris Inquiry, Epstein testimony, and Poznanski 2001, 57–60.

26. Paris Inquiry, André Ballot, Nov. 29, 1945; AAN, letter in Berger's handwriting to his comrades, Paris, Aug. 22, 1945. Also Vilner-Fanstein testimony in Poznanski 2001, 59, and 194–195. Compare with Yonatan Gruenbaum, unpublished manuscript; Frister 1987, 283–284.

27. AAN, letter in Berger's hand to his comrades, Paris, Aug. 22, 1945; Paris Inquiry, André Ballot; Yonatan Gruenbaum, unpublished manuscript; Frister 1987, 283–284. Compare with the version of Jean Jerome (1986, 50–52), who supports Gruenbaum's claim that he decided not to flee because he did not want to endanger his fellow-prisoners, and his assertion about his central role in camp life.

28. AAN, Berger-Gruenbaum testimony 15087; Berger testimony, Aug. 13, 1945, Jacques Furmanski testimony, June 25, 1945; AAN, letter in Berger's hand to his comrades, Paris, Aug. 22, 1945.

29. AAN, letter in Berger's hand to his comrades, Paris, Aug. 22, 1945; Paris Inquiry,

testimony of Léon (Leib) Epstein, testimony of Daniel Finkelkraut, testimony of Ijziykléar Oléar, testimony of Herman Freilich. Compare with the testimony of Jacques Furmanski, who criticized Eliezer's leadership at Beaune-la-Rolande because of what he said about the Soviet Union: AAN, Furmanski testimony, June 25, 1945.

30. AAN, Berger-Gruenbaum testimony 15087. On underground activity and aid to those in need see Poznanski 2001, 59ff.

31. Paris Inquiry, André Ballot, Nov. 29, 1945, 101–108 in the file; Paris Inquiry, Epstein and Finkelkraut testimonies.

6. *Auschwitz, Auschwitz-Birkenau, July 1942–March/April 1944*

1. Letter from Mrs. Teresa Swiebocka, director of the archive at Auschwitz Museum, with attached lists, and letter of Wojciech Plosa, archivist there, to Tuvia Friling, June 6, 2006, regarding the number assigned to Eliezer Gruenbaum, who arrived from Beaune-la-Rolande to Auschwitz on June 30, 1942. Eliezer was included in shipment 5 on June 28, 1942, and was registered at Auschwitz on June 30. His number in the shipment was 282. His address in Paris (the clerks did not strike out this detail) was 40 rue des Boulangers. See also Yad Vashem, Arsolen lists, M.8\Bu-A178, G-182 ITS (International Tracing Service), master index.

2. Gutman 1957, 34, 36–37; Czech 1994, 363–378. On the numbers in the camp see also P. Levi 1989, 94–95; P. Levi 1987, 33–34, 39.

3. P. Levi 1989, 94–95.

4. Massuah Archive, Charles Papiernik testimony, undated.

5. On the types of trains, the nature of the journey, the differences between trains originating in different parts of Europe, and the humiliation involved, see inter alia P. Levi 1989, 85–86; P. Levi 1987, 23–25; Aly 2007, 69, 77–78, 104–108.

6. Massuah Archive, Charles Papiernik testimony, undated; Mark 1978, 261, n. 55; P. Levi 1989, 87–88; Aly 2007, 102; Czech 1994, 363–378.

7. Gutman 1957, 11–13; Baum 1962.

8. Czech 1994, 364; Langbein 1980, 273–275; Gutman 1957, 11–13.

9. Gutman 1957, 13–18; Mark 1978, 12; Langbein 1980, 273–275.

10. Gutman 1957, 16–17; Langbein 1980, 273–275; Baum 1949, chap. 1. On the crematoria see also "Yeled Gadal beAuschwitz" (from the memoirs of Leon Shlafsky, who was twelve years old when the war broke out) in Gutman 1957, 241–250, as well as the unsigned testimony "My Life during the Period of World War II," YVA M-1/E, 1787.

11. Piper 1994, 61–76.

12. Gutman 1957, 18ff.; Shlafsky memoir in Gutman 1957, 30–32; Czech 1994, 363–378.

13. Baum 1962, chap. 1; Gutman 1957, 18ff.; Shlafsky memoir in Gutman 1957, 30–32. On the shortage of water and great thirst see also the unsigned testimony "My Life during the Period of World War II," YVA M-1/E, 1787; Czech 1994, 363–378; P. Levi 1989, 25–26; P. Levi 1987, 80–81.

14. Mark 1978, 260, n. 21; Gutman 1957, 18.

15. Mark 1978, 259, n. 14; Baum 1962, chap. 1; Czech 1994, 363–378.

16. Gutman 1957, 30–32. The most recent counting of the Auschwitz victims is in Piper 1991; Piper 2002; Piper 1994, 61–76.

17. Paris Inquiry, André Ballot, Nov. 29, 1945, 101–108. For an entirely different account of Eliezer's appointment to block clerk see Massuah Archive, Charles Papiernik testimony, undated.

18. AAN 15087, 1–20; Massuah Archive, Charles Papiernik testimony, undated.

19. Massuah Archive, Charles Papiernik testimony, undated.

20. Mark 1978, 260, n. 21; Kornberg testimony, USHMM RG-50.030*0016; Shapiro testimony, Oct. 1989, YVA 036527 (English).

21. AAN, translated by Shmuel Katz; Massuah Archive, Charles Papiernik testimony, undated.

22. Gutman 1957, 21–26, and see there "Yeled Gadal beAuschwitz," 241–250; on the functioning of the *Stubendienst*, ibid. 50–53, 246; on the *Prominenten*, ibid., 50, 52–54, 73; Czech 1994, 363–378; Mark 1978, 12.

23. Paris Inquiry, André Ballot, Nov. 29, 1945, 101–108; AAN, Berger deposition, Aug. 13, 1945. On his appointment see also Mark 1978, 54–55; and Massuah Archive, Charles Papiernik testimony, undated.

24. Massuah Archive, Charles Papiernik testimony, undated.

25. "Yeled Gadal beAuschwitz" in Gutman 1957, 241–250; also Paris Inquiry, André Ballot, Nov. 29, 1945, 101–108.

26. Paris Inquiry, André Ballot.

27. Ibid. On Eliezer's bout with typhus see Paris Inquiry, Epstein testimony; Garbarz and Garbarz 1992, Czech 1994, 363–378.

28. AAN, Eliezer Gruenbaum in Berger deposition, Aug. 13, 1945.

29. Paris Inquiry, André Ballot, Nov. 29, 1945, 101–108; on Eliezer's appointment to head Block 20 see also Mark 1978, 54–55.

30. See Piper 2002 and Baum interview, USHMM RG-50.030*0017.

31. Paris Inquiry, André Ballot, Nov. 29, 1945, 101–108.

32. The ZWZ was a xenophobic nationalist party that had adopted an antisemitic platform at the end of the nineteenth century. It advocated a racially pure Poland. During World War I its representatives in the Sjem proposed a boycott of Jewish businesses and other antisemitic legislation. In the 1930s the party's younger members, influenced by Germany and Italy, adopted Nazi and fascist principles.

33. A Polish resistance group formed in part out of remnants of the Polish army, subordinate to the government-in-exile in London. After the merger of the underground forces on February 14, 1942, its became the Polish Home Army (AK).

34. Mark 1978, 34–36; Baum 1962, chap. 4.

35. Mark 1978; Baum 1962.

36. Mark 1978, 37.

37. Ibid., 37–38, 71.

38. Ibid., 73.

39. See P. Levi 1989, 115; P. Levi 1987, 94–95; Mark 1978, 40–41.

40. Mark 1978, 74–75, Langbein 1980, 295–296.

41. Mark 1978, 74–75. On Szpilski's defense of Eliezer see Jozef Szpilski files, AAN t.osob. 5775 (Jozef Szpilski), 79, 115, 119.

42. Gutman interview, USHMM RG-50.120 *056.

43. Mark 1978, 80–81.

44. Ibid.

45. Ibid., 84.

46. Ibid., 85–86.

47. See Massuah Archive, Charles Papiernik testimony, undated; and Mark 1978, 87 on other groups active in the camp.

48. See Paris Inquiry, Goldstein testimony.

49. Czech 1994, 363–378; P. Levi 1989, 34–41.

50. Mark 1978, 116–117. He also mentions the provision of medicines and other goods found on the victims to the rest of the camp. See also P. Levi 1989, 34–41, especially on "the death of the soul."

51. Mark 1978, 117–118.

52. Ibid.

53. Ibid., 118.

54. Ibid.

55. Ibid., 120.

56. Ibid., 120–121.

57. Ibid.

58. Ibid.

59. Ibid.

60. Ibid., 122–123; Czech 1994, 363–378.

61. Mark 1978, 123–124.

62. Ibid.

63. Ibid.

64. Mark 1978, 125–126.

65. Ibid., also 150–153; also Gutman interview, USHMM and Massuah, RG-50.120*056.

66. Mark 1978, 125–126, 150–153, and esp. 149–151.

67. Leventhal's diary, quoted in Mark 1978, 150.

68. Mark 1978, 126–132, 150–152, according to Leventhal's diary. On the rebellion see the unsigned testimony "My Life during the Period of World War II," YVA M-1/E, 1787; on other small-scale rebellions in the Sonderkommando see P. Levi 1989, 34–41.

69. Mark 1978, 126–133; P. Levi 1989, 34–41.

70. Mark 1978, 127–132; P. Levi 1989, 34–41. For a postwar account of the rebellion see YVA, Ben-Zion Arieli testimony 0.3/6121, 03/8934, Nov. 8, 1994; Swiebocki 1995, 104, 129–130.

7. Jawischowitz, March 1944–January 1945

1. Piper 2002, 248.

2. Strzelecki 1974, 171–234.

3. Piper 2002, 378.

4. Garbarz and Garbarz 1992; Strzelecki 1974; Moraud 1985; Strzelecki 1989; Kornberg interview, USHMM RG-50.030*0016; testimony of Victor Majzlik in Moraud 1985, 252.

5. Shapiro testimony, YVA 036527, Oct. 24, 1989; Liber testimony, YVA 11981, Nov. 13, 2001.

6. Ibid.

7. See in the list of companies that received construction and other services in Shapiro and Liber testimonies, ibid.

8. Strzelecki 1974. On work by the conveyor belt see Arieli testimony, YVA 0.3/6121, 03/8934, Nov. 8, 1994; Shachar (Schwarz) testimony, YVA 11231, March 10, 1999; Preizler testimony, YVA 12086, June 4, 2002; Z. Kohen testimony, YVA 03/7046, Nov. 8, 1994; Zalmanovitz testimony, YVA 03/9495, July 11, 1995. On the exploitation of forced laborers see Aly 2007, 55–63, and the example of the Daimler-Benz factories.

9. Strzelecki 1974.

10. See, for example, Victor Majzlik testimony in Moraud 1985, 254.

11. Strzelecki 1974; Majzlik testimony in Moraud 1985, 252–253; Kornberg interview, USHMM RG-50.030*0016. See also Liber testimony, YVA 11981, Nov. 13, 2001; Landau testimony, YVA 03/7048, June 10, 1993; Zalmanovitz testimony, YVA 03/9495, July 11, 1995.

12. Liber testimony, YVA 11981, Nov. 13, 2001; Majzlik testimony in Moraud 1985, 252–253.

13. Strzelecki 1974; Kornberg interview, USHMM RG-50.030*0016; Shapiro testimony, YVA 036527, Oct. 24, 1989.

14. On the food at the camp see, for example, Shachar (Schwarz) testimony, YVA 11231, March 10, 1999. See also Landau testimony, YVA 03/7048, June 10, 1993; Zalmanovitz testimony, YVA 03/9495, July 11, 1995; Shapiro testimony, YVA 036527, Oct. 24, 1989.

15. Shapiro testimony, YVA 036527, Oct. 24, 1989; P. Levi 1987, 47.

16. Kornberg interview, USHMM RG-50.030*0016; Shapiro testimony, YVA 036527, Oct. 24, 1989; Zalmanovitz testimony, YVA 03/9495, July 11, 1995.

17. See, for example, Shapiro testimony, YVA 036527, Oct. 24, 1989.

18. Strzelecki 1974; Icek Baum interview, USHMM RG-50.030*0017, July 5, 1994. See also Kornberg interview, USHMM RG-50.030*0016.

19. Strzelecki 1974.

20. Ibid.

21. Paris Inquiry, André Ballot, Nov. 29, 1945, 101–108.

22. Ibid.; AAN 15087, Berger-Gruenbaum file.

23. Paris Inquiry, André Ballot's interrogation of Oléar, as well as Oléar testimony, 108. For more on Oléar see the testimonies of Victor Jakobs, Eugéne Kawka, Henri Krasukci, Benjamin Rapoport, and Mendel Zlotnik in Moraud 1985.

24. Paris Inquiry, André Ballot, Nov. 29, 1945, 101–108.

25. Ibid.

26. Moraud 1985, Majzlik testimony, 250–260.

27. Moraud 1985, 107–117, and Majzlik testimony, 250–260.

28. See Strzelecki 1974; Strzekecki 1973; Moraud 1985, 256–259.

29. Moraud 1985, 104–107.

30. Majzlik testimony in Moraud 1985, 256–259.

31. Moraud 1985, 256–259; Arieli testimony, YVA 0.3/6121, 03/8934, Nov. 8, 1994; Shapiro testimony, YVA 036527, Oct. 24, 1989.

32. Moraud 1985, 256–259.

33. Ibid.; Shapiro testimony, YVA 036527, Oct. 24, 1989.

34. Moraud 1985, 256–259.

35. Strzelecki 1975, 244–245; Kulka 1984, 404–405.

36. Moraud 1985, 110; Strzelecki 1975, 244–245.

37. Moraud 1985, 110; Zalmanovitz testimony, YVA 03/9495, July 11, 1995.

38. Moraud 1985, 110.

39. See, at length, Moraud 1985, 218–240, 317–335, 378–284; Garbarz and Garbarz 1992.

40. Moraud 1985, 259. Moraud spells Achsen's name "Axen."

41. On the Parisian Jewish Communists at Jawischowitz see Moraud 1985, 259.

42. AAN 15087, Berger-Gruenbaum; Berger deposition, AAN 15087, Aug. 13, 1945, 1; Majzlik testimony, ibid., July 18, 1945.

43. Friling 2005, 1:125–135.

44. Gilbert 1981, 205–206.

45. P. Levi 1987, 95–96.

46. Gilbert 1981; Braham 1981, 708–716; Bauer 2005; Conway 1981; Karny 1994, 553–568.

47. Friling 2005, 2:71–85.

48. Paris Inquiry, André Ballot, Nov. 29, 1945, 101–108; AAN 15087, Berger-Gruenbaum; Berger deposition, AAN 15087, Aug. 13, 1945, 1; Moraud 1985, 256; Garbarz and Garbarz 1992, 71.

49. Friling 2005, 2:77–78.

50. P. Levi 1989; P. Levi 1987, 158–159; Zalmanovitz testimony, YVA 03/9495, July 11, 1995; Shapiro testimony, YVA 036527, Oct. 24, 1989.

51. Zalmanovitz testimony, YVA 03/9495, July 11, 1995; Shapiro testimony, YVA 036527, Oct. 24, 1989; Garbarz and Garbarz 1992, 221 ; P. Levi 1989, 3–4.

52. P. Levi 1987, 159–161, and to the end of the book; Shachar (Schwarz) testimony, YVA 11231, March 10, 1999; Zalmanovitz testimony, YVA 03/9495, July 11, 1995; Garbarz and Garbarz 1992, 221.

53. Prizler testimony, YVA 12086, June 4, 2002; Arieli testimony, YVA 0.3/6121, 03/8934, Nov. 8, 1994; Z. Kohen testimony, YVA 03/7046, Nov. 8, 1994; Shachar (Schwarz) testimony, YVA 11231, March 10, 1999; Landau testimony, YVA 03/7048, June 10, 1993; Zalmanovitz testimony, YVA 03/9495, July 11, 1995; Garbarz and Garbarz 1992, 221–230.

54. Arieli testimony, YVA 0.3/6121, 03/8934, Nov. 8, 1994; Z. Kohen testimony, YVA 03/7046, Nov. 8, 1994; Prizler testimony, YVA 12086, June 4, 2002; Shachar (Schwarz) testimony, YVA 11231, March 10, 1999; Landau testimony, YVA 03/7048, June 10, 1993; Zalmanovitz testimony, YVA 03/9495, July 11, 1995.

55. Kornberg interview, USHMM RG-50.030*0016.

56. Strzelecki 1974; Strzelecki 1973; Shachar (Schwarz) testimony, YVA 11231, March 10, 1999; Landau testimony, YVA 03/7048, June 10, 1993.

8. Buchenwald, January–June 1945

1. "Buchenwald" in Gutman 1990, 254–256; Gutman and Saf 1984.

2. Gutman and Saf 1984, 282, n. 4.

3. "Buchenwald" in Gutman 1990, 254–256; Gutman and Saf 1984.

4. Preizler testimony, YVA 12086, June 4, 2002; Landau testimony, YVA 03/7048, June 10, 1993; Shachar (Schwarz) testimony, YVA 11231, March 10, 1999.

5. "Buchenwald" in Gutman 1990, 254–256; Gutman and Saf 1984.

6. "Buchenwald" in Gutman 1990; Gutman and Saf 1984.

7. Yonatan Gruenbaum, unpublished manuscript.

8. Arolsen documents, YVA, ITS folio 1157, 2676.

9. Jerome 1986, 50–52.

10. Moraud 1985, 218–240; Jozef Szpilski files, AAN, t.osob. 5775.

11. Shapiro testimony, YVA 036527, Oct. 24, 1989.

12. AAN 15087, Berger-Gruenbaum file, Berger-Gruenbaum testimony, Aug. 15, 1945, 1–20.

13. Orbach's testimony is in Yiddish, but he used this Hebrew word, which in its Yiddish incarnation usually means "gentiles."

14. Interviews with Orbach, YVA 03/4808, undated, 19 in the first interview and 20, 27–28 in the second.

15. I am grateful to Dr. Lena Novotna for her generous assistance in searching out this information. Fučík 1995, comments, 214–118, Czech National Archives, III. Department (Nedvěd material), Praha-Chodovec.

16. AAN 15087, Berger-Gruenbaum file, Berger-Gruenbaum testimony, Aug. 13, 1945, 1–20.

17. Paris Inquiry, André Ballot, Nov. 29, 1945, 101–108. Gustloff-Werke was a German arms factory, liberated in April 1945 by the U.S. Army's Eleventh Division.

18. Yonatan Gruenbaum, unpublished manuscript, 2–3; Paris Inquiry, André Ballot, Nov. 29, 1945, 101–108; Preizler testimony, YVA 12086, June 4, 2002; Shachar (Schwarz) testimony, YVA 11231, March 10, 1999.

19. Yonatan Gruenbaum, unpublished manuscript, 2; Baumel-Tydor 1992, 191–218.

20. AAN 15087, Berger-Gruenbaum file, Berger-Gruenbaum statement, June 3, 1945, 1–20.

21. Arolsen documents, YVA no. 117.491, ITS folio 1157, 2676, liberation records of the military government in Germany, May 4, 1945, Buchenwald.

22. I. Schwarzbart, London, to Yitzhak Gruenbaum, Jerusalem, April 26, 1945, CZA A127/345. See also ibid., Prof. Shalom Goldelman to Yitzhak Gruenbaum, April 27, 1945.

23. I. Schwarzbart, London, to Yitzhak Gruenbaum, Jerusalem, June 2, 1945, CZA A127/345.

9. Warsaw–Paris, Paris–Warsaw: June–September 1945

1. Unfortunately, I have been unable to find any information about the process by which Kowalski and Eisner were appointed, the names of their superiors, and the precise affiliation and status of those superiors within the party and the administration.

Neither have I been able to find out why the party decided to pursue this inquiry or the nature of the order to commence this quasi-legal proceeding.

2. AAN 15087, Berger-Gruenbaum file, Berger-Gruenbaum testimony, Aug. 13, 1945, 1–8.

3. Ibid., June 3, 1945, 1–20.

4. Ibid.

5. Ibid.

6. Ibid.

7. Ibid.

8. Ibid.

9. See P. Levi 1987, e.g., 165–166.

10. AAN 15087, Berger-Gruenbaum file, Berger-Gruenbaum testimony, June 3, 1945, 1–20.

11. Ibid.

12. Ibid.

13. Ibid.

14. Ibid.

15. Ibid.

16. Ibid.

17. Ibid.

18. Ibid.

19. Ibid.

20. Ibid. And see Kraus and Kulka 1960, 46, 71. They maintain that Hammerle was chief of Block 7, not Block 5 as in Eliezer's testimony.

21. AAN 15087, Berger-Gruenbaum file, Berger-Gruenbaum testimony, June 3, 1945, 1–2; Swiebocki 1995, 242–252.

22. AAN 15087, Berger-Gruenbaum file, Berger-Gruenbaum testimony, June 3, 1945.

23. Ibid.

24. Ibid.

25. Ibid.

26. Ibid.

27. Ibid.

28. Ibid.

29. Ibid.

30. Ibid.

31. In another part of his testimony, Eliezer spoke about another transport from Radom, from Series 123.000. It is not clear whether it was the transport mentioned here or a different one.

32. AAN 15087, Berger-Gruenbaum file, Berger-Gruenbaum testimony, June 3, 1945, 1–20.

33. Ibid.

34. Ibid.

35. Ibid.

36. Ibid.

37. Ibid.; cf. Mark 1978, 122–123, 127.

38. AAN 15087, Berger-Gruenbaum file, Berger-Gruenbaum testimony, June 3, 1945, 1–20.

39. Ibid.

40. Ibid.

41. Ibid.

42. Ibid.

43. Ibid.

44. Ibid.

45. Ibid.

46. On this matter see, for example, Trunk 1979 and P. Levi 1989, e.g., 5–7, 22–23, 27–34, 42–50.

47. P. Levi 1989, 60–61.

48. AAN 15087, Berger-Gruenbaum file, Berger-Gruenbaum testimony, June 3, 1945, 1–20.

49. Ibid., Kowalski and Elsner, deposition of Berger, Aug. 13, 1945, 1–8.

50. Ibid.

51. Ibid.

52. Ibid.

53. Ibid.

54. Ibid.

55. Ibid.

56. Ibid.

57. Ibid.

58. Ibid.

59. Ibid.

60. Ibid.

61. Ibid.

62. Ibid.

63. Ibid.

64. Ibid. Eliezer also told them about other activities of his.

65. AAN 15087, Berger-Gruenbaum file, Furmanski testimony, June 25, 1945, 14.

66. Ibid. The testimony does not display Furmanski's signature.

67. Ibid., Finkelkraut testimony, Aug. 9, 1945.

68. Ibid., Freilich testimony, Aug. 20, 1945, 12, 23. Signed by Freilich, with his address in Paris.

69. Ibid., Szmulewski testimony, undated and unsigned.

70. Ibid., Mink testimony, undated and unsigned.

71. Ibid., Laks testimony, Aug. 6, 1945, signed by the witness. According to the testimony, Laks was in Birkenau from July 1942 to March 1943. Other sources indicate that he was a member of the camp orchestra until the autumn of 1944, when he was transferred to Dachau.

72. Ibid., Majzlik testimony, Aug. 6, 1945, signed by the witness.

73. Ibid., Napieracz testimony, Nov. 7, 1945, unsigned; and see also Berger's notes of Napieracz's testimony, 22–24, manuscript, ibid.

74. Ibid., Berger's questions to Majcher Langman, manuscript and typed version, 16–17 in the file.

75. Ibid., Berger's questions to David Szmulewski, manuscript, 25–27 in the file.

76. Ibid., Berger's questions to Jacques Furmanski, manuscript, 13; Berger's questions to Léon Epstein,13; Eliezer's initial testimony.

77. Ibid., Berger letter to Andrzej, April 3, 1945, 29 in the file (the date there is in error and should be July 1945, when Eliezer had been in Paris for a month).

78. Ibid., Berger letter to comrades, July 21, 1945, 30–32 in the file, manuscript and typed version.

79. Ibid., Berger letter to comrades, Aug. 22, 1945, 33–49 in the file, Berger's handwriting with his signature.

80. Ibid.

81. Ibid.

82. Ibid.

83. Ibid.

84. Ibid.

85. Ibid.

86. Ibid.

87. Ibid.

88. We have no confirmation from any other source that Eliezer served as assistant clerk in Block 13.

89. The documentation gives a clear impression that some of the participants in most of the ideological debates to which Eliezer refers simply did not understand the fine points of this debate because of profound discrepancies in their educational backgrounds and their acquaintance with Communist teaching.

90. Berger letter to comrades, Aug. 22, 1945, AAN 15087, Berger-Gruenbaum file, Furmanski testimony, June 25, 1945, 33–49 in the file, in Berger's hand and with his signature.

91. Ibid.

92. Ibid.

93. Ibid., report on Berger's case, 50 in the file.

10. *Paris, June 1945–May 1946*

1. About 77,000 out of the 320,000–350,000 Jews who had lived there in 1940.

2. Beevor and Cooper 1994, 165ff.

3. Ibid., 234–237.

4. Ibid., 179–182.

5. Ibid., 185–190.

6. Ibid., 240–247.

7. Ibid., 240–242.

8. Ibid.

9. Frister 1987, 290–291.

10. Ibid.

11. Ibid.

12. Compare Frister 1987, 291, with Yonatan Gruenbaum's version of events in his unpublished manuscript, 15. See also Collection of Dr. Jeannine (Levana) Frenk, Gebet and Pakin testimonies.

13. E. Shaltiel 2000, 186; Barzel 1998; Keynan 1995.

14. Yitzhak Gruenbaum 1964, July 15.

15. Yonatan Gruenbaum, unpublished manuscript, 3.

16. Ibid.

17. Ibid.

18. Ibid., letter from Eliezer to his mother, Miriam, Aug. 30, 1945.

19. *Annuaire des secrétaries et anciens secrétaries de la Conférence du Barreau de Paris*, Paris, 1998, 271; *La Vie Judiciaire*, Dec. 20, 1937, and Paris documents, private collection.

20. Paris Inquiry, 72–86 in the file; Collection of Dr. Jeannine (Levana) Frenk, report of Vézard Emilien to the department commissar, chief of la Cour de justice de la Seine, Paris, Oct. 12, 1945.

21. Collection of Dr. Jeannine (Levana) Frenk, Paris, 1945–1946, manuscript, testimonies from the hearing; Gebet testimony, Oct. 9, 1945.

22. Ibid., Zylberstein testimony.

23. Ibid., Loberstein testimony.

24. Ibid., Pakin testimony; see also there the testimony of Szlama Hezlikorwitz, a prisoner at Birkenau who never encountered Gruenbaum.

25. Ibid., examination and cross-examination, 51–54.

26. Ibid., cross-examination before Magistrate Maurice, Pakin's response. Yad Vashem's *Book of the Dead* includes the name of a man named Hirtz Pinkiert, born in 1904, sent from France on transport 20, who died on Jan. 21, 1943.

27. Ibid., Zylberstein testimony.

28. Ibid., Gebet testimony.

29. Ibid., Zylberstein, Gebet, and Pakin testimonies, and Eliezer's and Ballot's replies.

30. Ibid., testimonies from the hearings, 72–86, Oct. 19, 1945.

31. Yonatan Gruenbaum, unpublished manuscript, 16–17, quoting Yitzhak Gruenbaum's letter to his family, Oct. 13, 1945.

32. See Bulawko 1954.

33. Rayski, letter of March 17, 2007, in response to a letter from Re'ut Ben-Horin of March 15, 2007, in possession of author; on the meeting between Rayski and Yitzhak Gruenbaum see also Levana Frenk interview, conducted by Re'ut Ben-Horin, Feb. 13, 2007.

34. Rayski, letter of March 17, 2007, in response to a letter from Re'ut Ben-Horin of March 15, 2007, in possession of author; also his letter of March 22, 2007, to Ben-Horin and letter of Ben-Horin and Friling to Rayski, March 29, 2007, in possession of author.

35. Liblau 2005, 44–45.

36. Liblau met with the inspector at quai de l'Horloge, in the police and judicial compound at Île de la Cité.

37. Liblau 2005, 44–45.

38. Liblau 2005.

39. Ibid.

40. Ibid.

41. We cross-checked other names that Liblau used to ascertain whether he had been able to observe Eliezer firsthand. At various points in his life he called himself Chaskel Lichtblau. In the Auschwitz documents he is registered as Chaskiel Liblau: see item 3198702 in the Yad Vashem lists and Arolsen documents, Yad Vashem M.8\L-129 ITS, master index.

42. Haika Grossman interview, HaShomer haTza'ir Archive, 95-69 4 (4), 296–297.

43. Paris Inquiry, Léon (Leib) Epstein testimony; compare this with Epstein's testimony in the version contained in Collection of Dr. Jeannine (Levana) Frenk, Paris, 1945–1946, testimonies from the hearing — the two versions are almost identical.

44. See above, Chap. 9.

45. Collection of Dr. Jeannine (Levana) Frenk, Paris Inquiry, Finkelkraut testimony.

46. Compare with Finkelkraut testimony, Aug. 9, 1945, AAN 15087, Berger-Gruenbaum file.

47. Collection of Dr. Jeannine (Levana) Frenk, Paris, 1945–1946, testimonies from the hearing, Szmulewski testimony.

48. Paris Inquiry, Oléar testimony; P. Levi 1987, 93–106.

49. Paris Inquiry, Goldstein and Steg testimonies; see also Collection of Dr. Jeannine (Levana) Frenk, Paris, 1945–1946, testimonies from the hearing.

50. Collection of Dr. Jeannine (Levana) Frenk, translation certified by the Polish consul general in Paris, T. Riepka, Oct. 15, 1945, 141–143 in the file. The original is cited there as having appeared in *Pioner*, Wrocław, Lower Silesia, Sunday, Oct. 4, and Monday, Oct. 5, 1945, issue 60.

51. Paris Inquiry, letter from Association of Spanish Republican Volunteers, Polish Section, 79 boulevard Beaumarché [*sic*], to André Ballot, Dec. 14, 1945, 136; Paris Inquiry, M. Marchesseaux, Paris, Jan. 20, 1946, 13.735, 165–166.

52. Collection of Dr. Jeannine (Levana) Frenk, Paris, 1945–1946, testimonies from the hearing; Yitzhak Gruenbaum, letter to his family, in Yonatan Gruenbaum, manuscript of unpublished book, 9–10.

53. Letters from Yitzhak Gruenbaum to his wife and family, Oct. 23 and 31, Nov. 25, 1945, all quoted in Yonatan Gruenbaum, manuscript of unpublished book, 16–17.

54. Ibid., 17–18.

55. Yitzhak Gruenbaum to Hartglas, November 1945, ibid.

56. Paris Inquiry, André Ballot, speaking for Eliezer Gruenbaum, Nov. 29, 1945, 101–108.

57. Ibid.

58. Frister 1987, 292.

59. Ibid., 295–296.

60. Ibid.

61. Yonatan Gruenbaum, unpublished manuscript, 18; Yitzhak Gruenbaum to Meir Hartman, Jan. 12, 1946, quoted in Ben-Hanan 1989, 4–7; Frister 1987, 291–294, 297.

62. Yitzhak Gruenbaum to "Dear Mariosh" (his wife Miriam), Jan. 16, 1946, quoted in Frister 1987, 296.

63. Frister 1987, 292.

64. Yitzhak Gruenbaum, no recipient named, but apparently Moshe Sneh, Nov. 1, 1945, LA.

65. Frister 1987, 292.

66. Friling 2005, 1:125–135.

67. Ibid., 134–135.

68. Frister 1987, 292–293.

69. Yitzhak Gruenbaum, no recipient named, but apparently Moshe Sneh, Nov. 1, 1945, LA.

70. Yitzhak Gruenbaum to Meir Hartman, Nov. 2, 1945, quoted in Ben-Hanan 1989, 4–7. See also Yitzhak Gruenbaum, no recipient named, but apparently Moshe Sneh, Nov. 1, 1945, LA.

71. Frister 1987, 294; Yitzhak Gruenbaum interview, Jan. 12, 1966, by Natan Cohen, Oral History Division, Institute of Contemporary Jewry, The Hebrew University of Jerusalem, file 555/1, film 826.

72. Friling 2005, 2:209–213.

73. Ruth Aliav interview, Dec. 4, 1978, by Gershon Rivlin and Yigal Donyets, Oral History Division, BGHA.

74. Ibid.; Ehud Avriel interview, undated, by Yehuda Bauer, Oral History Division, Institute of Contemporary Jewry, The Hebrew University of Jerusalem, file 39 (4), interview no. 2, 5–13; Kliger-Eliav 1976; Butnaru 1993, 168–169.

75. Ruth Aliav interview, Dec. 4, 1978, by Gershon Rivlin and Yigal Donyets, Oral History Division, BGHA.

76. Ibid., 36–37, 43–44.

77. Ibid., 57–58. See also Avizohar 1987, 253–270. On the second visit see Teveth 2004, 642–645.

78. Collection of Dr. Jeannine (Levana) Frenk, Paris, 1945–1946, manuscript, testimonies from the hearing, handwritten (by Yitzhak Gruenbaum?).

79. Ochshorn (Okshorn) testimony, YVA TR 2/ PS 2429.

80. Paris Inquiry, Ochshorn deposition, documents of legal proceeding; Yitzhak Gruenbaum to Miriam, Feb. 13, 1946, in Yonatan Gruenbaum, unpublished manuscript, 18–19. Compare with Collection of Dr. Jeannine (Levana) Frenk, Paris, 1945–1946, testimonies from the hearing, Egon Yitzhak (Isaak) Ochshorn, Feb. 17, 1946. See also Ochshorn testimony, YVA, copy of original in Weiner Library, London, P.III.h. No. 557 (General), and his card in the Arsolen documents, master index, 0–57 ITS.

81. Paris Inquiry, André Ballot, summing up, 110–134.

82. Ibid.

83. Ibid.

84. Ibid.

85. Ibid.

86. Ibid.; Arolsen documents, master index, YVA L-163 ITS.

87. Paris Inquiry, André Ballot, summing up, 110–134.

88. Ibid. On Tillard at Matthausen see Arsolen documents, YVA T-45 ITS, and documents at the Holocaust Museum, Paris.

89. Ibid. To lend further credence, Ballot is quoted in *Forfaits Hitlériens* 1945, 295.

90. Paris Inquiry, André Ballot, summing up, 110–134.

91. Ibid.

92. Ibid.; Jerome 1986.

93. Paris Inquiry, André Ballot, summing up, 110–134.

94. Ibid.

95. Paris Inquiry, signed at Kinneret on Oct. 16, 1945, in the presence of S. Branblum, lawyer, Tiberias. The testimony was confirmed by Asher Leviszky, lawyer and notary, Palestine.

96. Paris Inquiry, André Ballot, summing up, 110–134.

97. Yonatan Gruenbaum, unpublished manuscript, 18–19.

98. Paris Inquiry, Ministry of Justice, Directorate of the War Crimes Investigation Service, March 20, 1946, document from page 168; Paris Inquiry, letter from the director of the War Crimes Investigation Service to the legal aide to the court (*Commissaire du gouvernement*), 2805-ac-jm-52-334, office of M. Marchessaux.

99. Frister 1987, 296–297; on the opposition to issuing Eliezer a certificate see Eran Turbiner, private collection; and notes of a conversation with Gavriel Tsifroni, then a correspondent for the newspaper *HaBoker*, also in Turbiner, private collection.

100. Frister, 1987, 297.

101. Ibid., 297–299.

102. Ibid., 299.

103. Yonatan Gruenbaum, unpublished manuscript, 19; Frister 1987, 299.

11. *Jerusalem, May 1946–May 1948*

1. Yonatan Gruenbaum, manuscript of unpublished book, 19; Ben-Hanan 1989, 4–7; Frister 1987, 299–300; CZA A 127/359, from interview by A. Wartman with the signatories to the Declaration of Independence, 3.

2. Yitzhak Gruenbaum 1964; Yonatan Gruenbaum, manuscript of unpublished book, 18–19; Frister 1987, 299–300.

3. Yitzhak Gruenbaum 1964; Frister 1987, 299–300; Yitzhak Gruenbaum interview by Natan Cohen, Jan. 12, 1966, Oral History Division, Institute of Contemporary Jewry, The Hebrew University of Jerusalem, 6; Rivka Gruenbaum interview by Glasner-Heled, Glasner-Heled collection.

4. On Ben-Gurion at the end of April and early May see Ben-Gurion diary, BGA. See also Ze'ev Tsahor to Eran Turbiner, Turbiner private collection.

5. Atty. Zvi Kalmantinovsky to Yitzhak Gruenbaum, May 6, 1946, CZA A 127/345. See there also about the article on the gathering in *Iton Meyuhad*.

6. Rubin, editor of *HaMashkif*, to Yitzhak Gruenbaum, May 21, 1946, CZA A 127/345.

7. Ibid.

8. Chairman and secretary of the Committee to Aid the Jews of Bialystok to Yitzhak Gruenbaum, Tel Aviv, June 13, 1946, CZA A 127/345.

9. Glasner-Heled and Bar-On 2004, 123, n. 59, conversation with Gershon Handel, journalist. See also Rosenfeld 1998, 2–10.

10. Summary by Eran Turbiner, Turbiner collection; Frister 1987, 301.

11. Frister 1987, 301; Rivka Gruenbaum interview by Glasner-Heled, Glasner-Heled collection.

12. Summary by Eran Turbiner, Turbiner collection; Frister 1987; Rivka Gruenbaum interview by Glasner-Heled, Glasner-Heled collection.

13. Ben-Gurion termed the British operation a pogrom and "a first lesson or preliminary" to violent attacks by the British in the near future. There is no doubt that this was the case. Sharett wrote to Sneh, characterizing Ben-Gurion's position as "all hope is lost." But Sharett wrote that "it isn't lost," and others agreed with him.

14. See, for example, Teveth 2004, 740–760.

15. Tahon 1969 (1927).

16. Ben-Hanan 1989, 4–7; Rivka Gruenbaum interview by Glasner-Heled, Glasner-Heled collection; Eran Turbiner notes, Eran Turbiner collection.

17. Ben-Hanan 1989, 4–7; Rivka Gruenbaum interview by Glasner-Heled, Glasner-Heled collection; Eran Turbiner notes, Eran Turbiner collection; Frister 1987, 300–301.

18. Ben-Hanan 1989, 4–7; Rivka Gruenbaum interview by Glasner-Heled, Glasner-Heled collection; Eran Turbiner notes, Turbiner collection; Frister 1987.

19. Yonatan Gruenbaum, unpublished manuscript; Eliezer (Itche) Gruenbaum, *Be-Hatzerot haMavet*, diary, in Avinoam 1952.

20. Ibid.

21. Ibid.

22. Ibid.

23. Ibid.

24. Ibid.

25. Ibid.

26. Ibid.

27. Ibid.

28. Glasner-Heled and Bar-On 2004, 140–142.

29. See Oren 1993, Oren 2007, 381–411.

30. Rozenman 1980, 41–45.

31. Ibid.

32. See Blatman 1993, 69–97.

33. Rozenman 1980, 42–43. On the appeal to bomb the camps and access roads see Friling 2005, 2:3–85.

34. Ostap Dluski, director of the Overseas Department (KC, PPR), Central Committee of the Polish Workers' Party, to Comrade Lewikowski, Party Oversight Committee, Jan. 8, 1948, AAN; Ostap Dluski to Lewikowski, director of the Party Oversight Committee,

Jan. 17, 1948, AAN; Yitzhak Gruenbaum to the Party Oversight Committee in Warsaw, Oct. 14, 1947, from Paris, on official Jewish Agency stationery, Paris office, AAN.

35. Ami Gruenbaum interview by Glasner-Heled, Glasner-Heled collection.

36. Frister 1987; interviews of Rivka and Ami Gruenbaum by Glasner-Heled, Glasner-Heled collection.

37. Frister 1987; Tsahor and Tsifroni in Eran Turbiner, private collection.

38. No record of Yitzhak Gruenbaum's request has been found in the Ben-Gurion Archive or in Ben-Gurion's diary, but the fact is that Eliezer was called up. Cooper 2006.

12. *Ramat Rachel, May 21–22, 1948*

1. Lapidot 1992, 269; Levi (Levitseh) 1986; Shiloah 1990, 109–112.

2. IDFA 121/50/208, Account of battle, p. 8; IDFA 500/48/34, Report on the Battles in Jerusalem's Southern Neighborhoods, p. 7; Shiloah 1990, 109–112.

3. IDFA, 121/50/208, Account of battle, p. 8; IDFA 8284/49/405, 32–33; JIA 38/9–473/168, Ramat Rachel battles, p. 3; Shiloah 1990, 109–112.

4. Memoirs of Abdallah al-Tal, quoted in Lapidot 1992, 134–135; Levi (Levitseh) 1986, 256; Shiloah 1990, 109–112.

5. IDFA 121/50/208, Account of battle, p. 8; IDFA 8284/49/405, 32–33; Shiloah 1990, 109–112.

6. IDFA 121/50/208, Account of battle, pp. 8, 9; IDFA 8284/49/405, 32–33. Levi (Levitseh) 1986, 256; also, Ben-Horin telephone conversation with Ya'akov Nitzan, Richie's brother, April 19, 2007. Transcript in possession of the author. According to Nitzan, the commander at Ramat Rachel, a resident of the kibbutz whose last name was Katz fled from the battle.

7. IDFA 121/50/208, Account of battle, pp. 8, 9; IDFA 500/48/34, Report on the Battles in Jerusalem's Southern Neighborhoods, p. 7.

8. JIA 38/9–473/168, Ramat Rachel battles, p. 3.

9. IDFA 121/50/208, Account of battle, pp. 8, 9; IDFA 500/48/34, Report on the Battles in Jerusalem's Southern Neighborhoods, p. 7; testimony of Lt. Col. Yeshoshafat Harkabi (aka "Gold") March 16, 1953, IDFA 922/78/290, 3–4.

10. JIA 38/9–473/168, Ramat Rachel Battles, "The Battle that Saved Jerusalem," p. 8; Lapidot 1992, 134–135; Elitzedek 1949; Levi (Levitseh) 1986, 256, and in particular Shmuel Katz 1966, 428–429. Compare with Shiloah 1990, 109–112, and the account in D. Shaltiel 1981, 183–185.

11. Summary of telephone conversations with Micha Kaufman of the IDFA, Feb. 13, 21, 1996, by Galia Glasner-Heled, Glasner-Heled collection; Doron Avi-Ad, conversations with Re'ut Ben-Horin, March 26, 2007.

12. Levi (Levitseh) 1986, 256; Ben-Hanan 1989, 4–7, Lapidot 1992; Elitzedek 1949; Ya'akov Nitzan, brother of Richman, phone call with Ben-Horin, April 19, 2007; Shlomo Havilio, phone call with Ben-Horin, Feb. 21, 2007; Eli Vald (who rode in the armored car with Eliezer), phone call with Ben-Horin, Feb. 25, 2007. Vald said that about ten soldiers rode in the vehicle.

13. Levi (Levitseh) 1986, 256; Shlomo Havilio, phone conversation with Ben-Horin, Feb. 21, 2007; Ben-Hanan 1989, 4–7.

14. Ya'akov Nitzan, phone call with Ben-Horin, April 19, 2007; Shlomo Havilio, phone call with Ben-Horin, Feb. 21, 2007; Eli Vald, phone call with Ben-Horin, Feb. 25, 2007; Ze'ev Rivlin, phone call with Eran Turbiner, Turbiner collection.

15. JIA, IZL collection, file with unclear number but apparently 38/9–473/168, Jerusalem district, Ramat Rachel Battles, Reports, Surveys, Testimonies, May 22–25, 1948. According to the information at Beit HaPalmach — Palmach forces also participated in the combat at Ramat Rachel — twenty-six soldiers were killed and eighty-four wounded in four days of fighting. Shlomo Havilio told us that the bodies were evacuated under fire later in the day: Shlomo Havilio, phone call with Ben-Horin, Feb. 21, 2007.

16. Levi (Levitseh) 1986, 256. On the deaths of Richman and some of his men see also Lt. Col. Meir Sharvit ("Yarkoni") testimony, March 16, 1959, IDFA 922/78/290, 5–6, as well as Y. Cohen, testimony 44, June 28, 1959. Compare with Shiloah 1990, 109; on the wounded in the truck abandoning Ramat Rachel see Sa'adiah Caravani at the Beit HaPalmach site.

17. Lapidot, commander of the IZL force in the Ramat Rachel battle, conversation with Ben-Horin, Feb. 21, 2007; Eli Vald (who rode in the armored car with Eliezer), phone call with Ben-Horin, Feb. 21, 2007.

18. Ben-Hanan 1989, 4–7. See also Yehuda Lapidot, conversation with Ben-Horin, Feb. 21, 2007; Shlomo Havilio, phone call with Ben-Horin, Feb. 21, 2007; Ya'akov Nitzan, phone call with Ben-Horin, April 19, 2007; Shalom Dror, conversation with Ben-Horin, April 19, 2007.

19. The writer must have meant Talpiot — if Eliezer was close to the ground he would not have been able to see Rehaviah.

20. Ben-Hanan 1989, 4–7.

21. Yehuda Lapidot, conversation with Ben-Horin, Feb. 21, 2007. According to Lapidot, it would be difficult to determine the cause of death. The Israeli forces were barely able to evacuate the bodies of its dead soldiers, and there was no possibility of conducting an inquest.

22. Yizkor, memorial site for the IDF and the Ministry of Defense. The first publication about Eliezer in an official Israeli memorial book was in *Gevilei Esh*, vol. 1, 1952. The publication in *Yizkor*, vol. 1, came in 1955.

23. The article was first published in Yiddish in *Heint*, Montevideo, Uruguay, July 15, 1964.

24. A. Wortman, interview with the signers of the Declaration of Independence, CZA 127/359A, p. 6; see also Yitzhak Gruenbaum's letter to the president of Israel, CZA 127/345A.

25. Frister 1987, 302; Glasner-Heled and Bar-On 2004, 111–146.

26. Barnea 1986, 24–31.

27. Glasner-Heled and Bar-On 2004, 124–125 and nn. 70, 71. Family versions: Yonatan Gruenbaum, unpublished manuscript; *Ha'Ahian* (The nephew), film by Matti Regev (Eliezer's nephew) with Dov Kroytoro, broadcast April 8, 2002 (night of Holocaust

Memorial Day) on Israel's Channel 2. See also with Eli Vald (who rode in the armored car with Eliezer), phone call with Ben-Horin, Feb. 25, 2007.

28. Quoted in Glasner-Heled and Bar-On 2004, 124–125, and n. 71.

29. Turbiner, private collection.

30. Ya'akov Nitzan, brother of Richman, phone call with Ben-Horin, April 19, 2007.

31. Turbiner, private collection.

32. Ibid.

33. Eli Vald, phone call with Ben-Horin, Feb. 25, 2007.

34. Yehuda Lapidot, conversation with Ben-Horin, Feb. 21, 2007.

35. Yosef Ami to Yitzhak Gruenbaum, June 20 and July 11, 1962, CZA 127/345A.

36. Levi (Levitseh) 1986, 364.

37. On this possibility see Eli Vald, phone call with Ben-Horin, Feb. 25, 2007. Vald repeated this suggestion in a conversation with us and a reference to it also appears in Turbiner's collection. And see Cooper 2006.

38. Compare with Ben-Hanan 1989, 4–7, which quotes a letter from Yitzhak Gruenbaum to Meir Hartman, and Frister 1987, 301–302.

39. Frister 1987, 301–302.

40. Frister 1987; Rivka Gruenbaum, interview by Glasner-Heled, Glasner-Heled collection.

41. Frister 1987, 303; Ben-Hanan 1989, 301–302; Barnea 1986; Rivka Gruenbaum, interview by Glasner-Heled, Glasner-Heled collection.

42. Adek found Stefa in mortal condition after she took an overdose of pills. She was evacuated to a hospital, where an attempt was made to save her, but she died a few days later. Lotte Loker later related that Stefa left a suicide note in which she wrote that she had no more strength, that she was exhausted, that she had no more reason to live, and that she realized she was leaving a child behind but that even if she remained alive she would not be able to give him what he deserved and needed. Her young son was told that his mother had been killed in the bombardment of Jerusalem. He learned the truth only after reaching adulthood. Turbiner collection; Glasner-Heled collection; Ben-Hanan 1989; Frister 1987, 203.

13. *Postmortem: Israel, the First Decades*

1. This occurred on Sept. 10, 1950. See undated form letter from Yad leBanim and personal invitation to the family to be present at the transfer of the bodies from Givat Ram (the Hebrew name given to Sheikh Bader) to the Mount Herzl military cemetery, CZA, Gruenbaum files.

2. Sivan 1991, 123–124.

3. Ibid., 143.

4. Ibid.; Avinoam 1957.

5. Sivan 1991, 125–126.

6. Ibid., 55.

7. Ibid., quoted on p. 55.

8. Barnea 1986, 24–31. Barnea based himself on Rembah 1961a and b, about which more below.

9. Barnea 1986, following Rembah, see below. *Gevilei Esh* has three parts. In the third section, which contains short biographies of each soldier, Eliezer and Noam in fact appear side by side. Eliezer's article "Reshet Misharit 'Koloniyalit' shel haYehudim beYemei Qedem" appears on 284–285, and selections from his diary, *BeHatzerot haMavet*, appear on 437–440.

10. Barnea 1986, following Rembah, see below.

11. Y. Gruenbaum, former minister of the interior (as he characterizes himself in the letter), to the Department for Memorializing Soldiers of the Ministry of Defense, August 6, 1952. With the generous assistance of Doron Avi-Ad, IDFA, Documentation and Cataloging unit.

12. Miron 1988, 196–203; Bartov 1999, 148–175.

13. Miron 1988, 196–203.

14. Mony is the younger brother of Harry, the book's central character. His character is based on that of De-Nur's younger brother.

15. De-Nur 1988, 194–195.

16. Prisoners who dealt in cigarettes and other goods; see Primo Levi's (1987) depictions of covert commerce in the camp.

17. De-Nur 1988, 56.

18. Ibid., 55

19. Ibid., 57.

20. Ibid., 151–152.

21. "Bno shel haManhig haTzioni sheHolikh Yehudim leMasrefot," *Panim el Panim* 107 (28 Nissan 5721/1961): 10. The article is unsigned, but Menachem Gerlik told Re'ut Ben-Horin in a conversation with her on May 10, 2007, that it had been written by Menachem Hacohen.

22. See Friling 2005, 1:70–74.

23. Hacohen 1961.

24. Ibid.

25. Ibid.

26. Ibid. The article continues on p. 16.

27. Ibid.

28. Ibid.

29. Rembah 1961a, Sept. 10, 1961.

30. Rembah 1961b, Sept. 24, 1961.

31. Ibid.

32. Ibid.

33. Ibid. Rembah used the research and effort he had put into these two articles to produce a book, *Banim Akhlu Boser* (1973). The book cites even more cases in which children deviated from the path set by their parents and in doing so brought them disgrace. Among others on the list: Ahad Ha'am and Simon Dubnow.

34. Rivka Gruenbaum, interview by Glasner-Heled, Glasner-Heled collection, 9–10; Cooper 2006.

35. See, for example, Weitz 1995.

36. Rivka Gruenbaum, interview by Glasner-Heled, Glasner-Heled collection, 9–10.

37. See, for example, Friling 2003b, Introduction, 62–11, and the articles there by Aronson, 379–417 and Friling, 418–456; also Michman 1997.

38. See Rotem 2002.

39. On the younger Eliezer see Rivka Gruenbaum, interview by Glasner-Heled, Glasner-Heled collection; Menachem Gerlik to Eran Turbiner, Turbiner collection.

40. Hilary Strauweiss testimony, Dec. 1945, recorded by L. Sheftel, YVA 313 M.49.E.

41. Avraham-Berl Skakal testimony, Feb. 3, 1947, in Yiddish, to the Jewish History Committee, YVA M.49E 2250; see also the labor camp testimonies collected by the History Committee in Dünaburg, YCA M-1/E 105/911.

42. Rajcher testimony, April 25, 1958, YVA O.3/988, 2–6.

43. See also Yitzhak Alprovitch interview with Avraham Opochinski, Oct. 1987, YVA 03/4897.

44. Yeshayahu Lichtenstein testimony, YVA 03/8273, Jan. 23, 1995, p. 4.

45. Liblau 2005.

46. The Status Quo Agreement took the form of a letter sent by David Ben-Gurion, then the chairman of the Jewish Agency, on June 19, 1947, to Agudat Israel. On Yitzhak Gruenbaum's role in and position on one of the important issues involved in drafting the Law of the Return, the question of defining membership in the Jewish people, see Ohad 1987.

47. On the most recent research see Porat 1992b; Shalem 2007; Friling 2005, 1:125–135.

48. Wuzelman 1989, 233–242.

49. Ibid., 243.

50. Ibid., 246.

51. Broadcast on the night of Holocaust Memorial Day, April 8, 2002, Channel 2.

52. Gerlik told the same story to Eran Turbiner, Turbiner collection.

53. See: "My Life during World War II," anonymous testimony, YVA M-1/E, 1787, where the use of the method is attributed to a block chief named Tuvia Tzatzis. See also Gutman 1957, 22.

54. See Chapter 7, on Jawischowitz, and Garbarz and Garbarz 1984, which he wrote with his father.

55. All these quotes in this section come from a transcript of Kroytoro's film (2002).

56. Turbiner notes, Turbiner collection; Menachem Gerlik, interview by Re'ut Ben-Horin, May 10, 2007.

57. Turbiner notes, Turbiner collection. See also Yisraeli 1991.

58. Yonatan Gruenbaum, unpublished manuscript.

59. See Yonatan Gruenbaum 1985.

60. Rotem 2002.

61. Rotem 2002; Cooper 2006.

62. Regev 1989.

63. Ibid.; Cooper 2006.

64. Regev 1989.

65. Glasner-Heled and Bar-On 2004, 111–146; Rivka Gruenbaum interview by Glasner-Heled, Glasner-Heled collection; Cooper 2006; Menachem Gerlik to Eran Turbiner, Turbiner collection.

66. Glasner-Heled and Bar-On 2004, 111–146; Rivka Gruenbaum interview, by Glasner-Heled, Glasner-Heled collection.

14. History, Politics, and Memory

1. Trunk 1979.

2. These courts of honor imposed different kinds of punishments, among them forbidding the convicted person to hold positions in refugee organizations or institutions or depriving him or her of eligibility to receive assistance from Jewish aid organizations in immigrating to another country. See Trunk 1979, 487–498; and Sarna 1984, which also addresses Eliezer and the rumors about the circumstances of his death.

3. ABG, Minutes Division, Secretariat of the Histadrut Executive Committee, Sept. 5, 1945, Eliyahu Dobkin, 28–30.

4. Ibid.

5. Ibid.

6. Ibid.

7. Ibid.

8. Ibid.

9. Sarna 1984; Segev 1993, 259, and n. 8.

10. See Yablonka 1996, 135–152, and her reference, in note 31 on p. 147, to NA 6879/judgment 51/974; NA 6879c/judgment 51/2/1189.

11. Segev 1993, 258–260.

12. Yablonka 1996, 132, n. 10. Dozens of complaints of both types can be found in the Israel Police Archives; see, for example, IPA 100\47\ח\ \מ 2200\ל.

13. "*Hatza'at Hoq Neged Posh'ei Milhamah Yehudi'im*," *Ha'aretz*, Nov. 10, 1949, p. 4; Yablonka 1996, 140, as well as note 11. The entire correspondence, including the Ministry of Justice side, is in IPA 32\55 ח\פ\מ\2162ל.

14. Segev 1993, 258–260.

15. Yablonka 1996, 141–142.

16. Weitz 1996c, 271; Weitz 1996a, 163.

17. Yablonka 1996, 142; for a critique of the law see Muflah 1953.

18. Yablonka 1996, 142; Karsai 2004, 54–55.

19. The full names are not given to protect the privacy of the families of the accused.

20. Yablonka 1996, 145–146, n. 29; Segev 1993, 258–260. For the verdicts in trials of alleged kapos and the holders of other posts see *Piskei Din shel Batei Mishpat Mehozi'im*, vol. 5, 1951–1952, 146ff.; *Piskei Din shel Beit haMishpat haElyon*, vol. 13, 1959, p. 1056; *Piskei Din shel Beit haMishpat haElyon*, vol. 18, 1964, pt. 2, p. 85ff., as well as the daily press from the dates surrounding these trials. The press covered these trials intensively. Some examples, organized according to their defendants, are: YA: *Herut*, April 4, 1951; Blinder Max:

Herut, Jan. 26, March 7, April 30, 1951; YH: *Herut*, Jan. 6, 1951; MG-A: *Herut*, April 4, 12, 18, 1951; MB-M-Sh: *Herut*, March 12, 1951; MP: *Herut*, March 22, 27, 28, April 4, 1951; MG: *Herut*, Jan. 26, 1951; YSh: *Herut*, Feb. 23, 1951; MP: *Herut*, Jan. 18, March 5, 1951.

21. Yablonka 1996, 146; *Piskei Din shel Batei Mishpat Mehozi'im*, vol. 5, 1951–1952, 152ff.

22. Yablonka 1996; Weitz 1996a; I. Zertal 2005, 118–125; M. Shaked 2000; Glasner-Heled and Bar-On 2004, 111–146 and nn. 13–19.

23. *Divrei haKnesset*, 1149–1151; Yablonka 1996; Segev 1993; Weitz 1996a, 153–164.

24. On the danger of miscomprehending the complexity of the situation faced by those who lived within those historical circumstances see Weitz 1996a, 166; also *HB v. Attorney General*, Criminal Appeal 77/64, *Piskei Din shel Beit haMishpat haElyon*, vol. 18, 1964, p. 101.

25. Yisrael Bar-Yehuda, Aug. 1, 1950, *Divrei haKnesset*, 6:2394.

26. Ibid.; Yablonka 1996, 144; Segev 1993, 260–261.

27. Yosef Lamm, Aug. 1, 1950, *Divrei haKnesset*, 6:2395; Segev 1993, 260–261; Yablonka 1996, 144.

28. Yosef Lamm, Aug. 1, 1950, *Divrei haKnesset*, 6:2395; Segev 1993, 244–245.

29. Yablonka 1996, 144.

30. Ibid.

31. Ibid.

32. Stauber 2000, 85–116; Yablonka 1996, 143–144; Segev 1993, 260–261.

33. Yablonka 1996, 142–143; Weitz 1996a, 160–161; I. Zertal 2005, 97; Segev 1993, 260–261.

34. Weitz 1996a, 160–161.

35. Newspaper clipping in the author's possession; provenance unknown.

36. Friling 2005, 1:110–115; Baumel-Tydor 1999; Weitz 1996a, 163–164.

37. Stauber 2000, 85–86; Weitz 1996a, 153–164.

38. Stauber 2000, 84–85, 96.

39. See, for example, Rappel 2004; Balf 2008; Portugez 2005; Brug 2002; Balf 2005; Porat 2001.

40. On Yitzhak Gruenbaum's appearances and writings see, for example, "LaAhar 'Eser Shanim," his column in *Al haMishmar*, "Reshut haYahid beReshut haRabim," 1953. See also Stauber 2000, 132, n. 80. See also Yitzhak Gruenbaum's speech at the laying of the cornerstone of the Anielewicz memorial at Yad Mordechai, and the coverage of the ceremony in *Al haMishmar*, "Revavah beMa'amad haNisgav beYad Mordekai" (no author), *Al haMishmar*, May 4, 1951, p. 3.

41. P. Levi 1989, 22–24.

42. Porat 1995, 295–324.

43. Shalmon 1988, 8.

44. Ibid., 10, 13.

45. Ibid., 28, 92, quoted in Porat 1995, 300–302.

46. Porat 1995-5755. "Shutafav shel 'Amalek': HaAshamot haHaredim baAretz be-Shenot haShemonim klapei haTzionut beTekufat haShoah." *Hatzionut* 19:295–324.

47. Shalem 2007, 125–126; Shonfeld 1943.

48. Friling 2005, 1:125–135, as well as the chapters on the Rescue Committee in 1944–1945; Shalem 2007, 130–131.

49. Friling 2005, 2: 89–115, esp. 100–102, 104–105; Shalem 2007, 131–133.

50. See above, Chap. 10: Paris, June 1945–May 1946, on the "Triumvirate" and the "Parallel System," the secret Yishuv operational command to save European Jewry.

51. Friling 2005, 1:143–260.

52. Salomon 1987, 76–77.

53. See Salomon's interpretation, Salomon 1987, 75.

54. Hayim Shalem, *Et La'Asot leHatzalat Israel: Agudat Israel beEretz Israel leNokhah haShoah*, 101–102.

55. See, for example, Salomon 1987, 209.

56. Porat 2001, 315, 324.

57. M. Friedman 1990.

58. Ibid., 54–55.

59. Sompolinsky 1987, 502; M. Friedman 1990, 39; Nirel 1997; Porat 2001, 308.

60. On Neturei Karta see M. Friedman 1990 and Nirel 1997.

61. Fund 1989, 438, n. 321.

62. Shonfeld 1949, "Klapei Panim," *Digleinu*, Tevet 5709, reprinted in *Hashqafateinu beAspaqlariah shel Dorot*, 5738, no page numbers, reprinted in Fund 1989, 345–346. See also the comprehensive, well-reasoned, and organized version of Rabbi Tzvi Weinman, Weinman 1995.

63. Shonfeld 1954, "Lev Hakham leYemino," *Digleinu*, Tamuz-Av 5714, 2; Shonfeld 1981, "HaMilhamah bePA"Y Mitnahelet a"y GaDOT"T," *Hashqafateinu*, parts 4–5, 5741, p. 214, both found in Fund 1989, 380–381.

64. Fund 1989, 270–271.

65. Shonfeld 1975.

66. Shonfeld 1973, "Athalta deGe'ula o 'Ikvata deMeshiha," *Niv haMoreh*, Elul 5733, p. 10, quoted in Fund 1989, 472.

67. Ibid., p. 11, quoted in Fund 1989, 472, nn. 19–20.

68. Shonfeld 1948, "HaGiyus leTzion," p. 4. First published in *Digleinu*, Iyyar 1948, quoted in Fund 1989, 320.

69. Shonfeld, "Hashta 'Avdei leShanah haBa'ah Benei Horin," *Bein Eretz Yisrael le-Medinat Yisrael*, 12, 14, quoted in Fund 1989, 476.

70. M. Friedman 1990, 56–57. Among Shonfeld's extensive writings, alongside *Serufe haKivshanim Ma'ashimim* (Those burned in the furnaces accuse) and *Yaldei Teheran Ma'ashimim* (The Tehran children accuse), he also published *Bein Eretz Yisrael leMedinat Yisrael: Birurim Ra'ayoni'im veHashqafati'im al Tehom sheNif'arah vaGesher la Ein* (Between the land of Israel and the state of Israel: Ideological and philosophical studies on the abyss that has opened up and which has no bridge), 5735 (1975).

71. For other positions see, for example, Friling 2005, 2:195–219; Porat 1990, final chap.; Aronson 2004.

72. Porat 1995.

73. Porat 1995, 307–308.

Research Notes: From Clio's Elusive World

1. See www.leonberger-hunde.org/breed_history.html.
2. See http://boisdejustice.com/History/History.html.

BIBLIOGRAPHY

PRIVATE COLLECTIONS

Frenk, Dr. Jeannine (Levana), faculty of Yad Vashem and Ghetto Fighters' House, collection of, including:

Ochshorn, Egon Isaak, written statements, Feb. 2, 1946

Paris, 1945–1946, manuscript, testimonies from the hearing

Glasner-Heled, Galia, collection, including interviews of Rivka Gruenbaum and Bat-Ami Gruenbuam

Gruenbaum, Yonatan, manuscript of unpublished book. A portion of the manuscript is in the possession of the author. Portions of this manuscript that are not in the author's possession are quoted by other writers, as noted. The section *haTragedia shel Eliezer Gruenbaum* was kindly shown to the author by Matti Regev.

Paris Inquiry: Documentation of the Inquiry and Legal Proceeding Conducted in Paris, Sept. 1945–May 1946, private collection, including:

Archive file, pp. 165–166

Ballot, André (attorney), 158 boulevard Maleserbe, statement, Nov. 29, 1945, pp. 101–108

Epstein, Léon (Leib), testimony, unknown date.

Finkelkraut, Daniel, testimony, unknown date.

Goldstein, Haim Idel, forty-five years old, tailor, resident at 41 rue des Bois, Paris, Nineteenth Arrondissement, record of interrogation and cross-examination, Nov. 9, 1945, before M. Maurice, de la Seine Courthouse

Landau, David, testimony, October 16, 1945, in the presence of S. Branblum, lawyer, Tiberias. The testimony was confirmed by Asher Leviszky, lawyer and notary, Palestine.

Marchesseaux, M (Monsieur); statements by government commissioner, Paris, Jan. 20, 1946, 13.735

Oléar, Ijziykléar, garment cutter, resident at 397 rue des Pyrénées, Twentieth Arrondissement, testimony

Steg, Martin, fifty years old, Twelfth Arrondissement, testimony

A total of six testimonies conveyed to the judge of the preparatory bench, office of M. Maurice; signed by *inspecteur général*, Police Judiciaire
Document from page 168, Ministry of Justice, Directorate of the War Crimes Investigation Service, 48 rue Villejuste, Paris, Sixth Arrondissement, March 20, 1946
Turbiner, Eran, collection. Including interviews of Ze'ev Rivlin, Menachem Friedman, Ze'ev Tsahor, Gavriel Tsifroni, Menachem Gerlik; Rabbi Mordekhai Noigershal, and soldiers from Eliezer Gruenbaum's unit.

ARCHIVES

AA — Auschwitz Archive, Auschwitz-Birkenau National Museum, Poland, Oświęcim
AAN — Archiwum Akt Nowych (Central Archives of Modern Records), Poland
I. Documentation of the PPR party court, Archive of the Institute for Party History — the United Polish Workers Party (PZPR) of the Central Committee of the United Polish Workers Party, Poland, file number 15087, Berger-Gruenbaum file
Berger letter to Andrzej (no other name given), April 3, 1945, p. 29 in file (the date is in error — the letter was written in July 1945, when Eliezer could say that he had been a month in Paris)
Berger letter to party comrades, July 21, 1945, pp. 30–32 in file, in Berger's hand and in typescript
Berger questions to Léon (Leib) Epstein
Berger questions to Jacques Furmanski, handwritten
Berger questions to Majcher Langman, handwritten and typed version, pp. 16–17 in file
Berger questions to David Szmulewski, handwritten, pp. 25–27 in file
Berger-Gruenbaum testimony, Aug. 13, 1945, present: Kowalski, Eisner
Dluski, Ostap, director of Foreign Department (KC, PPR), Central Committee of Polish Workers' Party, to Comrade Lewikowski, Party Inspection Committee, Jan. 8, 1948
Finkelkraut, Daniel, testimony, Aug. 9, 1945
Freilich, Herman, testimony, with the addition of Freilich's address in Paris
Furmanski, Jacques, testimony, June 25, 1945
Gruenbaum, Eliezer, first testimony
Kowalski and Eisner testimonies
Laks, Simon, testimony, Aug. 6, 1945, signed by the witness
Majzlik (Malik?), Victor, testimony, July 18, 1945
Mink, Emmanuel, testimony, undated and unsigned
Notes of testimonies: Napieracz testimony, Nov. 7, 1945, unsigned by the witness
Notes of Napieracz's statement on Berger
Report on Berger's case, p. 51 in file
Szmulewski, David, testimony, undated and unsigned
II. Jozef Szpilski files (Jozef Szpilski) t.osob. 5775

BGHA — Ben-Gurion Heritage Archive
Aliav, Ruth Kluger (Kliger), interview by Gershon Rivlin and Yigal Donyets
BGD (Ben-Gurion diary), Diary Division
History Division
Minutes Division
Speeches and Articles Division
CZA — Central Zionist Archive
Letters and documents on the attempts to save Eliezer Gruenbaum, S46-344
Yitzhak Gruenbaum files, including 127/359A; 127/345A; 127/382/1A
HHA — HaShomer haTza'ir Archive, Yad Ya'ari
Grossman, Haika, interview, 69-95. 4(4), pp. 296-297
Yitzhak Gruenbaum files
IDFA — Israel Defense Forces Archives
Account of battle, 121/50/208, p. 8
Report on the Battles in Jerusalem's Southern Neighborhoods, 500/48/34; 8284/49/405
Testimony of Lt. Col. Meir Sharvit "Yarkoni," 922/78/290, March 16, 1959, pp. 5-6
Testimony 44, of Y. Cohen, June 28, 1959
Testimony of Lt. Col. Yeshoshafat Harkabi, "Gold," March 16, 1959, IDFA 922/78/290
IPA — Israel Police Archives
IPHA-UWPP — Institute of Party History Archive, United Workers Party of Poland
JIA — Jabotinsky Institute Archive
Files of IZL fighters in the Ramat Rachel battles
LA — Labor Archives, Lavon Institute
Moshe Sneh, personal archive
Massuah Archive
Papiernik, Charles, testimony (Montevideo), "The Truth about Eliezer Gruenbaum," undated
YVA — Yad Vashem Archive
Division M8, notes ITS. Arolsen
File M-1/E 105/911
File TR 2/ PS 2429
Yad Vashem Testimonies:
Arieli, Ben-Zion, 03/6121; 03/8934, Nov. 8, 1994
Brat Berek, Bodel Shushan, Yehoshua Ron, M.1/E 911 and M.1/E1787
"Camps" file, article 14, Yehoshua Ron, "Lisrod beTofet: Zikhronot miMahaneh haRikuz Auschwitz 2, Birkenau"
"Hayai beTekufat Milhemet 'Olam haShniyyah," testimony without name of the witness, M.49 E1313
Kohen, Zalman, 03/7046, Nov. 8, 1994
Landau, Dov, 03/7048, June 10, 1993
Liber, Itzhak, 11981, Nov. 13, 2001
Lictenstein,Yeshayahu, 03/8273, Jan. 23, 1995, p. 4

Ochshorn, Egon Isaak, 495, copy of the original in the Weiner Library in London
Opoczinski, Avraham, 03/4897, Oct. 1987, interviewed by Yitzhak Alprowitz
Orbach, Natan, 03/4808, undated, interviewed by Yitzhak Alprowitz, two interviews in the file
Preizler, Moshe Leib, 12086, June 4, 2002
Rajcher, Henoch, O. 3/988, April 25, 1958, pp. 2–6
Sakal, Avraham-Berl, Bialystok, Feb. 3, 1947, Yiddish, Jewish Historical Committee, M49E 2250
Shachar (Schwarz), Yoel, 11231, March 10, 1999
Shapiro, Joseph, 036527, Oct. 24, 1989 (English)
Strauweiss, Hilary, 1313 M.49.E, Dec. 1945, taken down by L. Sheftel
Zalmanovitz, Mordekhai Shlomo, 03/9495, July 11, 1995

ORAL DOCUMENTATION

Institute of Contemporary Jewry, The Hebrew University of Jerusalem, Mount Scopus Campus, Division of Oral History

Avigur, Shaul, interview by Aharon Kedar, (110)4, June 23, 1968
Avriel, Ehud, interview by Yehuda Bauer, (4)39, interview no. 2, pp. 5–13, undated
Gruenbaum, Yitzhak, interview by Natan Cohen, (4)33b

Interviews

Conducted by Dan Bar-On and Galia Glasner-Heled:

Eliraz, Shmuel, 1996
Frister, Roman Gershon Handel, and Micha Kaufman, 1996
Gruenbaum, Bat-Ami, 1996
Gruenbaum, Rivka, 1996
Handel, Gershon, 1996

Conducted by Re'ut Ben-Horin:

Avi-Ad, Doron, March 26, 2007
Dror, Shalom, Menachem Richman's commander in the Michmash Battalion (before Richman was sent on the mission on which he was killed), April 19, 2007, by telephone
Frenk, Levana, Feb. 13, 2007
Gerlik, Menachem, May 10, 2007
Havilio, Shlomo deputy commander of Eliezer's battalion, Feb. 21, 2007, by telephone
Lapidot, Yehuda commander of the IZL force in the Ramat Rachel battle, Feb. 21, 2007, by telephone
Nitzan, Ya'akov, Menachem Richman's brother, April 19, 2007, by telephone
Vlad, Eli (soldier who was in the armored car with Eliezer), Feb. 25, 2007, by telephone

Conducted by Tuvia Friling:

Steinfeldt, Irena, head of Yad Vashem's Righteous among the Nations Department, Aug. 9, 2007

Interviews from the United States Holocaust Memorial Museum, Washington, DC (USHMM)

Baum, Icek, interview by Randy Goldman, July 5, 1994, RG-50.030*0017

Gutman, Israel, interview, date not known, Israel, joint project of the USHMM and Massuah, RG-50.120*056

Kornberg, Morris, interview by Linda Kuzmack, March 15, 1990, RG-50.030*0016

BOOKS AND ARTICLES

Almog, Oz. 1997. *HaTzabar: Diyukan*. Tel Aviv: Am Oved.

al-Tal, ʿAbdallah. 1960. *Zikrhonot ʿAbdallah al-Tal*. Tel Aviv: Maʿarakhot.

Alterman, Natan. 1989. *ʿAl Shetei Derakhim: Dapim min haPinkas, Mahberot Alterman V*. Tel Aviv: HaKibbutz haMe'uhad.

Aly, Götz. 2007. *Into the Tunnel: The Brief Life of Marion Samuel, 1931–1943*. Translated by Ann Millin. New York: Metropolitan Books.

Annuaire des secrétaires et anciens secrétaires de la Conférence du Barreau de Paris. 1998. Paris.

Aronson, Shlomo. 2003. "Tziyonut vePost-ziyonut beYisrael: HaHeksher haHistori-Idiologi." In *Teshuvah leʿAmit Post Tziyyoni*, edited by Tuvia Friling, 379–417. Tel Aviv: Yediot Aharonot.

———. 2004. *Hitler, the Allies, and the Jews*. Cambridge: Cambridge University Press.

Arpaly, Boaz. 1992–5752. *HaʿIkar haShelili: Idiologiah vePoetikah be"Mikhan uMikhan" uve"Atzabim" leY. H. Brenner*. Tel Aviv: HaKibbutz haMe'uhad.

Avinoam, Reuven, ed. 1952–5712. *Gevilei Esh: Yalkut, Kolel Mivhar ʿEzvonam haSifruti-Omanuti shel haBanim sheNaflu beMilhemet haKomemiyut leYisrael*. Tel Aviv: Ministry of Defense.

———. 1955. *Yizkor: Parshiyot Hayeihem uMotam shel haNoflim beMaʿarkhot TZaHa"L*. Tel Aviv: Ministry of Defense.

———, ed. 1957. *Levavot Dovevim: Avot al Banim sheNaflu*. Tel Aviv: Ma'arachot.

Aviv, Yitzhak. 1991a. *Mahapekhah uMahapekhah shekeneged beSefarad: HaRepublika haShniyyah uMilhemet haEzrahim. 1931–1939*. Tel Aviv: Ministry of Defense.

———. 1991b. "Mahapekhah vaTeror beEzor haRepublikani." In Yitzhak Aviv, *Mahapekhah uMahapekhah shekeneged beSefarad: HaRepublika haShniyyah uMilhemet haEzrahim. 1931–1939*. Tel Aviv: Ministry of Defense.

Avizohar, Meir. 1987. "Bikur Ben-Gurion beMahanot haAquriom veTfesato haLeumit beTom Milhemet haOlam haShniyya," In *Yehadut Mizrach Eropah bein Shoa leTkuma*, edited by Benjamin Pinkus. Sde Boker: Ben-Gurion Research Institute for the Study of Israel and Zionism.

———. 2002. *Moriah beYerushalayim beTaSHa"H: Gedud haHI"SH haRishon beKravot Yerushalayim*. Lod: Mahbarot Lesifrut.

Avizohar, Meir, and Avi Bareli, eds. 1989. *Akhshav o leʿOlam Lo: Diyunei MaPA"I beShanah haAharonah laMandat haBriti, Mevo'ut veTe'udot*. Beit Berl: Beit Berl.

Azaryahu, Maoz. 1995. *Pulhanei Medinah: Hagigot haʿAtzma'ut veHantzahat haNoflim, 1948–1956*. Sde Boker: Ben-Gurion Heritage Institute.

Bacon, Gershon. 1999–5759. "Hikui veShelilah: Agudat Israel ve haTenu'ah haTzionit, 1912–1939." In *HaTzionut vehaHazarah leHistoriah: Ha'arachah Mehadash*, edited by Shmuel Noah Eisenstadt and Moshe Lissak, 497–508. Jerusalem: Ben-Zvi Institute.

———. 2000. "Politika Artzit veIdeologiah Shemeimit: Agudat Israel bePolish Nokhah 'Aliyat haNatzim leShilton beGermaniah." *Dapim leHeker haShoah* 16:57–67.

———. 2005–5765. *Politika uMasoret: Agudat Israel bePolin, 1916–1936*. Jerusalem: Zalman Shazar Center.

Balf, Micha. 2005. "Hantzahat haShoah baKibbutzim." *Ariel* 27.

———. 2008. *Kol shelo Ne'elam: 'Itzuv Zikaron haShoah veDarkhei Hantzahatah baTenu'ah haKibutzit*. Tel Aviv: HaKibbutz haMe'uhad.

Barnea, Nahum. 1986. "Melekh haYehudim uBanav." *Koteret Rashit*, Dec. 3, pp. 24–31.

"Bar Neherag beSefarad." 1961. *Ha'Olam haZeh* 2332.

Bar-On, Dan. 1999. *'Al ha "Aherim" beTokheinu: Temorot beZehut haYisraelit meNekudat Re'ut Tipologit-Hevratit*. Beersheva: Ben-Gurion University.

Bartov, Omer. 1999. "Kitsch veSadizm bePlanetah shel Ka-Tzetnik: No'ar Yisraeli Medamyen et haShoah." *Alpayim* 17:148–175.

Barzel, Neima. 1998. *'Ad Kalot umiNeged: HaMifgash bein Manhigei Mered haGeta'ot levein haHevrah haYisraelit*. Jerusalem: HaSifriyah haTzionit.

Bar-Zohar, Michael. 1977. *Ben-Gurion*. Tel Aviv: Am Oved.

Basok, Moshe, ed. 1947. *Sefer haMa'apilim*. Jerusalem: Histadrut haTzionit.

Bauer, Yehuda. 1971–5731. "Reshit Hithavuto shel Irgun She'erit haPleitah beBavariah." *Yad Vashem: Kovetz Mehkarim* 8:117–114.

———. 1980. "Nisayon leHavharah." *Iton 77* 22–23 (Sept.–Oct.): 571–572.

———. 2005. "HaProtokolim shel Auschwitz." *Yalkut Moreshet* 80:159–167.

Baum, Bruno. 1949, 1962. *Widerstand in Auschwitz*. Berlin: Kongress-Verlag.

Baumel-Tydor, Judith. 1992–5752. "MiBuchenwald le'Kibbutz Buchenwald': Hithavutah vePe'ilutah shel Kevutzat haHakhsharah haRishonah sheNosdah beGermania le'ahar Milhemet ha'Olam haSheniyah." *Yahadut Zemaneinu* 7:191–218.

———. 1997. *Kibbutz Buchenwald*. New Brunswick, NJ: Rutgers University Press.

———. 1999. *Bein Idiologidah leTa'amulah: Mishlahat haIZ"L beArtzont haBrit veShorshei haYamin haYehudi haMilitanti beAmerika*. Jerusalem: Magnes.

Beevor, Antony. 1982. *The Spanish Civil War*. London: Orbis.

Beevor, Antony, and Artemis Cooper. 1994. *Paris after Liberation, 1944–1949*. London: Hamish Hamilton.

Ben-Gurion, David. 1950. *BeHilahem Yisrael*. Tel Aviv: Mifleget Poalei E"I.

———. 1957. *BaMa'arachah*. Vol. 5. Tel Aviv: Mifleget Poalei E"I.

———. 1987. *Zikronot min ha'Izavon*. Vol. 6. Tel Aviv: Ben-Gurion Heritage Institue and Am Oved.

Ben-Hanan, Uriel. 1989. "Neched Min haMilhamah." *Al haMishmar, Hotem*, May 12, pp. 4–7.

Ben-Shlomo, Ze'ev. 1955. "Hovat haSifrut leOr Hurban haGaluyot: Re'eyon 'im Uri Tzvi Greenberg beKoblo Pras Bialik." *Zemanim*, July 15.

Benvenisti, David. 1980. *Siyurim beYerushalayim*. Jerusalem: Kiryat Sefer.

Berkowitz, Eliezer. 1987-5747. *Emunah Le'ahar haShoah*. Jerusalem: Shalem and Yad Vashem.

Birnberg, Yoav. 2005. "Shekarim sheSiprah Li Ima." *Yediot Aharonot*, May 3.

Bitan, Dan. 1996. "On Sagi Porae'ah: Mitosim 'al Gevurah Lohemet beReishit haTzionut. 1880–1903." In *Mitos veZikaron*, edited by David Ohana and Robert Westreich, 169–188. Tel Aviv: HaKibbutz haMe'uhad.

Blatman, Daniel. 1993. "HaBund bePolin baShanim 1939–1949." *Yehadut Zmaneno* 8:69–97.

Botser, Ahuva. 1997. "'Aliyato veNefilato shel ha'Iton Herut." *Kesher* 21:143–151.

Boyarin, Jonathan. 1986. *Polish Jews in Paris*. Ann Arbor, MI: University Microfilms International, 47–48.

———. 1991. *Polish Jews in Paris*. Bloomington: Indiana University Press.

Braginsky, Yehuda. 1965-5725. *'Am Hoeter el Hof: Hamesh-Esreh Shanah beSherut Aliyah Bet*. Tel Aviv: HaKibbutz haMe'uhad.

Braham, Randolph. 1981. *The Politics of Genocide: The Holocaust in Hungary*. 2 vols. New York: Columbia University Press.

Brenner, Lenni. 1983. *Zionism in the Age of the Dictators: A Reappraisal*. London: Croom Helm.

Brome, Vincent. 1965. *The International Brigades, Spain, 1936–1939*. London: Heinemann.

Brug, Muli. 2002. "Zekher Halom leBerakhah: Mordechai Shenhavi veRa'ayonot haHantzahah haRishonim shel haShoah beEretz-Yisrael, 1942–1945." *Yad Vashem* 30:241–269.

"Buchenwald." 1990. *HaIntzeklopediah shel haShoah*. Vol. 1, edited by Israel Gutman, 254–256.

Bulawko, Henri. 1954. *Les jeux de la mort et l'espoir, Auschwitz-Jaworzno*. Paris: Amicale des anciens deìporteìs juifs de France.

Butnaru, I. C. 1993. *Waiting for Jerusalem: Surviving the Holocaust in Romania*. Westport, CT: Greenwood Press.

"Cachin, Marcel." 2013. *The Columbia Encyclopedia*, 6th ed. Encyclopedia.com, http://www.encyclopedia.com/doc/1E1-E-Cachin-M.html (accessed Aug. 7, 2013).

Caplan, Kimmy. 2001-5761. "HaOmnam 'Nitzberu Harbeh Shekarim beSifrei haToldot?': HaShoah beHistoriografiah ubaToda'ah haHistorit haHaredit haAshkenazit beYisrael." *Yad Vashem Kovetz Mehkarim* 29:249–293.

———. 2001. "Klei haTikshoret beHevrah haHaredit beYisrael." *Kesher* 30.

Cohen, Natan. 2001. "'Itona'ut Yomit Yehudit bePolin." In *Kiyyum veShever: Yehudei Polin leDoroteihem*. Vol. 2, edited by Israel Gutman and Israel Bartal. Jerusalem: Zalman Shazar Center.

———. 2003-5763. *Sefer, Sofer, ve'Iton: Merkaz haTarbut haYehudi beWarsaw, 1918–1942*. Jerusalem: Magnes.

Cohen, Raya. 1999. *Bein Sham leKan: Sipurim shel 'Edim leHorban, 1939–1942*. Tel Aviv: Am Oved.

Conway, John S. 1981. "Der Auschwitz-Bericht von April 1944." *Zeitgeschichte* (Aug.-Sept.): 313–442.

Cooper, Hanoch. 2006. "Mi sheYitzhak Aharon." *Shofar News*, April 25.

Crossman, Richard H. S. 1950. *The God That Failed*. New York: Columbia University Press.

Czech, Danuta. 1990. *Auschwitz Chronicle, 1939–1945*. New York: Henry Holt.

———. 1994. "The Auschwitz Prisoner Administration." In *Anatomy of the Auschwitz Death Camp*, edited by Israel Gutman and Michael Berenbaum. Washington, DC, and Bloomington: United States Holocaust Memorial Museum and Indiana University Press.

Davidson, Eyal. 2003. *Yerushalayim mikol Makom*. Elkana: P. Asidon.

De-Nur, Yehiel [Ka-Tzetnik, pseud.]. 1988. *Kor'im Lo Piepl*. Tel Aviv: HaKibbutz haMe'uhad.

Diamant, David. 1979. *Combattants Juiffe dans l'Arméé Republicaine Espagnole, 1936–1939*. Paris: Éditions Renouveau, Paris.

Dinstein, Yoram. 1965–5725. *Hanhagah shel Tziyut leFekudah miGavoah baMishpat haBeinleumi*. Jerusalem: Magnes.

Don-Yehiya, Eliezer. 1983. "Mamlakhtiyut veShoah." In *BeShevilei haTehiyyah: Mehkarim beTzionut haDatit*, edited by Avraham Rubinstein, 167–188. Ramat Gan: Bar-Ilan University.

Dotan, Shmuel. 1991. *Adumim: HaMiflagah haKomunistit beEretz Yisrael*. Kfar Saba: Shevna haSofcr.

Dunun-Wasowicz, Krzysztof. 1982. *Ruch oporu w hitlerowskich obozach koncentracyjnych 1933–1945*. Warsaw: PWN.

Eisenberg Gotdiner, Mali. 2005–5765. *'Ed, Maz'ik, Meta'ed uMantziah: R. Moshe Prager vehaShoah: 1940–1984*. MA thesis, Bar-Ilan University, Ramat Gan.

Elath, Eliahu. 1979. *HaMa'avak 'al haMedinah: Washington (1945-1946)*. Tel Aviv: Am Oved.

Eldad, Y. 1951. "Bein Galut Malkhutit uMedinah Galutit." *Sulam*, Iyyar 5711.

Elgazi, Yosef. 2000–5760. "Milhemet haEzrahim haSefaradit beRe'i ha'Itonut ha'Ivrit beEretz Yisrael/Palastina." In *HaFashizm Lo Ya'avor: Milhemet haEzrahim beSefarad, 1936–1939*, edited by Ra'anan Rein, 272–305. Tel Aviv: Zemora Bitan.

Elitzedek, Ariel. 1949. "HaEmeth al Parashat Ramat Rachel." *Herut*, September 23.

Engel, David. 2002–5762. "'UBe'arta haRa' miKirbekha': LeBirur haMusag 'Shituf Pe'ulah' beTekufat haShoah beAspaklariah shel Mishpatei Michael Weichart." In *HaShoah: Historiah veZikaron*, edited by Shmuel Almog et al., 1–24. Jerusalem: Yad Vashem.

Epstein, Mortimer. 1931, 1932. *Statesman's Yearbook: Statistical and Historical Annual of the States of the Year*. London: Macmillan.

Fackenheim, Emil. 1978. *The Jewish Return into History: Reflections in the Age of Auschwitz and a New Jerusalem*. New York: Schocken.

Farbstein, Esther. 1998–5758. "He'arot Ahadot 'al Hatzalat haRabi miBelz." At *Da'at*, website for Jewish Studies and Humanities, Gush Etzion: Herzog College, http://daat.ac.il/daat/kitveyet/sde_chem/harabi.htm (accessed Aug. 7, 2013).

———. 2002–5762. *BeSeter Ra'am: Halakhah, Hagut, uManhigut beYemei haShoah*. Jerusalem: Mosad haRav Kook.

Fatran, Gila. 1992. *Ha'im Ma'avak 'al Hisardut: Hanhagat Yehudei Slovakiah beShoah, 1938–1944*. Tel Aviv: Moreshet.

Feldstein, Ariel. 1998. "Sheloshah Yamim beHodesh Iyyar TaSHa"H: 'Iyun Mehudas leOr haMekorot." *Iyunim Bitkumat Israel* 8:354–374.

Ference, Gergory C., ed. 1994. *Chronology of 20th-Century Eastern European History*. Detroit: Gale Research.

Fisher, Teresa. 2002. *Paris: Madrikh Spirali*. Tel Aviv: Kinneret.

Forfaits Hitlériens. 1945. Vols. 6–7 of *Cahiers de Traits*. No editor listed. Trois Collines.

Frank, Benis M. 1992. "The Jewish Company of the Shanghai Volunteer Corps Compared with other Jewish Diaspora Fighting Units." Paper given at the Conference "China and the Jewish Diaspora: A Comparative Historical Perspective on Acculturation, Economic Activity, Assimilation, Anti-Semitism," http://net.lib.byu.edu/estu/wwi/comment/svc.htm (accessed Aug. 16, 2013).

Frankel, Yitzhak Yedidyah, ed. 1953. *Sefer Linshits*. Hotza'at Olei Linshits beYisrael.

Freilich, Miriam. 1999. *Hitbolelut vePolonizatziah bekerev Yehudim bePolin bein Shetei Milhamot ha'Olam, 1918–1939: Hebetim Irguni'im, Hevrati'im, veFoliti'im*. PhD diss., The Hebrew University of Jerusalem.

Friedman, Menachem. 1990. "Mediniyut Yisrael keDilemah Datit." *Alpayim* 3:24–68.

———. 1991. *HaHevrah haHaredit: Mekorot, Megamot, veTahalikhim*. Jerusalem: Jerusalem Institute for Israel Studies.

Friedman, Philip. 1950. *Ashwientshim*. Buenos Aires: Tzentral Farband fun Polishe Yiden in Argentina.

———. 1973–5733. "HaHitnagdut haYehudit leNazism: Hebetim uTzurot." In *Shuat Yehudei Eropah: Reka', Korot, Mashma'ut*, edited by Israel Gutman and Livia Rothkirchen, 361–373. Jerusalem: Yad Vashem.

Friling, Tuvia. 1984. "BeZekhut haMevukhah: Ha'Im haYudenratim Hayu Bogdim?" *Kivunim* 23 (May): 105–118.

———. 2001. "HaTriumverat haBilti Mutzhar vehaMa'arekhet haMakbilah." In *HaShoah: HaYihudi vehaUniversali, Kovetz haYovel leYehuda Bauer*, edited by David Bankir and Dalia Ofer, 117–159. Jerusalem: Yad Vashem and Institute of Contemporary Jewry.

———. 2003a. "David Ben-Gurion vehaShoah: Shorashav veGilgulav shel Stereotip Shelili." In *Teshuvah leAmit Post-Tzioni*, edited by Tuvia Friling, 418–456. Tel Aviv: Yediot Aharonot.

———. 2003b. "Tahalikhim shel Havkarah beZehut Sedukah: Mavo." In *Teshuvah leAmit Post-Tzioni*, edited by Tuvia Friling, 11–62. Tel Aviv: Yediot Aharonot.

———. 2005. *Arrows in the Dark*. 2 vols. Madison: University of Wisconsin Press.

Frister, Roman. 1987. *Lelo Psharah*. Tel Aviv: Bitan.

———. 1993. *Diyukan 'Atzmi 'im Tzaleket*. Tel Aviv: Dvir.

Fuchs, Moshe, Noah Zablodawitch, and Moshe Kulka. 1952. *Der Hurban fun der Yidisher Kehilah Tshekhanow un der Heldisher Toit fun Roza Robota. Kehilat Ciechanów veHurbanah veMot haGiborim shel Roza Robota*. Tel Aviv: Irgun Yotzei Tshekhanow beYisrael.

Fuchs, Sarit. 1991. "Zeh Lo Mofa' 'Eirom, Zeh 'al haShoah." *Ma'ariv*, Sept. 8.

Fund, Yossef. 1989. *Agudat Israel mul haTzionut uMedinat Yisrael: Idiologiah uMediniyut*. PhD diss., Bar-Ilan University, Ramat Gan.

Garbarz, Moshe, and Elie Garbarz. 1984. *Un survivant: Pologne 1913–1929, Paris, 1929–1941, Auschwitz-Birkenau-Jawischowitz-Buchenwald 1942–1945*. Paris: Plon.

———. 1992. *A Survivor*. Detroit: Wayne State University Press.

Gelber, Yoav. 1990. "HaPegishah bein haHayalim haYehudim beTzava haBriti veShe'erit haPleitah." In *She'erit haPleitah*, edited by Israel Gutman, 60–80. Jerusalem: Yad Vashem.

Geshur, Benny. 2000. "HaMitnadvim leEzrat haAm, al ha-Brigadot haBinleumiyot beSefarad." www.e-mago.co.il.

Gilbert, Martin. 1981. *Auschwitz and the Allies*. New York: Holt, Reinhart, and Winston.

Glasner-Heled, Galia, and Dan Bar-On. 2004–5764. "Eliezer Gruenbaum: Havnayat Sipuru shel Kapo beMisgeret Zikaron haShoah haKolektivi beYisrael." *Alpayim* 27:111–146.

Goldberg, Amos. 1998–5758. "HaShoah ba'Itonut heHaredit: Bein Zikaron leHadhakah." *Yahadut Zemaneinu* 11–12:155–206.

Goren, Yair. 1997. *Kuzari beYerushalayim*. Jerusalem: Ilan.

Greilsammer, Ilan. 2004. *Léon Blum*. Or Yehudah: Dvir.

Gross, Jan Tomasz. 2000. "Themes for a Social History of War Experience and Collaboration." In *The Politics of Retribution in Europe: World War II and Its Aftermath*, edited by István Deák, Jan Tomasz Gross, and Tony Judt. Princeton, NJ: Princeton University Press.

Grossman, Haika. 1950. *Anshei haMahteret*. Tel Aviv: Sifriyat Po'alim.

Gruenbaum, Eliezer. 1962–5712. "BeHatzerot haMavet." In *Gevilei Esh*, vol. 1, edited by Reuven Avinoam. Tel Aviv: Ministry of Defense.

Gruenbaum, Yitzhak. 1953. "LaAhar 'Eser Shanim." *Al Hamishmar, Reshut haYahid beReshut haRabim*, n.d.

———. 1963. *Ne'umim baSejm haPolani*. Edited by Mordechai Halamish. Jerusalem: M. Neuman.

———. 1964. "Di Tragedia fun Mein Zun Eliezer." *Heint*, July 15.

Gruenbaum, Yonatan. 1985. "Lamut beKavod." *Al Hamishmar*, June 23, p. 15.

Guterman, Alexander. 1997. *Kehilat Warsaw bein Shtei Milhamot ha'Olam: Otonomiah Leumit beKavlei haHok vehaMetziut, 1917–1937*. Tel Aviv: Merkaz LeHeker Toldot haYehudim bePolin uMorashtam.

Gutman, Israel, ed. 1957. *Anashim veEfer: Sefer Auschwitz-Birkenau*. Merhaviah: Sifriyat Po'alim.

———. 1990. *Encyclopedia of the Holocaust*. New York: Macmillan.

Gutman, Israel, and Israel Bartal, eds. 2001. *Kiyyum veShever: Yehudei Polin leDoroteihem*. Jerusalem: Zalman Shazar Center.

Gutman, Israel, and Michael Berenbaum. 1994. *Anatomy of the Auschwitz Death Camp*. Washington, DC, and Bloomington: United State Holocaust Museum and Indiana University Press.

Gutman, Israel, and Avital Saf, eds. 1977. *Yehudei Warsaw, 1939–1943: Getto-Mahteret-Mered*. Tel Aviv: Sifriyat Poalim.

———. 1984. *The Nazi Concentration Camps: Structure and Aims, the Image of the Prisoner, the Jews in the Camps: Proceedings of the Fourth Yad Vashem International Historical*

Conference, Jerusalem, January 1980. Translated by Dina Cohen. Jerusalem: Yad Vashem.

Gutwein, Daniel. 1988. "Hafratat haShoah: Politika, Zikaron, veHistoriographiah." *Dapim Leheker haShoah* 15:7–52.

Hacohen, Menachem. 1961. "Bno shel haManhig haTzioni sheHolikh Yehudim leMisrafot." *Panim El Panim* 103 (28 Nissan 5721 — April 14): 10–11.

Hadari, Ze'ev Venja. 1991. *HaMossad le'Aliyah Bet: Yoman Mivtza'him, Paris 1947*. Beersheva: Ben-Gurion University.

Halamish, Aviva. 1990. *Exodus — haSipur haAmiti: Parshat Oniyat haMa'apilim "Yetziat Eropah TaSHA"Z*. Tel Aviv: Am Oved and Tel Aviv University.

———. 2007. "Yahaso shel Meir Ya'ari leHatzalah ule'Aliyah beTekufat haShoah." *Yalkut Moreshet* 83:25–51.

———. 2009. "Merhaviah veStalingrad! Lo Warsaw velo Metzadah: Meir Ya'ari Nokhah Shoat Yehudei Eropah veHashlahoteha." In *Shoah miMerhak Tavo: Ishim baYishuv haEretz-Yisraeli veYahasam laNazim velaShoah, 1933–1948*, edited by Dina Porat, 475–504. Jerusalem: Yad Yitzhak Ben-Zvi.

HaMeiri, Avigdor. 1935. "'Al haFascism veSi'o: HaMilhamah." Address at the opening of the Second Antipa National Conference, Mughrabi Hall, Tel Aviv, April 12. May, pp. 3–5, 7.

Hartman, Meir, Moshe Kalkheim, and Amikam Gurevitch. 1982. *Yitzhak Gruenbaum: Zokef Kumat 'Amo*. Tel Aviv: Amikam, for the Public Committee to Perpetuate the Memory of Yitzhak Gruenbaum.

"Hatza'at Hok Neged Posh'ei Milhama Yehudim." *Ha'aretz*, Nov. 10, 1949.

HB vs. Attorney General. 1964. Criminal appeal 77/64 to Supreme Court. *Piskei Din*. Vol. 18, p. 101.

Hemmingway, Ernest. 2006. *LeMi Tziltzelu haPa'amonim*. Tel Aviv: Sifrei Hemed, Yediot Aharonot.

Hopkins, James K. 1998. *Into the Heart of Fire: The British in the Spanish Civil War*. Palo Alto, CA: Stanford University Press.

Iishuni-Beri, Shoshana. 1996. "HaIsh she Hufkar Pa'amayim." *Yalkut Moreshet* 62: 201–211.

Jäckel, Eberhard. 1981. *Hitler's World View: A Blueprint for Power*. Translated by Herbert Arnold. Cambridge, MA: Harvard University Press.

Jerome, Jean. 1986. *Les clandestins. 1940–1944: Souvenirs d'un témoin*. Paris: Acropole.

"Jewish Volunteers in the Spanish Civil War: Spanish Civil War Veterans after World War II." n.d. Abraham Lincoln Brigade Archives. http://www.alba-valb.org/resources/lessons/jewish-volunteers-in-the-spanish-civil-war/jewish-spanish-civil-war-veterans-during-world-war-ii (accessed Aug. 13, 2013).

Kagan, Raya. 1957. *Nashim beLishkat haGehinom*. Merhavia: Sifriyat Po'alim.

Karmish, Yosef. 1991. "'Itonut haMahteret haYehudit beWarsaw." *Kesher* 9 (May): 32–51.

Karny, Miroslav. 1994. "The Vrba and Wetzler Report." In *Anatomy of the Auschwitz Death Camp*, edited by Israel Gutman and Michael Berenbaum. Washington, DC, and

Bloomington: United States Holocaust Memorial Museum and Indiana University Press.

Karsai, László. 2004. "HaShoah beHungariah kefi sheHi Mishtakefet beMishpatei Beit haDin ha'Amemi beBudapest." *Yad Vashem Kovetz Mehkarim* 32:54–55.

Katz, Shmuel, 1966. *Yom haEsh*, Tel Aviv: Karni.

Katz, Steven T. 1983. *Post-Holocaust Dialogues: Critical Studies in Modern Jewish Thought*. New York: New York University Press.

———. 1990. "Teguvot Filosofiyot veTe'ologiyot shel Yehudim 'al haShoah." In *HaIntziklopediah shel haShoah*. Jerusalem: Yad Vashem.

Ka-Tzetnik. *See* De Nur, Yehiel.

Keynan, Irit. 1995. *Lo Nirga'haRa'av: Nitzulei haShoah veShelihei Eretz Yisrael, BeGermaniah 1945–1948*. Tel Aviv: Am Oved.

Kliger-Eliav, Ruth. 1976–5736. *HaMiflat haAharon*. Tel Aviv: Am Oved.

Koblanov, A., ed. 1938. *Lema'an Sefarad haRepublikanit*. Jerusalem: Antipa and Hug ha'Ovdim haIntelektualim.

Kochavi, Arieh. 2007. *HaDerekh leMispatei Nirenberg: Gibush Mediniyut ha'Anishah Klapei Posh'ei haMilhamah*. Sde Boker and Jerusalem: Ben-Gurion Research Institute for the Study of Israel and Zionism and Yad Vashem.

Kraus, Otto, and Erich Kulka. 1960. *Beit Haroshet leMavet Auschwitz*. Jerusalem: Yad Vashem.

Kremish, Y. "HaMeri vehaMered baGeto." In *Intziklopediah shel Galuyot*, column 767.

Kroyanker, David. 1996. *Yerushalayim: Mabat Architectoni*. Jerusalem: Keter.

Kulka, Erich. 1984. "Escape of Jewish Prisoners from Auschwitz-Birkenau and Their Attempts to Stop Mass Extermination." In *The Nazi Concentration Camps: Structure and Aims, the Image of the Prisoner, the Jews in the Camps: Proceeding of the Fourth Yad Vashem International Historical Conference, Jerusalem, January 1980*, translated by Dina Cohen, edited by Israel Gutman and Avital Saf, 401–416. Jerusalem: Yad Vashem.

Laks, Szymon. 1989. *Music of Another World*. Evanston, IL: Northwestern University Press.

Langbein, Hermann. 1980. "Auschwitz: The History and Characteristics of the Concentration and Extermination Camp." In *The Nazi Concentration Camps: Structure and Aims, the Image of the Prisoner, the Jews in the Camps: Proceeding of the Fourth Yad Vashem International Historical Conference, Jerusalem, January 1980*, translated by Dina Cohen, edited by Israel Gutman and Avital Saf, 485–502. Jerusalem: Yad Vashem.

———. 1994. "The Auschwitz Underground." In *Anatomy of the Auschwitz Death Camp*, edited by Israel Gutman and Michael Berenbaum, 485–502. Bloomington: United States Holocaust Memorial Museum and Indiana University Press.

Laor, Dan. 1989. "'Od 'Al Shetei Derakhim." In *'Al Shetei Derakhim: Dapim min haPinkas, Mahberot Alterman V*, by Natan Alterman, 114–148. Tel Aviv: HaKibbutz haMe'uhad.

Lapidot, Yehuda. 1992. *'Al Homotayikh*. Tel Aviv: Ministry of Defense.

———. 1996. *BeLahav haMered: Ma'archot haIZ"L beYerushalayim*. Tel Aviv: Ministry of Defense.

Lavi, Zvi. 1987. "Va'adat haOrkhim: HaMitos vehaMetziyut." *Kesher* 1:11–34.

Lavsky, Hagit. 1990–5750. "She'erit haPleitah miObyekt leSubyekt: Megamot Mehkar." *Yahadut Zemaneinu* 6:25–43.

Lefebvre, Henri. 2005. *Yitzur haMerhav*. In *Tarbut Adrikhalit: Makuom, Yitzug, Nof*, edited by Rachel Kallus and Tali Hatuka. Tel Aviv: Resling.

Lerski, George J. 1996. *Historical Dictionary of Poland, 966–1945*. Westport, CT: Greenwood Press.

Lev, Yosef. 1991–5751. *VeEmenatkha baLeilot: Mispar 98661*. Bnei Brak: H. Lev.

Levi, Amnon. 1988. *HaHaredim*. Jerusalem: Keter.

Levi, Primo. 1987. *If This Is a Man*. Translated by Stuart Woolf. London: Abacus.

———. 1989. *The Drowned and the Saved*. Translated by Raymond Rosenthal. London: Abacus.

Levi (Levitseh), Yitzhak. 1986. *Tish'ah Kabin*. Tel Aviv: Ma'arachot.

Levin, Ruth. 1987. *HaYesharim Hayu Itah: Sefarad 1936–1939*. Tel Aviv: Ofakim.

Levinson, Avraham. 1953–5713. Toldot Yehudei Warsaw. Tel Aviv: Am Oved.

Liblau, Charles. 2005. *Les kapos d'Auschwitz*. Paris: Syllepse.

Lubitz, Ruth. 1985. *Baharti Lehiyot beMa'avak*. Tel Aviv: Shahar.

Lustiger, Arno. 2001. *Schalom Libertad: Judíos en la Guerra civil española*. Frankfurt am Main: Atheneum.

Mark, Bernard. 1978–5738. *Megilat Auschwitz*. Tel Aviv: Sifriyat Po'alim.

———. 1982. *Des voix dans la nuit: La résistance juive a Auschwitz-Birkenau*. Paris: Plon.

Markovitzki, Yaakov. 1995–5755. *Gahelet Lohemet: Giyus Hutz laAretz beMilhemet ha'Atzma'ut*. Tel Aviv: Ministry of Defense.

Marrus, Michael R., and Robert O. Paxton. 1995. *Vichy France and the Jews*. Palo Alto, CA: Stanford University Press.

Maybaum, Ignaz. 1965. *The Face of God after Auschwitz*. Amsterdam: Polak & Van Gennep.

McIroy, John, and Alan Campbell. 2005. "The British and French Representatives to the Communist International, 1920–1939: A Comparative Survey." *International Review of Social History* 50.2 (August): 203–240, http://journals.cambridge.org/action/displayAbstract;jsessionid=643BF9886E38316DCA91A69AC1ED98A5.journals?fromPage=online&aid=323359 (accessed Aug. 7, 2013).

Medin, Tzvi. 2000. "Franco: Tefisat haShilton uMisudah shel Afsut Politit, 1936–1945." In *HaFashizm Lo Ya'avor: Milhemet haEzrahim beSefarad, 1936–1939*, edited by Ra'anan Rein. Tel Aviv: Zemora Bitan.

Melman, Yossi. 1987. *Shutafut 'Oyenet: HaKesharim haSdofiyim bein Israel leYarden*. Tel Aviv: Mitam.

Melzer, Emanuel, ed. 1995. *Moshe Sneh: Ktavim. I. 1929–1939; II: 1940–1947*. Tel Aviv: Am Oved and the Chaim Weizmann Institute for the Study of Zionism, Tel Aviv University.

Menasche, Albert. 1947. *Birkenau (Auschwitz II): Memoires of an Eyewitness; How 72,000 Greek Jews Perished*. New York: I. Saltiel.

Michelson, Menachem. 1990. "'Itonut Haredit beYisrael." *Kesher* 8:11–22.

Mickiewicz, Adam. 1953. *Pan Tadeusz*. Tel Aviv: N. Twersky.

———. 1982–5742. *Sefer 'Âm Polnis Jerry Polnis*. Paris.

Mintz, Binyamin. 1945. "HaHishtatfut haHaredit beMered Ghetto Warsaw." *She'arim*, Oct. 11.

Miron, Dan. 1988. "Bein Efer leSefer." *Alpayim* 10:196–224.

Molho, Michael. 1948–1949. *In memoriam: Hommage aux victimes juives de Nazis en Grece, Salonique*. 2 vols. Salonique: N. Nicolaideìs.

Moraud, Henri, ed. 1985. *Jawischowitz, une annexe d'Auschwitz*. Paris: Amicale d'Auschwitz, section Jawischowitz.

Morris, Benny. 2003. *Korbanot: Toldot haSikhsukh haTzioni-ha'Aravi, 1881–2001*. Tel Aviv: Am Oved.

Muflah. 1953–5713. "HaHok le'Asiyat Din baNazim ube'Ozreihem, TaSH"Y 1950. Toldot Kishalon Harutz." *HaPraklit* 3:61–69.

Negev, Ayelet. 2006a. "Megilat Rut [Eliav]." *Yediot Aharonot, 7 Yamim*, March 24, pp. 68–74.

———. 2006b. "Milhemet Yesh Breirah." *Yediot Aharonot, 7 Yamim*, Sept. 8, pp. 108–112.

Netzer, Shlomo. 1980–5740. *Ma'avak Yehudei Polin 'al Zekhuyoteihem haEzrhiyot vehaLeumiot. 1918–1922*. Tel Aviv: Goldstein-Goren Diaspora Research Center, Tel Aviv University.

Nevo, Amos. 1996. "Nekmat haNitzolim." *Yediot Aharonot — Mussaf Yom Shishi*, Dec. 27, p. 46.

Nirel, Haim. 1997. *Haredim mul Shoah: HaAshamot haHaredim klapei haTzionut beAhrayut laShoah*. Jerusalem: Carmel.

Novenstern, Adi. n.d. "Meshorerim uMordim beFolin haRomantit: Historiah Intelektualit beFolin shel haMeah ha-19 derekh Demuto shl Adam Mizkovitch." Seminar paper under the direction of Dr. Raphael Vago.

Ofer, Dalia. 1988. *Darakh baYam: 'Aliyah Bet beTekufat haShoah: 1939–1944*. Jerusalem: Ben-Zvi Institute.

———. 1998. "Mah ve'Ad Kamah lizkir min haShoah: Zikaron haShoah beMedinat Yisrael ba'Asor haRishon leKiyumah." In *'Atzma'ut: 50 haShanim haRishonot*, edited by Anita Shapira, 171–193. Jerusalem: Shazar Center.

———. 2007. "She'erit haPleitah beHistoriorafiah haYisraelit." *Iyunim Bitkumat Israel* 17:465–511.

Ohad, M. 1987. "Neged haZerem." *Ha'aretz — Mussaf*, Feb. 6, pp. 12–13.

Oren, Neli. 1993. "Retzifut veTemurot beYahasei Yisrael-Polin: 1944–1951." MA thesis, Ben-Gurion University, Beersheva.

———. 2007. "Pe'ilut haMishlahat haPolanit baU"M beShe'elat Eretz-Yisrael." *Iyunim Bitkumat Israel* 17:381–411.

Ortner, Natan Yehuda. 1963. *Devar Hen: Sefer Zikaron leRav uleZugato*. Tel Aviv: L. Friedman.

———. 1982. "'Al Drasha Hasidit Belza'it: Teshuvah leMamaro shel Mendel Piekarz." *Kivunim* 14 (February): 145–149.

Oz, Amos. 2004. *A Tale of Love and Darkness*. Translated by Nicholas de Lange. London: Chatto & Windus.

Paczkowski, Andrzej. 1988. "'Itonut Yehudit bePolin bein Shetei Milhamot ha'Olam." *Kesher* 3 (May): 49–56.

Pappé, Ilan. 1995. "Mediniyut Artzot 'Arav Klapei haMahalakhim haDiplomatim beShe'elat Eretz-Yisrael, 1947–1949." *Iyunim Bitkumat Israel* 5:112–125.

Perlis, Rivka. 1987. *Tenu'at haNo'ar haHalutziyot beFolin haKevushah*. Tel Aviv: HaKibbutz haMe'uhad.

Piekarz, Mendel. 1981–5741. "Gezirot Polin uMenuhah veShalvah leYehudei Hungariah beDrasha Hasidit Belza'it beYanuar 1944 beBudapest." *Kivunim* 24 (May): 115–119.

Pinkus, Benjamin. 2005. "Mediniut Sovitit beNose haYehudi ve haEretz Israeli beHasot ha'brith haBilti Kdusha." In *'Olam Yashan Adam Hadash*, edited by Ėli Tsur, 44–45. Sde Boker: Ben-Gurion Research Institute for the Study of Israel and Zionism.

Piper, Franciszek. 1991. *Mispar haMegurashim leMahaneh haMavet Auschwitz-Birkenau uMispar haNispim Bo*. Yad Vashem 21: 41–85.

———. 1994. "The Number of Victims." In *Anatomy of the Auschwitz Death Camp*, edited by Israel Gutman and Michael Berenbaum. Washington, DC, and Bloomington: United States Holocaust Memorial Museum and Indiana University Press.

———. 2002. *Auschwitz Prisoner Labor: The Organization and Exploitation of Auschwitz Concentration Camp Prisoners as Laborers*. Oświęcim: Auschwitz-Birkenau State Museum.

Piskei Din shel Beit haMishpat ha'Elyon (Judgments of the Supreme Court). Vol. 1, 1948–1949–5708–5709); vol. 1b, 1949–5709–5710. Jerusalem: Ministry of Justice.

Piskei Din shel Batei haMishpat haMehoz'im (Judgments of the District Courts). Jerusalem: Ministry of Justice, n.d.

Polonsky, Antony, and Bolesław Drukier. 1980. *The Beginnings of Communist Rule in Poland*. London: Routledge & Kegan Paul.

Porat Dina. 1992a. "BeSelihah uveHesed." *Yalkut Moreshet* 12:9–33.

———.1992b. *The Blue and the Yellow Star of David*. Cambridge, MA: Harvard University Press.

———. 1995–5755. "'Shutafav shel 'Amalek': *haAshamot* haHaredim baAretz beShenot haShemonim klapei haTzionut beTekufat haShoah." *HaTzionut* 19:295–324.

———. 2000. *Me'ever laGashmi: Parshat Hayav shel Abba Kovner*. Tel Aviv and Jerusalem: Am Oved and Yad Vashem.

———. 2001. "Mahapkhanut beToch Kontzenzus: Parshanuto shel Abba Kovner leHistoriah haYehudit." *Yalkut Moreshet* 71:151–161.

Porath, Yehoshua. 1978. *MeMehumot leMeridah: HaTenuah haLe'umit ha'Aravit haFalastinit, 1929–1939*. Tel Aviv: Am Oved.

———. 2001. "Keitzad Nitzlu Yehudei Tzarfat? Skirat Bikoret al Sifrah shel Renée Poznanski, 'Lehiyot Yehudi beTzarfat." *Tekhelet* 11 (Autumn): 194–203.

Poznanski, Renée, ed. 2000–5760. *'Itonai Yehudi beParis haKevushah: Yoman 1940–1942*. Jerusalem: Yad Vashem.

———. 2001. *Jews in France during World War II*. Translated by Nathan Bracher. Waltham, MA: Brandeis University Press.

Prago, Albert. 1979. *Jews in the International Brigades*. New York: Jewish Currents reprint.

Rappel, Hagit. 2004. *UMi Yizkor et haZokhrim? Zikaron Kolektivi veZikaron Ishi beKibbutz Yad Mordekhai*. PhD diss., Ben-Gurion University, Beersheva.

Ravitzky, Aviezer. 1993. *HaKetz haMeguleh veMedinat haYehudim: Meshihiyut, Tzionut, veRadikalizm Dati beYisrael*. Tel Aviv: Am Oved-Ofakim.

Regev, Matti. 1989. "Lamah Leha'ashim et Elohim." *Hadashot shel Shabbat*, June 2, p. 27.

Rembah, Isaac. 1961a. "Ka'asher Lo Avot Ele Banim Okhlim Boser." *Herut*, Sept. 10.

———. 1961b. "Ma leProkhtenbaum ule-'Gevilei haEsh?'" *Herut*, Sept. 24.

———. 1973. *Banim Akhlu Boser*. Edited by Joseph Nedava. Tel Aviv: HaVa'ad haTziburi leHotza'at Kitvei Isaac Rembah.

Richman, Menachem. 1996. *'Alumim beTzel haSa'ar: 1924–1948*. Edited by Ami Shamir. Tel Aviv: Ministry of Defense.

Roos, Hans. 1966. *A History of Modern Poland*. New York: Knopf.

Rosen Ber, Y. 1988. "Rekviam leTalomatzkah 13: Mekomot Mifgash shel Itona'im Yehudim." *Keasher* 3 (May): 120–121.

Rosenak, Avinoam. 2000–5760. "Parshanut haTorah: HaShoah veHilul Hashem." *Shabbat Shalom* 152, Parshat Ki Tavo. Jerusalem: OzVeshalom-Netivot Shalom.

Rosenfeld, Shalom. 1998. "Ha'Itonut: Bein Basel leShinkin, miAltneuland leFarhaland." *Kesher* 23:2–10.

Rotem, Tamar. 2002. "Tir'u Mah Karah laBen shel Gruenbaum." *Ha'aretz, Gilayon Shishi*, April 5, p. B10.

Rozenman, Abraham. 1980. "Bikurav' shel Yitzhak Gruenbaum bePolin leAchar haShoah." *Massuah* 8 (April): 41–45.

———. 1988–5748. "Yitzhak Gruenbaum: Nusah Roman Frister." *Massuah* 16 (Nisan-April): 205–218.

Rubenstein, Richard L. 1966. *After Auschwitz: Radical Theology and Contemporary Judaism*. Indianapolis: Bobbs-Merrill.

Rubin, Amos. 2007. "Lo Nitan Lehastir et ha'Emet." *HaTzofeh*, March 16.

Rubinstein, Avraham. 1991. *Shivhei haBESH"T*. Tel Aviv: Reuven Mas.

Salomon, Yehezkel. 1987–5747. *Shoah miShamayim: HaEmunah beMivhan haShoah*. Bnai Brak: Torat Avot.

Sandler, Shmuel. 1979. "Ben-Gurion's Attitude towards the Soviet Union." *Jewish Journal of Sociology* 21, no. 2: 149–151.

Sarna, Yigal. 1984. "Yehudi 'im Shot uMagafayyim." *Hadashot shel Shabbat*, April 27, pp. 36–37.

Schatz-Oppenheimer, Rivka. 1984–5744. "Vidui 'al Saf haMisrafot ve'Aharit Davar': Rav Haredi Makeh 'al Het." *Kivunim* 23: 49–62.

Schueftan, Dan. 1986. *Optsyah Yardenit: HaYishuv haYehudi uMedinat Israel el Mul haMishtar haHashemi vehaTenu'ah haLe'umit haPalestinit*. Tel Aviv: Yad Tabenkin, HaKibbutz haMe'uhad.

Schweid, Eliezer. 1994. *Bein Hurban leYeshu'ah: Teguvot shel Hagut Haredit leShoah biZemanah*. Tel Aviv: HaKibbutz haMe'uhad.

Segev, Tom. 1983. "HaZaken vehaYoman. *Ha'aretz, Mussaf*, Sept. 7.

———. 1993. *The Seventh Million: The Israelis and the Holocaust*. Translated by Haim Watzman. New York: Hill & Wang.

Seidman, Hillel. 1957–5717. *Yoman Ghetto Warsaw*. New York: Die Yiddishe Wakh Press.

Shaary, David. 1983–5783/1984–5744. "HaTzionim 'haRadikalim,' 1923–1933." *Kivunim* 20:11–51; *Kivunim* 22:21–58.
Shaham, Nathan. 1954. *Heshbon Hadash*. Tel Aviv: Sifriyat Po'alim.
Shaked, Gershon. 1972. "HaYafim Hem Hayeinu haMelei'im Mahshavot 'al haMetim." *Bamah* 52:61–63.
———. 1996–5756. "Bein haKotel ubein Metzadah: HaShoah vehaToda'ah ha'Atzmit shel haHevrah haYisra'elit." In *Temurot Yesod be'Am haYehudi be'Ikvot haShoah*, edited by Israel Gutman, 511–523. Jerusalem: Yad Vashem.
Shaked, Michal. 2000. "HaHistoriah beBeit haMishpat uBeit haMishpat baHistoriah: Piskei-haDin beMishpat Kastner vehaNarativim shel haZikaron." *Alpayim* 20:36–81.
Shalem, Hayim. 2007. *'Et La'Asot leHatzalat Yisrael: Agudat Israel beEretz Yisrael leNokhah haShoah*. Beersheva: Ben-Gurion University.
Shales, Melissa. 2003. *Paris*. Tel Aviv: Steimatzky.
Shalev, Meir. 1993. "Mitz Petel." *Yediot Aharonot, Mussaf*, Aug. 6.
Shalev, Ziva. 2005. *Haika*. Tel Aviv: Moreshet.
Shalmon, Shalom. 1988–5748. *Pishae haZionot beHashmadat yehudi haGolah*. Published by the author.
Shaltiel, David. 1981. *Yerushalyaim TaSHa"H*. Tel Aviv: Ministry of Defense.
Shaltiel, Eli. 2000. *Tamid baMeri: Moshe Sneh, Biografiah*. Tel Aviv: Am Oved, Sifriyat Ofakim.
Shapira, Anita. 1981. *Berl*. Vol. 2. Tel Aviv: Am Oved.
———. 1988a. "Berl, Tabenkin, uBen-Gurion veYahasam leMahapekhat October." *Zemanim* 27–28:86–93.
———. 1988b–5748. "Mifgash haYishuv 'im She'erit haPleitah." In *HaHalikhah 'al Kav haOfek*, edited by Anita Shapira, 325–354. Tel Aviv: Am Oved.
———. 1992. *Herev haYonah*. Tel Aviv: Am Oved–Ofakim.
———. 1996–1997. "HaShoah: Zikaron Prati veZikaron Tziburi." *Zemanim* 57 (Winter): 4–13.
———. 1998–5758. "Kama He'arot shel Hovev Historiah leHokhmei Historiah." In *Hamishim Shenot Medinah*. Jerusalem: HaHevrah haHistorit haYisra'elit.
———. 2000–5760. "Mifgash Tzipiyot, Berihim shel Shetika: She'erit haPleitah veEretz Yisrael." *Massuah* 28:11–19.
Sharett, Moshe. 1958. *BeSha'ar haUmot: 1946–1949*. Tel Aviv: Am Oved.
Shiloah, Amnon. 1990. *Anu Lekha Humat Magen*. Tel Aviv: Ma'arakhot.
Shneiderman, S. L. 2001. *Notes for an Autobigraphy*. College Park, MD: University of Maryland Libraries, the S. L. Eileen Shneiderman Collection of Yiddish books.
Shoham, Chaim. 1983. "Ha'Kan' veha'Sham': 'Al haMahazai haYisraeli veTzilo haYehudi." *Moznaim* 57, nos. 1–2 (July): 61–63.
Shonfeld, Moshe. 1942. "Al Tehte'u baYeled." *HaDerekh*, Oct. 22.
———. 1943. "HaZe'ev beTafkid haRo'eh." *HaDerekh*, Jan. 14.
———. 1948. "HaGiyus leTzion." First published in *Digleinu*, Iyyar, p. 4.
———. 1949. "Klapei Panim." *Digleinu*, Tevet 5709. Republished in *Hashkafatenu beAspaklariah shel Dorot*. Bnei Brak: no publisher noted, 1978.

———. 1954. "Lev Hakham leYemino." *Digleinu*, Tamuz-Av, p. 2.

———. 1973. "Athalta deGe'ula o 'Ikvata deMeshiha." *Niv haMoreh*, Elul, p. 10.

———. 1975–5735. "Bifroa' Pra'ot beYisrael." In *Bein Eretz Yisrael leMedinat Yisrael: Birurim Ra'ayoniyim veHashkafatiyim 'al Tehom sheNeif'arah veGesher la Ein*. Bnei Brak: Hug Bnei Torah.

———. 1978–5738. *Serufe haKivshanim Ma'ashimim* (Those burned in the furnaces accuse). Bnei Brak: Hug Bnei Torah.

———. 1981. "HaMilhamah bePA"Y Mitnahelet a"y GaDOT"T." *Hashkafatenu*, parts. 4–5. Bene Brak: Hug Bnei Torah, p. 214.

"Simon Laks." n.d. Boosey & Hawkes. http://www.boosey.com/pages/cr/composer/composer_main.asp?composerid=18196 (accessed Aug. 7, 2013).

Sivan, Emanuel. 1991. *Dor TaSha"H: Mitos, Diyukan, veZikaron*. Tel Aviv: Ma'arachot.

Slotzky, Yehuda. 1972–5732. *Sefer Toldot haHaganah*. Vol. 3. Jerusalem: HaSifriya haTzionit.

Sompolinsky, Meir. 1987–5747. "HaMosdot haYehudi'im ba'Olam ubaYishuv beRe'I haHistoriografiah shel haYehudim haHaredim 'al haShoah." In *HaShoah baHistoriografiah: Hartza'to veDiyunim beKinus haBeinleumi haHamishi shel Hokrei haShoah*, edited by Israel Gutman and Gideon Greif, 497–516. Jerusalem: Yad Vashem.

Sperber, Rakuel. 2003. *Hem Lo Ya'avru! haBrigadot haBeinleumiot veLohameihen haYehudim beMilhemet haEzrahim beSefarad, 1936–1939*. Catalog of an exhibition at the National and University Library of Israel, Feb. 17–April 10.

Stauber, Roni. 2000. *HaLekah laDor: Shoah veGevurah baMahshavah haTziburit ba'Aretz beShnot haHamishim*. Jerusalem and Sde Boker: Ben-Zvi Institute and Ben-Gurion Heritage Center.

Stein, Sigemond. 1961. *Der birger-krig in Shpanye Zikhroynes fun a militsioner*. Paris.

Strzelecki Andrzej. 1973. "Das Nebenlager Jawischowitz." In *Hefte von Auschwitz*. Vol. 15. Oświęcim: Auschwitz-Birkenau State Museum.

———. 1974. "Podobóz Jawischowitz." *Zeszyty Oświecimskie* 15:171–234.

———. 1989. *Marsz Śmierci: Przewodnik po trasie Oświęcim, Wodzisław Śląski. Death March: A Guide along the Route from Oświęcim to Wodzisław Śląski*. Katowice: Towarzystwo Opienki nad Oświęcimiem. Auschwitz Preservation Society.

Sugarman, Martin. Undated. "Jews Who Served in the Spanish Civil War." Jewish Virtual Library. http://www.jewishvirtuallibrary.org/jsource/History/spanjews.pdf (accessed Aug. 7, 2013).

Swiebocki, Henryk. 1995. *Auschwitz, 1940–1945: The Resistance Movement*. Vol. 4. Oświęcim: Auschwitz-Birkenau State Museum.

Szmulewski, David. 1984–5744. *Zikhronos fun Widershasand-Auschwitz-Birkenau*. Paris.

Tahon, Y. 1969–5729. *Sefer Zikhronot Likhvod haD"R Shmuel Avraham Poznański*. Jerusalem: Board of Great Synagogue on Tłomacki. Original edition: Warsaw: Board of Great Synagogue on Tłomacki Street, 1927–5687.

Taikhtel, Yisaskhar Shelomo. 1983–5743. *Em haBanim Semehah*. Jerusalem: Pri Haaretz Institute.

Tarshish, Avraham. 1954. "HaGolah keMakor le'Arakhim Ruhaniyim uleSheflut Medinit, haGolah keMakom le'Atzma'ut Ruhanit veNafshit veleSheflut Medinit." *Lamerhav*, Sept. 8.

Teveth, Shabtai. 1986a. *HaDerekh leIyyar*. Tel Aviv: Ministry of Defense.

———. 1986b. "HaRatz leMerhakim Arukim." *Yediot Aharonot, Mussaf*, Oct. 3.

———. 2004. *Kinat David; Hayei David Ben-Gurion*. Vol. 4, *Ish Riv*. Jerusalem: Shocken.

Trunk, Ishaia. 1979. *Judenrat*. Jerusalem: Yad Vashem.

Tsahor, Ze'ev. 1986–5746. "Sotzializm uMashma'uto etzel Ben-Gurion." *Kivunim* 29:103–114.

———. 1994. *HaHazon vehaHeshbon: Ben-Gurion bein Idiologiah leFolitikah*. Tel Aviv: Sifriyat Po'alim.

———. 2005–5765. "Nitzulei haShoah vehaPolitikah haTzionit: Mi haMenatzel uMi haMenutzal." In *'Olam Yashan Adam Hadash: Kehilot Yisra'el beEidan haModernizatziah*, edited by Eli Tsur, 264–279. Sde Boker: Ben-Gurion Research Institute for the Study of Israel and Zionism.

Ungar, Michal. 2005. *Lodz: Aharon haGeta'to bePolin*. Jerusalem: Yad Vashem.

Vrba, Rudolf. 1998. *Barahti miAuschwitz*. Haifa: University of Haifa.

Weinman, Tzvi. 1995–5755. *MiKatovitz 'ad Heh beIyyar*. Jerusalem: Vatikin.

Weinryb, Elazar, ed. 1987. *Hashivah Historit*. Vol. 1. Tel Aviv: HaUniversitah haPetuhah.

Weiss, Aharon. 1978a–5738. "Birurim beShe'alat Ma'amadah ve'Emdoteiha shel haHanagah haYehudit beFolin haKevushah." *Yad Vashem* 12:243–266.

———. 1978b–5738. "HaMishtarah haYehudit beGeneralgouvernement ubeSilesiah Eilit beTekufat haShoah." PhD diss., The Hebrew University of Jerusalem.

Weitz, Yehiam. 1995. *HaIsh sheNirtzah Pa'amayim: Hayav, Mishpato, veMoto shel Dr. Yisrael Kastner*. Jerusalem: Keter.

———. 1996a. "HaHok le'Asiyat Din baNazim uve'Ozreihem veYahasah shel haHevrah haYisraelit beShnot haHamishim leShoah veleNitzoleha." *Cathedra* 82:153–164.

———. 1996b–5796. "'Itzuv Zikaron haShoah beHevrah haYisraelit beShnot haHamishim." In *Temurot Yesod ba'Am haYehudi be'Ikvot haShoah*, edited by Israel Gutman, 473–493. Jerusalem: Yad Vashem.

———. 1996c. "BeHeksher Politi: HaMemad haPoliti shel Zikaron haShoah beShnot haHamishim." *Iyunim Bitkumat Israel* 6:271–278.

———. 2007. "HaYom Bo Menachem Begin Hafakh leBiryon." *Ha'aretz*, Dec. 10.

Williams, Colin, Bill Alexander, and John Gorman. 1996. *Memorials of the Spanish Civil War*. Stroud, UK: A. Sutton.

Wuzeck, Ephraim. 1964. *Zikhrones fun a Botvinist* (*Memoirs of a Member of the Botwin Company*). Warsaw: no publisher.

Wuzelman, M. 1989–5749. *Ot Cain*. Edited by Menachem Gerlik. Tel Aviv: no publisher.

Yablonka, Hanna. 1996. "HaHok le'Asiyat Din baNazim ve'Ozreihem: Hebet Nosaf leShe'elat haYisraelim, haNitzolim, vehaShoah." *Cathedra* 82:135–152.

Yad Vashem. 1976–5736. "Lancicia." *Pinkas haKehilot*. Vol. 1. Jerusalem: Yad Vashem.

Yasani, A. Wolf. 1962. *Bukh fun der Tchekhanawer Yidisher Kehilah: Sefer Yizkor leKehilat Ciechanów*. Tel Aviv: Irgun Yotzei Ciechanów beYisrael un di Landmanshaft in Hutz La'Aretz.

Yehoshua, A. B. 1980. *HaShoah: Parshat Derakhim.*

Zaagsma, Gerben. 2001. "Jewish Volunteers in the Spanish Civil War: A Case Study of the Botwin Company." MA thesis, University of London.

———. 2006. *East European Jewish Communists in Paris during the Popular Front Era.* Amsterdam: European Social Science History Conference. http://www2.iisg.nl/esshc/programme9606.asp?selyear=8&pap=4481 (accessed Aug. 26, 2013).

Zait, David. 2002. *HaUtopiah haShomerit: HaShomer haTza'ir beFolin 1921–1931.* Beersheva: Ben-Gurion University.

Zekharyah, Shabtai. 2003. *Yerushalayim Shel Matah.* Jerusalem: Ariel.

Żelechower, Natan. 1968. *Siedem obozów. Seven Camps. Biuletyn Żydowskiego Instytutu Historycznego* 68:5–68.

Zentner, Yisrael. 1966. *MiMadrid 'ad Berlin.* Tel Aviv: published by the author.

Zertal, Idith. 1996. *Zehavam shel haYehudim.* Tel Aviv: Am Oved.

———. 2005. *Israel's Holocaust and the Politics of Nationhood.* Translated by Chaya Galai. Cambridge: Cambridge University Press.

Zertal, Moshe. 1980. *Ken Ne'urim: Pirkei haShomer haTza'ir beWarsaw, 1913–1943.* Tel Aviv: Sifriyat Po'alim.

Zerubavel, Gilad, ed. 1957. *Sefer haPaLMa"H.* Vol. 2. Tel Aviv: HaKibbutz haMe'uhad.

Zeruvabel, Yael. 1994. "Mot haZikaron veZikaron haMavet: Metzadah vehaShoah keMetaforot Historiyot." *Alpayim* 10:42–67.

Zuckerman, Yitzhak. 1990. *Shev'a haShanim haHen.* Tel Aviv: HaKibbutz haMe'uhad.

FILMS

Kroytoro, Dov. 2002. *HaBen shel Gruenbaum.* Broadcast on Israel Channel 2, eve of Holocaust Day, April 8, 2002.

Setton, Danny, Danny Faran, and Tor Ben-Mayor. 1999. *Kapo.* Israeli-German-Italian coproduction. First broadcast on the television program *'Uvdah*, Telad, Israel Channel 2.

Turbiner, Eran. 2000. *Madrid Lifnei Hanitah.* Broadcast on Israel Channel 1, Jan. 7, 2000.

INDEX